IT Project Management:
On Track From Start to Finish

Second Edition

Joseph Phillips

McGraw-Hill Osborne

Mexico City M New York Chicago San Francisco Lisbon London Madrid
ronto

The *McGraw·Hill* Companies

McGraw-Hill/Osborne
2100 Powell Street, 10th Floor
Emeryville, California 94608
U.S.A.

To arrange bulk purchase discounts for sales promotions, premiums, or fund-raisers, please contact **McGraw-Hill**/Osborne at the above address. For information on translations or book distributors outside the U.S.A., please see the International Contact Information page immediately following the index of this book.

IT Project Management: On Track From Start to Finish, Second Edition

8 9 0 DOC/DOC 0 1 9 8

Book p/n 0-07-223203-X and CD p/n 0-07-223204-8
parts of
ISBN 0-07-223202-1

Publisher Brandon A. Nordin	**Acquisitions Coordinator** Jessica Wilson	**Composition** Jean Butterfield, Tara A. Davis
Vice President & **Associate Publisher** Scott Rogers	**Technical Editor** Cyndi Snyder	**Illustrators** Kathleen Edwards, Melinda Lytle
Editorial Director Gareth Hancock	**Copy Editor** Lauren Kennedy	**Series Design** Roberta Steele
Project Editor Julie M. Smith	**Proofreader** Linda Medoff	**Cover Design** Greg Scott
	Indexer Valerie Perry	

This book was published with Corel VENTURA™ Publisher.

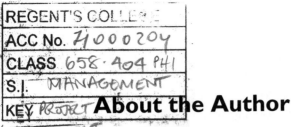
About the Author

Joseph Phillips, PMP, IT Project+, is the Director of Education for Project Seminars, a PMI Registered Education Provider. He has managed and consulted on projects for industries including technical, pharmaceutical, manufacturing, and architectural among others. Phillips has served as a project management consultant for organizations creating project offices, maturity models, and best practice standardization.

As a leader in adult education, Phillips has taught organizations how to successfully implement project management methodologies, information technology project management, risk management, and other courses. Phillips has taught for Columbia College, University of Chicago, Indiana University, and others. He is a Certified Technical Trainer and has taught over 10,000 professionals. Phillips has contributed as an author or editor to more than 30 books on technology, careers, and project management.

Phillips is a member of the Project Management Institute and is active in local project management chapters. He has spoken on project management, project management certifications, and project methodologies at numerous trade shows, PMI chapter meetings, and employee conferences. When not writing, teaching, or consulting Phillips can be found behind a camera or on the working end of a fly rod. You can contact Phillips through www.projectseminars.com.

About the Tech Reviewer

Cyndi Snyder is a professional consultant, facilitator, instructor, author and partner in Vista Performance Group. She is an experienced leader in developing strategic and operating plans that have resulted in organizational growth and maturity. Cyndi has 10 years of experience managing a variety of projects from public sector program development to acquisitions and system implementation.

Cyndi has experience in training for the corporate, public sector and academic environment. She currently instructs for UC Irvine, CalTech, and USC. Cyndi also participates in the UC Irvine Project Management Program Advisory Committee. In addition she was a contributor to the Project Management Competency Model which was published by the Project Management Institute.

Cyndi is a member of the Project Management Institute and is the Chair of the Chapter Leadership Development and Excellence Committee for 2003 – 2005. She received an award for Outstanding Chapter President of the Year for 2002. Cyndi is a certified Project Management Professional (PMP) and earned her Masters in Business Administration from Pepperdine University.

For my son, Kyle.

CONTENTS

The logo of the CompTIA Authorized Quality Curriculum Program and the status of this or other training material as "Authorized" under the CompTIA Authorized Curriculum Program signifies that, in CompTIA's opinion, such training material covers the content of the CompTIA's related certification exam. CompTIA has not reviewed or approved the accuracy of the contents of this training material and specifically disclaims any warranties of merchantability or fitness for a particular purpose. CompTIA makes no guarantee concerning the success of persons using any such "Authorized" or other training material in order to prepare for any CompTIA certification exam.

The contents of this training material were created for the CompTIA *IT Project+* exam covering CompTIA certification exam objectives that were current as of *December 2003.*

How to Become CompTIA Certified:

This training material can help you prepare for and pass a related CompTIA certification exam or exams. In order to achieve CompTIA certification, you must register for and pass a CompTIA certification exam or exams.

In order to become CompTIA certified, you must:

1. Select a certification exam provider. For more information please visit http://www.comptia.org/certification/test_locations.htm.

2. Register for and schedule a time to take the CompTIA certification exam(s) at a convenient location.

3. Read and sign the Candidate Agreement, which will be presented at the time of the exam(s). The text of the Candidate Agreement can be found at www.comptia.org/certification

4. Take and pass the CompTIA certification exam(s).

For more information about CompTIA's certifications, such as their industry acceptance, benefits, or program news, please visit www.comptia.org/certification

CompTIA is a non-profit information technology (IT) trade association. CompTIA's certifications are designed by subject matter experts from across the IT industry. Each CompTIA certification is vendor-neutral, covers multiple technologies, and requires demonstration of skills and knowledge widely sought after by the IT industry.

To contact CompTIA with any questions or comments:

Please call + 1 630 268 1818

questions@comptia.org

ACKNOWLEDGMENTS

Books, like projects, are never done alone.

I'd like to thank Cyndi Snyder for keeping me on track and focused on PMP requirements and test-centric ideas. A big thank you goes to Gareth Hancock for his patience, guidance, conversation, and overall support for this book. Thank you to Julie Smith for her keen organizational skills, attention to detail, and ability to keep me moving. Lauren Kennedy—thank you for tightening my writing, clarifying my thoughts, and helping me to be a better writer. Thanks also to Jessica Wilson, Paul and Linda Medoff, and the talented people in the production department for all of their hard work.

Thank you to my friends and colleagues for their encouragement as this book was created: Linda Barron, Brad Bobich, Stacey Beheler, Scot Conrad, Kallie Cremer, Emmett Dulaney, Rick Gordon, Greg Kirkland, Don Kuhnle, Nancy Maragioglio, Deanna Moreland, Heather Rippey, Phil Stuck and my brothers Steve, Mark, Sam, and Ben.

Managing a project is not unlike directing a movie, coaching a major league baseball team, or flying the space shuttle around the moon. Of course, if you were directing a movie you'd be working with superstars. If you were coaching a major league team, you might win the pennant. And if you were flying the space shuttle, you'd have a great view. But with project management, you get to experience some of the same thrills I'm sure directors, coaches, and astronauts experience.

Relax. This book will help you become the superior project manager you've dreamed of becoming. *IT Project Management: On Track from Start to Finish* will show you how to get started, get funding, and get the project done. You'll discover advanced project management techniques, the mechanics of project management, and inspiration to keep moving towards the end result of any technical project. I'll show you how you can direct your team to work together and independently. I'll show you how you can motivate team members, get management fired up about your project, and keep yourself from burning out. This book takes you from project management basics to advanced concepts on such topics as creating budgets, devising Work Breakdown Structures, and sustaining an exciting environment that will guarantee your success over and over.

As a project manager, you'll be challenged and forced to think on your feet, and you'll learn how to lead people rather than just manage them. Project management is a wonderful life experience that will stretch your brain and abilities further than you ever thought possible. Some people love project management so much they've dedicated their careers to it. These professionals love the exhilaration of finding a solution to a seemingly impossible predicament. They love the nirvana of resolving disagreements between coworkers—and watching their team become tight as family. They thrill over each success en route to the victory of completing the project on track and on budget.

My hope is that you'll become one of these people and that I can help get you there. This book is written based on my experiences as a project manager. How I wish a book of this caliber were available when I started my career! Fortunately for you, it's here now. You can (and I hope you do) read the book from cover to cover. Or, if you really want to, you can skip from chapter to chapter. Heck, read it backwards if it helps you! Regardless of your reading tactics, the best way to learn is by doing. Do yourself a big favor and complete the exercises at the end of chapter—they'll help to reinforce what you've read. If you're new to project management, try to discuss some of the issues in this book with an accomplished project manager. Once you've finished reading the book, teach someone else what you've learned. After all, teaching is just learning twice.

Finally, if you'd like to discuss any of the topics in this book, feel free to drop me an e-mail. I try to respond to as many as possible. You can reach me at itpm@josephphillips.com. I wish you my best in your career and your endeavors as a project manager.

Chapter 1

Initiating the Project

Welcome to information technology (IT) project management. IT project management is different from managing any other project you may have worked on in the past. In the world of information technology, we've got attacks on all fronts: ever changing business needs, hardware compatibility, software glitches, security holes, and network bandwidth, not to mention careers, attitudes, and office politics.

Don't be scared off! This is also the most challenging and exciting place to be in a company. What you do here will affect entire organizations, and have an impact on profits, and can boost your career, confidence, and life to the next level.

IT project management can be as exciting as a white water rafting excursion or as painful as a root canal; the decision is yours. What makes the difference between excitement and a sore jaw? Many things: leadership, know-how, motivation, and, among other things, a clear vision of what each project will produce, what it will cost, and when it will end.

This first chapter will help you build a strong foundation for managing successful IT projects. Like anything else in the world, adequate planning, determination, and vision are required for success. Ready to start this journey? Let's go!

Gathering Project Information

Everybody talks about project management, but what is it exactly? In some organizations, any task or duty is considered a project that requires someone to manage it. Puh-leeze! Project management is the ability to administer a series of chronological tasks resulting in a desired goal. Some tasks can't be completed until others are finished, while other tasks can be done in parallel. Some tasks require the skill of a single individual; other jobs in the project require that everyone chip in and lighten the load.

A project, technically, is a temporary endeavor to create a unique product or service. Projects are an undertaking outside of the normal operations of an entity. For example, you might roll out a new application, install new monitors, create a new portion of a web site, or establish a new call center for application support. In some organizations, such as ones comprised of application developers or consultants, or IT integration companies, everything they do is a project because they complete projects for other organizations. Consider a company that creates custom applications for other organizations. Their operation is an ongoing series of projects. The organization that completes the project work is called the *performing organization*.

IT project management is the ability to balance the love and implementation of technology while leading and inspiring your team members. Of course, the goal of project management is not technology for technology's sake, but rather a movement toward things like improved customer service, enhanced product quality, and increased profitability. As you can see in Figure 1-1, project management is a high-wire balancing act.

Establishing the Project Requirements

Before the actual project work can begin, the project manager must establish the project requirements with the project stakeholders. Stakeholders are any individuals, groups, or communities that have a vested interest in the outcome of the project. On some projects, the stakeholders may be just one department. On others, when projects may affect every department, the stakeholders may be throughout the entire organization. Identifying stakeholders is important because their input to the project requirements early in the project initiation can ensure the project's success.

Of course, on most projects there will be key stakeholders who influence the project's outcome: department managers, customers, directors, end users, and other folks who have direct power over the project work. With the input of these key stakeholders, specifically their requirements for the project, constraints on the project, and time and cost objectives for the project, the project manager will be able to gather the project requirements to begin building a project plan to create the project deliverables.

Clarity is paramount. When the decision has been handed down that your company will be implementing some new technology, and you'll be leading the way, you need a clear, thorough understanding of the project's purpose. Ambiguous projects are a waste of time, talent, and money. Before the project begins, you need to know what

FIGURE I-I

A project manager must balance the team and the technology.

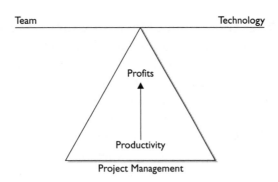

exact results signal the project's end. A project truly begins when you know exactly what the project will produce.

Once the project is defined, you need a clearly stated start and end date. The role of a project manager is not permanent but temporary. You, the project manager, are responsible for seeing the goal, developing the steps to get there, and then leading the way for your team to follow.

How will you know what the end result of the project is to be? Ask! Who do you ask? People like the project sponsor can answer these kinds of questions. More about that later! You must have a clear vision of the end result, or the project will drone on and on forever and you'll never finish. Too often IT projects can roll into project after project stemming from an original, indecisive, half-baked wish list. Whether you are a full-time employee within an organization or a contract-based project manager, you must have a clear understanding of what the end results of the project will be.

Imagine your favorite archeologist maneuvering through a labyrinth of pitfalls, poison darts, and teetering bridges to retrieve a golden statue. In the movies, there's always some fool who charges past the hero straight for the booty and gets promptly beheaded. Don't be that guy. Before you can rush off toward the goal of any given project, you've got to create a clear, concise path to get there.

To create this path, you'll have to interview the decision makers, the users the change will affect, and any principals involved in the development of the technology. These are the stakeholders—the people who will use the project deliverables on a daily basis or will manage the people who will use the project deliverables. You must have a clear vision of what the project takes to create it or you're doomed. Often projects start from a wish list and evolve into a catalog of complaints about the current technology. One of your jobs in the early stages of the project will be to discern valid input from useless gripes.

As you begin your project, consider these questions:

Does the Project Have an Exact Result?

Projects that are as indecisive as a six-year-old at an ice cream stand rarely are successful. As a project manager, you must ensure the project has a definable, obtainable end result. At the creation of the project, every project manager, project sponsor (the initiator of the project), and team member should know and recognize the end result of the project. Beware of projects that begin without a clearly defined objective.

While you should be looking for exact requirements that a project is to include, you must also look for requirements that are excluded from a project (for example, a project that requires all mail servers to be upgraded in the operating system, but

not the physical hardware). As the project takes form, the requirements to be
excluded will become obvious based on management, the time allotted for the
project's completion, and the given budget.

Are There Industry or Government Sanctions to Consider?

Within your industry there may be governmental or self-regulating sanctions
you will have to take into account for your project. For example, in a banking
environment there are regulations dealing with the security of the technology,
the backup and recovery procedures, and the fault tolerance for the hardware
implemented. Government regulations vary by industry, and if your company
is a government contractor, there are additional considerations for the project
deliverables.

Within your industry there may be standards and regulations. Regulations
are "must-haves" that are required by law. Of course, pharmaceuticals, utility
companies, and food packaging companies have regulations that dictate their
practices. If companies break regulations, fines and lawsuits may follow. Standards,
however, are generally accepted guidelines and practices within an industry.
Standards are heuristics, rules of thumb, which are not laws but are usually followed.
The project manager must be aware of regulations and standards that affect the
project's work and deliverables.

Does the Project Have a Reasonable Deadline?

Massive upgrades, software rollouts, application development, and system conversions
take teamwork, dedication, and time. Projects that don't have a clearly stated,
reasonable deadline need one. Projects should not last forever—they are temporary.
Acknowledge the work. Do the work. Satisfy the user with deliverables of the
project. Once you've accomplished this, the project is done.

We'll talk more about project scheduling in Chapter 7, but the project manager
must be aware of the project calendar and the resource calendar. The project
calendar defines the hours in which the project work can take place. For example,
if your project is to rewire an entire building with new network cable, the project
calendar may specify access to the building between the hours of 8:00 P.M. and
6:00 A.M. Resource calendars are specific to the project team members. They
take into consideration the hours employees are available, their vacations, and
company holidays.

In addition, the project manager must consider how many working hours their
project team members will be able to devote to the project in a given day. Six hours
of productivity is typical of an eight-hour day because of impromptu meetings,

phone calls, and other interruptions. These factors directly influence the project schedule and if the project can meet the project deadline with the given resources.

Is the Project Sponsor Someone Who Has the Authority to Christen the Project?

Most IT folks hate politics, but we all know politics, personal interests, and department leverage are a part of every company. Make certain the project sponsor is the person who should be initiating the project—without stepping out of bounds. Make certain this individual has the resources to commit to the implementation and has the support of the people up the flowchart. And do it with the full knowledge and support of management.

The project sponsor should be an individual within the organization who has the power to assign team members, allocate funds, and approve decisions on the project work. The project sponsor is typically above the functional managers of the project team members assigned to the project work.

Does the Project Have a Financial Commitment?

If you do not have a clear sense of a financial commitment to the completion of the project, put on your hard hat and don't stand under any fans. Technology costs money because it makes money. The goal of a project, in the corporate world, is the same goal of any company: to make or save money. A tech-centric project requires a financial investment for quality hardware, software, and talent. If the project you are managing has a budget to be determined somewhere down the road, you've got a wish list, not a project at all.

Is Someone Else Doing This Already?

In large companies, it's easy for two projects to be competing against each other for the same end result. This comes back to communication among departments, teams, and the chief information officer. In a perfect world, IT projects fall under one umbrella, information is openly shared among departments, and everyone works together for the common goal of a company (to make money). This process can be administered through a Project or Program Management Office where projects are tracked across the enterprise. Of course, that doesn't always happen. You should do some initial research to ensure this project isn't being accomplished elsewhere in the company before you invest time, finances, and your career in it.

Possessing Multiple Personas

Are you an optimist? A pessimist? A realist? A project manager has to be all of these. You have to be an optimist so you may lead your people, manage the resources, and implement the technology according to plan. You have to be a pessimist, secretly of course, because you need to look at the worst-case scenario for each piece of the technology implementation. You have to be a realist because you need to look at the facts of the projects completely, unattached, unemotional, and unencumbered.

When your project is developing, you should play devil's advocate to each cornerstone of the project. You need to question the concepts, the technology, and the time it may take for each step of the implementation. As you can see in Figure 1-2, you should question everything before you begin.

Questions to consider:

How Will This New Technology Affect Your Users?

Not all technology you implement has a direct effect on your users, but most of it does. Your life may be IT, but the accountant in the finance department doesn't like change. She likes everything the way it is now; that's everything from having to click OK on a redundant error message to installing her favorite screen saver. If your technology changes her world, you should let her know ahead of time; otherwise, she'll be certain to let you know after. Your primary objective must be to make her job easier.

As technology has become integrated in practically all areas of an organization, users are becoming more tech-sophisticated. They will want to know why the change is happening, why the change is needed, and how it will help them. This

FIGURE 1-2   Project managers must question all aspects of a project.

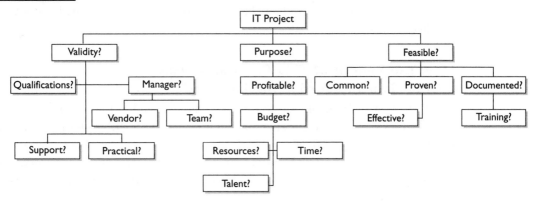

brings us back to requirements gathering and communication. Ninety percent of the project manager's job is communication. If the project manager wants buy-in from the stakeholders, particularly the users, he must communicate the benefits and rationale behind the technical project.

Will This Technology Have an Impact on Any Other Software?

How many times have you installed software without testing it, only to discover it disrupts something as unrelated as printing? I hope never, but it happens. You must question and test the ability of the new technology to work with your current systems. Of course, if you're considering a 100 percent change in technology, then there really isn't a software compatibility issue.

Will This Technology Work with Any Operating System?

How many operating systems are in your organization? While the goal may be just one, I'd wager you've got two or three different OSs floating around. Think about those graphic designers and their Macintoshes. Remember those salespeople and their Windows XP laptops? And what about those mainframe and server-based Linux users? If your company has multiple operating systems, you've got to question the compatibility of the technology for each.

What Other Companies Are Using This Technology?

The assumption is you are buying this solution rather than building it. Therefore, is it a bleeding edge solution? Are you first in line? No one likes to be first, but someone has to be. When embracing and implementing a new technology, ask that question of the vendor's salesperson. Hopefully, the salesperson will be happy to report about all the large companies that have successfully installed, tested, and implemented the vendor's product. That's a good sign. If someone else has done it, you can too.

Does the Vendor of This Technology Have a Good Track Record in the Industry?

From whom are you buying this technology? Has the vendor been around for a while and implemented its product many times over? Does the vendor have a history of taking care of problems when they arise? This is not to say you should not buy from a startup—every major IT player was a startup at some time in its history. You should feel fairly confident that the vendor selling the product today will be around to support it tomorrow.

What Is the Status of Your Network Now?

You may not always have to ask this question, but with so many network-intensive applications and new technologies today, it doesn't hurt. You don't want to install the latest bandwidth hog on a network that's already riding the crest of 90 percent utilization. You and your company won't be happy. By asking this question, you may uncover a snake pit that needs to be dealt with before your project can begin.

What If...?

Finally, you need to dream up worst-case scenarios and see if there are ways to address each. You need to find out how the technology will react when your servers are bounced, lines go down, and processor utilization peaks. You want to ask these questions and have answers for them now rather than when the crisis hits during your four-week vacation to Alaska.

No Other Choices?

At the start of a project, in its very genesis, ensure that the proposed technology is the correct technology. Of course, sometimes you have no control over the technology that is to be implemented because some vice president decision maker heard about the product from his golf buddy who is CIO at another large firm and is now having you install it everywhere. It happens.

Other times, hopefully most of the time, you have some input to the technology implemented to solve a problem. You are the professional, the IT guru, so you should have a definite say regarding the technology that you'll be in charge of delivering. You'll need to create a list of questions and then find the appropriate technology that offers the needed solution, works with your current systems, and fits within your budget. Having the right technology to begin with ensures success at project's end.

Interviewing Management

To have a successful project, you need a clear vision of the delivered result. You need to know why the project is being implemented. You need a strong commitment of management to the project. You need to share management's vision of how the end results will benefit the company. How will you discover these facts? Ask!

When your boss comes to you, for instance, and reports that you are to manage a project to upgrade the mail servers, you need to find out why. It may not be that the manager really wants the mail servers upgraded; he could just be having trouble opening a cartoon his frat brother from Utah sent him and blaming it all on the company's e-mail system.

When you approach management to find out why the project needs to happen, you aren't questioning their decision-making ability. You are, however, questioning what their vision is for the project. In your company, your immediate manager may be the most technically savvy genius in the world and her decisions are always right on target. In others, if not most, managers know that a technology exists and can be implemented. However, they don't know exactly which technology they're after. Figures 1-3 and 1-4 show the difference between effective decision-making abilities and poor decision-making abilities.

As the project manager, your job is to ensure the success of your project and your career, and a successful impact on the bottom line. When you speak with management about the proposed project, you are on a fact-finding mission. Ask questions that can result in specific answers. For example:

■ What do you want technology so-and-so to do?

■ Why is this technology needed?

■ How did you discover this technology?

■ What led you to the decision this was the way for our company to go?

Sometimes a manager may come to you with a specific problem for you to solve. In these instances, the project is wider, more open-ended, and you'll have to drill deeper into the problem presented. Let's say for example that a vice president is complaining about the length of time it takes her to retrieve information on customers through your database. She just wants it faster.

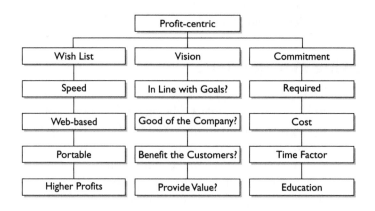

FIGURE 1-3

Well-informed decisions result in success for everyone, not just the project.

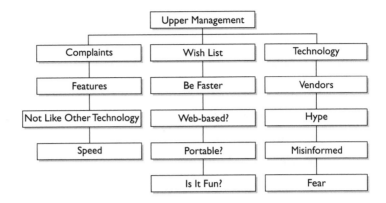

FIGURE 1-4

Decisions based
on complaints,
wishes, and
sales spiels
miss the mark.

Your questions may be something like this:

- Can you show me how the process is slow?
- Is it slow all the time or just some of the time?
- How long have you experienced this lag?
- Have others reported this problem?

There are several things we can do to increase the speed of the process. Each may require a financial commitment initially, but would result in faster responses for all of the database users. Do you want to investigate this route?

Notice how you're thinking like an executive. It's not technology for technology's sake. A new multiprocessor database server, gigabytes of memory, and faster switches are all cool stuff, but if they don't earn their keep, they are just toys. When you are inventing a project, think like an executive of a company and show how the investment in software, hardware, and talent can create more dollars by increasing productivity, safeguarding data, or streamlining business processes and ultimately making customers happy.

Interviewing the Stakeholders

As you know, stakeholders are individuals, groups, or organizations that have a direct interest in the outcome of the project. Your project's success or failure will directly affect the way they complete their work, use their existing technology, or continue to buy from your company. Stakeholders can include

- Management
- The project manager
- The project team
- Project sponsors
- Customers
- End users
- The community

In a technical project, the largest group of stakeholders is typically the users. Any project that has an impact on users needs to be discussed with them. This can be done several different ways. The most popular, and sometimes most disruptive, is a focus group. Fair warning: focus groups have a tendency to engage in gripe sessions about the problem rather than the solution. If you choose this route, take control of the discussion and keep the participants focused on the solution.

A focus group allows you to take a sampling from users from each affected department, present the project to them, and then listen to their input. You need to explain how the proposed technology will be better than the current, how it will solve problems, and, if necessary, why the decision is being made to change. Input from focus groups can alter your entire project for the good or the bad.

Another way to interview users is through an intranet site. This method can be an effective form of communication because users have the opportunity to share their opinions and have some say on your project. Of course, with this route, it's best to have your intranet site request responses to a survey so the results can be tallied quickly. See Figure 1-5 for an example of an online survey.

Some project managers rely on the Delphi Technique. This approach is often used in risk management, but can be applied to any consensus-gathering activity. The participants and their comments are anonymous. The participants are allowed to freely comment on the technology, their concerns, and desires for the requirements. All of the comments are then shared with all of the participants, and they can agree or discount them based on their opinions and experience. Because the process is anonymous, there is no fear of retribution or backlash, or offending other

An online survey
can quickly tally
users' input to a
new technology.

Workflow Creation Survey

Your Name: [   ]

Your shift hours: ○ Day ○ Night

Check the all activities that you use on a daily basis:
☑ Time reporting ☐ HR Reporting ☑ Fax submission
☐ Expense Request ☐ Expense Approval
☑ Room reservations ☑ Meeting Request
☐ Available time queries

Which form do you use the most? [Payroll request ▼]

Would you like to participate in the pilot testing group?
○ No ◉ Yes

[Send this survey]   [Cancel this survey]

participants. After several rounds of discussion, a consensus is formed on what is needed. An intranet site can automate the method and keep users anonymous.

Finally, learn how the users do their work now. This is especially important for situations like new software development, application upgrades, and new hardware technologies. This can be accomplished in a usability laboratory where mock screens, resembling the technology being implemented, are made available. Feedback from users helps design the solution to be implemented. By working with a user one-on-one, you can experience how the user is using the current technology, how the new technology will affect the user, and what the ultimate goal of a technical change should be: increased productivity and increased profits. Don't lose sight of that fact.

Identify the Project Needs

Thanks to Intel's Gordon Moore, it is a common belief that the processor chip speed of technology doubles every 18 months. This law has spread to practically all areas of technology, which, in turn, means the role of an IT project manager can be expected to change just as rapidly. IT project managers everywhere struggle with keeping teams, budgets, and goals focused. IT project management becomes even more tedious when you consider the economy, the instantaneous expectations of stockholders and management, the constant turmoil in the IT industry, and the flux of each team member's commitment to their own career.

According to the Standish Group, a respected IT industry analysis and research firm, IT project management is getting better, but still out of control. Consider these statistics from their 2004 version of the CHAOS report:

Project Attribute	1994 Statistics	2004 Statistics
Cancelled before completion	31 percent	23 percent
Missed deadline, over budget, or both	88 percent	51 percent
Average cost overrun	189 percent	45 percent
Schedule overrun	222 percent	63 percent

While this news is encouraging, it's still far from success. Some would argue that these tighter values put more requirements on the project manager because they have less "wiggle room" on their projects than just a few years ago. You could also make the argument, however, that the education, expertise, and granular approach to project management provides more successful projects than ever before.

Still, there's that 23 percent of project cancellations and the 51 percent of projects that are late, over budget, or both. How can this be? Why do so many projects fail from the start? Projects fail for many different reasons: other projects take precedence, team members lose sight of the purpose of the project, and project managers try to do the work rather than lead the team, among others. At the root is a fundamental problem: vision. Vision, in project management terms, is the ability to clearly see the intangible and recognize the actions required to get there. One of your jobs is to develop, nurse, and transfer the vision to everyone on your team. The project manager, however, cannot have a clear vision of the project if the project needs are never clearly established.

Creating Reasonable Expectations

Once you've discovered your vision, create a goal. A goal should be a clearly stated fact, for example, "The new database will be installed and functional by December 6 of next year." A goal sums up the project plan in a positive, direct style. Every member of your team should know and pursue the goal. It's not all up to you. The goal establishes the direct need and purpose for undertaking the project.

When creating a goal for your project, be reasonable. Just like it would be foolish for a fat man to say, "I'm going to lose sixty pounds this month," it would be as unreasonable for you to create an impossible goal.

A logical goal is not just an idea, a guesstimate, or some dreamy date to be determined. A goal is actually the end result of a lot of hard work. Each IT project will, of course, have different attributes that determine each goal. Let's say, for example, that your company is going to be migrating your servers and desktops to the latest and greatest operating system.

With this scenario, certain questions would have to be answered to determine the ultimate goal: Is the hardware adequate for the new OS? Will the applications work with the new OS? Will the team have adequate time to be trained and experiment with the new OS? These questions will help you create the end date for the goal.

Creating the Project Charter

Once you've determined the business needs for the project, it's time to create a project charter. A project charter is similar to the goal, but more official, more detailed, and in line with your company's vision and goals. Obviously, a project can stem from a broad, general description of an IT implementation. A goal narrows the description and sets a deadline. A project charter formalizes the goal and serves as a map to the destination. Above all, however, a project charter formally authorizes the project.

Not only does a charter clearly define the project, its attributes, and its end results, it also identifies the project authorities. The project authorities are usually the project sponsor, the project manager, and the team leaders (if necessary), and the charter specifies the role and contact information for each. See Figure 1-6 for the evolution of a project charter.

Why do you need a project charter? Why not just hop right in and get to work? In a small company, plowing right into the project may turn out just fine. However, in most companies, including smaller ones, a project charter is the foundation for success. Consider what the charter accomplishes:

- Authorizes the project
- Defines the business need in full
- Identifies the sponsor of the project

FIGURE 1-6

The project manager must lead the process to create a project charter.

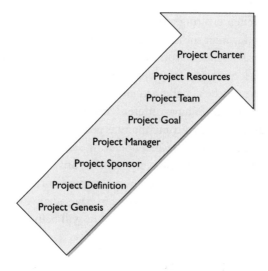

Project Charter
Project Resources
Project Team
Project Goal
Project Manager
Project Sponsor
Project Definition
Project Genesis

- Identifies the project manager
- Makes the project manager accountable for the project
- Assigns authority to the project manager on behalf of the project sponsor

Project Charter Elements

When you create the project charter, you can include just about any information on the project that you'd like. Generally though, consider these elements:

- Official project name
- Project sponsor and contact information
- Project manager and contact information
- Purpose of the project
- Business case for the project (reasons why the project needs to happen)
- High-level results and deliverables of the project
- General statement about how the team will approach the work
- Basic timeline of when the work will be implemented (A more detailed timeline will exist in the project plan.)
- Project resources, budget, staff, and vendors

Every project needs a charter. It authorizes the project, creates a sense of responsibility for the project manager, a sense of ownership for the sponsor, and a sense of teamwork for the project team. The project charter will save you headaches, establish who's in charge, and move you to your goal more quickly and with more confidence.

Following is an example charter, based on a fictional company called Best Enterprises. The company's network currently consists of 380 computers running Windows NT, 11 Windows NT 4.0 servers, and 5 Novell NetWare servers. It has made a decision to move all the workstations to Windows XP and all the servers, including the NetWare servers, to Windows 2003 Server.

Sample Project Charter

Project: Operating system upgrade: XP and 2003 servers
Project Sponsor: Sharon Brenley, Chief Information Officer (x. 233)
Project Manager: Michael Sheron, Network Administrator (x. 234)
Project Team: Edward Bass, Ann Beringer, Brad Bobich, Carol Fox, Charlotte Harving, Don Khunle, Casey Murray, Mick Suskovich, Mark Turner, Stephen Utmeyer

Project Purpose   All desktops will be upgraded to Windows XP by December 3, 2005. All servers will be upgraded and moved to five Windows 2003 Servers by December 20 of the following year.

Business Case   Windows NT has served our company for the past five years. We've learned to love it, embrace it, and grow with it. However, it's time to let it go. We'll be embracing a new technology from Microsoft, similar to Windows NT, but far superior: Windows XP. Windows XP will allow us all to be more productive, more mobile, more secure, and more at ease.

In addition, there are new technologies that work excellently with XP, such as infrared networking for our manufacturing shop floors and new accounting software that will be implemented later this year.

Of course, our company will continue to embrace our web presence and the business we've earned there. XP will allow us to follow that mindset and create greater opportunities for us all.

As our company has experienced over the past year, our servers are growing old, slow, and outdated. We'll be replacing the servers with six new multiprocessor servers loaded with RAM, redundant drives, and faster, reliable tape arrays—which means faster, reliable, more productive work for us all. The operating system we'll be implementing for all of our servers will be Windows 2003.

Windows 2003 will allow our users to find resources faster, keep our network up longer, and provide ever-increasing security.

Project Results

- Windows XP on every desktop and portable computer
- Windows 2003 Server installed on six new servers
- All implementation complete by December 20 of the following year

Basic Timeline

- **September** Test deployment methods, capture user and application status, finalize deployment image, and create scripts.
- **October** Initial deployment of 100-user pilot group. Test, document, and resolve issues. Redeploy 100-user pilot group with updated images and scripts. Begin Windows 2003 Server testing and design.
- **November** Begin month-long four-hour training sessions. While participants are in class, XP will be deployed to their desktops. Troubleshoot and floor support in coordination with Jamie Bryer, Help Desk Manager. Continue to test Windows 2003 Servers. Three Windows 2003 Servers will go live on November 15.
- **December** Finish deployment of XP. Install new 2003 servers and create infrastructure. Convert each existing server to Windows 2003. Project completed December 20 of the following year.

Project Resources

- Budget: $275,000 (includes XP, 2003 server, client access licenses, consultants, training)
- Test lab reserved for four-month duration
- On-site consultant from Donaldson Education

Your project charter can include as much or as little information as you deem necessary. Project charters are often shared with the entire company (with the exception of the budget) so you may have a few revisions before the charter is complete. Sharing a project charter with the entire organization, especially one that will affect all users as in the sample charter, can get everyone involved, excited, and aware of coming changes. A project charter also creates a sense of responsibility for all involved.

Your project team members will get distracted, pulled in different directions, and lose interest. Vacations pop up, kids get sick, people quit. Realize at the onset that not everyone will be as dedicated to your project as you are. Do your best to inspire, motivate, and lead. Set aside politics, egos, and aspirations and work toward the goal.

Finally, keep in mind that a charter can be called different things in different organizations and that the level of detail can vary depending on the company or the project being created. Most charters, however, accomplish two primary things: authorizing the project work and defining the project work.

Finding the Completion Date

There's a cartoon that's probably posted in every auto mechanic's garage. In the cartoon, there's a bunch of people rolling around laughing uncontrollably. Above all this mayhem is the caption, "You want it when?" Of course, as an IT project manager, you can't take that same approach, but a reasonable deadline has to be enforced.

A firm end date accomplishes a few things:

- Creates a sense of responsibility toward the project
- Gives the team something to work toward
- Signifies a commitment from sponsors, team members, and the project manager
- Confirms that this project will end

How do you find the completion date for a project and how do you know if it's reasonable? The magic end date is based on facts, research, and planning. In upcoming chapters, you'll get a more detailed look at project end dates and how you establish them. For now, know that projects are a sequence of steps, and each step will take time. The completion of each step will predict when a project should end.

Some project managers create a flexible deadline. Don't do it. If you allow yourself a deadline that is not firm, you'll take advantage of it. And so will your

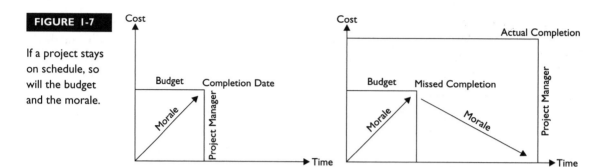

If a project stays on schedule, so will the budget and the morale.

team, your sponsor, and your management. Set a deadline based on an informed opinion, and then stick with it. The charts in Figure 1-7 demonstrate how a missed completion date is bad for the project, the company, and morale.

A rule of economics that affects scheduling is "Parkinson's Law." Parkinson's Law states that work will expand to fill the time allotted to it. In other words, if you give yourself extra time to complete a project, the project will magically fill the extra time. A firm deadline gives the project manager and the project team a definite date to work toward.

Some projects have a self-contained deadline. Remember the Y2K scare? With the year 2000 rolling in like a summer storm, every programmer and company found a way to make the deadline because it wasn't moveable.

Other factors can have impact on your projected deadline:

- **Business cycles**   Does your project deadline coincide with busy times of the year? Think of a retail giant. How willing do you think it would be to overhaul the database that handles shipping and store management around December?

- **Financial situations**   A company may be more (or less) willing to invest in new hardware or software at a particular time of the year due to taxes, fiscal year ending, or the advent of a new budget. You've got to consider these factors when you request finances for your project.

- **Times of the year**   When will your team members take vacation? How will their vacation plans coincide with your deadline? What other internal time commitments do they have? Will they be traveling to other sites? These factors can delay a project for weeks and months—ultimately resulting in a missed deadline. Work with your team members to ensure their availability coincides with their responsibilities within the project plan.

FROM THE FIELD

Interview with Kevin Kocis

Name: Kevin Kocis
Title: Manager of Information Technology
Years in the IT field: 10

Kevin Kocis has been working in the information technology field for over 10 years. He is currently the Manager of Information Technology for a division of a Fortune 100 company, where he develops strategies for network and server infrastructure, Oracle implementation, and platform interoperability issues (Windows, UNIX, and Macintosh).

Q: What is the best part about IT project management?

A: The best part about IT project management is leading an initiative that resolves a business need and/or contributes to business success. Another great part about IT project management is the challenge of leading new cross- functional teams.

Q: How do you start a new project?

A: The project is usually started in response to a broad objective or a business request. Once a performance analysis and feasibility study are completed, it can be determined whether the objective or request can be deemed a project. A project can also be initiated to optimize internal processes and to leverage return on investment.

Q: When you start a new project, what is the first thing you do?

A: The first thing to consider when starting an official project (assuming performance and feasibility tests are complete) is to gather requirements and document flowcharts to develop the project plan. Of course, requirements often change throughout the project, but the initial requirements will be based on current knowledge. Make it a priority to update the business champions and sponsors in regular project meetings.

Q: When starting a project, what's the most important thing a project manager should do?

A: When starting a project, the most important thing a project manager should do is to identify the business goal and determine the business champion or sponsor. The business sponsor needs to understand the project scope and help convey this process to the senior management team.

Q: How do you manage the relationship between upper management, your team, and the project?

A: The IT team manager manages the relationship between the upper management team and project by acting as interpreter. One of the challenges is that senior management may not understand the IT role for the project and vice versa. The project manager should debrief both groups to ensure a synchronous understanding.

Q: How important is a project goal?

A: The goal is always significant as it is essentially the initial reason for pursuing the project. However, the goal cannot be achieved without certain conditions. Factors such as scope creep, team relations, and communications will become important as the project progresses. These factors will contribute to the success of the project, so while a project manager must maintain a focus on the goal, she cannot ignore the factors contributing to the project's success.

Q: How necessary is it for project managers to create a project charter?

A: A project charter is very important for the project manager as it serves as a roadmap for the project. As its name suggests, the roadmap should define the key steps of the project, as well as the high-level deliverables. The roadmap should also include the relationship of the project to the business' operational or strategic goals. Project charters should be well publicized (such as through an intranet web site) in addition to the project's progress.

Q: Can you share an example of how you started a project and the steps it took for you to complete it?

A: One of my projects (that saw plenty of challenges) was an internal domain migration in preparation for Windows 2000. My company was one of the first to install Windows 2000 in its production environment, and with several hundred internal Windows NT domains, there was a strong need to consolidate to a handful of key domains. To simplify the process for the scope of this chapter, we communicated heavily with our business group management. I met with senior staff to inform them the migration was a corporate initiative that would simplify a later transition to Windows 2000. I also informed them that to mitigate potential risks, we would test the migration in our test lab.

FROM THE FIELD *(continued)*

Since the timeline for this project was short (weekend transition with one week scheduled for follow-up issues), no project charter was created. We tested the feasibility to perform the migration in our lab, working with an outside vendor for our domain migration software. We communicated the transition to the user community on a weekly basis, and on the Friday of the conversion.

Unfortunately, we did not plan for the unexpected power outage, nor the virus infection that occurred that weekend. As a result of these unforeseen events, our team had to branch out to maintain progress on the project. The only issues that resulted from the project were vagabond machines or users, and this essentially helped us prepare for our internal audit, so I considered this project quite successful.

Q: How do you work vendors into your timeline?

A: I always notify vendors during the project proposal phase as a courtesy when a project need is identified. This enables me to arrange project-planning windows around their turnaround times. Many hardware vendors do not build or prepare hardware until they are issued a purchase order, but advance notice can help expedite the process. Vendors (depending on the project) often work in parallel paths with the project team. For example, if we are looking to upgrade our servers by replacing them, the project team can plan communications and documentation while waiting for the hardware to be built and shipped.

Q: What do you do if vendors are late on delivery, which may disrupt your project completion date?

A: To avoid vendor delivery issues, the project managers should address contingency plans for any vendor-related critical path that exists in the project plan. By discussing the critical nature of the delivery, vendors can assist with providing an alternative solution before the schedule is critically impacted. These issues should be discussed prior to committing to the vendor.

Q: How do you balance the time between projects and your regular work duties?

A: Unfortunately, when it comes to balancing time, there is seldom a right or defined answer. Individuals balance time responsibilities differently. In my case, I prioritize the projects and weigh them against my daily duties. Some project meetings I may not attend, and assign a team member to represent me. For the team, I prioritize their project tasks and communicate with management to ensure there is understanding that daily tasks will not maintain their priority.

For example, if a desktop support person is involved in a critical stage of the project, daily support will not be able to maintain the same expectation level. This can be leveraged with additional resources if the business wishes to maintain its support expectancy.

Q: What's a common trap IT project managers fall into and how can they avoid it?

A: IT project managers often fall victim to making reactionary decisions based on a hardship or challenging situation. Often, the response time in light of a complication is limited, and if no contingency plan was developed or an unpredictable event occurred, the project managers may be forced to make a reactionary and critical decision without business support. To avoid this, make sure contingency and rollback plans exist for all projects. Listen to the project team, and form a consensus on the issue. The project managers may also have a tendency to become too hands-on or hands-off in the process if the plan is behind or ahead, respectively.

Q: What are characteristics of a successful project launch?

A: The characteristics for a successful launch include high publicity and management involvement. Start with a kickoff meeting (with goodies), and make sure *all* business management can participate, as well as the entire project team. Ensure that all communication standards are agreed to, and that management understands the goal of the project and its participants. Review the plan and its impacts in great detail. Listen to concerns and modify the project plan *only* if critically necessary.

Q: If a project has many steps to the final implementation, how do you keep the project moving and heading toward each milestone?

A: For long-term projects, accountability and strict deadlines are mandatory. A key to ensuring that the team does not burn out or fade is to acknowledge their successes at milestones, regardless of the size or magnitude of their contribution. Teamwork is critical for a successful project.

Q: What advice can you offer fellow IT project managers in regard to implementing new technologies?

A: My personal advice to fellow IT project managers regarding new technologies is to thoroughly understand the enhancements and changes. Make sure external resources exist (such as vendor training and demos). Test and document the technologies thoroughly.

FROM THE FIELD *(continued)*

Never underestimate how people (your users) are affected by change, even good change. Overcommunicate and focus on the positive results.

Q: What advice can you offer for aspiring IT project managers?

A: My advice to aspiring IT project managers is to remember that we grew from a certain "track." Some of us are (or were) developers, DBAs, systems engineers, and network engineers. We may not have led people from other tracks. Learn to listen and be fair. Don't be influenced by where you've been. Focus on teamwork.

CHAPTER SUMMARY

Did you ever see one of those movies with the ace reporter scrambling into the newsroom with just minutes to go before his deadline? He writes a fantastic article on the mayor, the mob boss, or the sports team with just seconds to spare. Meanwhile, his cigar-chomping boss is ranting about this reporter's usual skin-of-the-nose behavior.

That's how IT project management can be. The really awful part? Sometimes it's not even that close. Projects are consistently late, over budget, and half- cooked. IT project management is not about implementing a technology. It's about leadership, integrity, decision-making ability, planning, and time management.

To be a successful project manager, you have to start each project with a clear, concise vision of what the project will yield, when it will end, and how you can lead your team to that destination.

Project management is governed by business cycles, dedication, time, and sometimes weekends. Successful project management takes more than implementing the latest whiz-bang technology. To succeed in project management is to succeed in leadership.

CHAPTER QUIZ

1. What is project management?

   A. The ability to complete a task within a given amount of time

   B. The ability to complete a task with a given budget

   C. The ability to manage a temporary endeavor to create a unique product or service—on time and within budget

   D. The ability to administer a series of chronological tasks within a given amount of time and under budget

2. Which of the following determine the start of a project?

   A. Knowing the project sponsor

   B. Knowing the project budget

   C. Knowing the project completion date

   D. Knowing the project results

3. Which of the following is the most important element of a project genesis?

   A. Sponsor

   B. Team members

   C. Vision

   D. Project manager

4. Why must you interview the project decision makers before starting the project?

   A. To detail the budget of the project

   B. To determine the project results

   C. To gain their support and trust

   D. To determine the project completion date

5. What is the purpose of the project charter?

   A. To launch the project team

   B. To identify the project manager

   C. To assign a budget to the project

   D. To authorize a project

6. Why must a project manager question every facet of a new project? Choose two:

   A. To determine the project results

   B. To determine the validity of the project

   C. To determine the project budget

   D. To determine the project resources

7. Why are new technologies implemented within a company?

   A. To increase the speed of internal processes

   B. To be more competitive

   C. To be more profitable

   D. To be more technically savvy

8. When considering the type of technology to implement in any given situation, what are things a decision maker must consider? Choose all that apply:

   A. The steps required to implement the technology

   B. The users the change will affect

   C. The vendor's ability to provide support

   D. The business cycles the change may interrupt

9. What is a focus group?

   A. An interview process for elective team members

   B. An interview process by the team members to determine the success of a project manager

   C. A sampling of users affected by the proposed technology

   D. A sampling of management affected by the proposed technology

10. Why can a focus group be counterproductive?

   A. The participants may not understand the technology.

   B. The management involved may not like the technology being implemented.

   C. The participants may focus on the problems of the old technology rather than the goals of the project.

   D. Team members may have political agendas against the project manager.

11. A project manager would like to use an anonymous tool to gain a consensus on the needs of the project. Which tool is the project manager likely to use?

    A. A survey on an intranet site

    B. The Delphi Technique

    C. An e-mail message to all users within the organization

    D. A Monte Carlo simulation

12. Fill in the blank: Increased _____ results in increased profits.

    A. Technology

    B. Speed

    C. Productivity

    D. Bandwidth

13. What is a project goal?

    A. The end result of the project

    B. A statement of the project and its end date

    C. A statement of the project, its results, and its end date

    D. The mission statement

14. What does a firm completion date accomplish? Choose two:

    A. Creates a sense of urgency

    B. Signifies a commitment to the project from the sponsor(s)

    C. Signals a financial commitment to the project

    D. Confirms the project will end

15. Why is a flexible completion date bad?

    A. Allows the project to be delayed

    B. Signals the project will end eventually

    C. Increases time and cost, decreases morale

    D. Allows other projects to overlap this project

CHAPTER EXERCISES

Exercise 1

You are the project manager for Ogden Underwriters Insurance Company. This company has offices in Chicago, Des Moines, Seattle, Lincoln, and Atlanta.

You have been tasked with managing the rollout of a new web-based training program. You are to interview several members of your company to find out what their goals for the project are and work those into your plan as much as possible. As this is a simulated exercise, you'll find quotes from several key personnel in the following table.

To complete this exercise, analyze persons being interviewed, list their concerns about the project, and then record the objective of each.

Person	Title	Concerns	Objectives
Nancy Gordon	Chief Executive Officer	I am very excited about this project. All employees should have access to the web site, no matter where they are located in the country. The training should supplement our existing classroom training and provide new information as needed. I would also like to see videos of common tasks for quick review. Finally, the web-based training must be searchable, user friendly, and easy for learners to stop and resume lessons with ease. Have fun!	
Cory Owens	Accountant	Will this thing really work? Our network seems pretty slow already. I don't have time to be waiting on images to load, downloads, and other stuff like that. My computer is so old, and so is everyone else's in this department, that we can't take another software upgrade if we have to. By the way, when are we going to get new computers? Mine at home is faster than the one here at work. Sigh.	
Sarah Sullivan	Claims Adjuster	This is a great idea; I just hope I have time to use it. I get interrupted a lot so I'd need to be able to pause and restart if necessary. Will this web-based training work with my computer? I'm using Linux here and Windows NT at home. I will be able to access it from home, won't I?	

Person	Title	Concerns	Objectives
Michael Bogner	Chief Information Officer	Web-based training will allow for training on demand in modular pieces. The thing to remember though is that all users will need computers with at least an 800 MHz, 128MB RAM, and the latest version of Internet Explorer or Netscape to take advantage of this. In fact, there are 240 PCs that need to be replaced in six months. Go ahead and work that into your budget and your plan. They'll need to use Windows XP. I guess that'll mean these folks will need training on XP, too.	
Jill Vaughn	Web Design Manager	I've wanted to do WBT (web-based training) forever. My team will be using Macromedia's ColdFusion, Flash, Authorware, and Fireworks for everything. Make certain all the users have the correct plug-ins for their browsers.	
Jackson Dahl	Web Integrations Team Leader	We can do it—if a few things come true. We'll need a fatter pipe to our ISP if we're going to host the pages here. Of course, if users are coming from all over the country to this thing, we're going to need to talk about security, authentication, and types of access. We'll probably need another server for Jill's ColdFusion database.	

Exercise 2

Now that you've gleaned the key pieces of information from each of the key staff members, you need to write a charter for the project. Your sponsor for this project is Nancy Gordon. Here are some facts that must be included in your project charter:

- Official project name (use your imagination)
- Project goal
- Business case for the project
- High-level results of the project
- A basic timeline of how your team will implement the plan
- Required resources for the project (If you would like to find the prices of the new computers, software, and operating systems, you may, but they are not required for this exercise.)

QUIZ ANSWERS

1. **C.** Project management is the ability to manage a temporary endeavor to create a unique product or service on time, within budget. Answer D is incorrect because completing a project under budget is nice, but reflects inaccurate planning of what the budget should have been at the project outset. In addition, the project goal must be met.

2. **D.** When you begin a project, you must know what's expected at the end of the project. You wouldn't begin building a house without a plan; the same is true for project management. While knowing the project sponsor and the project budget is necessary, it still doesn't determine what the goal of the project is.

3. **C.** Before any effort is applied to the implementation of a project, the project manager and the team must have a vision of what the project will produce, how it will come about, and when it will be finished. Vision supercedes all other elements.

4. **B.** Again, you must have a clear understanding of what the decision makers' vision of the project results are before any other factor of the project implementation. After you have a clear understanding of the project vision, address issues such as budget and the completion date. Answer C is incorrect because you will gain the support and trust of the decision makers once you have obtained their vision of the project, not through an interview.

5. **D.** The purpose of the project charter is to authorize the project. Answer A is incorrect because the project team may not be selected until later in the project. Answer B, identifying the project manager, is also incorrect. The project manager is named and identified in the project charter, but the purpose of the charter is to authorize the project. Answer C is also incorrect; the project charter's purpose is not to assign a budget to the project.

6. **A, C.** A project manager must first determine the project results before beginning a new project. You must know the end results of a project before beginning a project; to do otherwise is asinine. Technology costs money because it makes money. You must know what is required to obtain the desired results. From this information you can form a required budget. Answer B, the validity of the project, is incorrect because answer A will determine that. Answer D is also incorrect because answer A will lead to D.

7. **C.** As information technology specialists, it is easy to lose sight of the link between technology and why it exists. The goal of a technological implementation is, generally, to lead to more productivity, which in turn leads to higher profits. If technology does not earn its keep, it should be considered an unwelcome houseguest.

8. **B, C, D.** Answer A is not a correct choice because that's why the decision maker has put you in charge of the project. The decision maker has made the decision and then delegated the implementation to you.

9. **C.** A focus group is a collection of users your project will affect. It should consist of a sampling from management and staff, not just management.

10. **C.** The participants may focus on the problems of the old technology rather than the goals of the project. An improperly organized focus group can result in a gripe session about the old technology and its flaws rather than the benefits and goals of the new project. A focus group requires a strong leader to help the participants focus on the future implementation rather than their complaints with the current technology.

11. **B.** The Delphi Technique allows for anonymous input from participants and provides rounds of discussion for consensus building. Answer A is incorrect because a survey on an intranet site may or may not provide anonymous input. Answer C, e-mail, is incorrect because it does not provide anonymous input from users. Answer D is incorrect. Monte Carlo simulation is a simulation tool testing variables, not a consensus building approach.

12. **C.** Technology can be counterproductive. Technology should increase productivity, allow for a quick learning cycle, and ultimately result in higher profits.

13. **C.** A goal is a clear, concise statement of the project. It should include the project end results and be positive in nature.

14. **B, D.** A firm completion date shows a commitment to the project from sponsors and it confirms that the project will end. A completion date does not, however, signal a financial commitment to the project. A completion date should create a sense of responsibility, but not a sense of urgency or panic.

15. **C.** A flexible completion date can result in the delay of the project. The delay of the project will result in higher costs and lower morale.

EXERCISE SOLUTIONS

Exercise 1: Possible Solution

Person	Title	Objectives
Nancy Gordon	Chief Executive Office	All employees should have access to the web site. Training should supplement existing training. Offer videos of common tasks. Site should be searchable. Users must be able to stop and resume lessons.

Person	Title	Objectives
Cory Owens	Accountant	Speed issues need to be addressed. Computer needs to be brought current.
Sarah Sullivan	Claims Adjuster	Users should be able to pause and resume lessons. Need to take multiple operating systems into account. Include access from home.
Michael Bogner	Chief Information Officer	Upgrade computers to at least 800 MHz, 128MB RAM. Upgrade browsers. Replace 240 PCs as part of project. Systems require XP operating system. XP training required.
Jill Vaughn	Web Designer	Include plug-ins for browsers.
Jackson Dahl	Web Integrations Team Leader	Need faster bandwidth. Keep in mind security issues. Need new web server for ColdFusion database.

Exercise 2: Possible Solution
Project Charter
Project Name: Click and Learn: Web-Based Training Initiative
Project Sponsor: Nancy Gordon, CEO
Project Manager: Your name here
Project Goal: A new web-based training program will be created and implemented company-wide by January 2003.

Business Case: There's something new and exciting happening at Ogden Underwriters Insurance Company, and it's not a new life insurance policy. It's web-based training (WBT). WBT will allow us to replace and supplement traditional classroom training on all topics.

No longer will you have to enroll in the same four-hour class because you've forgotten how to do one ten-minute task. No longer will you get hours and even days behind schedule because you needed to attend a class on the latest procedure for your department. No longer will you need to pester help desk staff, your neighbor, or your favorite computer nerd about how to write a macro.

Instead you'll just click and learn.

Our WBT service will allow employees from around the world to access the information it contains. That means each office and mobile user, and even those who work at home will be able to log in to our site and access the information they need anytime, day or night.

We'll provide forms, printable directions, and videos of various tasks for each department. Because this technology is web based, it doesn't matter what operating system your computer is running. It's going to be great.

You'll be able to search for a specific topic or take an entire structured course. And thanks to our modular approach, you'll be able to pause your training should you get interrupted and then resume it minutes or even days later.

Required Resources: Of course, with this technology there are fundamental changes that will affect all of us. For a start, all users will receive the latest version of Microsoft Internet Explorer and the additional software required to view the videos and complete the WBT classes. 240 computers will be replaced with new, speedy PCs running Windows XP.

Our web server farm will grow to add an additional database server. Additionally, our fractional T1 line will be replaced with a full T1 line starting next spring.

Timeline:

- **First 30 days**   Replace 240 older PCs with new computers. Begin offering classes on Windows XP as part of rollout. Work with web developers to create a schedule of course listings for each department.

- **Second 30 days**   Continue development of web courses. Order T1 installation. Install and work with Jill Vaughn and Jackson Dahl on integration for ColdFusion server and current web servers.

- **Third 30 days**   Begin creation of videos, streaming software, and bandwidth utilization issues. Work with Jill and Jackson on links for Microsoft Explorer upgrade scripts.

- **Final 30 days**   Go live with initial classes and test usage. Throttle servers and document results. As month progresses, continue to go live with additional offerings. Create form to request additional courses, troubleshooting, and support.

Chapter 2

Planning the Project

Picture this: You're an IT professional and your manager informs you that the entire network, from the physical cabling to the network cards in each machine, has to be replaced with something bigger, better, and faster.

After you recover from choking on your coffee, you ask, "Something? What exactly did you have in mind?"

And what does your boss say? "I dunno. Something faster. Just figure it out and let me know what'll work. By the way, we can't spend too much. See ya."

While this may not be a typical way for a project to begin, you can see before any implementation, charter, or budget talks get under way you've a ton of research and planning to do. Where does that planning begin and how can you formalize your results? This chapter will answer these questions and help you streamline your efforts.

How to Plan

Don't laugh. Many IT project managers, executives, and professionals don't know how to plan. Oh sure, they think they do, but the reality is they don't. When these folks begin planning, their efforts consist of searching the Web randomly, leafing through vendor brochures, and chatting with other professionals about similar problems they've encountered and how those problems were resolved. On the surface, this looks like a great effort. The Web, vendor brochures, and interviews are all essential elements to IT research. The trouble, however, is there's little rhyme or reason, little approach, and, most important, few results to show for the effort.

The goal of research is to come to a conclusion, a discovery, and hard-hitting facts, upon which a decision, a plan, or an implementation can be based. Now here is the key: good research stems from an organized, concentrated effort.

In order for projects to be successful, the project manager and the key stakeholders must know what it is the project will create. Often, especially in information technology, the customers of the project don't know what exactly your project will create. They may have a general idea of a scenario they'd like for you to create for them. Through interviews, quantitative analysis, and in-depth research, you'll propose solutions to them.

When creating a solution for a customer, the project manager must have the same vision the customer has for the final product. While there will, no doubt, be iterations and revisions as the project progresses, it's better to understand upfront what the project deliverables consist of. Root cause analysis allows the project manager and the customer to work together to find the solution for the problem, opportunity, or other condition the project is to resolve.

When you go about researching anything, from real-time transaction servers to RJ45 connectors, you must possess a plan of attack, maintain laser-like focus, and document your efforts. How do you plan? Here is a sure-fire, six-step method that works:

1. *Define the purpose of the research in writing.* Writing a concise Concept Definition Statement of the project helps form the research you are undertaking. The Concept Definition Statement will help you develop the laser focus you'll need for success. Keep that statement in plain view as you research. Don't lose track of your purpose, or you'll meander through your research like a lazy walk in the woods.

2. *Determine what resources you will use during this research.* Make a list of avenues of information you'll utilize. This is not to rule out any possible source of information, but to list your sources and then organize them in priority. Sources can include:

   - Prior experience
   - Experience of others
   - Qualified, quality Internet sites
   - Specific trade magazines
   - IT books directly related to the topic
   - Vendor brochures

3. *Delegate.* If you have team members in mind for this project, use them to help in the research. You'll need their expertise and experience to develop the best solution for the project purpose. Break down your planning into multiple components and then delegate portions of the research to team members. Many hands may lighten the load, but accurate workers with knowledge develop the plan.

4. *Get to work.* Begin reading, evaluating, and taking notes on your discoveries. If you use the Internet, bookmark useful pages you've found. Few things are worse than knowing there's a great page out there somewhere, but you can't remember when or where you saw it. Record the books and magazines you've

used and associated page numbers. This supporting evidence will help you later when you formalize your project plan.

5. *Organize and document.* Compile all of the information you and your team have gathered. This is the start of a feasibility plan. One key management skill is the ability to organize and recall the needed information at notice. A knowledge management system is ideal for any project manager.

6. *Evaluate and do more research.* Once your research has come together, determine if the collected data answers the research purpose. If it does, move on. If it does not, continue to research following these same six steps as your guideline.

This method of research is simple and direct, but will produce results. One key element is time; don't get bogged down in the research process. Of course, quality takes time, but set a deadline to reach step 5. As you can see in Figure 2-1, the steps to successful research also follow a projected timeline.

Creating a Feasibility Plan

A feasibility plan is a documented expression of what your research has told you. It helps you determine the validity or scope of a proposed project or a section of a project.

Feasibility plans are often written with upper management in mind, so they're direct, organized, and generally factual rather than opinionated. As you approach your project, keep in mind that the goal of any IT project is not technology for technology's sake, but to add value to the company. The feasibility plan determines if the proposed project can feasibly be accomplished.

FIGURE 2-1

Time management is crucial to effective research.

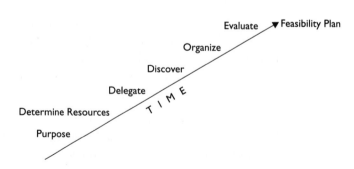

As you draft the feasibility plan, think like an executive and write with the business in mind and how the proposed technology will benefit the company. If you approach any project as if it is a business venture and you are the proprietor of the business, you'll be much more successful in your work. As the "project proprietor," you assume ownership and responsibility of the project and its success or failure.

Begin Writing

To begin writing the plan, refer to the Concept Definition Statement you used in the research phase. The Concept Definition Statement defines why you initiated the planning process and should reflect the proposed project. As Figure 2-2 demonstrates, the statement is the foundation of the feasibility structure.

For example, suppose an international company is investigating implementing a new, to-be-determined application that will need to manage multiple calendars, resources, and e-mail. The company's Concept Definition Statement at the start of the research reads as follows: "To determine the selection of a calendaring system that can provide resource management, e-mail, and workgroup collaboration, the application must be proven, able to integrate with our current network operating system, and address international time zones." This purpose statement would introduce the feasibility plan.

FIGURE 2-2

The Concept Definition Statement is the foundation of the feasibility plan.

Feasibility Structure

The feasibility plan is broken into five sections:

- Executive summary
- Product
- Audience impacted
- Financial obligations
- Recommended action

Each section is vital to the study and should be direct, full of facts, and provide references to the historical information and supporting evidence you've used to create the plan.

Executive Summary

At the start of the feasibility plan should be an executive summary, the purpose of which is twofold: to draw the reader into your findings and to define the key points of your plan. As its name implies, it provides a summary of your findings so the entire document doesn't have to be read. It should include a summation of each of the remaining sections in your plan.

Product

The product section describes the benefits of the technology you've investigated and are recommending. For example, the international company seeking the calendaring system may include in this section "ABC Server and the ABC Calendaring client software work together to provide a calendaring system that can be shared among all users. This client-server package allows for public and private calendars, free time lookups, room and resource reservations, e-mail, and international time zone calculations. In addition, the software allows application developers to create workflow applications, collaboration, and Web integration. Our current network operating system can be integrated with this solution." For this company, the ABC Server and client software is a logical solution as it meets every requirement of the Concept Definition Statement.

You should write the product section to pinpoint the audiences impacted by the proposed technology. The product section may also include

- Differences between the recommended product and a competitor
- Support for the recommended product

- How the recommended product may dovetail with the current technology
- Vendor history
- Other companies that have successfully implemented the product
- Any shortcomings or risks involved with the proposed product

Audience Impacted

The feasibility plan should address issues concerning the users who will be affected by the implementation:

- How much downtime will the audience experience because of the implementation?
- What is the learning curve of the new software?
- Will training classes be needed for all users?
- How will the recommended software transfer or work with your company's existing technology?
- How long before this software will be upgraded again?
- How long before it will be retired, obsolete, or no longer supported by the company?

Also in this section of the plan, you need to mention how the technology will be implemented. Consider if a portion of the company switches to the new technology before other parts of the organization. Will the technology have an impact on work and communication between the two parts of the company? How long will the technology implementation take?

Financial Obligations

This section of the feasibility plan provides an overview of the cost of the technology rather than a full-blown budget (Chapter 4 will detail budgets). Consider these factors:

- The price of the technology product
- The necessary licenses
- Training the implementation team

- Cost of labor to create or implement the solution

- Technical support from the vendor

- Outside talent and contractors to install the technology

- Monthly fees that may be associated with the technology (for example, service-related fees such as those for using a Tl line)

- Also consider the cost of not implementing the solution

The financial obligation section can also include return on investment (ROI) analysis. You should demonstrate how the technology will increase productivity, be easier to use, increase sales, or other relevant information. Of course, back your facts with references from your research.

Recommended Action

Within this section of the feasibility plan, you're ready to make your pitch for, or against, a technology to solve the problem. You should present a general overview of how the technology works, how it will be implemented, and what types of resources are required to make it work in your environment. You can also make a recommendation to investigate other options or newer technologies at this time— just be certain to explain why.

The solution and actions you recommend must be in alignment with the project purpose. A recommended action must address and satisfactorily answer the purpose of the project. Consider the reasons why the project may be initiated, including

- To solve an existing problem

- To increase productivity

- To become more efficient

- To reduce costs

- To increase revenue

- To become more competitive in the marketplace

Now that you know the different parts of the plan, take a look at the executive summary of a sample feasibility plan in the sidebar, "Executive Summary for Murray Enterprises." This company is considering replacing all of the current CAT5 cabling and upgrading its networks to something more current, faster, and reliable.

Executive Summary for Murray Enterprises

Written by Justin Case, IT Manager

Executive Summary The purpose of this feasibility study is to determine the type of cabling and related network devices required to improve the speed and reliability of our current LAN.

As we've all experienced, our current network is dated, sluggish, and unstable. A change of technology is required to increase the speed and reliability of our network.

- Proposed Technology: Install CAT5E cabling for our entire network.
- Install gigabit switches to segment and control network traffic.
- Upgrade wiring closet to gigabit equipment.
- Install 1000Base-T network cards in all compatible devices for faster throughput.
- Replace 850 PCs with new workstations that have gigabit compliant hardware.

Impact:

The change would affect all users. The new network cabling would be created and installed, while the existing network remains as is. The switch of the PCs to CAT5E-compatible NICs will happen by December 15. Users logon processes and usual workflow will remain constant, only the speed will be faster and more reliable.

Financial Obligations:

- The initial projected cost of the project materials: $11,400
- Cabling and connectors: $1800
- Switch: $1800
- Wall-mounted patch panels: $800
- 200 network cards: $5800
- Network installation kits: $1200
- 850 PCs will not be included in this budget but will be coordinated with normal operations.

Recommended Action:

Upon final approval, a project charter will be drafted and the team assembled. A plan of action will be created for the implementation. Upon arrival, the patch panels and switches will be installed and tested.

Cabling will begin at the top of the project. Next our team will complete the testing of the switches and network cards, and then connectivity will begin. No PCs in production will be connected to the new infrastructure until the new technology has been proven reliable and passed a quality audit. The workstations in production will cut over to the new infrastructure in waves. Upon successful cutover of all workstations to the new infrastructure, the original CAT5 cable will be removed.

The entire feasibility plan should detail each component and why the recommendations are being made. In addition, the financial obligation section should name the specific parts recommended.

Establishing Project Priority

As a project manager you'll likely find yourself managing multiple projects. You may also find yourself going head to head with other departments implementing similar projects, or worse, conflicting projects. Given every organization has different approaches to project management, your odds of success will increase if you know your organization's approach.

Project priority may shift from quarter to quarter or year to year. Project portfolio management is a process an organization takes to pick and choose which projects are needed, worthy, and should continue. Just as you might manage your financial portfolio, an organization has a responsibility to manage its portfolio of projects. The value, project champion current success rate of the project manager, and the purpose of a project are all factors a company may use to determine which project takes the highest priority.

Another approach to project management is the creation of a Project Management Office (PMO). The role of the PMO is twofold: it offers traditional project management services for an entire organization, or portion of an organization, and it serves as governing committee for all projects throughout an organization. If your organization were to participate in a PMO relationship, conflict resolution, budgeting, and the process of implementing projects and controlling projects would follow a system of checks and balances unique to your organization.

Your project sponsor should be as excited and motivated by the technology to be implemented as you are. The sponsor hopefully will be able to go to your defense, or

If you are fortunate enough to have multiple people helping you research the project, don't be tempted to micromanage. Assign research topics to the team members, give them objectives that their research should produce, and then give them a deadline. There is no need to watch someone research. Let your team complete their assignments, and wait for the results.

Once your team members have completed the research, create a way for the information to be compiled quickly and easily so it can be assessed and then decisions made. If you have the resources, and depending on the project researching, conduct a meeting and have the team members report their findings.

As the findings are being shared, have someone collect the notes and record any dialogue, controversy, or other information from the meeting. After the meeting, organize the collected data and disperse it to the team members. From the discussion on the collected research, the compiled report, and your own intuition, you should be ready to make an intelligent decision on how the project should move forward.

Contingency Plans

Every project needs at least one contingency plan. You may call these rollback plans, worst-case scenario plans, or disaster recovery plans. A contingency plan is a predetermined decision that will be enacted should the project go awry. If you ignore the creation of a contingency plan, you are tempting fate. A project that runs askew without a contingency plan will force your project to be late and most likely over budget.

As you complete the research and the foundation for your project develops, think about how you will react if any phase of the project falters. As most IT projects will certainly have multiple steps to completion, there are plenty of opportunities for things to go wrong. And they will. Figure 2-8 shows how contingency plans are used and built into a successful project.

As part of the project planning process, record reported troubles; document any conflicts with other technology, and bookmark any articles or web sites that offer warnings on the technology you're implementing. Researching the negative possibilities of your technology can keep the love of the implementation from overriding reason, and heighten the awareness that any technology can have flaws.

Use if-then statements such as the following to compose most contingency plans: "If the software conflicts with our video driver, then we'll write a driver that allows it to work." While this seems simple, a series of if-then statements can allow you to create a quick and concise contingency plan.

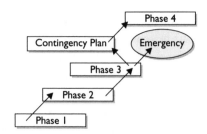

One of the primary reasons for creating contingency plans during the research phase of the project is in preparation of the next phase: dealing with management. Management loves to play devil's advocate. Some will swear they are the devil, but they aren't—usually.

By having a documented, logical contingency plan for each facet of your project, you are working with management prior to the face-to-face meeting with them. This will build trust, confidence, and support of your project even before they say, "Make it happen."

CHAPTER SUMMARY

Every project has its boundaries. Before you can begin to implement a project, assess budget dollars, or define a project goal, you must know the boundaries of the project. A project manager must know exactly what the project is to accomplish. The goal of project planning is to answer questions in regard to the project scope. Planning allows decisions to be made, teams to be assembled, and the wheels of productivity to begin to turn.

Create and evaluate a feasibility study to determine the project goal, the validity of the project, and the desired results of the project. Work together with your team to research, report, and develop the study. The feasibility study allows all parties to evaluate the project, its results, and its estimated ROI.

Establishing project priority, through researching the project, allows teams to work together for the good of the company. As conflicts, politics, and personal achievement arise, a set path of conflict resolution needs to be established between project managers, project sponsors, and upper management. The business champion should always win by putting the good of the company against the desire of others. In a perfect world, departments, management, and teams share information, work together, and strive to dovetail projects to create a powerful organization. It is achievable, but not always probable.

Financial obligations to a project should be considered during the planning phase. A successful project manager will evaluate the cost of the technology and the ROI. As a project manager, you must know the difference between value and investment and determine which technology will be the best investment.

You also have to be able to organize the tasks required to complete a project. Research must be organized and shared to determine the required tasks, required time, and required talent to complete an implementation.

Finally, for each major phase of a project you should create a contingency plan. A contingency plan allows you to make predetermined decisions in the event of project phases gone awry. Contingency plans allow a project team to work with management, allow for different variables to a project, and add a touch of realism to an expected flawless execution. As Henry Ford said, "Before everything else, getting ready is the secret to success."

FROM THE FIELD

Interview with Eric Chermely

Name: Eric Chermely
Title: Manager of Practice Support/IT
Company: Graydon Head & Ritchey LLP
Years as an IT project manager: 17

Eric Chermely, a certified project planner, earned his MBA from Xavier University with an IT concentration. Mr. Chermely serves as the IT manager for a law firm in Cincinnati, Ohio. He has managed many projects as an integrator as well as for the client side of the business.

Q: What is the best part about IT project management?

A: One of the advantages of IT is that it never stops changing. This makes each project new and exciting. If you like to be challenged at every turn, IT projects will meet that goal. No two projects are the same. Hardware, operating systems, and software products change every few months.

FROM THE FIELD (continued)

Q: How do you begin researching a new project?

A: The birth of a project should be the needs assessment. Many managers overlook the internal research and begin researching the newest technology—in particular, asking the question "What is the business need that the potential project should address?" Too often, IT managers jump to the "techie" stuff without looking at the business strategy. The first task is asking the right questions so that the team can begin to create the project's scope.

Q: How important is it to research a project versus going with the vendor's implementation recommendations?

A: Vendors can be your best source of knowledge. Just realize that vendors make money in some fashion. Knowing how they make their money and whom they represent is a key to the review of their recommendations. Help from e-mail listservs and industry associations are vital. If I know other law firms that have used an integrator, I might quiz the integrator about a specific project, but only with the consent of the other firm. That shows a potential vendor that I'm well connected and I've collected lots of "intelligence."

Q: When researching a new project, what's the most important thing a project manager should do?

A: Don't get hung up in the technology. Stay focused on the business need and how a particular project could provide a solution. Last, be objective and keep an open mind. If a new and very cool technology has no current application, put the research away and move on.

Q: How do you delegate research to team members?

A: Each person on a team has particular interests and an area of expertise. I will delegate accordingly. This process includes seminars, Internet research, or review of journal articles. I may circulate articles to team members just to expose them to a new area or product and then ask them to comment. The same people researching in their area of interest may end up with that piece of the project.

FROM THE FIELD *(continued)*

Q: What percentage of a project's time, on average, is given to research?

A: I consider research part of the planning phase. "Measure twice, cut once" is a good message for IT project planners too. For every one hour spent in planning, you save three during implementation. It is difficult to find an average percentage. Our team may spend 10 to 25 percent of the total time in the planning stage, but this will vary according to the scope and size of the project.

Q: How are projects introduced in the legal profession: through vendors, trade magazines, or the desire to create a solution?

A: Most are solution based. Usually, it's the desire to provide a solution to a business need. Then we perform the research to find possible alternative solutions. Again, knowing how other law firms solved similar business needs may help direct our research efforts.

Q: Should technical training be part of a project's research phase?

A: Yes. As long as you know the training will not go waste. It should be broad enough to expose the person to the technology as well as the product. Much of today's training is vendor sponsored. Keep an open mind even in training.

Q: How do vendors impact the research portion of your project?

A: Vendors are a great source of information for their product. You need to know how they make their money. If they represent all the products, a particular product margin may dictate their solution. Also, you will hear the good news, not the bad, and you should assume that you may not hear the whole story.

Q: How useful is the Internet when researching projects?

A: The Internet is a good place to start. Journals, articles, technical specifications, vendor information, and success (or failure) stories can be found on the net. It may be a good idea to look at vendors' support web sites to review the type of problems and solutions that current customers are seeing.

Q: What's a common trap IT project managers fall into and how can they avoid it?

A: Too many times, technology is the excuse for everything else. Make sure to take credit when due and share in the success too. Project creep, or adding items to the project after a project plan is in place and the charter approved, can ruin a project. A project manager has to learn to say no or at least "We'll look at that project later." Some sponsors will help you run the political defense.

Q: What are characteristics of successful research?

A: First, it's not just the technical knowledge but also the benefits to the business that must be researched. If everything is working, replacing Ethernet hubs with more advanced switches means nothing to a CEO. If the CEO knew that switches would provide the user population faster access to information when servicing clients on the phone and the savings could be quantified, that's the type of research that will make a difference to the CEO.

Q: What advice can you offer fellow IT project managers in regard to researching new technologies?

A: Technology professionals have a tendency to rush to the newest "bleeding edge" technologies. If a project has a large financial impact and changes the operations of a company, research it as if the company depends on the project's success.

The web server you propose must be reliable and easy to implement, and can be from any reputable software vendor. Your company has a fractional Tl line to the local LAN, and Janice, your manager, is concerned that more bandwidth is going to be needed to ensure reliability for all the company's clients.

Exercise 3

Based on your findings for the Caulfield Educational Supply Company, create an executive summary. Recall that an executive summary should include information on the recommended product, the audience impacted, financial obligations, and recommended action.

Possible solutions to these exercises appear at the end of the chapter.

QUIZ ANSWERS

1. **B.** The goal of planning is to arrive at a conclusion. While it may seem appropriate to discover which technology will make the company most profitable, that is not always the goal of research. Determining the cost of a project is part of research, but it is not the ultimate goal.

2. **D.** Organization and a concentrated effort is the key to good research. Without an organized focused approach, research has a tendency to ramble and be fruitless.

3. **A, D.** Experience with the proposed technology is the best resource anyone can ask for. The second best is information from the vendor touting what the product is capable of. An Internet search engine may be an excellent resource for finding information, but not a resource in and of itself.

4. **A.** Many hands lighten the load. Whenever possible, a project manager should delegate the planning among team members. The project manager rarely completes planning alone.

5. **B.** A feasibility study is a plan based on the project research. It contains a summary of the information you've discovered in an organized, factual document to determine if the project is feasible to complete.

6. **B.** Market research is not included in a feasibility study. An executive summary, information on the product, and financial obligations are included.

7. **C.** A project manager must evaluate any downtime caused by the product implementation. Downtime for users, whether through a learning curve or lack of productivity, is an expense for the company. Too high of a learning curve or long periods of inactivity due to lack of planning is unacceptable.

8. **B.** To implement the technology, an organization will have an initial cash outlay. The ROI will show how the technology can earn back the initial expense and more by increasing productivity. If the ROI is too little, the project may be scrapped.

9. **A.** A project manager may have multiple projects to manage. Project priority is the ability to determine which project takes precedence since it is most important to the success of an organization.

10. **C.** The goal of a project sponsor is to increase profits through the proposed project. A project manager will carry out the implementation of the project. A project sponsor may manage a project manager, but it should not be her goal to do so.

Chapter 3

Working with Management

Management. That very word conjures up so many different visions for project managers. For some, it brings up the image of the irate and belligerent boss who's always unhappy with someone about something. For others, it's the image of the boss who hides away, dreading to make a decision on anything. Still for some, management is not a bad word at all. To these people, management is a mentoring, guiding presence that wants projects to succeed.

Whatever type of management you're stuck with, you have to deal with them, work with them, and usually answer to them. If you're fortunate to have a good manager, count your blessings. There are plenty of people out there who would trade you places any day.

The thing to remember about management is that it's not necessarily an "us-against-them" mentality. Management's job is to support the vision of the company. Their role is to cut costs, increase productivity, increase revenues, and ensure that the requirements of upper management are met.

This chapter will examine how you, the project manager, can work with management toward success. Here you'll learn how to present a plan to management, get management involved in the plan, and then work with management as the project progresses.

Defining the Organizational Structure

The way your organization is structured determines the communication requirements, responsibilities, and reporting structure you have with management. Because all organizations and projects are different from one another (thankfully), they can be broken down into one of three different organizational structure models: functional, matrix, and projectized.

Working in a Functional Organization

Functional organizations are fairly common. These types of organizations are segmented by departments and their "functions." For example, you may have "Sales," "Accounting," "Legal," "IT," and so on throughout your organization. In a true functional environment, all team members, including the project manager, report to their functional manager.

The project manager in a functional organization has very little power. Decisions flow through the functional manager—he's the one running the show. The advantage of the functional organization, however, is there's a reduction in anxiety and a reduction in communication demands, and team members stay within their departments to complete the project work.

Working in a Matrix Organization

A matrix organization model allows a project team to incorporate resources from around the organization regardless of which department employees may work in. Project team members can be recruited, from anywhere or anyplace, within the organization. In contrast to the functional structure, this model blends the project team based on team members' individual contributions and abilities.

Technically a matrix structure has three different flavors:

- **Balanced** The project manager and the functional manager have equal power and autonomy over the project team.
- **Strong matrix** The project manager has autonomy over the project and the project team.
- **Weak matrix** The functional manager has autonomy and power over the project team members.

There are some downsides to the matrix structure. Communication demands increase for the project manager because he'll likely be required to keep all of the project team members' bosses up-to-date on how the project is moving and how the team members are doing on it. Another downside of this structure is that team members have to report to at least two bosses: their functional manager and the project manager. In addition, team members can expect to be on multiple projects at one time, which, of course, increases their responsibilities, communication requirements, and workload. Further, team members may be expected to complete their regular job duties along with additional responsibilities on the project.

Working in a Projectized Organization

In this structure, the project manager works with complete autonomy over the project. The project team is on the project full-time and reports only to the project manager.

The project manager has the most authority in this structure. There are many advantages to this structure:

- The project team is on the project full time.
- The project team reports to one boss for the duration of the project.
- The project manager has the power over the project.
- Communication demands are reduced.

However, this can lead to redundancy in some functions, such as tech support, accounting, purchasing, legal, and so on. Additionally, team members do not get the experience they gain when they work in an environment of their peers. This is particularly true for technical fields.

Using Project Management Power

The project managers are the power on the project team. While there may be some resistance of the project team to cooperate with the project manager, complete assigned duties, or participate as requested, the project team should realize the project manager is the project authority. There are five types of powers the project manager yields:

1. Expert. The authority of the project manager comes from experience with the technology the project focuses on.

2. Reward. The project manager has the authority to reward the project team.

3. Formal. The project manager has been assigned by senior management and is in charge of the project. Also known as positional power.

4. Coercive. The project manager has the authority to discipline the project team members. This is also known as "penalty power." When the team is afraid of the project manager, it's coercive.

5. Referent. The project team personally knows the project manager. Referent can also mean the project manager refers to the person who assigned him the position; for example, "The CEO assigned me to this position so we'll do it this way." This power can also mean the project team wants to work on the project or with the project manager due to the high priority and impact of the project.

Presenting the Project to Management

It's been said that the number-one fear most people have is public speaking. Above anything else, from crocodiles to death, public speaking is the most dreaded. And with good reason. Everyone has witnessed someone making a terrible job of delivering a presentation, so you know the dilemma. The fellow is sweaty, speaking low, and tripping over every word while he's searching for the next. Poor guy.

Chances are, though, if you were to talk to this person over a cup of coffee about the same ideas, he'd be rational, personable, and able to express his thoughts without a single "um" or "uh." What he's got is stage fright, and it's curable—with practice. The most important thing in a presentation? The message, not the messenger! If you know exactly what you want to say, you can say it much easier.

Presentations can be powerful, inspiring, and informative sessions. An effective speaker can captivate and motivate the audience to action. The core of an excellent presentation is the speaker's intimacy with the topic. The more familiar you are with the topic you are speaking on, the more convincing you will be. You must know your topic to speak effectively. Figure 3-1 shows the building blocks to an effective presentation.

Start at the End

When you begin a presentation, you want to capture your audience's attention. You want to hook them and reel them into your project idea. One of the most effective

FIGURE 3-1

An effective presentation must sell the project through effective reasoning.

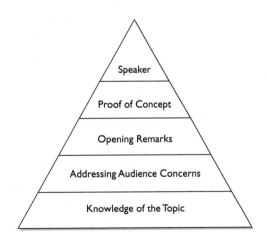

ways to do this is to start at the end. Tell your audience first what the proposed project will deliver. Forget all the techno-babble—that only impresses geeks. Management wants to hear facts.

For example, Susan is implementing a real-time transaction server for databases across the United States. She could go on about how long each transaction will actually take, the number of processors in each server, and the network connecting each site—but who cares (other than IT folks)? To grab the attention of management, she needs to open with the end result: "Our company will be 33 percent more productive by implementing this technology. From coast to coast, our customers can buy more products in real time with a guarantee of when they'll ship. Of course, this means our company will be more savvy, more advanced, and more profitable than our competitors."

Wow! Now Susan really has management's attention. She now has to back up her statements with the proof she's already gathered from her initial research. Once she has delivered the "punch line," Susan should immediately "show her cards" as to why she's so confident the implementation is a good thing. A slideshow or charts to show the expected growth would be most excellent—and most convincing—but it's easy to fall in love with the medium, not the message. Slide shows (ahem, PowerPoint) can be painful to sit through, boring, and overdone when they incorporate flashy animations that aren't relevant to the message. Keep it simple.

The WIIFM Principle

The WIIFM, or "What's In It For Me," principle is the ability to make a presentation touch the audience members so that they see how they will benefit from the proposal. When an IT project manager pitches an idea, he has to show the audience, typically management, how this technology will make customer lives better, improve profitability for the company, and make the company superior.

Professional sales people call this selling the benefits of a product, not just the features. If you do present a feature, always back it up with a benefit. For example, "This new system has a gigabyte of memory (feature), which will enable each user to increase productivity by twenty percent."

Obviously, whenever you get an idea to implement a new technology, you've got some personal reasons: productivity, an easier workload for you, an opportunity to work with technology, career advancement, and maybe some personal reasons you wouldn't say out loud and deny even if you were asked. Management will have similar reasons for implementing, or not implementing, your plan. You have to realistically look at four major points in the WIIFM principle to determine if your plan is viable:

- **Profitability** If the ROI on your project is small or nonexistent, proceed with caution. Remember, all businesses exist to make money; make certain your project helps that goal.

- **Productivity** Examine how your project can increase the productivity of the company. Not all projects will increase productivity for everyone, but at the minimum it should not hinder productivity.

- **Personal satisfaction** At the core of WIIFM is the ability to personalize the project. Find attributes of profitability, credit for implementing the technology, new sales channels, and other benefits that will make management (and you) happy to implement the plan.

- **Promotion** Think of how the project can promote the company's products, but also think how it can promote careers—not only yours, but the decision maker who will see the advantage of the project and may become your project sponsor.

WIIFM is not all about greed. It's thinking for the other parties. It's showing them the need that they may not see. WIIFM is creating a win-win solution for the parties involved. There's nothing wrong with thinking about the interest of the parties you are pitching your presentation to—in fact, it's required if you want their approval.

In many instances, the project manager gets the project dumped in her lap, a slap on the back, and a hearty handshake. In other words, there's no pitch to management, or anyone else, to get the project off the ground. An effective project manager, however, should investigate why this project is needed, how it helps the organization, and what exactly the project must deliver.

Tailor the Presentation

If you are speaking to a group of executives who have but a few minutes to hear your proposal, you need to quickly get to the point in terms they can understand. Forget about processors and bandwidth altogether with this crowd—focus on the benefits. If you're pitching to a group of managers who have a background in technology, then show them the details of the technology and how it increases productivity, profitability, and sales. Figure 3-2 shows the overlapping scopes a project manager

Project managers
must address
several factors in
a presentation.

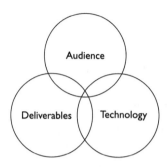

must consider when addressing an audience. The point is, know your audience
ahead of time and tailor your presentation to that audience.

If you are presenting your plan to a group composed of upper management,
middle management, and your immediate supervisors, always address your presentation
to the decision makers—typically upper management. Whomever you are speaking to,
tailor your presentation to what they want, and need, to hear to make a decision. Here
are five tips to help you do so:

- *What is your track record?* If you've gained approval in the past but blew the
  implementation, that's experience for you and them. If you've worked as a
  project manager before and failed miserably, management is going to be less
  excited to give you another opportunity until you can prove yourself again
  as a team player in other project implementations. Consider the Lessons
  Learned from the prior project and how it can help you on this new project.
  You may want to approach your immediate boss and discuss the proposal
  with her help.

- *Do they really want to listen?* You need to determine if this is the best time
  to even be talking about new ideas. If the company is in turmoil, financially,
  emotionally, or technically, your chances are diminished for implementing
  new projects—unless your project can resolve the turmoil.

- *Are they listening?* Remember, you've got to speak the language your audience
  needs to hear. Describe your project and its deliverables in the business
  terminology your audience speaks, and you will be heard.

- *And who are you again?* If you're low on the totem pole, you may have big
  ideas, but little track record. In this instance, your idea may be valuable but
  you aren't recognized—yet. Partner with someone in the company who is

a valuable leader and work with that person to pitch and manage the project. Use teamwork.

■ *How does this help?* If you are getting this question from your audience, then you are not starting at the end. Show them, in their language, exactly how this helps. Show them how this increases profitability, what the ROI is, and why it should be implemented.

■ *Are you following the rules?* Does your organization have formal or informal guidelines and procedures to pitch new projects? If so, follow the rules. Other organizations, and people, have enough on their plates that they don't dream of starting a new project until they can catch their breath on their current assignments. Find the rules to make a project a reality and follow them.

For each presentation, it would behoove you to have handouts of your overheads, charts, graphs, and any other pertinent data. Your feasibility plan is ideal for this collection of handouts if you've had the opportunity to complete one. Whatever you decide to disperse, always include an executive summary near the front of the plan so the reader can skim over the details and get the hard-hitting facts first. Of course, you should write the executive summary with your audience in mind.

Role of a Salesperson

Robert Louis Stevenson, the author of *Treasure Island,* said, "Everyone lives by selling something." No matter what you do for a living, you are selling something: time, wrenches, advice, a service, or a product. When it comes to presenting your idea to management, you have to slip into the role of salesperson.

When you think of sales, dismiss the sleazy, used-car salesperson image. A good salesperson is someone who identifies a need and then helps to fulfill it. That's what you have to do here. You've identified a need through your research, and now you may have to show management where that need exists and how this technology will fill it.

When selling an idea, speak in direct, simple terms. If it takes you longer than five minutes to express the reason for the technology, you're talking way too long. In fact, an excellent summary of the technology and its benefits should take less than a minute. For example, if you've determined the solution to the problem you've been presented with is to implement Macromedia Dreamweaver for your web designers, provide the supporting evidence for your recommendation. You have done the research, interviewed the developers, and explored the cost of the decision, right?

To open the presentation, you'd say something to the effect of, "Macromedia Dreamweaver will increase productivity, streamline the efforts of our web designers, and allow for collaboration of in-house and external developers. The time saved alone will pay for the product in less than a month." This is assuming you have the evidence to support this statement.

Again, you're starting at the end, but the whole idea and pitch is done in less than a minute. You need to capture your audience's attention and draw their interests into the plan. Everyone wants to be part of an investment that works. Show them immediately how your plan will work and then invite them to participate.

Part of presenting to management is also an informal presentation. You may know this as the infamous elevator speech. You know the drill: the CEO sees you in the elevator and asks, "So what are you working on these days?" And then you can sum up your project in 20 seconds or less on your elevator ride. This elevator speech is handy to summarize your project to anyone anywhere—not just for your favorite CEO in your favorite elevator.

Defining Management's Role

Management, to some, is a necessary evil. Sure, there are plenty of bad, heartless bosses in this world, but not every manager is bad. The majority of managers want to be good bosses, they want to be well liked, and they want to do a good, thorough job. While management should show an interest in the project you're implementing, their role should be one of support, not one of implementation. Management should not be peering over the shoulder of a technician trying to install video cards and memory. That's as obnoxious as family members watching doctors perform an appendectomy.

Project sponsors, however, do have an active role in the project management experience. Figure 3-3 shows the relation between the project sponsor, the project manager, and management. Project sponsors need to be informed of the status of the project, who is completing which portion of the project, and how the project is doing on time and finances.

Project sponsors have invested their credibility in the implementation, and they are relying on you to report progress and to complete the work. Project sponsors, like management, should not be peering over technician's shoulders, but should,

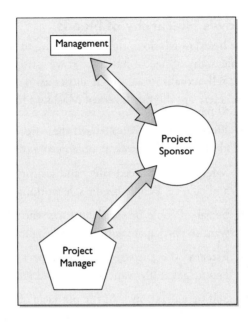

FIGURE 3-3

Project sponsors are mediators for project managers and management.

in some cases, attend team meetings, be involved with the project planning phases, and have input on the project implementation. Don't be afraid to ask questions and share concerns with your project sponsor—the sponsor is on your side and wants you to succeed with the project.

In fact, if you are going to present the project, it is in your best interest to talk with the project sponsor ahead of time and get coaching on the presentation. Find out the hot buttons, allies, showstoppers, and so on. Then you can tailor your presentation to incorporate this information. If you are pitching a project that does not yet have a project sponsor, see if you can get some input from a likely sponsor, or a friendly person in senior management. It always helps to stack the deck in your favor a little bit.

Management Theories

Your relationship with management, and how management sees their relationship with their employees, has been theorized and debated for years. These management theories can not only help the project manager realize how management views him, but also help him manage his own project team more successfully.

Maslow's Hierarchy of Needs

You've heard of Maslow, right? According to Maslow, people go to work to satisfy their hierarchy of needs. Basically, if we satisfy our most basic needs, we can strive toward self-actualization, which allows us to contribute and use our skills and talents. Here are the five layers of Maslow's hierarchy:

- **Physiological**   People need these necessities to live: air, water, food, clothing, and shelter. People need a place to work.

- **Safety**   People need safety and security; this can include stability in life, work, and culture. People need a safe working environment—with job security.

- **Social**   People are social creatures who need love, approval, and friends. People want to participate with their colleagues and peers—and to be liked at work.

- **Esteem**   People strive for the respect, appreciation, and approval of others. People generally want to do a good job and complete their projects.

- **Self-actualization**   At the pinnacle of their needs, people seek personal growth, knowledge, and fulfillment. People want to excel and work at something they enjoy and feel that is valuable.

Herzberg's Theory of Motivation

Frederick Herzberg, a psychologist and authority on the motivation of work, believed two agents affect people and their views toward their careers and work:

- **Hygiene agents**   These elements are the expectations all workers have: job security, a paycheck, clean and safe working conditions, a sense of belonging, civil working relationships, and other basic attributes associated with employment.

- **Motivating agents**   These elements motivate people to excel. They include responsibility, appreciation of work, recognition, the chance to excel, education, and other opportunities associated with work beyond financial rewards.

Herzberg's theory says the presence of hygiene factors will not motivate people to perform given they are expected. However, when the factors are absent, it demotivates workers. The motivating agents inspire workers to strive for success.

McGregor's Theory of X and Y

In Douglas McGregor's Theory of X and Y, management's view of their workers is broken down into two categories: bad and good. X people are lazy, must be micromanaged, and generally cannot be trusted. Y people are wonderful people who are self-led, motivated, and can accomplish new assignments proactively.

Ouchi's Theory Z

William Ouchi's Theory Z is based on participative management. His theory states that workers are motivated by the commitment, opportunity, and advancements the organization employing the workers provides. Workers have a lifetime-employment mind-set and learn the business by moving up through the ranks of the company.

Expectancy Theory

The Expectancy Theory states that people will behave based on what they expect the results of their behavior to be. In other words, people will work in relation to the reward they expect for their work. If the reward is desirable to the worker, she will work to receive it. In other words, people expect to be rewarded for their efforts.

Delegate Duties

In this discussion of how a project manager works with management, it also needs to be acknowledged that project managers are now part of management. If your organization has an us-versus-them mentality toward management, then it's up to you to bridge the gap. As a project manager, your team, especially a newly created team, may not fully trust you at the project's conception. Which may be too bad, considering your team will probably be made up of your friends and colleagues. You'll need to do your best to work with them, not against them—and earn their trust and respect.

One of your first challenges will be delegation of duties. Delegation is necessary. You are the project manager, and you cannot do every task required of a project. Once the team has been created, you need to follow the path the management and the project sponsor have taken: put your trust in others that they can do the job you've assigned to them.

Have you ever had the experience of someone asking you to do a task, only to stand over your shoulder and question every move you make? Or worse, have a boss watch you without saying a word? It's frustrating, to say the least. As a project manager, don't do it.

Once you have pitched the idea to management and your project has been approved, it's up to you to make it happen. It's easy to be tempted to do every piece of the project planning, or at least the exciting parts, but it's not wise to yield to that temptation. An effective project manager assembles the team, assigns tasks based on qualifications and credentials, and then trusts his team to perform.

Chapter 5 will detail the complete process of assembling and working with a team. For now, know that you are also management once you're titled the project manager. All those nasty thoughts and dislikes you have harbored for some managers can very easily be sent your way now from your team. As you start the project, consider these points to being an effective project manager:

- *Follow management.* Take management's lead and delegate as they've delegated. If you like the way certain managers have treated and challenged you in the past, follow their lead and do the same for your team. If you don't like the way some managers have delegated duties, find a role model and follow that manager's lead.

- *Delegation is necessary.* You are not Superman or Wonder Woman. By delegating duties, you are showing respect, trust, and wisdom to your team. As you move further and further into project management, you also move further and further from technology. Soon there will be a gulf between what you know and the present technology. A successful IT project manager must release the reigns of the implementation to the project team members; they're closest to the project work.

- *You are in charge.* From the onset, as you delegate activities, be fair—but also remember you are in charge of the project. Establish the flow of communication from your team to you, not around you.

- *Remember the users.* As your project develops, don't forget to consistently address the needs of the users impacted by this technology change. Often it's easy to overlook the individuals affected by the project you are managing. At each phase on the project, remember to ask how this impacts the users of the technology.

- *Keep the big picture in mind.* As a project manager, you need to make decisions on trade-offs and resources that benefit the company as a whole, not just you, your team, or your project. Develop the ability to see the macro environment and the details. This will take some getting used to, but it is an ability that will serve you well.

■ *Learn how to speak different languages.* At times you will need to present the status of your project to senior managers. They speak a language of ROI, productivity, and competitive advantage. However, your team members communicate in techno-speak. Make sure you are speaking appropriately to the various audiences you address.

■ *Delegate, delegate, delegate.* As a project manager, you will have plenty of work to do: following each team member's success and failures, tracking the status of the project, meeting with management, meeting with the team, and meeting with team members one-to-one. You need to delegate the tasks and leave them delegated. If a team member is having trouble with a task, then offer your assistance.

You are responsible for the project's success, the motivation of the team, and the communication to management. If this project fails, it is your fault. If the project succeeds, then everyone shares the glory. That's just the nature of the beast.

Focusing on the Results

Management's role is to help you, the project manager, focus on the end results. From the 1940s through the mid-1980s, management decided what task needed to be done, who would do it, when they would do it, and how it would be done. To complicate matters more, management would often supervise each step of the process to ensure that it was being done right. You know this, no doubt, as micromanagement.

Today's management philosophy is more laissez-faire, a hands-off, empowering approach to allowing teams to accomplish a goal. Management today is more concerned with results, rather than the process of getting there. As a project manager, you, too, must adopt this strategy. You must recruit your team, and then let the team do the work. Focus on the results, be available when you are needed, but allow the team to work.

Of course, this all sounds wonderful, but in reality is hard to implement. It's hard to allow others to continue with a project you've created. It's hard for others to have the same passion and drive that you do about a project. It's hard to put your future and your project's success in the hands of others. But remember you are not giving up ownership or control, you are allowing your team to do the job that you've asked of its members.

One of the best ways to create a team with drive and charisma is to, if at all possible, involve the team from the conception. By recruiting team members early and giving them responsibility early on, you have given them ownership in the project's success. A project manager, keeping the project results in mind, must have

- The ability to encourage participation from all members
- The ability to empower team members
- The ability to inspire team members and management

Inventing a Project Kickoff

Every project requires a project kickoff. So what is it, how do you get one, and why is it needed? A project kickoff is a meeting—or an event—to introduce the project, the management backing the project, the project manager, and the team members. It should be friendly, yet authoritative; organized; and used as a mechanism to assign ownership of the project to the team.

A project kickoff is needed to establish the launch of the project, who's in charge of the project, and who's in control of the project team. The kickoff is an event to allow management to rally the troops, organize the team, and get everyone excited about the upcoming plans. It's also an opportunity to convey to everyone that the trip ahead is going to have its challenges, but it'll be rewarding at its completion. It's a bon voyage party—but not for the Titanic.

Set the Stage

Depending on your project or your company, your team may comprise long-time colleagues or complete strangers. Use this opportunity to create a team—or at least the start of one. As the project manager, you are responsible for this collection of individuals, so you need to create a social environment ownership, and teamwork.

In this first meeting, you can set the tone for the entire project. Most project managers want a sense of camaraderie, but also a sense of formality to the project. Here are some recommendations of how you can create both for your project kickoff:

- It's an event! Have some fun. Create a simple theme and have some prizes or handouts for the team that are relevant to the project. For example, using the theme "Together we grow," give each member a small plant at the meeting, and tell the team that as the plants grow, so will the project. Remind them the project needs daily nurturing, just like the plant.

- Get excited! It's okay to have fun at these meetings. If it's a major project, hire the local professional cheerleaders to "cheer on the team." Have someone from the local zoo bring in some animals to jump-start the event. Do something creative and unexpected. It's worth it!

- Invite someone from the vendor you are buying the technology from, such as Novell or Oracle, to give a pep talk to the team at the kickoff meeting.

- Have someone take candid photos of team members as they enter the room and then a group photo. Create an intranet page with each member's photo, bio, and contact information.

- If you can, schedule the meeting close to breakfast or lunch and order in food. Food has a wonderful way of bringing down walls and allowing people to mix and mingle.

Project kickoff meetings can be boring and stuffy. Do something exciting, invigorating, and memorable. Create alliances between you and management and the project team. Invoke excitement, assign ownership of the project, and ask for a commitment to excellence. There is no reason why kickoff meetings can't be exciting. Anyone who says otherwise is a bore.

How Management Fits In

At this meeting, invite all of the managers involved in the decision. Their presence signifies their commitment to the project. They don't have to stay for the whole meeting, but they should at least make an appearance to rally the troops and have a donut.

The project sponsor, however, should stay for as much of the meeting as possible. Ideally, the project sponsor should initiate the more formal part of the meeting by calling things to order and introducing the project scope. The project sponsor should speak for a few minutes on the value of this project and what it means to the company. Then the project sponsor should introduce you as the manager of the project.

This approach signifies a role of authority among the team members without having to say who's in charge. Obviously the project sponsor is the management most closely associated with the project, but the central line of contact between the team and the project sponsor is through the project manager. There needs to be a clearly defined path of who is in charge of the project. Projects are not a democracy; each team member should have input and some autonomy, but the success of the project rests on the shoulders of the project manager, so this individual must establish his authority.

Defining the Purpose

Once the project sponsor has introduced you to the team, you're on. Now is your opportunity to establish many things. Prepare yourself prior to the meeting of what message you want to convey to your team. Your opening remarks should do several things:

- Establish your role as the project manager.
- Clearly state the goal of the project.
- Define the objective of the project.
- Set the tone of how you'll manage the project.
- Express the impact that the project will have on the company.

In these opening remarks, you will establish the purpose and importance of the project and assign that ownership to the team. Don't drone on and on about the project—the project's already been approved and there's no reason to continue selling.

If possible, a slideshow of what the project will include would be ideal. You can walk the team through a five- to ten-minute overview of the project's origin to the deliverables that signify the project has reached its end. There's no need to have a detailed step-by-step plan yet. A simple timeline of each of the major milestones will be fine.

Once you've defined the purpose of the project, showed the team members the big game plan, and given them a sense of ownership, you can quit talking. You should be able to do all of this in fifteen minutes or less. Yes, fifteen minutes or less. Preferably less. The project team is already going to know much of what the project is designed to accomplish. This is an opportunity for the project team, management, the project sponsor, and you to all agree what the project should accomplish.

Finally, show how management fits into the plan. Show how a financial commitment has been made to the success of the project. Show how this team is responsible for the success of the project and how everyone is counting on them.

If possible, share the news of how much failure would cost the company and the impact any delays may have on the project. This isn't to scare the team into submission, but rather to create a sense of responsibility for the success. Of course, also share with them the benefits the company will reap when the team does succeed.

Creating Management Alliances

You and management are also a team. Just like you want your project team to be dedicated, to trust you, and to work with you—the same applies in your relationship to management. You and management are working together for the good of the company, striving in unison toward an obtainable goal. Figure 3-4 shows how your relationship with management can be reflective of how you manage your own project team. While it may not always feel like you and management are part of the same team, you are.

When management and you agree, either by your choice or theirs, to implement a new project together, a team has been created. Hopefully, your management will be as supportive of you as you are of your own team.

Creating the Communications Plan

In order to create solid management alliances, you'll need to communicate. In order to communicate effectively, you'll need a communications plan. Based on stakeholder analysis, the project manager and the project team can determine what communications

FIGURE 3-4

A working relationship with management is required for project success.

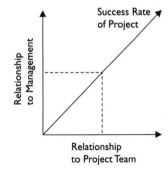

are needed. There's no advantage to supplying stakeholders with information that is not needed or desired. Time spent creating and delivering unneeded information is a waste of resources.

A communications plan can organize and document the process, types, and expectations of communications. It provides:

- A system to gather, organize, store, and disseminate appropriate information to the appropriate people. The system includes procedures for correcting and updating incorrect information that may have been distributed.

- Details on how needed information flows through the project to the correct individuals. The communication structure documents where the information will originate, to whom the information will be sent, and in what modality the information is acceptable.

- Information on how the information to be distributed should be organized, the level of expected detail for the types of communication, and the terminology expected within the communications.

- Schedules of when the various types of communication should occur. Some communication, such as status meetings, should happen on a regular schedule; other communications may be prompted based on conditions within the project.

- Methods to retrieve information as needed.

- Instructions on how the communications plan can be updated as the project progresses.

Working Together

The first step in this team of you and management is the ability to work together. Whether you like the immediate management you are working with or not, you have to work with them. Keep in mind that your goal, the success of the project, can be impacted by the management you are working with. Likewise, the success of your project can impact the management you are working with. In other words, it's a symbiotic relationship—you both need each other to be successful.

The solution to working together is to create a channel of communication. You and management must be able to talk, to discuss the project, and to report on the status of the work, the finances, and expectations.

Your Communications Plan will dictate how often you and management will need to communicate. In some organizations, it's weekly; in others, it's monthly. How will you know? Ask management what their expectations are. In some instances, conditions within the project will prompt immediate communication.

Intermediary communications in the shape of e-mails, an intranet site, or voice mail would be another avenue to keep management involved with the status of the project. By keeping a flow of communication open through you to management, you are ensuring management's involvement—but at a happy distance. Project managers must report both good and bad news. Don't candy-coat your findings; reporting both the good and the bad on an equal scale will build trust between you and management.

There are some problems that management and project managers together need to avoid. One of the largest complaints IT project managers have is that management will circumvent their position and go directly to the project team with instructions, input, and advice. In some instances, such as disciplining a team member, this action may be appropriate. The organizational structure of your organization will influence how project sponsors and other stakeholders communicate with the project team. Ideally, project sponsors should follow the same flow of communication through the project manager to the team.

While this requires delicate handling, it's not impossible to achieve. At the conception of the project and prior to the project kickoff meeting, the project manager should express to the project sponsor that she would like to handle all avenues of communication and management of the project. If you're new to project management, this may not be granted, although it's not unusual. Most professionals respect the line of command from management to project managers to the individuals on the team.

If for some reason members of management do bypass you and work directly with your team, and this is disrupting the project, you must address the issue. Report to your project sponsor that this confuses the project team about what the role of project manager is and whom they are to report to, and it undermines your authority with the team. Don't be confrontational, but do be factual.

Dealing with Challenging Bosses

Remember the boss who was a complete jerk? The one who thought he was still in the Marines and you were a new recruit? Or the one who would disappear for days and avoid any decision making? Do you still work for one of those?

While most Neanderthal behavior is not tolerated in today's workplace, a fair amount of it still exists. Management has tended to shift into a more team-building, empowering, goal-orientated style of leadership than in past years. However, there are still plenty of managers who don't relate well to people.

Unfortunately, most of these managers stem from IT backgrounds, and they lack social skills. Or they're traditional managers and lack IT skills. As an IT project manager, it can be tough and confusing to deal with either type.

The manager who comes from an IT background may feel threatened that new technology is coming onto the scene to replace the work and implementation he did so many years ago. Due to his current position, he's lost touch with the rapid pace of technology and feels frustrated by it.

Other managers who stem from traditional roles often have no grasp of technology and of what it can or cannot do. These managers often hide from decision-making responsibilities, overanalyze every phase of the project, or immerse themselves in the project in an attempt to learn as much or more as the IT project manager.

As a project manager, you will have to find a way to deal with different types of management. Here are six types of managers you'll likely encounter and how to deal with each:

- ■ **Managers who won't listen**   Managers who won't listen are either not interested in what you are saying or have a general lack of respect for others. The best way to deal with these people is to document what you have to say. Often these managers only put their confidence in something that is in writing, as it's on record. Use e-mail, letters, and memos to confirm conversations you've had with the manager.

- ■ **Managers who are aggressive**   Managers who yell, stomp, and are outrageously rude have become less popular in today's workplace; however, these bullies still exist. The best way to deal with these managers is to befriend them, as much as you can, and let them know that when they act the way they do, it offends you. Don't cower before them, and if the behavior persists, seek help from the human resources department.

- ■ **Managers who avoid decisions**   These managers are afraid of making the wrong decision, so they make no decision. They request more research, cancel meetings, and delay their way out of any forward progress. The best way to deal with these managers is to set deadlines with them on when the next phase of the project will commence. These deadlines don't have to be exact dates; they can even be the accomplishment of key milestones within the project. Put the deadlines in writing and try to get a commitment from them. As an alternative, present them with the decision you suggest, and let them know if you don't hear from them by a certain date, you will implement your recommendation. Make sure this is documented and that you give the manager a final head's up before going ahead with your recommendation.

- **Managers who micromanage**   These managers are typically perfectionists, feel that no one else can do the job as well as they can, or don't trust anyone else to do the task at hand. The best way to deal with these managers is to politely let them know that they are micromanaging. They just need to be told they aren't allowing you to do your work. Many of these managers don't realize that they are guilty of micromanaging and need to be told to back off. Of course, you'll then complete the task proficiently and with excellence to show the manager you can do the activity without his hovering.

- **Managers who rotate the discipline**   These managers think someone always has to be in trouble at any given time, and they will discipline someone once a week just to remind everyone else that they are in charge. Your department may refer to it as being in the doghouse, called on the carpet, or your turn. The best way to deal with this is to confirm the cycle of discipline and then confront the manager about it. You should always follow your organization's human resource practices concerning confrontations in the workplace. You don't want to create more trouble.

Working with Good Bosses

Just as plenty of bad bosses exist in the world, there are also a large number of truly good bosses. These individuals are caring, hard-working, goal-orientated individuals. They have the good of the company in mind, know how to lead, and treat people fairly. If you are fortunate to have a good boss, let him know. Let this person know that you appreciate the way he offers advice, listens to what you have to say, and treats you with respect.

Working for a good boss, however, can often be mistaken for working for a passive boss. If you can imagine another project manager working for a boss with a temper, that person's inspiration to work hard is to not get yelled at, publicly embarrassed, or put in the doghouse. On the other hand, some who have a kind boss may be tempted to become more lax because they know their manager would never yell or embarrass them. If you have a good boss, don't take advantage of her. Continue to work hard, to work persistently, and lead your team.

Learn from your boss. As an IT project manager, you can learn from either type of boss that you may have. A bad manager is showing you how not to manage, while an excellent manager is showing you how it's really done. Find the attributes of your manager that work and then repeat those skills with your project team. Not only will you become an effective manager, you'll also become an effective leader.

FROM THE FIELD

Interview with Jennifer Arndt

Name: Jennifer Arndt
Title: Senior Project Manager, PMP Certified Professional
Organization: American Chemical Society
Years as an IT project manager: 5

Jennifer Arndt worked at Metrocall, Inc., an Alexandria, VA–based wireless communications company. Jennifer began by managing projects for the telecom group, and eventually became the Manager of IS Operations Project Management. Currently Jennifer is the Senior Project Manager for the Publications Division of the American Chemical Society.

Q: What is the best part about IT project management?

A: The best part about IT project management is the challenge. There is a delicate balance between having enough technical expertise to understand the project at all levels, and having the people skills to ensure that no toes are stepped on.

Q: Why do IT project managers dread the thought of working with management?

A: Management holds power: power over budget, staff, and political sway. Management can also be slow to embrace project management processes, and may have difficulty with making documented decisions for which they must then be held accountable. Project managers are often viewed by management as competing for limited resources, rather than partners in the overall success of the business.

FROM THE FIELD *(continued)*

Q: What's the best way to form a partnership with management to ensure that a project will succeed?

A: When I first learn about a new project, I begin by identifying the departments and resources that will be involved. I then meet individually with the managers to discuss their goals for the project.

We also discuss which of their resources will be available for the project, and how much time they will be able to devote. One of the best ways to achieve management buy-in is to make sure that they are intimately involved in the early stages of the project. By instilling a sense of project ownership in management, and clearly communicating goals and concerns, you are more likely to create a cooperative atmosphere for the project.

Once I have obtained individual input from the managers, I hold a kickoff meeting. Managers and staff expected to participate in the project are all involved, so that expectations can be set and discussed with all interested parties. The most important way to form successful relationships with management is to keep the lines of communication wide open. Management concerns should be addressed as quickly and decisively as possible. Finally, project managers should ensure that they can be easily approached, and that communications are kept confidential where appropriate.

Q: When you prepare to approach management about a new IT project, what do you do first?

A: First and foremost, I do my homework. I research the project carefully, and do a preliminary assessment including

- Project summary
- Cost estimate
- Time estimate
- Risk analysis
- Resource identification
- Summary of project goals

I put together a presentation, and then schedule a meeting to discuss these items with the appropriate parties.

FROM THE FIELD *(continued)*

Q: How important is it to have the complete backing of management when starting a new IT project?

A: It is critical to have management backing for a project. All managers who will be affected should be contacted and interviewed before the project kickoff takes place.

Managers wield a great deal of political power within an organization. Even if managers' resources will not be required to implement the project, and their department will not be directly impacted, they still have the ear of those who can interfere with the success of the project.

Q: How do you manage the relationship between IT, management, and the good of the company?

A: One of the best ways to define this relationship in an enterprise environment is in terms of dollars. In fact, in many cases the "good of the company" can be primarily defined as "minimal cost and maximum profit to the company." If it can be clearly shown that an IT project will bring a significant return on investment, management buy-in is generally a given.

Acting as a liaison between management and IT staff can be challenging. Although most IT staff can clearly see the benefits to implementing new technology, they often have a hard time understanding the motivations of management. It often appears to them that managers change their minds about project scope on a whim, without thought to the ramifications. To a certain extent, I shield IT staff from management where appropriate, and work with managers to make sure that they understand why certain detailed technical decisions were made.

Q: In your experience, what has been the most difficult part of working with management on IT projects?

A: The most difficult part has been a lack of understanding of the capabilities and costs associated with IT projects. It can be quite difficult for managers to understand why something that seems like a simple modification can be very complex in terms of budget and manpower.

Q: What has been the most pleasant thing about working with management on any given project?

A: Management tends to have the "big picture" view of an organization. Managers are some of the best sources for information on the history of an organization, which often helps give perspective on the current environment. Working with management also gives the project manager the opportunity to gain visibility within an organization.

Q: What can a project manager do when the immediate management of some team members is not as committed to the project as others?

A: Engage those managers who are strong advocates for the project. In clear, nonjudgmental terms, show them where you are running into hurdles on the project path. If you allow them to draw their own conclusions about who is causing problems, they will often take it to the appropriate level for you.

Also, maintain good relationships with the staff of the manager in question. Even if the manager doesn't support the project strongly, the support of her staff can help to compensate for the lack of management backing.

Q: What's a common trap IT project managers fall into when working with management?

A: It's easy to conceptualize a project as "your baby," when in fact your role is more akin to that of a midwife. The people who conceived it, have ultimate responsibility for it, and will live with it once it's completed are the management and their staff.

Q: What are characteristics of a successful relationship between a project manager and management?

A: There has to be an underlying foundation of trust. Management needs to be able to trust you to handle the project details properly from inception through evaluation and development, and into implementation. You must be able to trust management to be honest with you about the challenges facing you with the project, and to make decisions in the best interest of the overall organization. There must also be respect. If the management and project manager cultivate respect for their roles and responsibilities, the project process becomes a pleasant experience.

CHAPTER SUMMARY

To begin working on a project, you need two fundamental things: dedication from you and approval from management. Often, to gain the approval of management, you will have to conduct a presentation in which you sell management on the idea of implementing your plan. This plan has to be condensed into the language that all management speaks: profit. Once you've got the plan condensed, create and tailor your presentation to management based on the audience in your presentation.

The organizational structure will determine your level of autonomy on a project. A functional structure restricts the amount of power the project manager has. This structure assigns the power to the functional manager. The matrix structure has three levels of power for the project manager: balanced, weak, and strong. When the project manager and the functional managers work in a matrix structure, they may struggle for project power and control. The projectized environment affords the project manager the most power and authority.

Just like your opening lines on a first date are crucial, so are the opening remarks at a presentation for new technology. By starting at the end of a project and exposing what the project will deliver, you'll capture your audience's attention and have them clamoring for more. Hopefully.

Once the project has been approved, you must continue to work with management and keep them informed of the project's progress. Management's role in the project is that of support, not implementation.

At the onset of the project, you, the project manager, must bring management and your project team together. At this kickoff meeting you'll create a sense of camaraderie and excitement for both management and your assembled project team. Have fun! Invite management and project clients to press the flesh and snack on a donut. Create excitement to make the kickoff an event and build immediate morale.

Finally, as the project begins to move forward, you'll need to work with your management. Just as there are different types of people, so there are different types of managers. Learn how to work with your manager, not for your manager. Mutual respect must be present or the project will be grounded. No matter what type of boss you have, good or otherwise, learn from her. Mimic her good attributes and avoid her bad. Bosses come and go, leaders remain.

CHAPTER QUIZ

1. What is the most important thing in a presentation?

   A. The audience

   B. The message

   C. The technology being presented

   D. The length of the presentation

2. In which organizational structure does the functional manager have the least amount of project power?

   A. Functional

   B. Weak matrix

   C. Strong matrix

   D. Projectized

3. Which management theory states that workers are either lazy and unwilling to work or they are self-led and willing to work?

   A. Herzberg's Theory of Motivation

   B. Maslow's Hierarchy of Needs

   C. McGregor's Theory of X and Y

   D. The Expectancy Theory

4. When presenting an idea to create a new project to management, which one of the following is going to help management make a decision?

   A. Time

   B. Team

   C. Profits

   D. Start-up costs

5. When speaking to executives, what topic should the IT project manager focus on?

   A. The results of the project

   B. Productivity

   C. Speed of technology

   D. The project manager's track record with the company

6. When creating audience handouts for the presentation, what information must be included in the handouts?

   A. Information on the profits

   B. Information on the project manager

   C. An executive summary

   D. An implementation plan and timeline

7. How long should a summary of a technology take?

   A. No more than 1 minute

   B. No more than 5 minutes

   C. No more than 10 minutes

   D. No more than 15 minutes

8. What role does management play in project management?

   A. Hands-on implementation

   B. Authoritarian

   C. Support

   D. Financial watchdog

9. When a project manager threatens to punish his project team if they don't complete all of their work on time, he is using which kind of project power?

   A. Expert

   B. Reward

   C. Coercive

   D. Formal

10. Of the following, which three are things an effective project manager does?

    A. Assembles the team

    B. Holds daily meetings with management

    C. Assigns tasks to team members

    D. Trusts team members to complete their assignments on time

11. Why must management communicate through the project manager to the team rather than directly to the team members? Choose two:

   A. It would offend the project manager.

   B. It would undermine the authority of the project manager.

   C. It would undermine the authority of the project sponsor.

   D. It would confuse the team members as to who is in charge of the project.

12. Whose fault is it if the project fails?

   A. The project manager

   B. The project sponsor

   C. The project team

   D. Management

13. In today's business world, what is management most concerned with in regard to IT projects?

   A. The technology implemented

   B. The process of completing the project

   C. The project deliverables

   D. The project manager's ability to perform

14. What is a project kickoff meeting?

   A. It is the assignment of tasks to the team members.

   B. It is the introduction of the project sponsor.

   C. It is the launch of a project.

   D. It is the commencement of the new project manager.

15. When creating a project kickoff meeting, what types of activities should be included in the meeting? Choose two:

   A. Discussion from management on finances

   B. Socialization

   C. Introduction from the project sponsor

   D. Discussion from management on profits

CHAPTER EXERCISES

Exercise 1

In this exercise, you will create an opening statement for a presentation to management. Recall that an opening statement should start at the end of the project—focusing on the project deliverables instead of the process to get there.

You are a network administrator for TriStar Manufacturing. Your network currently consists of two Windows NT 4.0 servers and 287 Windows 95 workstations. Most of the workstations are Pentium 433 MHz machines with 64MB of RAM. Users are constantly complaining that the network, their computers, and new applications are very slow and often crash.

Management has asked for your opinion on the technology and what can be done to improve the situation. You've decided it's past time for the company to upgrade. You have done some initial research and would like to recommend the following hardware and software upgrade for your company:

Hardware	Features
3 Windows 2003 Servers	Each server equipped with two 2.7 GHz processors, 1GB of RAM, and 200GB of disk space
300 Windows XP workstations	Each workstation equipped with a 2.0 GHz processor and 1GB of RAM, and CD-RW drives
3 network switches	Used to segment the network
3 network storage utilities	600GB storage each

Based on this information, create an opening statement for your presentation. Your opening statement should be snappy, captivating, and focused on how this upgrade will increase productivity.

Exercise 2

Congratulations! Your opening statement and presentation to upgrade the company's hardware is a hit, and management wants you to proceed. They've agreed that you will be the project manager for the rollout, and you've handpicked 15 people to be on your project team.

You've completed the feasibility study and are now ready for your project kickoff meeting. The following table will help you create an event for your kickoff.

Management has allotted a whopping $500 for the event. Have fun, and make it exciting and inspiring!

Questions	Action
Who should attend this meeting?	
When will the meeting take place?	
What is the theme of the project?	
What type of project-related handouts will you have?	
What fun things do you have planned?	
How will you inspire the team?	

Questions	Action
Who will speak first?	
What are your opening remarks to the team?	
What are some of the topics you'll cover in your team presentation?	
How long will your presentation take?	
What will you spend the $500 on?	

Exercise 3

Excellent kickoff party, er, meeting. The project team and your project sponsor had a good time—everyone thought it was great. Well, everyone but Peter Abbot, the company crank and, unfortunately, your immediate manager. Peter is less than thrilled about your new project and thinks technology generally gets in the way of any real work getting done. He would be happier with a chisel, a cave wall, and maybe an abacus.

Your assignment in this exercise is to record how you would react to different scenarios old Peter Abbot brings up. Enjoy.

Scenario	Your Response
Peter Abbot is getting increasingly cranky about the time you'll need to be spending on your "pet" project. He's insisting that you focus less on that technology stuff and help more users clean their workstations' mouse, monitor, and keyboard.	
Now you need Peter's help. He has to make a decision about when you can have the testing lab for the new PCs and operating systems. You need to create rollout scripts, test software compatibility, and work with servers. The equipment has arrived but Peter just doesn't want to make a decision on when you can use the testing lab for your project.	
Today is Frank's turn to be in Peter's doghouse. It was your turn last week, and next week it'll be Mary's. Every week someone on your team is in trouble with Peter. This whole cycle of Peter being angry with someone every week is demoralizing to your team, prohibiting progress, and generally frustrating.	
Now guess what? Peter Abbot has relapsed to his early Neanderthal days when he actually did draw on cave walls. He's yelling at anyone who comes into his office, threatening to "write you up," and acting very unhappy with any task you try to do. Yesterday he embarrassed Sam and made Jane cry.	

QUIZ ANSWERS

1. **B.** The most important thing in a presentation is not the audience, it is the message. The presentation must be clear, concise, and to the point. The technology being presented and the time of the presentation are both important elements, but they are not the most important things in the presentation.

2. **D.** The functional manager has the least amount of project authority in a projectized environment. The project manager has the authority over the project and the project team in a projectized structure. Incidentally, the project manager has the least authority in the functional structure— the environment where the functional manager has the most authority.

3. **C.** McGregor's Theory of X and Y says that X workers are lazy and unwilling to work. Y workers are self-led, have initiative, and are willing to work.

4. **C.** Management is concerned with the profitability of the project for the audience being addressed. When you are selling management on the project, time, team, and start-up costs are attributes of a project, but not direct benefits.

5. **A.** Executives are not going to have much time to listen to your technical ideas and implementation plans. When you are pitching a project to executives, always open with the deliverables and how they relate to profitability. While productivity, speed of technology, and the project manager's track record are important, show management the future state of the organization once the project is completed.

6. **C.** Always include an executive summary. As you give your presentation, the executive summary allows the audience to read over the quick facts of the project and get an idea of where the project will end. It also documents the goals and overview of the project for individuals who may not be able to attend your presentation.

7. **A.** You should be able to sum up any project in one minute. If it takes five minutes or more, you'll lose your audience. If the audience wants more details, you can then go into more depth. A project manager should always start with the end results of the technology and then broaden the discussion if more details are requested or needed.

8. **C.** Management should be supportive but not authoritarian or hands on.

9. **C.** When a project manager threatens the project team into doing their work, he is using coercive power.

10. **A,C,D.** An effective project manager assembles the team, assigns tasks to members, and then trusts team members to complete their assignments without micromanaging.

11. **B,D.** Management should follow the path of communication through the project manager to the project team. While bypassing the project manager may offend the project manager, the more relevant choices are the results it has on the team.

12. **A.** If the project fails, the project manager is to blame. The success or failure of a project lies on the shoulders of the project manager.

13. **C.** What does the project deliver? Executives are less concerned with the technology, the process, and the project manager than they are with the deliverables of the project.

14. **C.** A project kickoff meeting is the launch of a new project. It is used to meet the team and management, and inspire everyone to commit and own the project.

15. **B,C.** The project kickoff meeting should provide some socialization so the project team, management, the project manager, the project sponsor, and key stakeholders can meet each other before the project work begins. An introduction from the project sponsor grants the project manager referent power because he is now acting on behalf of the project sponsor.

EXERCISE SOLUTIONS

Exercise 1: Possible Solution

Your opening statement may be fashioned like this one:

By upgrading our servers and our workstations to current technology, we can increase productivity by 47 percent and increase morale by 100 percent. This implementation would allow all of us to work smarter, faster, and with less frustration.

Exercise 2: Possible Solution

Here is a sample of how a fun, informative project kickoff meeting could go:

Questions	Action
Who should attend this meeting?	Management, the project sponsor, the project manager, key stakeholders, and all of the project team members.
When will the meeting take place?	Early morning; breakfast will be provided.

Questions	Action
What is the theme of the project?	"Working on the Future."
What type of project-related handouts will you have?	Everyone will receive a hammer with the theme "Working on the Future" printed on the handle. Construction hats, breakfast food, and drinks will also be provided.
What fun things do you have planned?	Construction hats will be handed out at the door. Orange cones and sawhorses will lead the way into the meeting room. "Construction" workers from the computer and software vendor will be on hand to meet and greet the attendees.
How will you inspire the team?	In the opening statement, the project manager will relay the theme of "Working on the Future" by laying out the goals of the project.
Who will speak first?	The project sponsor.
What are your opening remarks to the team?	"Construction sometimes has a bad reputation, but everyone is happy to see the end results of the work."
What are some of the topics you'll cover in your team presentation?	Goals of the project. Project deliverables. Flow of communication.
How long will your presentation take?	One hour from start to finish.
What will you spend the $500 on?	Hammers, plastic construction hats, food.

Exercise 3: Possible Solution

The following table presents possible responses to the different scenarios with old Peter Abbot:

Scenario	Your response
Peter Abbot is getting increasingly cranky about the time you'll need to be spending on your "pet" project. He's insisting that you focus less on that technology stuff and help more users clean their workstations' mouse, monitor, and keyboard.	"Peter, I understand how you feel in regard to the computer upgrade process. There really is not a pressing need to clean the workstations, as we'll be replacing those within a few weeks anyway."

Scenario	Your response
Now you need Peter's help. He needs to make a decision about when you can have the testing lab for the new PCs and operating systems. You need to create rollout scripts, test software compatibility, and work with servers. The equipment has arrived, but Peter just doesn't want to make a decision on when you can use the testing lab for your project.	Document and date that the room is needed for the project rollout testing and planning. Send the document not only to Peter Abbot, but also to the project sponsor. By documenting the problem, you've created a paper trail that Peter may be more responsive to.
Today is Frank's turn to be in Peter's doghouse. It was your turn last week, and next week it'll Mary's. Every week someone on your team is in trouble with Peter. This whole cycle of Peter being angry with someone every weekend is demoralizing to your team, prohibiting progress, and generally frustrating.	Take Peter to lunch and explain that the cycle of discipline is unnecessary. You are all adults, and his behavior is interrupting the progress of the project and demoralizing your team. Be sure to buy.
Now guess what? Peter Abbot has relapsed to his early Neanderthal days when he actually did draw on cave walls. He's yelling at anyone who comes into his office, threatening to "write you up," and acting very unhappy with any task you try to do. Yesterday he embarrassed Sam and made Jane cry.	The project manager, Sam, and Jane should all take Peter to lunch and discuss his behavior. Acknowledge that he is your manager, but his actions will not be tolerated. After lunch, document the conversation in an e-mail and send it Sam, Jane, and Peter.

Chapter 4

Creating the Budget

T his chapter is about money. Have you ever noticed how people bristle when that word is mentioned? In some circles, it's not money; it's finances, working capital, currency, or funds. Whatever you want to call it, it's a large part of what you need to get your project done. Your project will need a budget to create the product or service your project customer expects. The resources you'll need, such as software and hardware, cost money. The labor you need, you know, the developers', database experts', and network engineers' time, as well as the brute force required to install the hardware and software, also costs money.

Your project needs a budget to determine just how much money, er, capital, needs to be allotted, and when it needs to be available, so you can reach the project goal. Your project needs a plan to create estimates and predict the total cost of the project. Your project's budget needs proof of why it will cost the amount you say it will, input from vendors, quotes from suppliers, and estimates on work hours committed to the project. And your project needs a time-phased budget that ties the resources needed with the project schedule.

Budgets may seem to be a necessary evil required by any project manager to get a project off the ground and into implementation. In reality, they're needed so the project stakeholders can see how much it will cost to create the deliverable they desire. In addition, a budget is needed to confirm the project manager truly knows what it is he is to deliver. A dreamy project goal is snapped into reality when management wants to hold you accountable for the cost of the project deliverables. With that in mind, let's get started.

Budget Basics

You need a budget to control and document project expenses—before the project work begins. When you are creating a feasibility plan, you'll no doubt include facts on the cost of the project and any ROI for the project. Now, once the project has been approved, or approved based on the financial obligations, you have to do a touch more research. Any bean counter in your company wants to know what exactly your project will cost. As any project manager who has worked on IT implementations will tell you, "It's not as easy as it looks."

You also need a budget to get your arms around the scope of the project and what you can afford to include in your implementation. There will be instances when your budget won't be approved and you'll have to cut any extras or settle for less to complete the project. In other scenarios, the project may have to be delayed until funds are available to continue. The worst-case scenario, of course, is that the project is approved but the funds to support the project are nonexistent.

A budget will serve as a financial guide to where the project is headed. Project managers who do their homework will have a clear vision of what the deliverables of the project will be and what it takes to reach those deliverables.

As you begin to create a budget, you need to come up with a plan of attack. There are numerous ways to create a budget, some better than others. One approach IT project managers have a tendency to use is to write down a list of all the products that the company needs to purchase to complete the project and add up the cost for each. At first glance, this seems like a viable solution; however, it opens the door for potentially overlooking important details, lack of true planning, and error. A better approach is to divide your project into phases and extract cost estimates for each phase of the project. This approach, called *phased gate estimating*, is ideal for large projects.

Phased gate estimating allows project managers to forecast the exact expenses for the pending phase of a project and provide more general estimates for phases downstream. The immediate actions of a project should be foreseeable, as opposed to actions that will happen way off in the future. For example, you probably know what you're doing this weekend, but don't know your plans a weekend a year from now. Because IT changes so rapidly, accurate estimates are available for actions in the present tense, and less so for those in the future.

A key factor in any project is the Work Breakdown Structure (WBS). The WBS is a deliverables-orientated decomposition of the project. From these lists of deliverables, the project manager can derive the activities required to deliver each component of the project. The major deliverables of the project, often called *project milestones*, are ideal for using as phases within a project. For example, a project to create a new application will have some logical, visible milestones between its beginning and completion. A project manager using phased gate estimating can predict the cost of the project through the next foreseeable milestone.

When a project calls for phased gate estimating, the WBS will reflect the approach as well. A software development project has some obvious phases just like a hardware roll-out project will as well. A WBS in these instances can reflect the deliverables within the immediate phase with a nod to downstream phases that will come later in the project.

Determine the Estimate Type

There are three different categories of estimates the project manager needs to be familiar with. These estimates will dictate how much detail the project manager will need to provide in order to create an accurate estimate. The three estimate types are

- **Rough order of magnitude** This estimate is "rough" and is used during the initiating processes and in top-down estimates. The range of variance for the estimate can be –25 percent to +75 percent.

- **Budget estimate** This estimate is also somewhat broad and is used early in the planning processes and also in top-down estimates. The range of variance for the estimate can be –10 percent to +25 percent.

- **Definitive estimates** This estimate is one of the most accurate. It is used late in the planning processes and is associated with bottom-up estimates. The range of variance for the estimate can be –5 percent to +10 percent.

Implementing Bottom-Up Cost Estimates

IT project managers love estimates; accountants don't. One of the toughest parts of your job as an IT project manager is to accurately predict the expenses your project will generate. As an IT professional, you know this is true because there is so much to IT that fluctuates: RAM, new versions of software, the size of hard drives, the speed of processors, and just about any other facet of the IT world. Intel's Gordon Moore is known for "Moore's Law," where he predicts processing power doubles every 18 months. This law, which is generally accepted as true, has spread to all areas of technology. Everything becomes more efficient with technological advances.

The old adage that time is money is never more true than when it comes to information technology. While the speed and price of hardware and software may fluctuate, one of the largest expenses in an IT project is time. Why? Basically, if you, or your team, are not adequately prepared to implement the technology, the estimated time to install and roll out a plan can double or even triple. A project manager must take into account the learning curve to implement and manage the new technology.

A project manager cannot always know her team's ability to implement a given technology. For example, a project manager assigns Jim to the development of an application. Jim does have a proven track record with developing applications in Visual Basic; however, this application will have hooks into a SQL database. If Jim does not have a clear understanding of the procedures to communicate with the SQL database, his reported estimated time might well be lower than the actual time used to create the application. Worse still, Jim doesn't understand SQL at all and needs additional weeks to ramp up on the technology to make his application design flesh in with the existing SQL database. Jim's weeks of training may incur additional expenses from your project budget and delay other workers and tasks that require Jim to complete his portion of the project first.

The cost of team development needs to be included in your project budget, both from a training and learning curve perspective. In other words, if you have a QA tester that will be using new software for error detection, not only do you have to figure in the cost of training, but you also have to remember that productivity on that piece of testing software will be about 60 percent of capacity in week 1 versus 90+ percent capacity in week 10. If the project team lacks the skills to deliver, it must be trained. Lack of knowledge to do the project work guarantees project failure. It's no great discovery that so much of the knowledge surrounding information technology is disposable, although it's necessary for the imminent project. Consider all the old and discarded information you and your project team have learned about DOS, OS/2, and Microsoft's products. At the time, the information was of incredible value; as technology changed, however, the information's value waned. The value of the training and knowledge to complete the project is what's important, not its value years from now.

Another fluctuating expense is hardware. Generally, hardware is at a fixed price and decreases in cost as newer, faster, better hardware becomes available. However, there are times when demand outweighs supply and the hardware costs increase. Also, as laptops, desktops, and servers drop in price, the demand for parts to manufacturers increases; this can cause hardware prices to remain steady, but the hardware itself to be significantly back-ordered. This, of course, throws your entire implementation plan askew.

To avoid these pitfalls, a project manager should implement bottom-up cost estimates. A bottom-up estimate does not mean you pour a shot of your favorite brew and yell, "Bottoms up!" Bottom-up cost estimating is the process of creating a detailed estimate for each work component (labor and materials) and accounting for each varying cost burden. As Figure 4-1 illustrates, a project can be divided into phases, and then each phase can be assigned a cost value.

A project divided into phases allows each phase to be assessed a cost value.

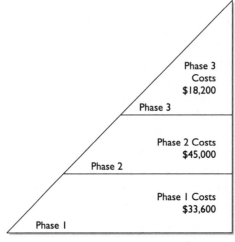

Phase 3
Costs
$18,200

Phase 3

Phase 2 Costs
$45,000

Phase 2

Phase 1 Costs
$33,600

Phase 1

Total Project Budget: $97,000

For example, an application development project can be divided into three phases. Within each phase, the work to complete the phase relies on time, software, and hardware. The project manager can assign each of these factors a monetary value to complete the total phase of the project.

In other words, the project manager is starting from the bottom of the project—the genesis—and working toward the project deliverables. Each component of the project has a monetary requirement assigned to it to ultimately predict the final cost. When you begin to create your budget, here are some issues to consider:

- *Divide your project into phases.* By segmenting the entire project into phases, it's easier to identify milestones and assign the amount of work and materials required to complete each phase. Once you break the project into phases, you'll find assigning dollars to each phase is more manageable than assigning one lump sum to an entire project.

- *Address the integration phase.* By prepping the production environment for the onset of the implementation, budgetary concerns can address downtime, lag, required work hours, and the time the project manager requires to oversee that the tasks are being completed to keep the project on schedule.

- *Consider the fully burdened workload required to complete each phase of the project.* A fully burdened workload is the amount of work, in hours, required by the staff to complete each phase of the project. Part of the budget must include the man hours necessary to complete any given phase. Team members should have a dollar amount assigned to their work hours to predict the true expense of the implementation. (In some instances, it may be, unfortunately, beyond your control to predict the hourly rate of workers due to your company's human resources department policy.) Additionally, when some work is outsourced, the hourly rate may include overhead, general and administrative expenses, a risk load factor, and a profit load. As a project manager, you should be aware of what ancillary, or additional costs, go into a true project cost.

■ *Consider the costs for any specialized services.* Will you be using subject matter experts? Will the project include training for the implementation team? Will the project include a pilot team of ordinary users? Any of these special services are easy to overlook when calculating a project's budget, but they will come back to haunt you if you don't plan for their expenses before the project begins..

■ *Consider the costs for equipment.* Of course, if you are purchasing new hardware, this is easy to account for. However, consider the value of leasing versus purchasing new hardware. Consider the impact of equipment dedicated to the project on any production machines that may be affected by the project's implementation—such as test servers, workstations reserved for testing, application development machines, the percentage of processor utilization, memory usage, and bandwidth impact.

■ *Consider production costs.* Any project will have fringe costs such as photocopying expenses, creating rollout manuals and user manuals, designing and developing web pages, and development.

■ *Consider quality requirements.* The project needs to account for the level of testing that needs to be done. How much regression testing, integration testing, and so forth, should be included to meet the customer's quality standards?

■ *Consider risk.* Just as with the budget, risks are vague in the initial stages of a project. As the planning evolves, so does information on risks and risk management. You will need money for rework, risk mitigation, schedule delays, and workarounds.

■ *Consider reserve amounts.* All projects run into challenges. Smart project managers plan for the unknown "unknowns," and for uncertainty. One way to plan for those things we can't know for certain is to keep a reserve amount to handle unforeseen circumstances. This is like the same idea as the personal savings account we keep for emergencies, only this reserve amount is for our project. The amount may, or may not be under your control, but it is useful to understand the concept, and how to plan for it.

Once you've taken into consideration these different aspects of your project implementation, you're ready to begin calculating expenses. After you've broken your project plan down into phases, create an evolution of expenses for each phase. For example, in phase 1 of a project, consider the expenses required to complete this stage of the project:

- Hardware to be purchased
- Software to be purchased
- Licensing issues
- Consultants
- Internal developers' time
- Percentage of time required by each team member to complete this phase of the project
- Risk and reserve funds
- Other expenses pertinent to your project

In the first phase of the project, you can complete the expenses required and then use the same template to move on to the second phase, the third phase, and so on, to create a table of expenses for each phase of the project.

Allowance for Change

When using bottom-up cost estimates, you need to calculate some allowance for change. When calculating time and costs for expenses, a project manager should create an average estimate for each phase of the project by factoring best- and worst-case scenarios into components that may fluctuate on price. Here's an example of an implementation phase for a new server-based application:

Component	Best Case	Worst Case	Average
New server (fixed price)			$7500
Application software (fixed price)			$2500
Application license (fixed price)			$3500
Development	40 hours	100 hours	70 hours
Testing and resolution	40 hours	120 hours	80 hours
Rollout to users	40 hours	80 hours	60 hours
Documentation	$4000	$6000	$5000
Training	120 hours	240 hours	180 hours

By including the best- and worst-case scenarios into your bottom-up cost estimates, you are factoring in an allowance up to the maximum amount, but predicting an average amount. Figure 4-2 depicts a simple predicted average for a project's expense. Most expenses within your project can follow this formula.

Some elements of your estimates will not come close to the worst-case scenario, or even the average cost. Others will no doubt reach the worst-case scenario and perhaps even pass it. How do you determine the amount of time and the price value associated with each component? Here are factors that you should call upon to estimate your budget:

- **Prior experience**   If you've worked with similar projects in the past, you'll call upon your experience to predict how similar phases of work will fit within the scope of this project.

- **Historical information**   Similar projects may have historical information that helps guide your current project's budget. In addition, are there mentors or other project managers you can call on for advice? Ask others how long certain elements took when they implemented similar projects within the company or in their work history. Project team members may have experience with key areas of your plan, so their input is needed.

FIGURE 4-2   Worst- and best-case scenarios allow for average amount predictions.

Best	Worst	Probable Average
$1400	$2100	$1750

■ **Fixed quotes** Vendors should be able to offer a fixed quote or a not-to-exceed (NTE) price on a deliverable. Typically, a fixed quote is for a product rather than a service, and it is valid 30 days from the time of the quote.

■ **Standard costs** Your budget department may have preassigned "standard costs" for labor to do tasks such as programming lines of code, installing hardware, or adding a new server. The cost of these activities may be found in a company-wide charter of accounts that represent types of work and their associated costs. This preassignment of values helps you estimate labor costs for a project easily, and without having to justify each labor expense as a line item. Hours to perform the task still may be a point of contention.

We'll talk more about time estimating in Chapter 5, but you should be keenly aware that time and money are interrelated. Time is money. In some organizations, the cost of the employee completing the work is not seen as a cost attributed to a project. In other organizations, however, the employee's time is billed to the project's customer. For example, an IT project to create a sales automation program may bill the sales department for the application developer's time. While the cost of the developer may not reflect the hourly rate of the employee, dollars are shifted from the sales department's budget to the IT department to account for the developer's time.

Tolerance for Budget Variance

As the cost of hardware, software, and services can fluctuate, project managers and management must agree on a tolerance level for the project's budget to be plus or minus a percentage of the predicted costs. Depending on your project and its budget, this may be only 1 to 2 percent or as large as 10 percent. Any variance in your project's budget can be unsettling, as it may reflect a lack of planning. Typically, management is more eager to deal with budgets under the predicted total costs than ones that are over. Beware: projects that finish significantly under budget are not reasons to celebrate; it often indicates a lack of proper planning for project costs.

To circumvent any disagreements, management and the project manager must agree on the range of variance for your project. Don't use the range of variance as an additional cushion for your purchases—you may need that percentage you spend now later in the project. In some companies, a variance in the budget can reflect the monetary rewards assigned to a project's success.

Using Top-Down Estimating

A top-down estimate allows a project manager to take a very similar project's budget, work some financial math magic, and arrive at a reasonable budget for the current project. Top-down budgets are often used by organizations that complete IT projects for other companies. Consider IT integrators who install servers, network cable, and network equipment. They'll have similar projects they can refer to when predicting the cost of current projects.

Within an organization, IT project managers also have projects that are similar to other projects they've completed in the past. Consider a project to roll out a new operating system using a disk-imaging server. If the project manager has rolled out other operating systems in the past using the disk-imaging server, he'll have a pretty good idea of how the current project will go. This historical information on proven, completed applications allows the project manager to save the time of doing a bottom-up estimate; he can work from prior successful projects

The problem with top-down estimates in the IT world, however, is that most IT projects have never been done before. Specifically, because IT changes so quickly and each environment is generally customized, top-down estimates are not as reliable or useable as bottom-up estimates.

Using Analogous Estimating

If you find that you're launching projects that are similar to past accomplishments, analogous estimating may be your best bet. Analogous estimating relies on historical information to predict the cost of the current project. It is a type of top-down estimating. The process of analogous estimating takes the actual cost of a historical project as a basis for the current project. The cost of the historical project is applied to the cost of the current project with respect to the scope of the current project, its size, and other known variables.

This estimating approach takes less time to complete than other estimating models do, but is also less accurate. This top-down approach is good for fast estimates to get a general idea of what the project may cost.

Here's an example of analogous estimating: You completed the design and installation of an application for the sales department to track incoming phone calls from clients. Your IT help desk now wants you to create an application to track phone calls from internal users. The project deliverables are technically different, but both have fundamental characteristics that can guide you to create a reasonably reliable project cost estimate.

Using Parametric Modeling

Another approach to top-down estimating is Parametric Modeling. Parametric Modeling uses a mathematical model based on known parameters to predict the cost of a project. The parameters in the model can vary based on the type of work being completed. A parameter can be cost per cubic yard, cost per unit, and so on. A complex parameter can be cost per unit with adjustment factors based on the conditions of the project. Further, the adjustment factors may have additional factors depending on additional conditions.

For example, if you're managing an application development project, you may create a cost estimate based on the number of years of experience the application developer has with a given software language. Bob may have eight years of experience while Sam only has two years of experience. Sam doesn't cost as much as Bob because he's considered less experienced than Bob. Sam can still get the work done; it just may take him slightly longer than if Bob did the work.

When you think of parametric modeling, a parameter is generally used: cost per unit installed, cost per machine delivered, and so on. This approach doesn't always lend itself to IT projects because of the variables within the technology. Consider function point analysis—lines of code are not always reflective of the productivity, the number of servers, or even the number of programmers assigned to an activity.

Budget at Completion

The Budget at Completion (BAC) is the sum of the budget for each phase of your project. This is the estimated grand total of your project. If a project manager breaks down a project into phases, and she should, then each phase can be reflected with a dollar amount that needs to be allotted to that phase. The benefit of this approach is that a company does not need to allot all of the BAC at the project's conception, but rather the initial amount required to set the project in motion, and an amount as each phase is completed.

The primary advantage of this approach is that an entity can continue to use the capital earmarked for the project until the next phase of the project is ready to proceed. A secondary advantage of the BAC is that it allows everyone involved in the project to examine the costs of each phase of the project and then its grand total. So rather than seeing "Server upgrade costs: $25,128," management sees this:

Phase 1	Start Date	Costs
Server 1	November 3	$4578
Server 2	November 3	$4578
	Phase 1 total	$9156
Phase 2	**Start Date**	**Costs**
Initiate clustering servers	November 10	$6526
Install switch	November 12	$1592
	Phase 2 Total	$8118
Phase 3	**Start Date**	**Costs**
Add RAID 5 tower	November 17	$7854
Test and document	November 19	$0
	Phase 3 Total	$7854
Phase 4	**Start Date**	**Costs**
Migrate data from old servers to new (performed at night)	November 21	0
Put servers into production	November 22	0
	Phase 4 Total	0
	Budget at Completion	$25,128

As you can see, this approach to budgeting allows all parties to get a sense of what each phase will cost, when the monies will need to be allocated (in advance of the implementation date, of course), and the total cost of the project. This cash flow approach to project management creates a cooperation between the project manager, the project customer, and management. The project manager should include phases that do not require any outlay of cash. In some situations, you may be required to add the number of hours estimated to complete each phase of the project to factor in the cost of an employee's or a consultant's time. The preceding sample only shows the hardware expense.

Zero-Based Budgeting

Another concept you'll likely encounter is zero-based budgeting. *Zero-based budgeting* means that the budget for a department or program to be created must always start at zero, rather than a dollar amount from a similar project, and then the new expenses factored in. This long-winded approach generally is required each fiscal year. As Figure 4-3 depicts, zero-based budgeting requires a zero balance at the genesis. In other words, you can't take last year's budget for all projects in the IT department, add 20 percent to it, and claim that this new number is this year's upgrade budget. Zero-based budgeting forces a project manager to reflect the true costs of each project.

While this approach may seem similar to a bottom-up estimating, it's often used for a series of projects, an entire department, or a long-term project that may last over several years.

The biggest complaint IT project managers have with zero-based budgeting is that it feels as though you're doing your work twice. In reality, it forces you to ensure the cost of goods and services have not changed—and if they have, the budget reflects the change in costs. Zero-based budgeting creates a sense of accountability for the project manager with regard to getting an accurate cost of the services and hardware to be purchased.

Some IT project managers will, however, rely on similar budgets and fudge their way through a new budget. Don't take this route! Why? Why not just take last year's figures, check out any major changes, and go with the number predicted? Well, it could cost the company money and you your project and your job.

Imagine that you take last year's budget for server upgrades, add 20 percent to the budget, and claim it as this year's project budget. When it comes time to actually purchase the hardware, what will happen if the cost of the hardware from last year

FIGURE 4-3

Zero-based budgeting requires a zero balance at the genesis.

Budget Built from Zero

Training = $12,900

Hardware = $38,900

Software = $47,000

Labor = $24,000

Zero at Genesis

has increased due to supply and demand? Or what if the servers you used last year are no longer available and the next step requires purchasing a server that costs 30 percent more than a similar server last year? You'll have much explaining to do.

When you are asked to use zero-based budgeting, use it. Even if the project is identical to a previous project, investigate the costs of goods and services required to complete the project and report them accurately. It's not always fun, but that's why it's called work.

Determining Project Expenses

On the surface, it's easy to predict what a project will cost. Take the hardware required, add it up, and there's the amount needed, right? We all know it's not that easy. There are other factors involved in predicting the cost of a project.

When predicting the project expenses, a project manager has to look at employees, the combination of employees working together or alone, hardware expenses, the determined scope of the project, and the necessary hardware to implement the plan. The total of these variables make for long planning, calculating, and educated guesses as to the expense of a project. Careful planning and experience are the two best ingredients for cooking up an accurate budget.

The Cost of Goods

If you wanted to purchase one floppy disk, it would be easy to determine the cost of that one disk. However, if you need to purchase two clustered servers, with 64GB of RAM, 200GB of hard disk space, two NICs each, and loaded with eight processors, the calculation would be a little tougher. You could leave it all up to the manufacturer or your favorite salesperson, but would you get your dollars' worth?

Would it be better to assemble the servers yourself? Would it be better to have the manufacturer assemble the board and NICs, and then you add the RAM and the cluster RAID later on your own? What about installing any operating systems through the manufacturer? Is your staff prepared and knowledgeable enough to assemble everything on their own? And is it even worth the time to assemble such a clustered server onsite? How much time will it take? These type of make or buy decisions should be based off of the WBS. Each deliverable should be analyzed to assess whether it should be made or bought, or if there is an option to make or buy that requires further investigation.

The decision to make or buy a product is a fundamental aspect of management. In some conditions, it is more cost effective to buy—while in others it makes more sense to create an in-house solution. The make-or-buy analysis should happen in the initial scope definition to determine if the entire project should be completed in-house or procured. As the project evolves, additional make-or-buy decisions are needed.

The initial costs of the solution for the in-house or procured product must be considered, but so too must the ongoing expenses of the solutions. For example, a company may elect to lease a piece of equipment. The ongoing expenses of leasing the piece of equipment should be weighed against the expected ongoing expenses of purchasing the equipment and the monthly costs to maintain, insure, and manage the equipment.

For example, Figure 4-4 shows the mathematical approach to determining whether it is better to create a software program in-house or buy one from a software company. The in-house solution will cost your company $25,000 to create your own software package and, based on historical information, another $2,500 per month to maintain the software.

The development company has a solution that will cost your company $17,000 to purchase, but the development company requires a maintenance plan for each software program installed, which will cost your company $2,700 per month. The difference between making the software and buying the software is $8,000. The difference between supporting the software the organization has made and allowing the external company to support their software is only $200 per month.

The $200 per month is divided into the difference between creating the software internally and buying the software—which is $8,000 divided by $200, or 40 months.

FIGURE 4-4

Make-or-buy formulas are common practices in project management.

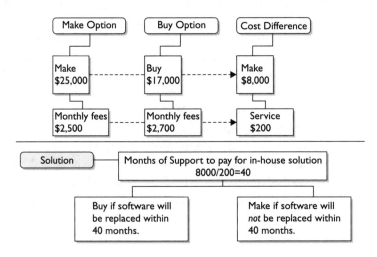

If the software is to be replaced within 40 months, the company should buy the software. If the software that will be created will not be replaced within 40 months, it should build the software.

There are multiple reasons why an organization may choose to make versus buy. A project team can make or buy as much as it needs to complete the project scope. Here are some common examples or reasons to make or buy:

Reasons to Make	Reasons to Buy
Less costly	Less costly
Use in-house skills	In-house skills aren't available or don't exist
Control of work	Small volume of work
Control of intellectual property	More efficient
Learn new skills	Transfer risks
Available staff	Available vendor
Focus on core project work	Allows project to focus on other work items

As you can guess, or maybe you've experienced, there are lots of avenues to consider when purchasing hardware that will need to be assembled and configured. In some instances, off-the-shelf hardware will be an appropriate solution for a project, while other times it will be more cost effective to assemble the hardware onsite. How can you know the difference? Figure 4-5 shows that the cost of hardware assembled by the manufacturer should not be higher than the time it takes to assemble the hardware in-house.

FIGURE 4-5

The vendor's cost should not outweigh the cost of internal resources.

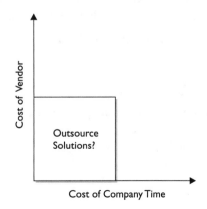

You need to consider other factors when allowing hardware to be assembled through the manufacturer versus piecing the hardware together in-house:

- *How long will the assembly take?* If you or a staff member has experience assembling hardware components, an accurate prediction can be made as to the length of the assembly process. From that information, you can calculate the cost of the assembly process. This dollar amount, assigned to the assembly process, can help you determine if it is more cost effective to assemble the hardware in-house versus allowing the vendor to assemble the hardware.

- *What other tasks can the technician do?* Consider the technician's time, the cost of the time, and the other responsibilities the technician could handle on the project. It may be more valuable to the project if the vendor assembles the hardware and the technician moves onto other aspects of the project.

- *Will the vendor guarantee the work?* If the vendor is to assemble the hardware, that vendor should guarantee their work. Incorrectly configured hardware by the vendor could bring your project to a grinding halt. A vendor that is assembling the hardware you are purchasing is going to charge you adequately for the time and materials it takes to build the component according to your specifications. The vendor's contract should include a guarantee that the hardware will arrive in working order and work in your environment.

- *Is it worth the headache?* The headache factor sometimes outweighs the money saved by doing the work in-house. In some instances, especially when the savings from doing the work in-house are nominal, it is more effective to allow the vendor to assemble the hardware. Let the vendor deal with installing the RAM, processors, and BIOS upgrades and configuration. Often it's not worth the headache to do the work in-house. Will making it in-house create a new competency that can be leveraged for other projects?

- *Do you have additional labor capacity? Not enough labor capacity?*

Software Licensing

Not all project expenses are going to be hardware related—if any at all! Software expenses can be unrelenting and tally up a huge bill before any software has even been installed or configured. Figure 4-6 shows an example of the two most popular licensing modes, per device and per user.

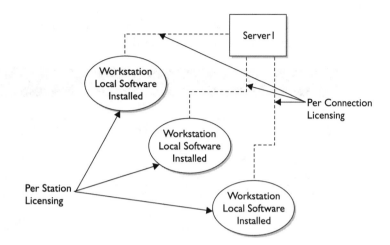

FIGURE 4-6

Per station and
per connection
are common
licensing tactics.

Software expense generally works in a few different licensing modes:

- **Per station**   A license covers the software application at the workstation where it is installed. Think of Microsoft Office installed on each workstation within an organization.

- **Per connection**   A license is required for each workstation-to-server connection. This scheme allows a maximum number of connections to a server. Think of the connection required for each user to access a share on a Windows 2000 Server using Microsoft's "per server" licensing.

- **Per station (server-based)**   This allows an unlimited number of connections to a server covered by the licensing plan. Each additional server would require its own licensing to allow connections to it.

- **Per usage**   This licensing plan allows a user to run an application for a preset number of days or times, or the user is charged a fee for each instance that the application is used. An example is a subscription to a web-based directory service.

To get an idea of how expensive software licensing can be, consider the following table. It represents the cost of imaginary software installed on servers that require a license fee for each connection. It is typical of licensing fees to decrease as the number of licenses increases. Regardless, you can see the impact that licensing fees, even simple connection fees such as this one, can have upon your budget.

Number of Licenses	Fee	Cost
100	$50	$5000
250	$40	$10,000
500	$30	$15,000
1000	$25	$25,000
1500	$20	$30,000
2000	$15	$30,000

Consider network operating systems such as Windows 2003 or Novell NetWare. Each requires the administrator to choose the type of licensing required for using the product on the network. For example, in a Windows 2003 environment, you may choose to use the per server licensing agreement, which requires that each connection to the server have a client access license purchased to allow the connection. Another type of licensing is the per device or per user method, which allows unlimited connections to the server from any seat in the network. The size of your network will determine the type of licensing you will want to use. Both Microsoft and Novell have enterprise-type licensing agreements that can save thousands of dollars in some instances.

Outsourcing

One of the most popular trends in information technology has been to outsource practically any project. On some levels this is not only cost effective, but also extremely productive. In organizations where there is no full-time IT manager, it is ideal to outsource the simplest of IT problems to a team or consultant. When you consider the cost of hiring a full-time IT professional at $77,000 per year base salary versus outsourcing to an integrator to service the computers and printers for $40,000, it's an easy decision. However, this opportunity, as with any industry, has created some less-than-desirable businesses. It's incredibly easy for anyone to market themselves as an IT expert, land a few accounts, and take advantage of otherwise unknowing clients. Not that this would happen to you.

When outsourcing a project, or considering outsourcing a project, ask the following questions:

- *Is it cost effective?* Consider the time, learning curve, implementation process, and the dollar amount associated with each variable and compare that to the figures from the vendor proposing to do the work.

- *Is it productive?* Again, consider the time of doing the work internally versus hiring an outside agency to complete the tasks. You should not only consider the dollar amount, but also the time involved to complete the project.

- *Is the vendor reputable?* Ask the vendor for references of similar work it has done before. Ask it for industry credentials from Microsoft, Novell, Lotus, CompTIA, and others.

- *Is this an HR decision?* Outsourcing a technology project may not even be the project manager's decision. HR and management may have created contracts and agreements with staffing agents to complete the project work while you, the internal project manager, are to manage the external workers.

- *Consider culture differences.* Internal resources are familiar with the politics, priorities, and procedures within your organization. A vendor may have a completely different set of priorities, or a different definition of quality or immediate deadlines.

Outsourcing is not always the best solution, but sometimes it's the sexiest to management. This is because the cost considerations, the internal learning curve, and other projects that may be on the horizon could conflict with the outsourced job. If you decide to consider outsourcing a project, get a fixed cost from the vendor—especially when proposing a budget to management. You may need to work with the vendor, or several vendors, to negotiate a fair cost for services and manage the purchase of the hardware separately to get a better sum price. Many vendors will give you a break on the price if you buy the hardware and the implementation through the same source.

Estimating Work Hours

What's the most expensive element in any project? If you said time, you are correct! Time is the one component of a project that is the most difficult to predict, the hardest to manage, and the easiest to lose control of.

Think about your own day as an IT professional. How many times have you set out to complete a task—for example, something as simple as troubleshooting a printer for a particular user—only to be summoned for more tasks along the way? You go to the printer to make certain it's turned on, you check the power, pop open the printer, and check the toner. While you're there, two folks begin asking you questions about how to create a macro for column numbering. Now your pager goes off, reporting that the SQL server is running out of disk space and the transaction log needs to be cleared.

The printer looks fine, but the user still can't print. You get to her desk only to discover that Marcy, her neighbor, reports that her mouse won't work. Get the picture? Or is it too close to reality? It's just one thing after another all day long—and that user still can't print.

As an IT project manager, your time is very valuable and has to be guarded from interruptions by users, pagers, and yet more users. I can hear you now, "Yeah, sure." Seriously, think about the percentage of your day that is committed to putting out fires in proportion to the percentage of your day that can be dedicated to a project. Now think of the people on your project team and the same interruptions and activities that may delay them from completing their project tasks.

While you, the IT project manager, may not be the individual performing each step of the project's implementation, you do have to be available to work with your team, resolve issues pertinent to the project's success, and have time to track and report the status of the project. In some companies, you may have to wear several hats, as you'll be supporting the users, working on each phase of the project, and tracking the project status. In others, you may have the luxury (or headache) of delegating the phases to individuals and managing several projects at once. In either situation, your ability to manage your time, and the time of your team, is crucial to the success of the project.

When you are budgeting a project, use the worst- and best-case scenarios for predicting team members' time. Most project managers have a range of variance assigned to labor costs. For example, the cost of labor will be $4,000 +/– $400. In the following table, examine how much team members' average hourly rates cost the company from best- to worst-case scenarios to do a given task.

Team Member	Average Hourly Rate	Best Time (Hours)	Cost	Worst Time (Hours)	Cost	Average Time (Hours)	Cost
Sally	$32.00	16	$512.00	24	$768.00	20	$640.00
Fred	$35.00	20	$700.00	28	$980.00	24	$840.00
Jane	$40.00	24	$960.00	35	$1,400.00	29.5	$1,180.00
Sam	$20.00	40	$800.00	49	$980.00	44.5	$890.00
Holly	$15.00	32	$480.00	41	$615.00	36.5	$547.50

As the table illustrates, you can accurately predict the cost associated with each team member's time by using the individual's hourly rates, the time you predict it will take the team member to finish the task, and the best, worst, and average scenarios. This worksheet has been created for you in an Excel document called Time Cost Worksheet that is on the CD-ROM. You will be using the worksheet in an upcoming exercise.

Another advantage of this worksheet is that it can help you determine what tasks should be assigned to what users. For example, you may not want to assign Jane, who has an hourly rate of $40.14, to pulling cable—a mundane and tiresome chore. A bigger bang for your budget dollars would be to assign this task to Holly or Sam. If you could, you may assign the task to both Holly and Sam, who have a combined hourly wage of $34.51. This would put two workers on the task and would cost less per hour than Jane's hourly rate. In addition, two people could, in this instance of pulling cable, finish the job in nearly half the time, or better, than one individual. Of course you'll have to consider two things when assigning resources to tasks:

- *Consider productivity.* Can a higher paid resource complete the job more quickly and more cost effectively than a lower paid, less experienced resource?

- *Consider the Law of Diminishing Returns.* Just because you can add more resources to a particular task doesn't mean the task time can be exponentially reduced. For example, adding two people to pulling network cable may ensure the activity is completed more quickly, but assigning four people to the same job doesn't mean it'll get done four times as fast.

Using PERT

While finding the best- and worst-case scenarios is a quick and easy way to arrive at an average cost, you can use a slightly more sophisticated method. It's called the Program Evaluation and Review Technique, also known as PERT. PERT is ideal for time estimates to complete activities. PERT uses a weighted average to predict how long the activity may take. You'd say that as, "pessimistic plus the optimistic, plus four times the most likely, divided by six." It's divided by six because of one count for pessimistic, one count for optimistic, and four counts for most likely. The following table shows this formula in action (it's also included on the Time Cost Worksheet on the CD):

Activity	Pessimistic	Optimistic	Most Likely	PERT Estimate
Configure servers	36	29	31	31.50
Install LAN hardware	35	22	29	28.83
Install NICs on all servers	23	12	19	18.50
Test database connectivity across network	40	25	35	34.17
Complete application update	34	20	28	27.67
Test application in production	17	10	14	13.83
Finalize application	33	22	29	28.50

Tracking Budgetary Expenses

It is very easy for expenses to spiral out of control. Imagine that you are buying a new server. You're talking with your favorite vendor and he's showing you that for a couple hundred dollars more you can have two processors instead of one. And you say, "Might as well." Then the vendor shows how for a couple hundred more you can add 200GB more storage. And you say, "Might as well." Then the vendor shows how for just a little more you can really up the RAM. Again you say, "Might as well."

"Might as well" are some dangerous words when it comes to shopping, aren't they? It's so easy to tack on some bells and whistles for just a few dollars more. Before you know it, those few dollars more have stretched your budget so thin you'll either have to ask for more funds or skimp on other areas of the project. And it's just not shopping that can ruin your budget. It's also manpower, human error, lack of planning, hidden costs, and general lack of research.

Not only do you need a detailed budget prior to any purchases, but you also need a detailed method to track expenses as they are incurred. This is called working toward your BAC. By documenting each purchase as it's made, you can check the purchase price against your initial budget to confirm that what you planned for is what's actually implemented.

Runaway Projects

A runaway project, as its name implies, is a project that starts out well, gains speed, momentum, and scope, and then causes runaways with your budget, man hours, and possibly your reputation or career. The biggest element of a runaway project is the budget. Project managers often try to throw money at a problem, rather than completing root cause analysis. Too often in project management, there is an attitude of solving problems by spending more money.

Runaway projects happen for several reasons:

- **Lack of planning**   Failure to plan for all aspects of the project. Projects fail in the beginning, not the end.

- **Lack of vision**   Failure to create a definite purpose for the project.

- **Scope creep**   Management and departments continue to add details and extras to an existing project scope. Recall that the project scope is all of the required work—and only the required work.

- **Lack of leadership**   Without leadership, the project is bound to wander aimlessly and incur additional expenses.

- **Lack of a Change Control System (CCS)**   A CCS is a formal process to evaluate, approve, or decline proposed changes and additions to the project scope.

You can prevent runaway projects by creating a definite, nearly unmovable plan for the project's implementation, budget, and scope as depicted in Figure 4-7. Any additional attributes of the project that are not key to its success should be set aside regardless of the requestor. In all projects, however, there needs to be a process that will allow adamant changes to the project plan. Chapter 9 will discuss this change management in great detail.

Here is an example of what appears to be a simple change to a project's scope: You are managing a project that will create an application with hooks into a SQL or Oracle database. The application will allow salespeople to place an order, check that order against warehouse inventory, and predict a ship date for the customer based on inventory or production.

FIGURE 4-7

Many factors
can cause
projects to run
away from the
original scope.

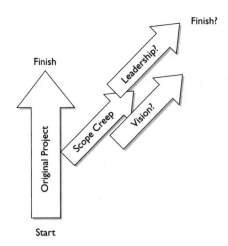

The original plan of the application called only for tight coupling of the application and the database. (*Tight coupling* means the application has to be connected to the database to run.) Now, several weeks into development, management asks that you change the application to allow loose coupling. (*Loose coupling* allows the application to run without being directly connected to the database.) Can you see the problem now? Several weeks of development have been centric to tight coupling; now what appears to be a simple change does not reflect the work hours invested in the original application.

In this scenario, management is suddenly adamant about the loose coupling because it enables the salespeople to take their laptops into the field, take orders and store them locally, and then, once they are connected to the network in the office, actually synchronize the orders with the warehouse. The project manager must first meet with management and discuss the change and explain to management how the request will increase the scope of the project. When the scope of the project increases, additional funds will be required, in most instances.

Next the project manager will have to meet with the developers and discuss the new application plans with them. The developers will, no doubt, curse management, slam their keyboards a few times, drink some sugar-rich soda, and then start working the new plan into their project. Because of lack of planning, the project scope has increased, time has been wasted, dollars have been spent, and morale has suffered.

Keeping Track of Expenses

Before the project actually begins, you'll need to work within your organizational policies on how project expenses will be tracked and monitored. In some organizations, budgetary concerns are handled by management with some input from the project manager. In other organizations, the project manager is responsible for the day-to-day accounting of the project budget. There are multiple tools available to help you track the project expenses, but whichever one you use to keep track of your project expenditures, you'll need to include some basic elements:

■ **Work hours**   Time is one of the most expensive elements in any project, so you should have a plan for team members to report their hours working on a given project. If you are working with vendors or consultants who will be billing by the hour, create a method for them to report their hours as well. You may need to create a formula to reflect overtime and weekend pay if that is applicable to your organization. Functional managers of your project team members will also want some accountability of their employees' time on your project.

■ **Procured goods**   Keep track of all hardware, tools, software, cables, and any other item that is purchased directly for your project. Your accounting software should have a method for entering any of these items. Also include petty cash items such as pizza, dinner, and miscellaneous items your team needs.

■ **Software licensing**   If your IT project includes software-licensing fees, be sure to document them. In some organizations, the IT department may pay for the initial licensing of the software, but as the software is released throughout the company, other departments have to pay to use the software from their budget. An IT project manager should know how these fees are handled and from whose budgets these funds will flow.

■ **Workstations and servers**   If your IT project includes workstations and servers as part of the plan, document the purchase price and installation date of the computers. Obviously, in some plans the implementation of the workstations or servers may in itself be the project. The reason to document the actual expense of the computers is so that if they are recycled into other servers or workstations for future projects, you can reflect the original paid price of the PCs and then diminish the value of the computers in the new project. You likely won't have to get into the details of single-line deductions versus dual-declining deductions for tax purposes, but your company's accounting department may query your decisions and choice to recycle hardware. Often an older workstation can be used as a terminal for Citrix or Windows Terminal Services. Rather than purchasing new PCs, you can incorporate the value of the older but usable PC.

■ **Actual variances**   Throughout your project, you may have small variances from what was estimated and the actual cost of the deliverable. For example, you may order supplies for the project at $440 and the actual invoice is $480. While it's only a $40 variance, it's still a variance that's going to add up and count against your budget at completion.

Here is an example of an Excel spreadsheet to keep track of budgetary expenses. This spreadsheet is for the first of three phases for a software upgrade. The actual Excel spreadsheet, named Budget, is available on the CD-ROM.

Each project will, of course, have different needs for computing the expenses committed to that project. This example shows work hours, hardware and software purchased, and any incidentals. The formulas reflect a running total of each week of the project and a total for the project's expense at the phase the project is currently in. You will get a chance to practice creating a budget spreadsheet in an upcoming exercise.

Phase One						
Budget for phase	$160,000.00		Amount spent to date	$159,897.89		
			Variance	$102.11		
Work Hours	**Hourly Rate**	**Week 1 Hours**	**Week 2 Hours**	**Week 3 Hours**	**Hours to Date**	**Cost to Date**
Steve	$21.63	37.0	30.0	39.0	106.0	$2292.78
Sally	$30.53	27.0	25.0	26.0	78.0	$2381.34
Jane	$32.81	38.0	37.5	29.0	104.5	$3428.65
John	$32.31	29.0	40.0	37.0	106.0	$3424.86
Fred	$30.38	35.0	40.0	26.0	101.0	$3068.38
Totals	$147.66	166.0	172.5	157.0	495.5	$14,596.01
Purchases	**Cost**	**Number of Units**	**Totals**			
Server 1	$7854	2	$15,708			

Phase One						
Application	$89	950	$84,550			
Licenses	$45	950	$42,750			
Total			$143,008			
Incidentals	Cost	Number of Units	Totals			
Network card	$21	2	$42			
Sound card	$45	4	$180			
Mouse	$37	2	$74			
Video card	$69	3	$207			
RAM	$268	5	$1340			
Team dinner	$150	3	$450			
Total			$2293			

As you can see, this project has ended phase 1 with a surplus of $102.11—an excellent reflection of planning and predicting by the project manager. While a surplus of this little amount is acceptable, a surplus of 10 percent or more of the predicted project phase budget is not a reason to celebrate.

Some IT project managers congratulate themselves for coming in under budget. However, there are several problems with large budget surpluses. The first problem is that it reflects poor planning on behalf of the IT project manager. An accurate plan will keep any surplus within 3 to 5 percent of the original budget, including the agreed upon range of variance for the project. The second problem with surpluses is that it creates an attitude of spending. Organizations with surpluses do not feel obligated to return the funds, but rather feel obligated to spend them to justify their original budget and to ensure that their budgets will be as fat on the next project. Poor planning is not a reason to celebrate.

FROM THE FIELD

Interview with Greg Kirkland

Name: Gregory A. Kirkland
Title: Information Systems Manager
Company: Katz, Sapper & Miller, LLP
Years as an IT project manager: 10

Greg Kirkland has earned a BA in computer information science from Franklin College. He started writing COBOL financial applications out of school, then switched to PC and network support. He worked for a Fortune 200 company in that capacity for 5 years. Greg is now working in one of the largest regional CPA firms in the country as an IS manager. He oversees all technology operations, including infrastructure, O/S, support, and training.

Q: What is the best thing about IT project management?

A: I think getting my hands on the new "toys" is the most fun. Trying new technology and making the recommendations to deploy that new technology is very rewarding.

Q: When you begin to create a budget for an IT project, what things do you consider first?

A: I try not to focus on the cost. I work for a CPA firm, and they are going to analyze the proposed budget expenditures to the Nth degree. What I try to do is look at what the best solution to the problem is. I consider the best products and services on the market, because I truly believe that you get what you pay for, and spending a little extra up front can save you additional expenses and headaches later.

Q: How can IT project managers get their visions of superb technology in alignment with company budgets?

A: The best way that I have found to accomplish this is to develop a three-year technology plan. We may be dreaming of what we want to do technologically in the future, so I put it in the plan for next year or the year after. That gives me many more opportunities to get our top management time to "warm up" to the idea of spending that cash when it counts.

FROM THE FIELD *(continued)*

Q: Working as an IT professional in an accounting firm must be frustrating at times with your budget. What advice can you offer in regard to preparing budgets for IT projects?

A: When I wrote my first IT budget three years ago, it was a very frustrating experience. I now know that every partner that looks at my budget is going to scrutinize it like they would their clients' financial statements. I'm not an accountant, but I have been trained to think like one.

I've divided my budget spreadsheet into Capital and Noncapital Expenditure sections. That tells us what our out-of-pocket expenses are this year versus what can be amortized over the life of the product, like a PC. Next, I create categories that match the General Ledger numbers for the firm's master budget, such as Hardware, Training, Maintenance, and Supplies. Know this—software and software licenses are handled differently! Software is a capital expenditure that is expensed in the current year and software licenses are noncapital expenditures that can be amortized. Share that with your CFO, and they'll know what you are talking about.

Aligning the categories with G/L allows our managing partners to compare budget numbers to last year's actual numbers. I even do my homework to find out those totals before I propose my budget. It helps me avoid arguments where my recommendations are on target or under last year's amounts. That leaves me with only one battle to fight—new projects where we spent more than last year.

Q: What key component does management want to see in an IT budget?

A: My management is not technically savvy. I can share with the managers RAID-5 this and SCSI that, and they would think that I'm speaking a foreign language. They need to understand the benefit of the end result, not necessarily what hardware or software product allows us to accomplish that result. I accomplish that by using lay terms and save the "geek speak" for when I'm back in my department. What they most appreciate is that my recommendations are well thought out, that I've considered other alternatives, and that we can get it for a fair price.

I break down the budget report format much like an invoice indicating quantity, price, annual price, description, and an explanation of that description. It goes through a first round cut, and then I add columns for Proposed Cuts, Cut Comment, and Revised Budget. (Secret: Ask for more than you want so that you at least get what you need.)

Additionally, they want to see the spreadsheet printed out in an easy-to-read format, with subtotals and totals that foot (add up) and are easy to follow. I typically improve the readability by highlighting category headings and totals in color and printing the spreadsheet on a color printer.

Q: Why do technology implementation projects always seem to cost more than expected?

A: I think failure to plan for the unexpected results in more time being spent, either internally, or with a consultant. The hardware and software costs should be predictable, so just the implementation costs are what is variable.

Q: What should project managers do when they are about to run over budget?

A: Honesty is always the best policy. Consult with your senior management to let them know what is going on. More than likely, you got their blessing before starting on the project. Help them remember the benefits of the project to get additional funds and time to complete the project successfully.

Q: In what ways can a project manager control cost?

A: Work absurd amounts of overtime by doing it yourself. OK, only slightly exaggerated. I do believe that an IS team should try to do all that it can internally (fixed cost if salaried) before outsourcing. Knowing your system and how to maintain it is very important. Don't hand over all of the control to the outside folks.

Q: How do you show return on investment for technology implementations?

A: We're in the services business. "Time is money," so they say, and it is true. Our company realizes the value in our investment in technology in that they can do more in less time. More billable hours means more money to the bottom line. "Investment" is definitely the key word. It isn't just an expense. We are getting the value out of our technology by improved efficiencies.

FROM THE FIELD (continued)

Q: How do you address risk in regard to new technology?

A: We try before we buy. We've got a test lab that we set up to simulate our production environment. Then we can test new products to see how they interact with our setup. We're definitely conservative in our approach. Our IS staff and our internal technology users group will try out the new gear before we roll it out to the rest of the firm. The tech group are the "guinea pigs."

Q: What is the most expensive part of IT budgets?

A: Capital expenditures for new hardware make up the biggest line item on our budget. New servers, PCs, printers, hubs, cables, and so on, that keep our firm on the leading edge of technology cost more than all of the other categories combined.

Q: How does a project manager defend a much-needed technology implementation when management doesn't agree?

A: I've found that management won't approve a project just because IS says it is "cool." A typical cost-versus-benefit analysis is normally necessary to help persuade them to see it your way. If they understand and appreciate the benefits, then finding a reasonably priced solution is your last hurdle.

Q: How do you factor variances of cost into your budget planning?

A: I was really fortunate this year in that the cost of the PCs that I put in the budget at the beginning of the year was much lower by the time I purchased them early in the fourth quarter. I look like a genius for saving so much money. I don't recommend padding your budget to get that effect, however. I get real quotes from the vendors I plan to do business with, then hope that prices are the same, if not lower, when I go to buy those items later in the year. In my experience, I've not seen any equipment get more expensive later in the year. I've got this saying, "Better, faster, cheaper," and it usually works out to my favor.

CHAPTER SUMMARY

Technology is not an expense, but an investment. One of your roles as a project manager is to safeguard the investment dollars and ensure that the project is implemented successfully and within budget. This includes the planning, testing, integration, and, ultimately, the implementation phases. In some instances you will be forced to alter the plan, which will most likely alter the budget.

An effective project manager can work with bottom-up cost estimates to accurately predict each phase of a project and what expenses will be associated with each phase. Typically, zero-based budgeting will determine estimates for IT projects, and this will require you and your project team to research the true costs of each component of the project to ascertain an accurate price for the product implementation. In some instances, a best- and worst-case scenario should be used so you can predict an average amount of time, cost, and dollars needed to implement the technology.

Finally, you will need a good flow of communication among vendors, team members, and consultants to keep an accurate record of time invested, dollars committed, and incidental expenses incurred in a project. By tracking budgetary expenses, you can see weekly, or even daily, expenses incurred throughout a project. This will also allow you to see a running total of a project's phase and predict any overrun or the possibility of a budget surplus.

CHAPTER QUIZ

1. What type of project estimating must account for every expense within a project before the work begins?

   A. Bottom-up estimating

   B. Top-down estimating

   C. Zero-based budgeting

   D. Parametric estimating

2. You are the project manager of the JHN Project. You have estimated the project will cost $129 for each unit installed. There are 1,200 units on this project. What type of estimate is this?

   A. Bottom-up estimate

   B. Top-down estimate

   C. Analogous estimating

   D. Parametric estimating

3. What is a bottom-up cost estimate?

   A. Last year's budget plus 20 percent to equal the current year budget

   B. This year's budget with a 20 percent plus or minus shift in the bottom line

   C. The process of working toward a zero balance as the bottom line in a budget

   D. The process of creating a detailed estimate for each work component in a project plan

4. Finish the sentence: One of the largest fluctuating expenses in IT is _____.

   A. Time

   B. Hardware

   C. Licensing

   D. Software

5. What should a project manager do to an IT implementation to accurately predict the total cost of the project?

   A. List all of the expenses and add them up using a best- and worst-case scenario for each expense.

   B. List all of the expenses, including labor, and add them up using an average-case scenario for each expense.

    C. Divide the project into phases and assign a dollar amount to each phase.

    D. Divide the project into phases and estimate a dollar amount for each milestone within a phase.

6. What is a fully burdened workload?

    A. It is when an employee has reached his maximum number of hours allotted for any given project.

    B. It is when a consultant has reached her maximum number of hours allotted for billable time for a project or task within the project.

    C. It is the prediction of the number of hours required by staff to complete each phase of the project.

    D. It is the record of the number of hours required by staff to complete each phase of the project.

7. Why should an IT project manager use best- and worst-case scenarios when calculating the time required for a task?

    A. Some staff members will take longer than other staff members to do the same type of work.

    B. Each staff member will have a dollar amount assigned to the work hour. The best- and worst-case scenario can predict which staff member is the most valuable.

    C. Best- and worst-case scenarios allow an IT project manager to predict the average time expense required to complete a task.

    D. Best- and worst case scenarios allow an IT project manager to predict the average amount of labor required to complete a task.

8. What are factors that a project manager can use to predict time for tasks within a project? Choose two:

    A. Call upon prior experience.

    B. Complete the task and see how much time the task requires.

    C. Call upon other IT professionals and ask for their advice.

    D. Leave the task time value open until the task has been completed.

9. What is a primary advantage of an IT project manager requiring a vendor to deliver a fixed quote?

    A. It locks the vendor into the project.

    B. It prevents the vendor from adding any additional features to the implementation.

    C. It allows the project manager to use the quote for up to one year.

    D. It allows the project manager to incorporate the quote into a proposed budget.

10. What is the Budget at Completion (BAC)?

    A. It is the total amount of the budget for each phase of the project.

    B. It is the amount of the total project before the project is done.

    C. It is the amount of each phase as the phase is completed.

    D. It is the grand total of the project once the project has been completed.

11. What is Program Evaluation and Review Technique (PERT)?

    A. It is a method for tracking time and costs.

    B. It is a time estimating technique that accounts for any variances between the optimistic and most likely estimates.

    C. It allows the project manager to use a similar project's budget as the "zero" starting point.

    D. It is a time-estimating method that accounts for the pessimistic, optimistic, and most likely estimates to complete an activity.

12. Of the following, which is a not a factor in the budget of an IT project?

    A. Labor of employees and consultants

    B. Upcoming software releases

    C. Hardware upgrades

    D. Software licensing

13. True or False: It is always better to purchase hardware already configured than to take the time to assemble it in-house.

    A. True

    B. False

14. Of the following, which is an example of a per connection licensing fee?

    A. The organization is charged for unlimited connections to a server.

    B. The organization is charged a fee each time an application is used.

    C. The organization is charged a fee for each connection to a server.

    D. The organization is charged a set fee for all the connections to a server.

15. Of the following, which is an example of a per station licensing fee?

    A. The organization is charged for unlimited connections to a server.

    B. The organization is charged a fee for each PC on which the application is installed.

C. The organization is charged a fee for each connection to a server.

D. The organization is charged a set fee for all the connections to a server.

CHAPTER EXERCISES

Exercise 1

In this exercise, you will complete the Time Cost Worksheet to predict and calculate the cost of each team member. Microsoft Excel is required to use the formulas to automatically predict the cost of each task. If you do not have Microsoft Excel, you can use the alternate worksheet called Manual Time Cost Worksheet to enter the values manually.

Scenario: You are the IT project manager for Harding Enterprises. The project you are managing is an installation of new network cable, network cards, servers, and workstations throughout the entire company. In this first part of the budget planning exercises, you need to calculate the hourly rate of each worker.

Follow these steps to complete Exercise 1:

1. Insert the CD-ROM included with this book into your CD-ROM drive.

2. Open Windows Explorer and navigate to the drive that represents your CD-ROM.

3. Within the CD-ROM, open the folder called Chapter 4.

4. Within the Chapter 4 folder, open the Microsoft Excel file called Time Cost Worksheet by double-clicking it.

5. The Excel document has two spreadsheets: Instructions and Time cost analysis. On the Instructions spreadsheet, hover your mouse over the red marker in cell A5. You'll see some general directions on how this spreadsheet works in case you want to use it in production. Click the spreadsheet titled "Time cost analysis" to move to the second sheet.

6. Hover your mouse over the comment marker in cell A1 and read the comments. Click in cell A2, enter **Rick Gordon**, and then press TAB to move to cell B2.

7. Hover your mouse over cell B1 to read the comment. In cell B2, enter Rick Gordon's yearly salary, **73500**, and press TAB to move to cell C2.

8. Rick Gordon's hourly rate is calculated for you based on his annual salary, divided by 52 weeks, and then divided again by 40 hours. Press TAB again to move to cell D2.

9. For this first task, enter **4.5** to represent four-and-a-half hours for the best value time. Press TAB to move to cell E2.

10. Note that 4.5 hours equates to $159.01 for Rick's time. Press TAB again to move to F2. For the worst time, enter 7 to represent seven hours and press TAB. The cost for seven hours is calculated. Press TAB to move onto cell H2.

11. Notice that cell H2 has already calculated the average time for Rick Gordon and the average cost for Rick to complete the assigned task.

12. Complete the remainder of the spreadsheet with the following information:

Team Member	Yearly Salary	Best Time (Hours)	Worst Time (Hours)
Samantha Murray	67500	5	9
Bradley Kiser	43200	9	15
Harriet Sutherland	37600	12	19
Fred Stephens	57600	8	16

1. Based on your entries, answer the following questions:

   A. What is the average cost of Samantha Murray's time on the assigned task?

   B. What is the cost of Bradley Kiser's time if he takes the worst amount of predicted time?

   C. What is the cost of Harriet Sutherland's time if she beats the best time estimate by two hours?

   D. What is the average cost of Fred Stephens' time?

2. Review your work and then close the document. You can save the spreadsheet to your hard disk if you would like to review your work again later.

Exercise 2

In this exercise you will create a budget for phase 1 of a hypothetical project. You will be using the Microsoft Excel spreadsheet called Budget to complete the exercise.

If you do not have Excel, you can use the alternative spreadsheet, Manual Budget, to complete the exercise.

Scenario: You are the IT project manager for Harding Enterprises. The project you are managing is an installation of new network cable, network cards, servers, and workstations throughout the entire company. In this exercise, you will be calculating ongoing expenses related to the purchase and installation of Category 5 UTP cable, switches, patch panels, and the servers. Follow these steps to complete the exercise:

1. Insert the CD-ROM included with this book into your CD-ROM drive.

2. Open Windows Explorer and navigate to the drive that represents your CD-ROM.

3. Within the CD-ROM, open the folder called Chapter 4.

4. Within the Chapter 4 folder, open the Microsoft Excel file called Budget by double-clicking it.

5. Hover your mouse over cell A1 to see the comment that has been added.

6. Hover your mouse over cell B2 to see the comment that has been added.

7. Navigate to cell E6, the third week's hours for Steve Ledbetter. Weeks 1 and 2 have been completed for you. Enter 27 for Steve's hours and press ENTER.

8. Notice that several things have happened: The hours to date and the cost to date have increased. Also, the amount in cell F2, the amount spent to date, has increased. Finally, the figure in cell F3, the amount until the budget has been reached, has decreased.

9. Move back to cell E6 and enter 37 for Steve's work hours and press ENTER. Notice the changes throughout the spreadsheet.

10. Enter the following figures for the rest of the team members' third week hours on the project:

Team Member	Week 3 Hours Worked
Sally Dehority	28
Jane Chambers	39
John Maxwell	21
Fred Hoffman	37

11. Navigate to cell B14. Enter **7854** as the amount of the server that will be purchased and press TAB.

12. In cell C14, enter **2**, and press TAB. The amount of the servers has been calculated and the spreadsheet has been updated to reflect your changes.

13. Navigate to cell B15, enter **1800** for the amount of the network cable, and press TAB to move to cell C15.

14. In cell C15, enter **3** and press TAB. Again, the spreadsheet is updated to reflect the changes.

15. Navigate to cell B16, enter **21.34**, and press TAB.

16. For the number of cards purchased, enter **227** and press TAB to see the spreadsheet updated.

17. Navigate to cell B20. Enter **27.80** as the amount of the PC tool kit and press TAB.

18. In cell C20, enter **5** as the number of tool kits purchased and press TAB.

19. In cell B21, enter **98.78** as the cost of the RJ-45 connectors and press TAB.

20. In cell C21, enter **2** and press TAB.

21. In cell B22, enter **49** and press TAB.

22. In cell C22, enter **4** and press TAB.

23. In cell B23, enter **150** and press TAB.

24. In cell C23, enter **3** and press TAB.

25. Review your work and then close the document. You can save the spreadsheet to your hard disk if you would like to review your work later.

QUIZ ANSWERS

1. **A.** Bottom-up estimating requires the project manager to account for all expenses within the project to arrive at a grand total for the project.

2. **D.** This is an example of a parametric estimate. The units will cost $129 each; this is the parameter. As there are 1,200 units on the project, the estimate is calculated by multiplying the parameter of $129 by the total number of units needed, 1,200, for an estimate of $154,800.

3. **D.** Bottom-up estimating is a process that requires the project manager to create a detailed estimate for each phase of a project. The project manager starts at the beginning of a project and works toward the project's completion to determine the actual financial obligations required to complete the plan.

4. **A.** Time is one of the largest fluctuating expenses within a project plan. Who is completing a task, that person's skill set, the type of work being completed, and other factors can determine the length of time required to complete the task.

5. **C.** The project manager should not create one grand total for a project. In order for the project manager to see a true picture of the work, she should segment the project into phases and assign each phase a dollar amount based on the work to be completed within it.

6. **C.** A fully burdened workload is the prediction of the number of hours required by the team members to complete a given project. This process allows the project manager to predict the financial obligations corresponding to time and create a sense of urgency as to when each task must be completed.

7. **C.** The best- and worst-case scenarios allow a project manager to predict the average amount of time the team member requires to complete a task. The project manager uses this value to assign a dollar amount to the work to be completed.

8. **A, C.** This is historical information. The experiences of the project manager or other IT professionals are two of the best methods to predict the length of time a task may take.

9. **D.** A fixed quote allows the project manager to use that dollar amount in a budget to predict the funds required to complete a project. It can also be used to determine which vendor will actually be awarded the job based on the price and hours to complete the work.

10. **B.** The Budget at Completion (BAC) is the predicted amount of the entire project before the project has been completed.

11. **D.** The Program Evaluation Review Technique (PERT) is a time-estimating formula that accounts for the optimistic, pessimistic, and most likely estimates. The formula is P+O+(4ML)/6.

12. **B.** Future releases of software are not a concern during the budget creation process. While it is possible that information about new software being released could impact the entire project, it will not change an existing budget based on plans that have been already created.

13. **B.** False. It is not always better to purchase hardware already configured from a vendor. Oftentimes, it will be more cost effective to configure the hardware in-house rather than assigning the task to a vendor to complete it.

14. **C.** Per connection licensing fees are assigned to each connection from a workstation to a server. Network operating systems, such as Windows 2000, use a licensing plan such as this.

15. **B.** Per station licensing is typical of applications installed on each workstation. Part of the licensing agreement requires that each workstation have a license to use the software.

EXERCISE SOLUTIONS

Exercise 1

At the completion of Exercise 1, your spreadsheet should look like this table:

Team Member	Yearly Salary	Hourly Wage	Best Time (Hours)	Cost	Worst Time (Hours)	Cost	Average Time (Hours)	Average Cost
Rick Gordon	$73,500	$35.34	4.5	$159.	7.0	$247.	5.75	203.
Samantha Murray	$67,500	$32.45	5.0	$162.25	9.0	$292.05	7	227.15
Bradley Kiser	$43,200	$20.77	9.0	$186.93	15.0	$311.55	12	249.24
Harriet Sutherland	$37,600	$18.08	12.0	$216.96	19.0	$343.52	15.5	280.24
Fred Stephens	$57,600	$27.69	8.0	$221.52	16.0	$443.04	12	332.28

Exercise 1 included four questions pertaining to the Time Cost Worksheet. Here are the answers:

A. Samantha Murray's average cost for the assigned task is $227.16.

B. If Bradley Kiser takes 15 hours to complete the task, the cost will be $311.54.

C. If Harriet Sutherland beats her predicted best time by 2 hours, the cost will be $180.77.

D. The average cost of Fred Stephens' time is $332.31

Exercise 2

At the completion of Exercise 2, your spreadsheet should look like this:

Phase I						
Budget for phase	$42,000.00		Amount spent to date	$41,694.87		
			Amount from budget	$305.13		
Team Members	Hourly Rate	Week 1 Hours	Week 2 Hours	Week 3 Hours	Hours to Date	Cost to Date
Steve Ledbetter	$21.63	37.0	30.0	37.0	104.0	$2249.52
Sally Dehority	$30.53	27.0	25.0	28.0	80.0	$2242.40
Jane Chambers	$32.81	38.0	37.5	39.0	114.5	$3756.75
John Maxwell	$32.31	29.0	40.0	21.0	90.0	$2907.90
Fred Hoffman	$30.38	35.0	40.0	37.0	112.0	$3402.56
Total						$14,559.13
Purchases	Cost	Number of Units	Totals			
Server 1	$7854.00	2	$15,708.00			
Network cable	$1800.00	3	$5400.00			

Phase 1						
Network cards	$21.34	227	$4844.18			
Total			$25,952.18			
Incidentals	Cost	Number of Units	Totals			
PC tool kit	$27.80	5	$139.00			
RJ-45 Connectors (box)	$98.79	2	$197.58			
Line testers	$49.00	4	$196.00			
Team dinner	$150.00	3	$450.00			
Total			$982.58			

Chapter 5

Creating a Work Breakdown Structure

Remember when you were a kid and you bought your first model car? You opened the box, sorted all the pieces, put the decals aside for safekeeping, and gathered all your tools. Of course, you read the directions completely and carefully assembled each piece of the model with just the right amount of glue, patiently waited for it to dry before proceeding, and then finally applied the decals with a pair of tweezers.

Doesn't sound quite right? Were you more like the kid who ripped the box open, tossed the directions aside, and ended up gluing your fingers together? What's the lesson here? With experience you became more like the kid in the first example: meticulous, careful, patient, planning, and savvy with a tube of glue. The same is true with project management—except for the glue thing. You, the project manager, need a detailed plan of the work, what phases are required in the work, and then what tasks are required within each phase. Just as it was building the model car, taking the proper steps won't be easy, but if you plan for success, you will reach your goal.

Defining the Work Breakdown Structure

An IT project manager cannot, and should not, do every piece of work in a project. On some projects it would be physically impossible for one person to do every task. Of course, with a project team, a project manager can delegate tasks to team members and let them get to work. But how will the team members know if their assigned tasks can begin before other team members' tasks end?

For example, your project is to create an application that allows web users to search a database of all the different cowboy boots your company makes—and have it in place before the Christmas shopping season begins on November 1. Customers must be able to search for their boots by size, color, style, and price.

A Work Breakdown Structure (WBS) allows you to answer these questions, get your arms around the project, and assign jobs to your team members. A WBS is a deliverables-orientated collection of project components. It is a categorization and decomposition of the project deliverables. A WBS to install a new network, for example, may offer high-level deliverables such as LAN, WAN, extranets, and intranets. Each of these high-level deliverables is broken down into a more defined deliverable that comprises the high-level components. At the lowest level of the structure, you have the work packages. These are the smallest deliverable within a WBS, and they will be further decomposed into activities in the project schedule.

A WBS is important in all projects. It is necessary because it serves as input to five key project management activities:

- Cost estimating
- Cost budgeting
- Resource planning
- Risk management planning
- Activity definition

Working with a WBS

There's no right or wrong way to create a WBS. You can draw an elaborate decomposition on a whiteboard, sketch it out on a cocktail napkin, or be more technical and use a piece of software such as Microsoft Project or even Excel, Visio, or PowerPoint. It is best, however, to use some common terminology when addressing your WBS.

A project, of course, is a complete piece of work that has a definite end date, produces a defined set of deliverables, and is an investment by an organization. For example, the software application that allows web users to search a database of boots requires a scope, defined deliverable, commitment of resources, and targeted end date.

Within the project there are phases. Well, technically there don't have to be any phases, but most projects have clear identifiable phases that segment the project work. A *phase* is a portion of the project that typically must be completed before the next phase can begin. Each phase has a set deadline. For example, the cowboy boot database project could have four phases: creation of the database, creation of the application, creation of the web interface, and troubleshooting and implementation. Typically, phases do not overlap each other in production, but it is possible that they can as they do in this example; each phase, while reliant on the others, could be completed in parallel rather than sequentially.

Within each phase, there are work packages. A *work package* is the smallest deliverable within the WBS. The project's activity list can be derived from the work packages. For example, within the cowboy boots project, the phase to create the database encompasses several work packages required for completion. A database administrator needs to create the database with the application designer to ensure consistency, a system needs to be built to enter the different attributes of the boots for searching, hooks need to be made between this database and an existing database production uses to create the boots, and probably more. Figure 5-1 shows the different components of a WBS.

When you do break down deliverables, keep in mind that the smallest layer of decomposition consists of work packages. Again, with the cowboy boots database, the work package representing the different attributes of the boots could consist of several tables for sizes, colors, styles, and prices with keys linked to other tables to create the relational database. In other words, a boot called the "Montana Boot" can be searched for by color, size, and price. The creation of these tables could, and most likely would, be considered a single task.

Coordinating WBS Components

Some project managers would recommend that you continue to break down each task until you cannot break down the activity anymore. However, conventional wisdom contradicts a continual decomposition of any activity, as it eventually leads to units of work that are too small. While some control over the work to be completed is required, a project manager needs to put faith in her team to complete the tasks necessary to finish the job.

As a rule, find an acceptable amount of time that will serve as the smallest increment of work. For example, with a small project, you may only break work down into days. With a larger project, you may choose to break work down into weeks. The key is to not continue to break down each activity into tiny, unmanageable tasks. A heuristic you can rely on is the "8/80 Rule." The 8/80 Rule suggests that the

FIGURE 5-1

A WBS consists of the project, phases, work units, and tasks.

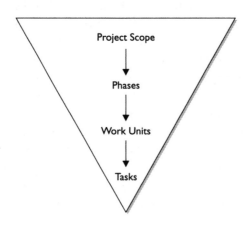

smallest work package take no more than 80 hours of time to complete—or no less that eight hours to complete. While this rule can apply to most projects, it's not always applicable. For example you may have a work package that represents a sub-project or part of your project that you'll be outsourcing to a vendor. The group completing the activities will likely decompose these work packages into their own WBS.

Why You Need a WBS

You may be tempted to skip the process of creating a WBS—especially on smaller projects. Don't yield to that temptation. By creating a WBS, even on small projects, a project manager can accurately predict several things:

- *A WBS defines the required work to complete the project.* How many times have you started any project only to uncover activities that you had totally forgotten about? Or worse, realized that a component was needed that didn't exist and had to be created before your project could continue? A WBS ensures that a project manager knows all of the required work for the project to be complete.

- *A WBS creates a sense of urgency.* By creating a WBS, a project manager and his team are working toward the project deliverables. Because the WBS is broken down at its lowest level into work packages—and the activity is derived from the work packages—the tasks can then be assigned start and end dates The WBS is needed to ensure proper scheduling and sequencing for the identified activities to create the project deliverables. The project can maintain its momentum—and its schedule—if all members complete their tasks on time. A WBS allows a project manager to track the success or failure of team members based on the completion of activities, which in turn creates the deliverables the WBS identifies.

- *A WBS can help prevent scope creep.* When management and departments try to add new features for an existing project, a WBS can ward them off. Because a WBS is a baseline that maps out each activity on the road to completion, it becomes easier for a project manager to rule out additions and new features to a project that has already started. It is possible, however, to add new features to a WBS, but the schedule will have to be adjusted to reflect the new additions, as will the budget.

- *A WBS provides control.* As a project manager, you may be in charge of several different IT projects. A WBS can allow you to graphically view the status of any project and how progress is being made. You can easily hone in on a particular phase, work unit, or task and make adjustments, counsel team members, or adjust the schedule as needed. Control is good.

■ *The WBS is the scope baseline.* Work that is not in the WBS is not in the project. It provides a point of agreement between the project manager, the customer, the sponsor, the team members, the vendors, and other stakeholders on what is in the project, and what is not in the project.

Examining a Sample WBS

Before you get into the inner workings of creating a WBS, take a moment and examine an existing WBS. Figure 5-2 is a WBS created in Microsoft Visio. This WBS is for a fictional company named Donaldson Investments and Holdings. The project is an implementation of a new mail server and the mail clients on all of the workstations.

In this example, only the work has been identified; the project manager has not yet assigned the tasks to team members. In addition, the task durations have been identified here, but they would not be identified in a true WBS. This WBS was created in Microsoft Project and the file is saved on the CD-ROM under the name Donaldson if you would like to examine it more closely.

Task Name	Duration
Phase One: Servers	9 days
W2003 Servers (3)	2.5 days
Exchange Server (3)	2.33 days
Exchange Server	4.17 days
Server links	1.17 days
Test user accounts	2 days
Mailbox rules	1 day
Phase Two: User configuration	5.83 days
Installation packages	3.33 days
Test workstation	1.17 days
W2003 policy	1.33 days
W2003 policy for different Ous	2.33 days

Task Name	Duration
Test policy installation	2.5 days
CD image for remote access users	1.33 days
Test CD image	1.17 days
Phase Three: Pilot users training and rollout	23.17 days
Pilot users class	13.5 days
Class workbook for training	2.17 wks
Pilot users training class (groups of ten)	5.5 days
Image to pilot users	9.67 days
Roll image to pilot users	1 day
Pilot users forum to discuss usage	2.17 days
Install image	2 days
Feedback from pilot users	1 day
Finalize and test images	1 day
Phase Four: User training and rollout	25 days
20 students per day	25 days
Rollout based on attendance	25 days

FIGURE 5-2   A WBS decomposes the project deliverables into manageable components.

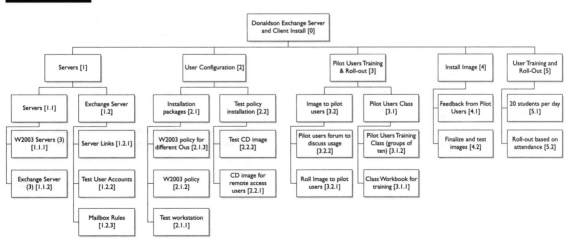

It is difficult to see the progression of work in an outline form as provided in this example. Figure 5-3 shows the work in Microsoft Project. Project allows you to see your project through a Gantt chart. This chart displays the intersection of dates until completion and the tasks within a project. Henry Gantt, an engineer and social scientist, invented this method of tracking deliverables in 1917.

Creating a WBS

Remember when you first began to go about the process of creating the project? You created the project scope, which defined all the required work—and only the

FIGURE 5-3   Gantt chart visualizes the flow of work.

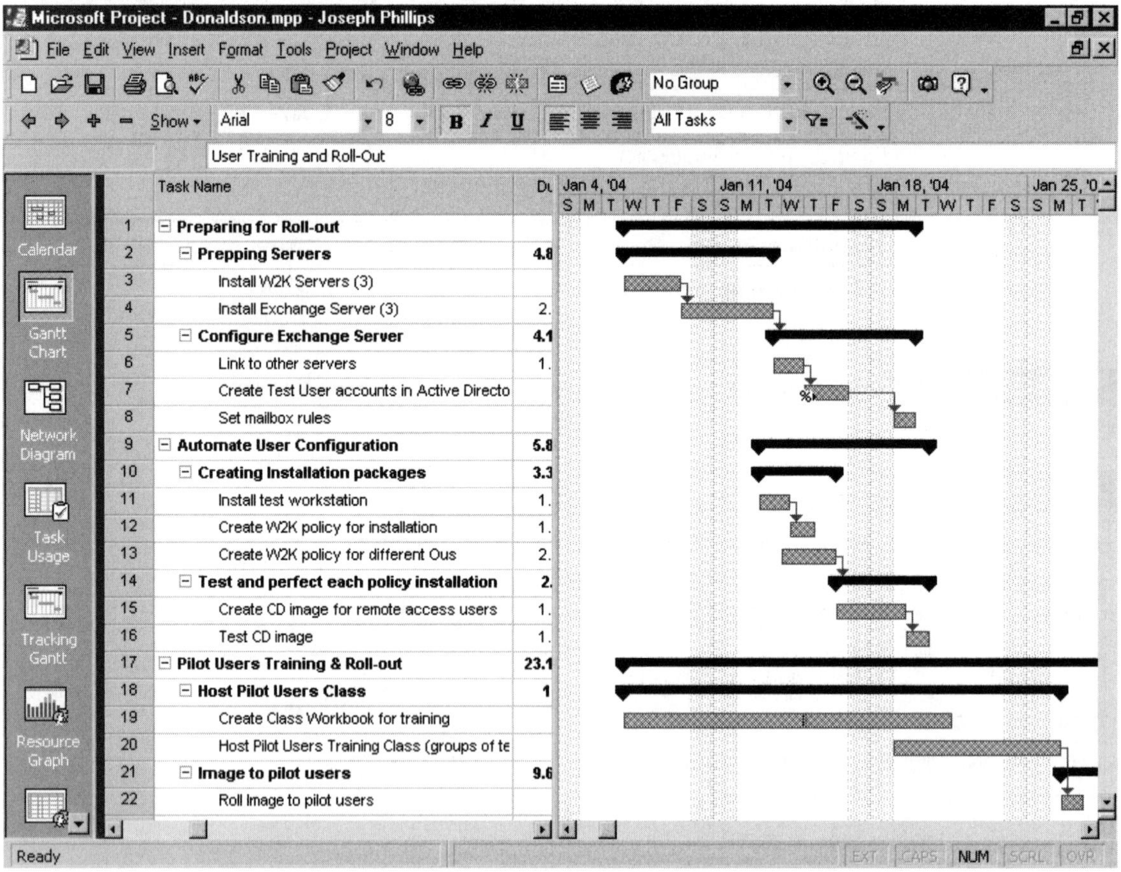

required work—for your project. Those deliverables are what you are working toward. The WBS is a compilation of the components you and your project team will create to reach the end of the project. Once the WBS is created, you can create the activity list—the actual work to create the deliverables.

A WBS also provides you with a means of assigning tasks to team members and associating a time value with each task. Once you have created the WBS, you'll use it to develop the scheduling and sequencing of your project work. The WBS is not the project plan, the schedule, or even the activity list. You will use the WBS to help you schedule and assign resources. A WBS is a process, as well as a visual representation of the work, to help you organize and plan the action that must be completed for the project to come to an end.

There are two broad methods used to create a WBS: top-down and bottom-up. The top-down approach uses deductive reasoning because it starts with the general and moves to the very specific. Bottom-up moves from the very specific toward the general. Figure 5-4 depicts the difference between the top-down and bottom-up methods.

Both methods have their advantages. The bottom-up method is ideal for brainstorming a solution to a problem. Imagine that a project team is trying to find a solution to connect a network in Chicago and a network in Phoenix without having to spend much money. The bottom-up method would call for very specific solutions without delving into all of the details of each solution. The method could investigate the use of new software, a new service provider, or practically any implementation that is still open for discussion on the actual work to be implemented.

FIGURE 5-4

There are two methods used to create a WBS.

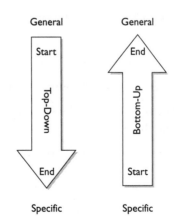

The top-down approach requires more logic and structure, and is generally the preferred method for creating a WBS. A WBS using the top-down approach would identify a solution first and then dissect the solution into the steps required to implement it. You probably use the top-down approach in your daily life. For example, when making a decision to purchase a car, you'd decide what kind of car to buy: SUV, sports car, sedan, mini-van. And then what can you afford? What color? What about the bells and whistles? This process of thinking begins with a broad approach and then narrows to specifics.

The Process of Creating a WBS

The process of creating the WBS is usually not a solo activity. Typically, it requires the involvement of the project manager and the project team. On some occasions, it may require the project sponsor or other stakeholders—though typically by this juncture the team has been given the go-ahead and management supervision is not required. Depending on the size of your project team, gathering around a computer screen to build a WBS is not ideal. What is ideal is to assemble the team and lead them through the process of creating the WBS together. Here's how:

For starters, make certain you have a whiteboard, plenty of markers, sticky notes, and control of the meeting. Instruct your staff that this process will help you to first determine the activities that need to be completed to reach the project goal. You'll start with the top-level objectives first. These are usually the phases of the project, but they can also be the major deliverables, categories of the project that may span the calendar phases, and so on. For this example, we'll assume that the deliverables are contained within each logical phase. If your budget has not been created or did not include project phases, determine what the project phases are by asking these questions:

- Are there logical partitions within this project (such as dates or activities)?
- Are there identifiable milestones that could represent phases?
- Are there business cycles within your organization that need to be considered during this project?
- Are there financial obligations or restraints within this project that could signify phases?

- What factors within the company project life cycle will impact the project?
- What processes are currently in place for system development within your organization?

Once you have the phases identified, write each one down on a sticky note and attach it to the whiteboard in the order of the phases. Now within phase 1, you'll decompose the components into smaller deliverables. You'll continue to decompose the project deliverables until they are at a manageable work package: the smallest unit within the WBS.

Decomposing the project deliverables requires some fine-tuning; you do not want to get too granular with the tasks, but you do want to break the components down so that you may allocate time and resources to the activities that must be completed to create each component. This is where you'll reference the 8/80 Rule: no task should be larger than 80 hours or smaller than 8. If you remain general and acknowledge the work to be completed rather than describe the actual mechanisms required to create each component, you'll be fine.

After you finished phase 1, or the first major deliverable, move on to the next component and repeat the process, and so on, until all of the deliverables have been broken down into work packages, and then the work packages have been broken down into the necessary tasks. What you'll have on your whiteboard may appear to be a very messy collection of sticky notes, but in reality, it represents your project from start to finish.

Introducing Microsoft Project

Microsoft Project is a software tool that allows you to create and manage an entire project from start to finish. While it is an excellent resource, it does not replace the ability to successfully manage a project, lead a team, and keep expenses under control.

Microsoft Project Server works with Microsoft Project and enables the entire project team to work together to report tasks, schedule updates, and record time spent on each project. It allows a project manager to enable multiproject tracking, share and track resources among multiple projects, and work with dependent projects.

Microsoft Project is also a fine tool for creating the WBS. Again, you may want to create the WBS outside of any software application and then set up the work inside your Project Management Information System. Once the project has been broken down into phases, work units, and tasks, you should enter the breakdown into Microsoft Project. By doing so, you can accomplish several things:

- Streamline the remainder of the WBS creation.
- Establish the sequence of events with each phase.
- Assign time estimates to each task within a phase to predict completion dates.
- Prepare to assign team members to tasks.

Within Microsoft Project, you can take the sticky-note organized structure on your whiteboard and begin to convert it into a digital format. The process is very similar to how you created the WBS on your whiteboard; only some of the terminology is different.

Examine the Deliverables

When a project is first created, it has a vision, a deliverable, and offers a clearly recognizable sign that the project is finished. When creating a WBS, the project manager will break the project down into identified deliverables. Within each phase there should also be deliverables that signify the end of a phase and the start of another.

For example, if a company is upgrading its network, servers, and workstations, there would be several phases within this massive overhaul. For simplicity's sake, assume the phases are the network upgrade, the server upgrades, and the workstation upgrades. Within each phase there most likely will be additional milestones signifying each phase is moving toward its completion.

When creating a WBS, you will need to examine each phase's major deliverables; these milestones will prove that the team and its leadership are moving in the right direction. The milestones should, however, have discreet completion criteria that represent the compilation of individual tasks required to reach this deliverable.

Again, within the scenario of overhauling the network, workstations, and servers, there are several obvious phases and not so obvious phases. The scrutiny of the deliverables will reveal the phases and the smaller victories within each phase. Figure 5-5 demonstrates the formula used to predict a timetable. A project manager should look at the deliverables to determine the time and tasks required to obtain them.

at is the best thing about IT project management?

ave a holistic vision of web development, which means that I've done everything from
tion to HTML design to web programming to search engine optimization. But that
ns that I'm a jack-of-all-trades and a master of none. Web project management lets me
vide range of experience to facilitate communication between manager, programmers,
gners, who don't often see eye-to-eye.

hen you begin to create a WBS, what do you do first?

y projects are based on a lifecycle of major phases, like definition, design, build, test,
nch. I begin the WBS process by identifying and defining all the deliverables that will be
ed under each project phase. Deliverables should be general descriptions of functionality
mpleted during the project. Then I decompose all the deliverables into actual work
ments.

hat is the most important element in a WBS?

emember that while you might know all the high-level deliverables and activities, you
not know all the lower-level activities that will complete your WBS. If you don't know
break down a higher-level activity, don't guess your way through and don't ignore that
go out and ask the people who will be responsible for the activity to tell you what the
nents of that activity are.

Do you use a software package to create your WBS?

personally use a flowchart program called Visio, because it's a really powerful program.
ver, when I have to collaborate with people who do not have Visio, I use the design and
harting tools that come with Microsoft PowerPoint to create my charts. It's not as
ful and intuitive as Visio, but at least the program is more widely diffused.

When creating a WBS, do you work in phases or do you attack the whole project?

I work the WBS in iterative cycles, since it's exceedingly difficult to map out all your activities
e fell swoop. Start with your main deliverables in the first cycle, and then decompose down to
gh-level activities, for example, define requirements. Validate that you have broken down every
erable into all the high-level activities required to complete that deliverable. Then decompose

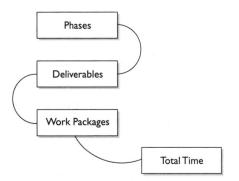

Obtaining Management Approval

Once the WBS has been initially created, it must pass through management for a
final sign-off. In some instances, such as when the project manager and the project
team are consultants or vendors integrating the technology into an existing enterprise,
the project manager probably won't have to pass every work unit within the WBS
through management for approval.

Presenting to the Project Sponsor

The project sponsor, the advocate of the project, will be the first stop on the road to
approval of the WBS. The project manager must be prepared to explain any phase
of the WBS to the project sponsor. If the project manager has fully researched and
skillfully planned the WBS around business cycles and the team members' schedules,
there should be few revisions to the schedule.

However, if the project manager has failed to work with the team, consider business
cycles, or take into account other implementations within the company, the project
sponsor can (and should) work with the project manager to correct these timings.
You can imagine the frustration that could ensue if the WBS has to be re-created
because of poor planning and an inadequate understanding of other activities within
the IT realm of an organization. Not to mention that failure in creating the WBS
does nothing to gain the confidence of your project sponsor and the project team.

Presenting to Key Stakeholders

Once the project sponsor has approved the WBS, the project manager should present the WBS to the key project stakeholders. Depending on your organization, this may be the customer of the project, another department within your company, or management. As always, tailor the presentation for the audience you are speaking to. The WBS presentation does not need to go into great detail for each task represented within each phase. To begin the presentation of the WBS, start at the deliverables of the project. By again reminding the stakeholders what the project will produce, you'll be reinforcing their decision to move the project forward. The whole point of presenting the WBS to management is to confirm that your project includes all of the deliverables they've requested for the project. Again, this will serve as the scope baseline for the project, therefore, everyone's agreement is essential.

Once you've established the deliverables, reveal the phases required to reach them. It would be most effective to show a timeline, perhaps created in PowerPoint, of the start and the finish dates of the project. As each phase is revealed, superimpose an arrow over the timeline to show where each phase will put you in relation to the project completion. This will allow your audience to visualize how your plan has been well conceived and how each phase will produce a deliverable, moving your team, and the company, toward the end result of the project. Figure 5-6 features an example timeline.

Within each phase, you may wish to show a few of the highlights to convey the activity that is required. It is not, however, necessary to illustrate every task required to complete each phase unless the stakeholders explicitly ask for it. You should be prepared to discuss each phase in detail, and it would serve you well to have an alternate presentation that does include each task of each phase of the project.

Generally, stakeholders do not want to know about each task associated with installing a cable, replacing a workstation, or upgrading a server. You should, however, always share with management any phase of the project that may require any downtime of IT components, even if it is over a weekend. Part of the WBS should address these downtimes, if they exist, so that the stakeholders are aware of the impact. Always take into consideration, through audits and logging, the type of activity that occurs over weekends or at nights due to remote users, international users, and users who work late and long hours. Don't assume anything.

If management does not approve the WBS, the project manager should immediately address any areas of concern. In some instances, management may approve on the condition of a few revisions. In other circumstances, management

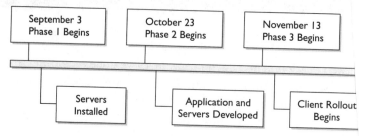

may delay your approval in order to study the WBS in approval meetings in accordance with what's the norm management always delays decisions to begin projects, on the implementation. Plan the WBS approval meetii management to review and revise your plan.

If your WBS needs to be approved immediately, stre the schedule must be implemented within x number of with the first phase of the schedule, then perhaps at leas begin while management reviews the later details.

FROM THE FIELD

Interview with Geoff Choo

Name: Geoff Choo
Title: Project Manager
Company: Invisible Site
Years as an IT project manager: 5

Geoff Choo is a project manager for Invisible Site, an Italian interactive a freelance business and technology writer. In his spare time, he helps pr Report (www.netstatistica.com), a free monthly newsletter with Internet stats at a glance. He contributes regularly to Gantthead.com and is a cont Europemedia.net. He has previously worked as a project manager and wel IconMedialab. You can get in touch with Geoff at geoff@netstatistica.com every activity into more granular activities in iterative cycles. At the end of every cycle, remember to validate that you've included every subactivity required to complete that higher-level activity.

Q: How do you predict how long each task may take?

A: From personal experience, or by using historical data from our time-tracking tools, or by simply asking the team member who will be responsible for completing that task.

Q: What methods do you use to assign tasks to team members?

A: My company built a project-tracking tool in Outlook using Microsoft Team Folders. I use the task assignment tool in Outlook to assign and track status on tasks.

Q: How important is it for a project to have a WBS?

A: Running a project without a WBS is like going to a strange land without a roadmap. A WBS provides you with a concise roadmap for reaching your destination. If you know which steps you have to take and which path you have to follow, it's going to be easier to get to where you want to go.

Q: How granular should a project manager get when creating the WBS?

A: Decompose the WBS as deeply as you need. There are no hard and fast rules to how granular a WBS should get. It all depends on the complexity of the project, the level of risk, how skilled your team is, and how much detail you need to maintain the necessary level of control. If you're working with a skilled team, you could probably get away with a shallow WBS. If you need more control on a complex project, the WBS should be decomposed as deeply as you can go. Generally, the deeper the WBS gets, the smaller (and shorter) the activities become.

But don't go too deep. You should decompose the WBS as deeply as you need, but there is a logical limit to how deep you should go and how small (or large) an activity should be. A general guideline that I like to follow is that each lowest-level activity in the WBS should be assigned to a single individual, and that individual should be able to complete the activity between one to ten working days. Anything smaller than one day and you'll end up with a 100-level deep WBS with a huge list of five-minutes tasks. Anything bigger than ten days and you might not have enough level of detail to effectively control the status of that activity.

Q: When should a project manager map out each step of an activity for a team versus identifying goals and allowing the team to create the solution?

A: The WBS is at its core a hierarchy of deliverables or tangible outcomes. Each deliverable or outcome will have a set of related activities, and each lowest-level activity will have one individual responsible for it. It is not a to-do list of every possible thing we can think of that needs to be done in the project. Rather it lists the assignments we will hold members of the project team accountable for delivering.

Whether you're working with an inexperienced team or a veteran team who can do things in their sleep, the important thing to keep in mind is that you must have enough granular detail to let you track status and progress on your projects. It's not just a matter of mapping out things for an inexperienced team or identifying the high-level goals for a veteran team and then letting them fill in the blanks.

Q: When creating the WBS, how much involvement is required from the project team?

A: I don't generally micromanage my team members and tell them all the things they have to do. I give them the high-level objectives and results I want from them, give them the tools to do it, agree on a metric to track progress, and then leave them to their own devices. This means that while I define the deliverables and high-level activities, the team members will fill in the blanks with the lower-level activities. I work with them to write down the lowest-level activities that I will use to track their progress.

Q: What method can a project manager use to confirm that he's not missed a step of the project?

A: Create the WBS in iterative cycles and constantly reevaluate the hierarchy of deliverables, activities, and subactivities. Always ask yourself and your team members, "If I had all these deliverables, would I achieve the planned objectives for the project? If I do all these activities, will I complete that deliverable? If I do all these subactivities, will I complete that activity?" If the answer is no, retrace your steps and fill in the missing step(s).

Q: What does a project manager do if he realizes a component has been left out of the WBS and adding it will throw the WBS off schedule?

A: Do what you would do if you were behind on a project:

■ Reevaluate your timing to see if your people can perform some of their activities faster. Or try to add additional people to perform the activities faster.

FROM THE FIELD *(continued)*

- Cut your scope down to the bare minimum.
- Renegotiate your deadlines and schedule.

Q: What advice can you offer to aspiring project managers in regard to creating a WBS?

A: A WBS is like the outline your teacher always made you do before writing your report in grade school. You know what you have to do, but your head is swimming with a huge list of ideas and things to do. It's hard to begin doing something if you don't know where to start. Writers call this the dreaded blank page syndrome. Staring at a blank page doesn't usually make the words flow out; neither will sitting at a desk trying to figure out how and where to start building your project.

Like an outline, a WBS helps you organize all your thoughts in a structured way, giving you something to start with and a list of steps to help you write your report or deliver a project. Start with the high-level outcomes that you have to achieve, for example, "create a user interface." Then think about what things you have to do to complete that deliverable, for example, "find out what users want, create a user interface prototype, and test the user interface for usability." Next break down those activities into more granular subactivities, such as "interview users and capture business processes." Then go deeper and deeper until you have reached the desired level of detail.

CHAPTER SUMMARY

Any organized activity, from football to cooking, requires a plan of action. A Work Breakdown Structure helps you create the plan of action. It allows you to define the top-level deliverables, the phases, and then break them down into work packages.

The process of breaking down the project deliverables into a logical order is called decomposition. As a rule, work packages do not need to be broken down into granular step-by-step tasks, but rather tight, individual units that provide a clearly defined expectation of the task for team members without micromanaging them on each click and CD-ROM to insert into the server they perform.

There are multiple ways to create a WBS, and any combination can be used as long as the end result depicts the start and end dates and the activities to be completed between the two. A WBS, once completed, needs approval from the project sponsor first to confirm the series of activities and how they mesh with an organization. Once you and the project sponsor are in sync on the plan, the key stakeholders need to sign off on the WBS to ensure that all of the project deliverables are accounted for as they're defined in the project scope.

CHAPTER QUIZ

1. You are the project manager for a project that will develop an in-house software used to monitor computer parts inventory. Your project sponsor asks that you begin working on the WBS. What is a WBS?

   A. A breakdown of the project work activities

   B. A decomposition of the project deliverables

   C. Weekly deadlines for the project

   D. A topology of the project team's responsibilities

2. In regard to a WBS, what is a work package?

   A. A unit of work that must be completed before the next unit can begin

   B. The smallest unit of work that can be performed by the team as a whole

   C. The smallest decomposed object in the WBS

   D. One of the three parts of any project: the introduction, the implementation, and the project wrap-up

3. What is the 8/80 Rule?

   A. How long a phase should last.

   B. A heuristic that says a project should last more than 8 months or less than 80 days.

   C. A heuristic that says a task should not last more than 80 hours or less than 8 hours.

   D. A description of a collection of tasks within one phase

4. Why must a project manager and the project team create a WBS?

   A. The WBS allows the project manager to work backward from the targeted date to assign tasks.

   B. The WBS allows the project manager to assign resources to tasks.

   C. The creation of the WBS ensures that all of the project deliverables are fully identified and decomposed so that the necessary resources may be obtained and assigned to the work.

   D. The WBS allows the project manager to assign multiple team members to multiple tasks to speed up the implementation.

5. You are implementing a small network and would like to create a WBS. Todd, your assistant, does not want to create a WBS for such a small project. Why should you create a WBS for every project?

    A. To ensure maximum billable hours

    B. To ensure the project is complete and whole at finish

    C. To ensure Todd performs all of his responsibilities

    D. To work toward a definite deliverable

6. You have finished creating the WBS, and the project sponsor asks to see the schedule in a Gantt chart format. What is a Gantt chart?

    A. A Gantt chart represents the total time involved for each team member.

    B. A Gantt chart represents the total time involved for the entire team.

    C. A Gantt chart illustrates the project activities visually in a timeline format.

    D. A Gantt chart illustrates the WBS in relation to the finances committed to the project.

7. Of the following, which two statements are accomplished by creating a WBS?

    A. A WBS defines all of the deliverables the project will create.

    B. A WBS identifies the sequence of activities within the project.

    C. A WBS can help control the project.

    D. A WBS illustrates the time involvement of each team member.

8. When you create a WBS, there are two main methods you can use. What are they? Choose two:

    A. Top-down

    B. Bottom-down

    C. Double-down

    D. Bottom-up

9. Of the different methods available to create a WBS, which requires the most logic and structure?

    A. Top-down

    B. Bottom-down

    C. Double-down

    D. Bottom-up

10. Of the following, which would not help a project manager determine the phases of a project?

    A. Project deliverables

    B. Obvious milestones within the project

    C. Business cycles

    D. Number of team members available

11. Of the following, which is a benefit of using Microsoft Project to create the WBS?

    A. Microsoft Project is easier to use than a whiteboard.

    B. Microsoft Project is required to prove the sequence of events within each phase.

    C. Microsoft Project streamlines the creation of the WBS.

    D. Microsoft Project reduces the overall cost of the project.

12. Which one of the following is not needed when creating a WBS?

    A. Project team members

    B. A preferred sequence of project activities

    C. A project scope

    D. Identified project deliverables

13. You are the IT project manager for a project to install a new mail server. Which of the following best describes the best approach to creating the WBS?

    A. Create a sample WBS and give it the project team to complete.

    B. Work with the project team to create a sample WBS and give it to management.

    C. Work with the project team and the key stakeholders to create the WBS.

    D. A project of this size does not need a WBS.

14. Why should the project scope be guarded against even simple additions?

    A. It adds additional team members to the project.

    B. It distracts the team members from the project.

    C. Additions, even simple ones, can greatly impact the success of a project.

    D. Additions, even simple ones, must be approved through the project sponsor.

15. What should signify the end of each phase?

    A. A milestone that has been reached

    B. A party for the project team

    C. A date that has been established within the WBS

    D. A definite deliverable result

CHAPTER EXERCISES

Exercise 1

In this exercise you will complete a Work Breakdown Structure. To assist you in the WBS and the research phase, questions will prompt you to complete the work decomposition. In addition, you can use the exercise solution at the end of this chapter as a guide to complete the WBS.

You are the IT project manager of a network upgrade project. The network will consist of 187 workstations, 5 servers, and 17 network printers. The network will be segmented through switches. The 187 workstations and printers will be on one segment and the servers on the other.

The 4 servers on the network will be replaced with 4 new Windows 2003 Servers; 3 servers will be domain controllers and the rest will be mail servers.

In addition to the creation of the network infrastructure, each workstation will be replaced with a new PC. Each PC will be configured identically with Windows XP and will use DHCP to receive its IP address.

Complete this table to begin the creation of the WBS:

Question	Answer
Are there any major deliverables within this project?	
What are the deliverables you see? (Hint: There are at least three.)	
In what order should the phases take place, and does it matter at this point of the WBS? Why or why not?	
Which components are within the first deliverable?	

Question	Answer
Which components are within the second deliverable?	
Which components are within the third deliverable?	
How do you break down the components within the first major deliverables into work packages? Break down a few.	
Do your work packages conform to the 8/80 Rule?	
Can you identify activities from each of the deliverables that can happen in tandem with other work packages?	
What method(s) can you use to roll out the Windows XP OS to the workstations?	
Which task needs to be completed first: the installation of the workstations or the installation of the servers? Why?	
How long would you estimate the entire project will last?	

Question	Answer
How many team members are required to complete this installation? Why?	
What method would you use to communicate with your team members?	
What method would you use for your team members to report their progress to you? Why did you choose this method?	

Exercise 2

In this exercise you will use Microsoft Project 2003 to build a WBS. This exercise is based on the possible solution to Exercise 1 and will walk you through each step to create the WBS in Microsoft Project.

1. Open Microsoft Project 2003 and, if necessary, click the View menu and choose Gantt chart.

2. Click File and choose Save. Name the file **Network Upgrade** and click Save.

3. Click in the first cell under the column heading Task Name.

4. Type **Phase 1: Network Infrastructure** and press ENTER. Note that the duration and the start and finish dates are also completed automatically. Those will change as you add more tasks.

5. In the second cell under Task Name, type **Creation of network map** and press ENTER.

6. Note that you are now in the third cell under the column heading Task Name. Type the following tasks and press ENTER after each one:

   ■ Installation of CAT5e cable

   ■ Installation of RJ-45 wall jacks

- Termination and testing of each cable
- Installation and testing of patch panel
- Installation and testing of network switch

7. You should now have six entries below phase 1. Click on the second entry and drag your mouse over the tasks to highlight the activities. On the Formatting toolbar, locate the green arrow pointing to the right. This is the Indent button. Click it once to indent the highlighted tasks under the first phase. The tasks should align under the phase 1 entry.

8. Now you will edit the duration of each task. Click in the duration cell for the task called Creation of Network Map. Type **3d** and press ENTER. You should now see the 3d changed to 3 days and the duration of phase 1 expanded to 3 days.

9. Use the following table to enter the remaining information to reflect the length of each of the tasks in the project.

Task	Duration
Installation of CAT5e cable	5 days
Installation of RJ-45 wall jacks	1 day
Termination and testing of each cable	2 days
Installation and testing of patch panel	1 day
Installation and testing of network switch	1 day

1. Great! Now the actual start of the whole project needs to be changed to reflect the true start and end dates for each task. From the Project menu, choose Project Information. Within the Project Information dialog box, set the Project Start date to March 6 and then click OK to adjust the calendar start date for the whole project to reflect the start date for each of the tasks.

2. Some of the tasks you've assigned within the first phase cannot begin until others have finished. For example, the first task, creating the network map, must be completed before the installation of the CAT5e cable can start. To reflect this within the WBS, you will link the tasks. Click the first task within phase 1, the task to create the network map. Click and drag down one cell to also select the second task, installing the CAT5e cable.

3. Now that both tasks are highlighted, click the Link Tasks symbol, represented by a chain icon, on the Standard toolbar. Notice how the start date for the installation of the CAT5e cable has been adjusted to begin when the first task ends.

4. The installation of the wall jacks cannot start until at least some of the cables have been situated throughout the office. Schedule this task to begin a few days after the start of the cable installation. You can do this by changing the start date to March 15. Notice how a calendar icon appears next to this task? This represents an explicitly set start date for the activity.

5. The next task, the termination and testing of each cable, can't begin until the wall jacks have been installed. Create a link between task 4 and 5 by highlighting them and using the Link Tasks command.

6. Now set the start date of the patch panel installation to coincide with the end of the cable installation. You can do this by creating a link to the two tasks. Because the tasks are not located directly next to each other, you will have to select them independently. Click task 3 first. Hold your CTRL key down and then click task 6. Click the Link Tasks symbol to link the two tasks together.

7. Now create a link between the installation and the testing of the patch panel to the last task, the installation and testing of the network switch.

8. In the middle of the project management screen, a gray dividing bar separates the tasks you've entered and how they look in a Gantt chart. Click and hold the dividing bar and drag it to the left to open a larger view of the Gantt chart.

9. The chart you are viewing is the start of the WBS for this project. You've not assigned users to complete the tasks or the remaining phases, but it's still very impressive. Hover your mouse over the black duration bar at the top of the chart. See how it gives the details on the project? Hover your mouse over any of the blue boxes to see a description of the task.

10. On the View taskbar, or from the View Menu, choose Calendar to see how the tasks look mapped out day-by-day. Click the Gantt chart view again.

11. Save your work, as you will be using this project in the next exercise.

Exercise 3

In this exercise you will continue with the Network Upgrade project you created in the previous exercise. Now that you have entered the task for the first phase, you will need to add resources to complete the project. Resources can be tools, components, and team members.

1. Confirm that the Network Upgrade project is open. If it is not, open it from the location you saved it in.

2. Click the Resource Sheet icon or choose Resource Sheet from the View menu.

3. In the cell directly under the column heading Resource Name, type **Henry Mikev** and press TAB.

4. Note that the Type of resource is Work, which means it is measured in hours. Press TAB.

5. The material label represents the type of material being used. Leave this field blank by pressing TAB.

6. Change the initials to HM, if necessary, and press TAB.

7. In the Group field, type **Full Time** and press TAB.

8. In the Max units field, leave the value at 100% and press TAB.

9. Set the standard rate to 43.78 and press TAB.

10. Set the overtime rate to 65.67 and press TAB.

11. Leave the Cost Per Use field blank, as Mike does not bill a fee per each usage. (Consultants may have a set fee for each appearance, but full-time employees do not.)

12. Leave the Accrue At value set to Prorated and press TAB.

13. Leave the Base Calendar value set to Standard and press TAB.

14. You've just entered the first resource for this project. Enter the following information as seen here:

Resource Name	Group	Std Rate	Ovt. Rate
Sally Dehority	Full Time	25.76	38.64
Mary Watkins	Full Time	43.24	64.86
Sam Arnold	Full Time	23.00	34.50
Mike Murran	Consultant	130.00	195.00
Sherri Webstein	Consultant	120.00	180.00
Cody Hyatt	Electrician	80.00	120.00

1. Excellent! You've just entered the project team members and their associated rates. You will now begin to assign tasks to users. Change back to the Gantt Chart view.

2. Within the Gantt Chart view, your screen is split between the graph of the Gantt chart and the view of the Gantt chart entries. Arrange your screen so that you can see most of the Gantt chart entries by dragging the divider bar to the right of the screen.

3. On the task called Creation of Network Map, follow the row all the way to the right until you see the column heading Resource Names. You will now assign a resource to this task.

4. Click in the cell under the Resource Names column heading. Click the drop-down arrow in the cell and choose Sam Arnold. Notice Sam Arnold has been assigned the task in both views of the Gantt chart.

5. Now you will assign four people to the installation of the CAT5e cable. To do so, move down one cell and click the drop-down arrow. Choose Henry Mikev and then type a comma and a space to separate the additional names. Choose Mary Watkins, Mike Murran, and Cody Hyatt by typing a comma and a space between each name. After Cody, simply press ENTER.

6. Assign the following tasks to the remaining team members:

Task	Team Members
Installation of RJ-45 wall jacks	Cody Hyatt
Termination and testing of each cable	Sherri Webstein, Mike Murran
Installation and testing of patch panel	Sally Dehority, Sam Arnold
Installation and testing of network switch	Henry Mikev, Cody Hyatt

7. Notice how the names of the team members are reflected within the Gantt chart to show their responsibilities.

8. Save and close the file.

QUIZ ANSWERS

1. **B.** A WBS is a decomposition of the work required to complete the project. It serves as input to five key processes within a project: cost estimating, cost budgeting, resource planning, risk management planning, and activity definition.

2. **C.** A work package is the smallest decomposed object within the WBS.

3. **C.** The 8/80 Rule is a guide that says a project activity should not be decomposed less than 8 hours or last more than 80 hours.

4. **C.** A WBS is a deliverables-orientated decomposition of the project work. It is a process to ensure that all of the required deliverables are identified and broken down into manageable components so resources and labor may be assigned to complete the project work.

5. **B.** A WBS, even on small projects, ensures that all tasks are complete and whole. It does not necessarily ensure maximum billable hours, nor does it promise work toward a definite deliverable—these would be accomplished through the project plan. The project manager is responsible for ensuring that Todd performs all of his duties, not the WBS.

6. **C.** A Gantt chart represents the WBS in a visual format. It depicts the start and end of phases and tasks. It does not represent the time involved for each team member. Although a Gantt chart could depict the total time involved for an entire team, that is not its true purpose. Finally, a Gantt chart does not reflect finances committed to the project.

7. **A, C.** A WBS does identify all of the deliverables the project will create. It can help control the project by referencing the WBS for resource planning, cost estimating, risk management planning, and activity definition.

8. **A, D.** The process of creating a WBS uses either top-down or bottom-up methods. Recall that the top-down method uses deductive reasoning and the bottom-up method uses inductive reasoning.

9. **A.** A WBS using the top-down method involves deductive reasoning, which requires logic and structure.

10. **D.** A WBS does not necessarily need to revolve around the number of team members available. Project deliverables, project milestones, and business cycles will have impact on the WBS.

11. **C.** Microsoft Project is an excellent software tool to finalize your WBS. A whiteboard is still ideal to use during the project planning phases. Microsoft Project can be used to prove the sequence of events, but a whiteboard can accomplish the same task in less time. Microsoft Project does not necessarily reduce the overall cost of the project, though it can help organize and streamline the effort to map out the project schedule.

12. **B.** The WBS is not concerned with the order of activities. Activity sequencing and scheduling, however, will be concerned with the order and relationship of activities.

13. **C.** Creating a WBS is not a solo activity. The project manager should work with the project team and any key stakeholders to create a WBS.

14. **C.** Additions to the project scope can have huge impacts on the deliverables of a project. Often additions are tossed into the plans without adequate foresight or care so their consequences can throw a perfect plan off balance. Do not change the scope of an existing project unless it is absolutely required.

15. **D.** Just as each project produces a definite deliverable, so should each phase. A milestone does not necessarily signify a phase has ended, as there can be multiple milestones within each phase. A party for the project team (while always an excellent idea) does not prove that a phase has officially ended. Dates, while targets for completion, do not signify the end of a phase—the deliverable proves the end of a project phase.

EXERCISE SOLUTIONS

Exercise 1: Possible Solution

Here is a completed worksheet that demonstrates the possible answers for the WBS process. Your chart may be slightly different from the answers presented here.

Question	Answer
Are there any major deliverables within this project?	Yes, there are three major deliverables.

What are the deliverables you see?	The three major deliverables are
	    The installation of the network infrastructure
	    The installation and configuration of the Windows 2003 Servers
	    The installation and configuration of the Windows XP workstations

In what order should the phases take place, and does it matter at this point of the WBS? Why or why not?	The phases would logically follow the installation of the network infrastructure, the servers, and then the workstations. There are multiple parts to each phase that could be simultaneously completed with the other phases. During WBS creation, however, activity sequencing is not crucial.

Question	Answer
Which components are within the first deliverable?	The first deliverable has many requirements to produce the desired results: the creation of a network topology to map out the path for each network cable and drop; the installation of a suitable and speedy network cable that follows installation code, such as plenum-grade cable, installation hooks, and wall jacks; the termination and testing of each cable to ensure reliability; and the installation of patch panels, switches, and connections between the network elements.
Which components are within the second deliverable?	The second deliverable requires five primary components: the planning and implementation of the Windows 2003 Server operating system on all five of the servers; the planning and implementation of the Windows 2003 Active Directory infrastructure; the planning and installation of the Exchange Servers and their role within Active Directory; the planning and implementation of the Windows 2003 user names and auto-configuration of the associated Exchange Server mailboxes; and domain security, policies, group creation, and access permission to resources such as home folders, printers, and data.
Which components are within the third deliverable?	The third deliverable requires these work units: the planning and implementation of delivery of Windows XP to each workstation; the configuration of the Windows XP workstation for network access, applications, and user profiles; and the development, testing, and implementation of a system to automate the rollout of the Windows XP Professional environment to each workstation.
How do you break down the components within the first major deliverables you've identified into work packages??	The installation of suitable network cables, plenum installation procedures, and the creation of wall jacks could be broken into three separate work packages. The installation of patch panels, switches, and connections between the network elements could be broken down into three separate work packages as well.
Do your work packages conform to the 8/80 Rule?	The WBS work packages should not take more than 80 hours to complete; if they do, the work packages should likely be further decomposed.

Question	Answer
Can you identify activities from each of the deliverables that can happen in tandem with other work packages?	The primary tasks of planning and configuring the Windows XP Professional environment may be done in tandem with other work packages. Other team members can easily complete this work while the servers are being installed and configured. In addition, the team members responsible for creating a method to roll out the Windows XP image to the clients can develop a plan of attack for this work unit as well. However, activity sequencing is not really a concern of the WBS creation.
What method(s) can you use to roll out the Windows XP OS to the workstations?	Windows administrators can use unattended methods to install the operating systems. There are also third-party packages such as Ghost or DeployCenter to "push" the operating system to the workstations.
Which task needs to be completed first: the installation of the workstations or the installation of the servers?	The servers need to be completely installed prior to the installation of the workstations.
Why?	The servers will control the security, access to data, and access to printers. Without the centralized administration of the servers, the network won't be functional.
How long would you estimate the entire project will last?	Once the hardware is physically on site, phase 1 could take seven days, phase 2 could take five days, and phase 3 could take five days. A coordinated effort could complete the project in three weeks optimistically, five weeks pessimistically.
How many team members are required to complete this installation. Why?	Six to eight would be an adequate number of IT professionals working on the project. In phase 1, all eight individuals could pull wire, terminate cables, and install the wall jacks based on their experience and ability. In the second phase, only two administrators are needed for the Windows 2003 Server implementations, though a third, an Exchange Server expert, could work with the other administrators to coordinate the efforts between Exchange and Active Directory. In the third phase, two individuals could work together to create and test an image for the Windows XP installation. Two or three additional team members could test and document each image and how the applications fare on the installation.
What method would you use to communicate with your team members?	Weekly meetings, daily interactions, e-mail updates, and an open door policy for team members to speak with me.

Question	Answer
What method would you use for your team members to report their progress to you? Why did you choose this method?	For this project, Microsoft Project Server could allow the team members to chart their progress online. Another acceptable approach would be e-mail updates or meetings each week. Given this project's implementation is somewhat short, an overextended reporting process isn't really required.

Exercise 2: Possible Solution

This exercise required the use of Microsoft Project 2000 to create the first phase of WBS for a network upgrade. At the completion of this first phase of the project, your Gantt worksheet should look like the file called Exercise 2 solution located within the CH5 folder on the CD-ROM.

Exercise 3: Possible Solution

Exercise 3 required you to complete the first phase of the WBS by assigning resources to tasks. At the completion of this phase, your Gantt worksheet should look like the file called Exercise 3 solution located within the CH5 folder on the CD-ROM.

Chapter 6

Organizing a
Project Team

Think of your favorite spy caper movie. Remember how the team in the movie is assembled? Each member has a specialty: explosives, gadgets, luck with the opposite sex, and other necessary skills to get the job done. Notice how there's never just an extra character walking around slurping coffee, dodging work, and whining about how tough his job is? Unfortunately, in the world of IT project management, you'll have both types of characters.

As a project manager, you will recruit the die-hard dedicated workers who are genuinely interested in the success of the project. These team members are exciting to be around as they love to learn, love technology, and work hard for the team and the success of the project. The other type of team members you'll encounter are nothing less than a pain in the, er, neck. These folks could care less about the project, the success of the company, or anyone else on the team. Their goal is to complete their required hours, draw a paycheck, and get on with their lives.

The reality is, however, most people want to do a good job. Most team members are generally interested in the success of the project. If you get stuck with one of the rotten apples, there are methods to work with them—and around them. This chapter will focus on how you, the project manager, can assemble a team that works well together. Your team may not be in any spy movies, but parts of the project can be just as exciting.

Assessing Internal Skills

Whether you get to handpick your project team or your team is assigned to you by management, you will still need to get a grasp on the experience levels of each team member. If you have an understanding of what your team members are capable of doing, the process of assigning tasks within the WBS and creating the project plan will go much easier for you.

As a project manager, you must create a method to ascertain the skills of your team. It would, no doubt, be disastrous to your project if you began assigning tasks to team members only to later learn they were not qualified to do the work assigned to them. In some cases, this will be easier to do than others, especially if you've worked with the team members before, interviewed the team members, or completed a skills assessment worksheet.

Experience Is the Best Barometer

As you gain experience as a project manager, you will learn which people you'd like on your team—and which you wouldn't. If you are a consultant brought into the mix to manage an IT implementation, you'll have to learn about the team members, their goals, and their abilities.

You must use strategies to recruit and woo knowledgeable and hard-working team members onto your team. This means, of course, you'll have to do fact-finding missions to gain information on your recruits. As Figure 6-1 demonstrates, you have available to you many methods to assess internal skills.

Once you've started your fact-finding mission, rely on multiple methods to assess internal skills:

- ■ **Prior projects** Obviously if you've worked with your team members prior to this project, you'll have a good idea who's capable of what tasks. You'll also have a record, through historical information, of who's reliable, dependable, and thorough, and has other traits of a good worker.

- ■ **Organizational knowledge** You may not have worked directly with particular team members who have been assigned to your project, but you might have a good idea of their track record. Let's face the facts: in your organization, it's likely there are people you haven't worked with, but you know the type of workers they are by their reputation, their ability to accomplish, and what others say about them. Gossip is one thing, but proven success (or failure) is another. The best way to learn about someone, of course, is not through hearsay, but to work with him or speak directly with his manager.

- ■ **Recommendation of management** You may not have the luxury of selecting your team members like you're picking a kickball team at recess. You'll probably

FIGURE 6-1

Assessment of internal skills is derived from multiple sources.

Team Members

Management Input

Reputation of Workers

Experience

be able to recruit some members of your team, but not all of them. Functional or Senior Management will have an inside track on the abilities of employees and can, and will, recommend members for your project. Management will also be able to select individuals who can commit time to the project.

■ **Recommendation of team members** Most likely, you will have other IT professionals within your organization whom you trust and confide in. These folks can help you by recommending other winners for your team. These individuals are likely in the trenches working side-by-side with other IT pros. Use their "scouting" to find excellent members to work on your project.

Resumes and Skill Assessments

Another source, if you have privy to the document, is the resume for each team member. A resume can quickly sum up the skill set of a team member. You may want the project team to create quick resumes for you in order to learn about the experiences of individual members. Use caution with this approach, however. Resumes have the connotation of getting, or keeping, a job, and your team members may panic. If you want to use this method but are uneasy using the word "resume," have the team members create a list of projects they have worked on, their skills, and other past accomplishments. This will give you a way to quickly understand the collection of talent and then assign work to the team.

A collection of skills will also allow you to determine if you have the resources to complete the project. For example, if you're about to create a database that will span 18 states, with multiple servers, and provide real-time transactions for clients, it'll be tough to do if none of your team members have worked with relational databases before.

Create a Roles and Responsibilities Matrix

A Roles and Responsibilities Matrix is a method to identify all of the roles within a project and the associated responsibilities to the project work. This matrix is an excellent way to identify the needed roles for the project participants, identify what actions they'll need to take in the project, and, ultimately, determine if you have all of the roles to complete the identified responsibilities. Here's a quick example of a matrix for a software rollout project:

	Project Manager	Application Developer	Network Engineer	ZenWorks Expert
Create the application	A	C	P	
Test the application	A	P	P	
Package the application	R		R	P
Test the application release	R	R		C
Push the application to the workstations	A		P	C

Here's the legend for this matrix:

A = Approves

R = Reviews

P = Participant

C = Creator

The Roles and Responsibilities Matrix can help the project manager identify the needed resources to complete the project work—and determine if the resources exists within the organization's resource pool. Later in the project, the project manager will use an even more precise matrix called the Responsibility Assignment Matrix (RAM) to identify which tasks are assigned to which individuals. We'll talk more about this coming up.

Learning Is Hard Work

Within the IT world, a requirement for certification has become practically mandatory. Certifications such as the PMP, Microsoft Certified Systems Engineer, Oracle DBA, and even industry certifications like CompTIA's A+ and Network + are proof of knowledge in a particular area of technology.

Individuals can earn these certifications based on training, experience, or a combination of both. Certifications are certainly a way to demonstrate that individuals have worked with the technology, understand the major concepts, and are able to pass the exam. Certifications do not, however, make the individual a master of all technologies. As Figure 6-2 demonstrates, a balance of certification and experience is desirable.

FIGURE 6-2

A balance of certifications and experience proves expertise.

Within your team, whether there or certifications or not, you'll need to assess if the members need additional training to complete the project. Training is always seen as one of two things: an expense or an investment. Training is an expense if the experience does not increase the ability of the team to implement tasks. Training is an investment if the experience greatly increases the ability of the team to complete the project.

When searching for a training provider, consider these questions:

- What is the experience of the trainer?
- Can the trainer customize the class to your project?
- Would hiring a mentor be a better solution than classroom training?
- What materials are included with the class?
- What is the cost of the course?
- Is there an in-house training department that can deliver the training, provide assistance in developing the curriculum in-house, or assist in contracting with an outside trainer?
- Would it be more cost effective to host the training session in-house?

These questions will help you determine if training is right for your project team. In some instances, standard introductory courses are fine. Typically, the more customized the project, the more customized the class should be as well. Don't assume that just because a training center is the biggest that it's also the best. No matter how luxurious a training room, or how delicious the cookies provided, or how slick the brochures are, the success of the class rests on the shoulders of the trainer.

Creating a Team

You can't approach creating a team the way you would baking a cake or completing a paint-by-the-numbers picture. As you will be dealing with multiple individuals, you'll discover their personalities, their ambitions, and their motivations. Being a project manager is as much about being a leader as it is managing tasks, deadlines, and resources.

You will, through experience, learn how to recognize the leaders within the team. You'll have to look for the members who are willing to go the extra mile, who do what it takes to do a job right, and who are willing to help others excel. These attributes signal the type of members you want on your team. The easiest way to create teams with this type of worker? Set the example yourself.

Imagine yourself as a team member on your project. How would you like the project manager to act? Or call upon your own experience: what have previous project managers taught you by their actions? By setting the example of how your team should work, you're following ageless advice: leading by doing.

Defining Project Manager Power

Project managers have responsibility. And with that responsibility comes power. When it comes to the project team you are seen as someone with some degree of power. Get used to it, but don't let it go to your head. While the project manager must have a degree of power to get the project work done, the extent of your power is also likely relevant to the organizational structure you're working in. For example, recall that a functional organization gives the power to the functional manager and the project manager may be known as just a project coordinator.

A project manager does, however, wield a certain amount of power in most organizations. The project team can see this power, correctly or incorrectly, based on their relationship with you. Their perception of your power—and how you use your project management powers—will influence the project team and how they accomplish their project work. The five types of project manager powers are

- **Expert**   The project manager's authority comes from having experience with the technology the project focuses on.
- **Reward/penalty**   The project manager has the authority to give something of value to team members, or to withhold something of value.

- **Formal** The project manager has been assigned by senior management and is in charge of the project. This is also known as positional power.

- **Coercive** The project manager has the authority to discipline the project team members. This is also known as penalty power. When the team is afraid of the project manager, it's coercive.

- **Referent** The project team personally knows the project manager. Referent can also mean the project manager refers to the person who assigned him the position; for example, "The CEO assigned me to this position so we'll do it this way." This power can also mean the project team wants to work on the project, or with the project manager, due to the high priority status and impact of the project.

Hello! My Name Is...

If your team works together on a regular basis, then chances are the team has already established camaraderie. The spirit of teamwork is not something that can be born overnight—or even in a matter of days. Camaraderie is created from experiences of the teammates. A successful installation of software, or even a failed one, creates a sense of unity among the team.

It's mandatory on just about any project that team members work together. Here's where things get tricky. Among those team members, you've got ambition, jealousies, secret agendas, uncertainties, and anxiety pooling in and seeping through the workers of your project. One of your first goals will be to establish some order in the team and change the members' focus to the end result of the project. Figure 6-3 illustrates the detrimental effect personal ambitions have on the success of a project.

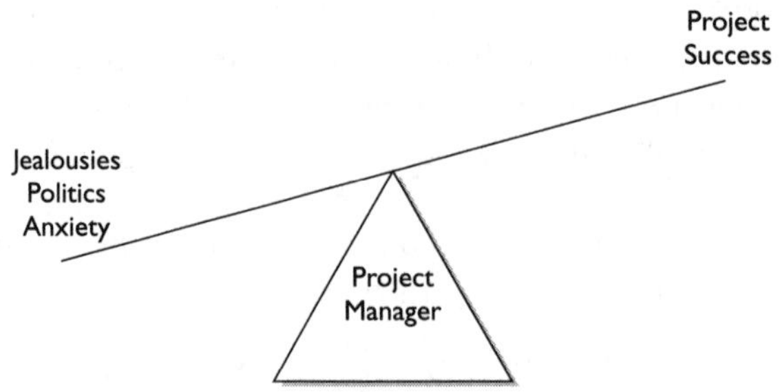

FIGURE 6-3

Personal ambitions must be put aside for the success of the project.

By motivating your team to focus on the project deliverables, you can, like a magician, misdirect their attention from their own agendas to the project's success. You can spark the creation of a true team by demonstrating how the members are all in this together. How can you do this? How can you motivate your team and change the focus from self-centric to project-centric? Here are some methods:

- *Show the team members what's in it for them.*   Remember the WIIFM principle— "What's In It For Me." Show your team members what they personally have to reap from the project. You may do this by telling them about monetary bonuses they'll receive. Maybe your team will get extra vacation days or promotions. At the very least, they'll be rewarded with adding this project to their list of accomplishments. Who knows? You'll have to find some way for this project to be personal for each team member.

- *Show the team what this project means to the company.*   By demonstrating the impact that this implementation has for the entire company, you can position the importance of the success (or failure) of the project squarely on the team's shoulders. This method gives the team a sense of ownership and a sense of responsibility.

- *Show the team why this is exciting.*   IT project managers sometime lose the sense of excitement wrapped up in technology. Show your team why this project is cool, exciting, and fun, and the implementation will hardly be like work. Remember, IT pros typically love technology—so let them have some fun! It is okay to have a good time and enjoy your work.

- *Show the team members their importance.*   Teams need to know that their work is valued and appreciated. You can't fake this stuff. Develop a sense of caring, a sense of pride, and tell your team members when they do a good job. Don't let them feel like they are as valued as the slave labor used to build the Egyptian pyramids. Let them own the technology, use the technology, and be proud of their work.

Where Do You Live?

In today's world, it's typical of a single project to span the globe. No doubt it's difficult for team members to feel like they are part of the same team when they're in London and their counterpart is in Phoenix. Ideally, collocated teams communicate better, work together better, and have a sense of ownership. Reality, however, proves that noncollocated teams exist in many organizations, and the project manager must take extra measures to ensure the project succeeds, regardless of the geographical boundaries. When dealing with noncollocated teams, your team will likely be built around subteams. A *subteam* is simply a squadron of team members unique to one task within the project or within each geographical area.

For example, as depicted in Figure 6-4, a company is implementing Oracle servers throughout its enterprise. The company has 12 locations throughout the world. Some of the same tasks that need to be accomplished in Madison, Wisconsin, will also need to be performed in Paris, France.

Rather than having one team consisting of six members fly around the globe, the project manager implements 12 subteams. In this example, each subteam has six members. Of the six members, one is the team leader for that location. All of the team leaders report to the project manager, the 73rd member of the team. The team members in each location report to their immediate team leader. Implementation of the Oracle servers at each location will follow a standard procedure for the installation and configuration. The path to success should be the same at each location regardless of geography.

Certainly not all projects will map out this smoothly. Some sites may not have the technical know-how of others, and travel will be required. In other instances, some sites will require more configuration than others, or an increase in security, and other

FIGURE 6-4

Subteams are crucial to large implementations.

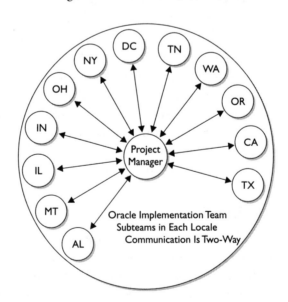

variances. The lesson to be learned is that when teams are dispersed, a chain of command must be established to create uniformity and smooth implementation. The phrase "out of sight, out of mind" often proves true when dealing with dispersed project teams.

Finally, when working with multiple subteams, communication is paramount. Team leaders and the project manager should have regularly scheduled meetings either in person or through teleconferences or videoconferences. In addition, team leaders should have the ability to contact other team members around the globe.

In some instances, team members from different teams will need to work together as well. For example, the communication between two servers has to be configured. The teammates responsible for this step of the configuration will need to coordinate their configurations and installation with the teammates who have identical responsibilities in other locations.

Building Relationships

When an individual joins your team, you and the individual have a relationship: project manager to team member. Immediately the team member knows his role in the project as a team member, and you know your role in relation to the team member as the project manager.

What may not be known, however, is the relationships between team members. You may need to give some introduction of each team member and explain why that person is on the team and what responsibilities that person has. Don't let your team members just figure things out for themselves. In a large project, it would be ideal to have a directory of the team members, their contact information, and their arsenal of talents made available to the whole team.

On all projects, your team will have to work together very quickly. It's not a bad idea to bring the team together in some type of activity away from the workplace. Examples of team building exercises:

- A bowling excursion
- A hike and overnight stay in the wilds
- A weekend resort meeting to learn about each other and discuss the project
- A trip to your local pool hall for an impromptu round of team pool

Don't discount out-of-the-office team-building exercises. Professional team building exercises are available around the globe:

- **Rhythm Journey (www.africanpercussion.com)**   Led by Paulo Mattioli, these team-building programs help teams find and thrive on their synergy.

- **Project Adventure, Inc. (www.adventureinbusiness.com)**   This company creates exciting staff development programs specifically for your organization.

- **Outdoor Adventure River Specialists (www.oars.com)**   Get out of the conference room and onto the river where you will become a team.

- **ETD Alliance (www.etdalliance.com)**   This web site provides more information on experiential training and development. An excellent starting point for locating team-building activities for your company.

Interviewing Potential Team Members

Remember your first big interview? You shined your shoes, made certain your hair was just right, brushed your teeth, and had a breath mint just in case. Your goal was to get the job, so you did your homework: you researched the company, investigated the position, made certain your resume and references were up-to-date, and then gave it your best shot.

Guess what? As a project manager, you may find yourself conducting interviews to woo internal employees onto your project team. You're mission will be twofold: impressing the candidates while at the same time learning about them to see if they are the right fit for your project team.

Why You Need Interviews

If you are one of the lucky project managers and you get to handpick your project team, you'll need to interview potential project team members. You, or you and the project sponsor, may discuss which employees should be placed on the project and why. The type of work to be completed will serve as your primary guide for the talent needed on the project. You may also need to look for other attributes such as aptitude, track record, and current workload.

An interview will help you ascertain each prospect's level of ability before you invite that person onto the project. Or, in the instance the individual has been assigned to the project, an interview helps you learn about her abilities and how they may contribute to the project.

Interviews for IT projects can be completed formally, with resume, or informally conducted over lunch or coffee. Regardless of how the interview is completed, you'll need to learn if the prospective team member will be able to complete the type of work you have in mind. This means, of course, that you're looking for a specific type of worker based on your planning.

An interview, even if it's a simple, informal meeting, allows you to discuss the prospective team member's abilities and how they can help on the project, and it gives you an insight into the person's goals, ambitions, and outlook regarding work. Interviews allow project managers to learn about the team members, their assets for the project, and how much of a learning curve may be required if the interviewee is to join the team.

How to Interview

Your goal when interviewing potential team members (or team members who have been assigned to your project) is to determine what their role in the implementation may be. Any project is only as good as the people completing the work. Your team will be a direct reflection on your own abilities, so this task is one of the most important you'll have on the entire project.

When interviewing potential team members, you'll need a job description for each open team position. A job description is needed for two reasons:

- So that you may share with the prospect what role needs to be filled
- So that you can focus on the attributes of the ideal team member

A job description is more than a title for a role on the team. A job description details the activities of the role, the scope of the position, the responsibilities, and the working requirements of the team member. A job description should be clear, concise, and easily summarized. For example, here is a job description for the role of a team member responsible for creating logon scripts: Logon script creator—This team member will be responsible for the creation, testing, and implementation of logon scripts for several thousand users. The logon script creator will be responsible for following the logon guidelines as assigned by management, updating current logon script procedures, and documenting the various logon scripts created.

You will also need selection criteria to determine which prospect is the best fit for the team role. The selection criteria will stem from the job description, as it should be a set of requirements that, if met, indicates the individual would be able to wholly complete the tasks of the job description. Selection criteria can include

- Education
- Knowledge on the tasks
- Experience with the tasks
- Skill sets applicable to the tasks
- Accomplishments within the company
- Other essential qualities such as aptitude, leadership, and the ability to work with others

Many project managers balk at completing interviews. Don't. They are not difficult if you've prepared. Interviews can help you properly assign tasks to team members during resource assignment and scheduling. To prepare for an interview, develop good questions. When interviewing, there are several question types that you should know and use:

- **Closed question**   These questions must be answered with a yes or no. For example: "Have you ever created a batch file before?"

- **Essay questions**   These questions allow the candidate to tell you information—and they allow you to listen and observe. For example: "Why are you interested in working on this project?"

- **Experience questions**   These questions focus on the candidate's behavior in past situations, and they allow you to see how a candidate has acted to predict how he may act in future situations that are similar. For example: "How did you react when a teammate did not complete a task on a past project and you had to do his work for him to complete your own? How was the situation resolved?"

- **Reactionary questions**   These questions evolve from the candidate's answers. When you notice a gap or an inconsistency in an answer, use a follow-up question that focuses on the inconsistency without directly calling it a lie. This gives the candidate the opportunity to explain herself better or flounder for an explanation. Reactionary questions also allow you to learn more information that may be helpful on your project. For example: "You mentioned you had experience with Visual Basic. Do you also have a grasp on VBScript?"

- **Questions not to ask**   In the United States, it's illegal to ask candidates questions that aren't related to their capacity to do a job. Basically, avoid questions that center on child care, marital status, religion, racial background, or physical disability. Use common sense, and this area of the interview should not be a problem.

Interviews are a great tool for learning about your potential team members. They are also an opportunity for potential team members to learn about you. Invite the candidate to ask you questions about your role on the project and the importance of the project. When conducting an interview, allow the candidate to do most of the talking so you can do most of the listening.

Managing Team Issues

Without a doubt, people will fight. Fortunately, in most offices, people are mature enough to bite their tongues, try to work peacefully, and, as a whole, strive to finish the project happily and effectively together.

Most disagreements in IT project management happen when two or more people feel very passionate about a particular IT topic. For example, one person believes a network should be built in a particular order, while another feels it should be constructed from a different approach. Or two developers on a project get upset with each other about the way an application is created. Generally, both parties in the argument are good people who just feel strongly about a certain methodology of their work. Figure 6-5 demonstrates how arguments over technical implementations take a project off schedule.

FIGURE 6-5

Arguments take a project off schedule and increase costs.

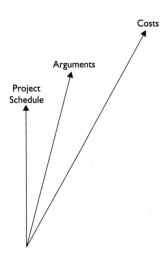

There are, of course, a fair percentage of contrary and pessimistic people in the world. These people don't play well with others, and are obnoxious at times. They don't care about other people's feelings, and much of the time they don't care about the success of your project.

Unfortunately, you will have to deal with disagreements, troublemakers, and obnoxious people to find a way to resolve differences and keep the project's momentum.

Dealing with Team Disagreements

In most projects there will be instances when the project team, management, and other stakeholders disagree on the progress, decisions, and proposed solutions within the project. It's essential for the project manager to keep calm, to lead, and to direct the parties to a sensible solution that's best for the project. Here are seven reasons for conflict in order of most common to least common:

- Schedules
- Priorities
- Resources
- Technical beliefs
- Administrative policies and procedures
- Project costs
- Personalities

So what's a project manager to do with all the potential for strife in a project? There are five different approaches to conflict resolution:

- **Problem solving** This approach confronts the problem head-on and is the preferred method of conflict resolution. You may consider this approach as "confronting." It calls for additional research to find the best solution for the problem, and is a win-win solution. Problem solving can be used if there is time to work through and resolve the issue, and it works to build relationships and trust.

- **Forcing** With this approach, the person with the power makes the decision. The decision made may not be best for the project, but it's fast. As expected, this autocratic approach does little for team development and is a win-lose solution. Forcing is used when the stakes are high and time is of the essence, or if relationships are not important.

- **Compromising** This approach requires both parties to give up something. The decision is a blend of both sides of the argument. Because neither party really wins, it is considered a lose-lose solution. The project manager can use this approach when the relationships are equal and it's impossible for one party to "win." This approach can also be used to avoid a fight.

- **Smoothing** This approach "smoothes" out the conflict by minimizing the perceived size of the problem. It is a temporary solution but can calm team relations and boisterous discussions. Smoothing may be acceptable when time is of the essence or any of the proposed solutions will work. This can be considered a lose-lose situation as no one really wins long-term. The project manager can use smoothing to emphasize areas of agreement between the stakeholders within a disagreement, minimizing the areas of conflict. Smoothing is used to maintain relationships and when the issue is not critical.

- **Withdrawal** This approach is the worst conflict resolution tactic because one side of the argument walks away from the problem—usually in disgust. The conflict is not resolved and it is considered a yield-lose solution. The approach can be used, however, as a cooling off period, or when the issue is not critical.

Phases of Team Development

Teams develop over time, not instantaneously. As a project team comes together, there are likely people on the project team who have worked with one another before just as there may be people on the project team who have never met. Because projects are temporary the relationships among project team members are also often viewed as temporary. The project manager can see, and sometimes guide, the natural process of team development.

The goal of team development is not for everyone to like each other, have a good time, and create life-long friendships. All of that is nice, but the real goal is to develop a team that can accurately and effectively complete the project scope. Within team development there are four stages the project team will pass though:

- **Forming** This stage allows the project team members to come together and learn about each other. They feel each other out and find out who's who and what each other is like.

■ **Storming**   This stage promises action. There's a struggle for project team control and momentum builds as members vie to lead the project team. It is during this phase that people figure out the hierarchy of the team, and the informal roles of team members.

■ **Norming**   In this stage, the project team's focus shifts toward the project work. Control on the project team has been established, and people learn to work together.

■ **Performing**   In this stage, the project team members have settled into their roles and are focusing on completing the project work as a team. During this stage, a synergy is developed; this is the stage where high-performance teams come into play.

Project Management Is Not a Democracy

Despite what some feel-good books and inspiring stories would like to have you believe, project management is not a democracy. Someone has to be in charge, and that someone is you, the project manager. The success of the project rests on your shoulders, and it is your job to work with your team members to motivate them to finish the project on schedule.

This does not mean that you have permission to grump around and boss any member of your team. It also does not mean that you should step in and break up any disagreement between team members. Among the team, you should allow some discussion and some disagreement.

This is what teams have to do: they have to work things out on their own. Team members have to learn to work together, to give and take, to compromise. Figure 6-6 shows the power of team decisions. Step back and let the team first work through disagreements before you step in and settle issues. If you step into the mix too early, then your team members will run to you at every problem.

FIGURE 6-6

Teams can make decisions on their own.

Ultimately, you are in charge. If your team members cannot, or will not, work out a solution among themselves, you'll be forced to make a decision. When you find yourself in this situation, there is an approach to working through the problem. Here are recommended steps to conflict resolution:

1. **Attention**   Meet with both parties and explain the purpose of the meeting: to find a solution to the problem. If the two parties are amicable to each other, this meeting can happen with both parties present. If the team members detest each other, or the disagreement is a complaint against another team member, meet with each member in confidence to hear that person's side of the story.

2. **Listen**   Ask the team members what the problem is, allow each to speak their case fully without interrupting, and then ask questions to clarify any of the facts.

3. **Resolve**   Often if the meeting takes place with both team members, a resolution will quickly boil to the surface. Chances are that you won't even have to make a decision. People have a way of suddenly wanting to work together when a third party listens to their complaints. They both realize how foolish their actions have been and one, or both, of the team members will cheer up and decide to work together.

4. **Wait**   If this is not the case in your meeting, don't make an immediate decision. Tell the team members how important it is to you, and to the project, that they find a way to work together. Sometimes even this touch of direction will be enough for the team members to begin compromising. If they still won't budge, tell them you'll think it over and then you will make a decision within a day or two—if the decision can wait that long. By delaying an immediate decision, you allow the team members to think about what has happened and you give them another opportunity to resolve the problem.

5. **Act**   If the team members will not budge on their positions, then you will have to make a decision. And then stick to it. If necessary, gather any additional facts, research, and investigations. Based on your evidence, call the team members into a meeting again and acknowledge both of their positions on the problem. Then share with them, based on your findings, why you've made the decision that you have made. In your announcement don't embarrass the team member who has

been put out by your decision. If the losing team member wants to argue his point again, stop him. Don't be rude, but stop him. The team members have both been given the opportunity to plead their case, and once your decision has been made, your decision should be final.

Dealing with Personalities

In any organization, you'll find many different personality types, so it's likely that there are some people in your organization who just grate on your nerves like fingernails on a chalkboard. These individuals are always happy to share their discontent, their opinion, or their "unique point of view." Unfortunately, you will have to find a way to work with, or around, these people.

Here are some personality types you may encounter and how you can deal with them:

Personality	Attributes	Resolution
The Imaginary Leader	These individuals think they are managing the project this week and will be running the company next week. You know the type, always first to raise their hands in school and remind the teacher if she forgot to assign homework.	These people really do want to lead—they just don't know how! Give them an opportunity by allowing them to conduct an occasional team meeting or organize upcoming activities. If you can, try to show them how to lead with tact instead of their rudeness.
The Mouse	These individuals are afraid of doing any activity on the project without explicit directions from you. They're so afraid they'll make a disastrous mistake, they require your guidance on each part of their work.	Encourage these types to take charge of their duties. Tell them that you have confidence in them to do the tasks that you've assigned to them. If they do make a mistake, work through it with them to build their confidence.
Your Favorite Uncle (or Aunt)	This persona is the office clown. Always playing gags, streaming toilet paper around someone's cubicle, telling jokes, and sharing stories around the office. Not only are these types of people great fun, but also they're great time wasters.	Often these folks don't have enough to do, and so they assume everyone else is under the same workload that they are. Give these people more assignments, and they'll have less time to kill. If that doesn't work, politely share with them that their jovial activities are appreciated, but not always necessary.

Personality	Attributes	Resolution
The Cowboy	These people love excitement. They are happy to try anything out (like rebooting a server mid-morning) just to see what happens. Their experience may be great, but their swagger, ten-gallon hat, and stunts aren't always well thought out.	To deal with the Cowboy types, encourage their enthusiasm but discourage their ability to make on-the-spot decisions without thinking about the results of their actions. These individuals are generally smart and eager to help, but need a touch more guidance from you.
The Prune	These sourpusses are as much fun as pocket full of thumbtacks. They don't care about your project, think the technology sucks, and take their hourly breaks every twenty minutes.	Granted, these folks are hard to work with. They've got more problems personally than the project you are managing. You can start by befriending them and then sharing the value of their work on the project with their superiors. This transfers some responsibility of the work onto those Prunes. And tell them to smile a little.

Use Experience

The final method for resolving disputes among team members may be the most effective: experience. When team members approach you with a problem that they just can't seem to work out between themselves, you have to listen to both sides of the situation.

If you have experience with the problem, then you can make a quick and accurate decision for the team members. But what if you don't have experience with the technology, and your team members have limited exposure to this portion of the work? How can you make a wise decision based on the information in front of you? You can't!

You will need to invent some experience. As with any project, you should have a testing lab to test and retest your design and implementation. Encourage your team members to use the testing lab to try both sides of the equation to see which solution will be the best.

If a testing lab is not available, or the problem won't fit into the scope of the testing lab, rely on someone else's experience. Assign the team members the duty of researching the problem and preparing a solution. They can use books, the Internet, or other professionals who may have encountered a similar problem. Experience is the best teacher, as Figure 6-7 demonstrates.

FIGURE 6-7

A method for
resolving issues
by testing should
be implemented.

Disciplining Team Members

No project manager likes the process of disciplining a team member—at least they shouldn't. Unfortunately, despite your attempts at befriending, explaining the importance of the project, or keeping team members on track, some people just don't, or won't, care. In these instances, you'll have little choice other than to resort to a method of discipline.

Within your organization, you should already have a process for recording and dealing with disciplinary matters. The organizational procedures set by human resources or management should be followed before interjecting your own project team discipline approach. If there is no clear policy on team discipline, you need to discuss the matter with your project sponsor before the project begins. In the matter of disciplinary actions, take great caution—you are dealing with someone's career. At the same time, discipline is required or your own career may be in jeopardy.

As you begin to nudge team members onto the project track, document it. Keep records of instances where they have fallen off schedule, failed to complete tasks, or have done tasks halfheartedly. This document of activity should have dates and details on each of the incidents, and it doesn't have to be known to anyone but you. Hopefully, your problematic team members will turn from their wicked ways and take your motivation to do their jobs properly. If not, when a threshold is finally crossed, then you must take action.

Following an Internal Process

Within your organization there should be a set process for how an unruly employee is dealt with. For some organizations, there's an evolution of a write-up, a second write-up, a suspension of work, then ultimately a firing. In other organizations, the disciplinary process is less formal. Whatever the method, you should talk with your project sponsor about the process and involve her in any disciplinary action.

In all instances of disciplinary action, it would be best for you and the employee to have the project sponsor or the employee's immediate manager in the meeting to verify what has occurred. This not only protects you from any accusations from the disgruntled team member, but it also protects the team member from your disappointment by having a member of management present.

Removal from a Project

Depending on each situation, you may discover that the team member cannot complete the tasks required of him on the project, and removal from the project may be the best solution. In other instances it could be that the team member refuses to complete the work assigned to him for his own reasons and is a detriment to the success of the project. Again, removal from the team may be the most appropriate action.

Removing someone from the project requires tact, care, and planning. A decision should be made between you and the project sponsor. If you feel strongly that this person is not able to complete the tasks assigned to him, rely on your documentation as your guide. Removal of a team member from a project may be harsh, but it's often required if the project is to succeed.

Of course, when you remove someone from the project, you need to address the matter with the team. Again, use tact. A disruption in the team can cause internal rumblings that you may never hear about—especially if the project team member that was removed was everyone's best friend. You will have created an instant us-against-them mentality. In other instances, the removal of a troublemaker may bring cheers and applause. Whatever the reaction, use tact and explain your reasons without embarrassing or slandering the team member who was removed.

Using External Resources

There comes a time in every organization when a project is presented that is so huge, so complex, or so undesirable to complete that it makes perfect sense to outsource the project to someone else. In these instances, no matter the reason why the project is being outsourced, it is of utmost importance to find the right team to do the job correctly.

Outsourcing has been the buzz of all industries over the last few years—and certainly IT has been a prevalent reason for companies to "get someone else to do it." There are plenty of qualified companies in the marketplace that have completed major transitions and implementations of technology—but there are also many incompetents that profess to know what they're doing only to botch an implementation. Don't let that happen to you.

Finding an Excellent IT Vendor

Finding a good IT vendor isn't a problem. Finding an excellent IT vendor is the problem. The tricky thing about finally finding excellent vendors is that they keep so busy (because of their talented crew), they are difficult to schedule time with. So what makes an excellent vendor? Here are some attributes:

- Ability to complete the project scope on schedule
- Vast experience with the technology to be implemented
- References that demonstrate customer care and satisfaction
- Proof of knowledge on the project team (experience and certifications)
- Adequate time to focus on your project
- A genuine interest in the success of your organization
- A genuine interest in the success of your project
- A fair price for completing the work

Finding an excellent vendor to serve as your project team, or to be integrated into your project team, is no easy task. Remember, the success of a project is only as good as the people on the project team. It's not just the name of the integrator, but the quality of the individuals on the integrator's implementation team that make the integrator great (or not so great). Never forget that fact. Figure 6-8 demonstrates how a vendor can be integrated into your project team. The success of the project is dependent on the payment of the vendor. The project manager should oversee the process.

FIGURE 6-8

A vendor must have vision and dedication to the success of the project.

Success of the Project
Project Vision

Process Overseen
by Project Manager

Vendor
Their Invoices

Size doesn't always matter. Those monstrous integrators and technical firms that have popped up in every city over the past few years don't always have the best people. Some of the best integrators you can find anyway are small, independent firms that have a tightly knit group of technical wizards. Do some research and consider these smaller, above-average tech shops. You may find a diamond in the rough.

To begin finding your integrator, you can use several different methods:

- ■ **References**   Word of mouth from other project teams within your organization, contacts within your industry, or even family and friends are often the best way to find a superb integrator. A reference does something most brochures and sales letters cannot: it comes from a personal contact and lends credibility.

- ■ **Internet**   If you know the technology you are to be implementing, hop on the Internet and see whom the manufacturer of the technology recommends. Once you've found integrators within your community, peruse their web site. Use advanced searches to look for revealing information about them on other web sites, in newsgroups, or in newspapers, or magazines. Know whom you are considering working with before they know you.

- ■ **Yellow pages**   When all else fails, open the phone book and call and interview the prospective team over the phone. Prepare a list of specific questions that you'll need answered. Pay attention to how the phone is answered, what noise is in the background, and how professional and organized the individual on the phone is. Is he rude? Is he happy to help? Take notes and let the other person do much of the talking.

- ■ **Trade shows**   If you know your project is going to take place in a few months, attend some trade shows and get acquainted with some potential vendors. Watch how their salespeople act. Ask them brief questions on what their team has been doing. Collect their materials and file them away for future review.

- ■ **Previous experience**   Never ignore a proven track record with a vendor. Past performance is always a sure sign of how the vendor will act with your project.

Interviewing the Vendor

Once you've narrowed your search to two or three vendors, it's time to interview each one to see to whom the project will be awarded. In the interview process, which the vendor will probably consider a sales call, remind yourself that this is a first date—it's a chance to find out more information about the vendor.

Document all parts of the meeting: How difficult was it to arrange a meeting time? How polite was the salesperson? Did the salesperson bring a technical consultant to the meeting? All of these little details will help you make an informed decision. In such meetings, pay attention to several things about vendors' representatives:

■ Do they pay attention to details? Are they on time? Dressed professionally and appropriately for your business? Are their shoes shined and professional? How vendors pay attention to the details in their appearance and presentation to win your business will be an indicator of how they will treat you once they've won your business.

■ How organized are their materials? When a salesperson opens his briefcase, can he quickly locate sales materials? Are the brochures and materials well prepared and neat, and not wrinkled or dog-eared? Again, this shows attention to detail, something every project requires from the start.

■ What is their body language saying? Pay attention to how they are seated, where their hands are, and how animated their answers become. A salesperson should show genuine interest in your project and be excited to chat with you. If she seems bored now, she will likely be bored when you call to discuss concerns down the road.

■ What does your gut say? Gut instinct is not used enough. The meeting with the salesperson should leave you with a confident, informed feeling. If your gut tells you something is wrong, then chances are something is. If you're not 100 percent certain, and you probably shouldn't be after one meeting, do more research or ask for another meeting with the project integrators.

Looking for a STAR

When you are interviewing the potential integrators, you need to ask direct, hard- hitting questions to slice through their sales spiels and get to the heart of the project. One of the best interview techniques, especially when dealing with

FIGURE 6-9

STAR is an
interview
methodology.

potential integrators, is the STAR methodology. Figure 6-9 demonstrates that STAR means Situation, Task, Action, Result.

When you use the STAR method, you ask a situational question, such as "Can you tell me about a situation where you were implementing a technology for a customer and you went above and beyond the call of duty?"

The vendor should answer with a specific Situation, followed by the Task of the situation, the Action he took with the task, and then the Results. If the potential vendor doesn't complete the STAR, add follow-up questions, such as "How did the situation end?" to allow the vendor to finish the STAR question.

This interview process is excellent, as it allows the project manager to discern fact from fiction based on the vendor's response. Try it!

Know What You Want

When you procure materials or resources from vendors, know exactly what you want from the procurement process. In the Statement of Work (SOW), the seller fully describes the work to be completed and/or the product to be supplied. The SOW becomes part of the contract between the buyer and the seller. It is typically created as part of the procurement planning process, and allows the seller to determine if it can meet the written requirements of the SOW.

Particular industries have different assumptions about what constitutes a SOW. What one industry calls a SOW may be called a Statement of Objectives (SOO) in another. A SOO is a document describing a problem to be solved by the seller. Some specific terms the project manager should be familiar with are shown next.

Document	Purpose
Bid	From seller to buyer. Price is the determining factor in the decision-making process.
Quotation	From seller to buyer. Price is the determining factor in the decision-making process.
Proposal	From seller to buyer. Other factors—such as skill sets, reputation, or an idea for the project solution—may be determining factors in the decision-making process.
Invitation For Bid (IFB)	From buyer to seller. Requests the seller provide a price for the procured product or service.
Request For Quote (RFQ)	From buyer to seller. Requests the seller provide a price for the procured product or service.
Request For Proposal (RFP)	From buyer to seller. Requests the seller provide a proposal to complete the procured work or provide the procured product.

Cinching the Deal

When you've just about made your decision, it's time to follow up with a phone call to a few references. Now most references that you'll be given by the vendor will no doubt be excellent and prepped. Not that anything's wrong with that; everyone wants to put her best foot forward. Ask the vendor what type of work was performed for the client and when the work was done.

If the work the vendor completed for the client is not directly associated with your project, ask if that vendor can provide you with another reference where similar work was done. In addition, the date of the work should be fairly recent, hopefully within the past six months.

Once you've called the references, reviewed your research, and have narrowed the field down to at least two integrators, ask for a quote in response to your Request For Proposal (RFP) by a specific date. Be firm about your deadline, but at least a week from the request is adequate time for a vendor to complete and return a proposal to you.

An RFP is a formal request from your company inviting the client to create a proposal of the work to be completed and provide you with a cost estimate. An RFP does not guarantee anyone the job; it simply formalizes the proceedings of the selection process.

Once you have the vendor's proposal in place, read it. If the technology to be implemented is not within your grasp or the grasp of anyone in your department, ask for a second opinion. Hire an IT consultant whom you trust, who is somewhat familiar with the technology to be implemented, and have him read the proposals and rate them. Having another set of eyes look over the proposals can help you make a more informed decision.

Once you have made your decision on which vendor the project is awarded to, get the scope of the project in writing, including the price, in the form of a contract. The vendor may, and should, have their own contract that they use whenever implementing technology. Review the vendor's contract, and if necessary have your attorney look it over and make any amendments or changes.

As painful as contracts are, they protect you and the integrator. Contracts should require that the vendor guarantee their work for a specified amount of time. The technology to be implemented will determine the amount of time expressed in the warranty and the type of guarantee provided.

There are many different types of contracts available. Based on the project work, the expected duration of the project, and the relationship between the buyer and seller, the contract type will be determined. Here's a quick overview of the common contract types and their attributes:

Contract Type	Attribute	Risk Issues
Cost Plus Fixed Fee (CPFF)	Actual costs plus profit margin for seller.	Cost overruns represent risk to the buyer.
Cost Plus Percentage of Cost (CPPC)	Actual costs plus profit margin for seller.	Cost overruns represent risk to the buyer. This is a dangerous contract type for the buyer.
Cost Plus Incentive Fee (CPIF)	Actual costs plus profit margin for seller.	Cost overruns represent risk to the buyer.
Fixed Price (FP)	Agreed price for contracted product. Can include incentives for the seller.	Seller assumes risk.
Lump Sum	Agreed price for contracted product. Can include incentives for the seller.	Seller assumes risk.
Firm Fixed Price (FFP)	Agreed price for contracted product.	Seller assumes risk.
Fixed Price Incentive Fee (FPIF)	Agreed price for contracted product. Can include incentives for the seller.	Seller assumes risk.

Contract Type	Attribute	Risk Issues
Time and Materials (T&M)	Price assigned for the time and materials provided by the seller.	Contracts without not-to-exceed (NTE) clauses can lead to cost overruns.
Unit Price	Price assigned for a measurable unit of product or time (for example, $130 for an engineer's time on the project).	Risk varies with the product. Time represents the biggest risk if the amount needed is not specified in the contract.

Before any implementation begins, and once the contract details have been worked out, do some prep work before the project begins. For example, if the project is an operating system upgrade on your servers, create a full backup or system image of your servers. If the technology is a new application to be developed with hooks into your database, assign the appropriate levels of access security to the database for the developers, but don't give the developers greater permission than what they need to accomplish their work. In other words, prepare for the worst-case scenario, but hope that you never have to use it.

After Hiring the Consultant

Consultants know what they know—and what they do not know can hurt them and your project. In other words, consultants need to learn about your environment, how your standard operating procedures work, who they should talk to, and so on. Consultants need to know how to get things done within your organization. You cannot throw a consultant into your organization and expect him to have the same level of detail, same level of expertise, and same organizational knowledge that you have. It takes some time and some guidance.

For this reason alone you should demand and require that the consultant attend project meetings, be located close to the project team, and take an active role in meeting the project team members and stakeholders. He needs to get involved in order to be successful and productive. Most consultants and experts, if they are worth anything at all, will be eager to follow these rules and requirements. Often it's the project manager who wants the consultant to feel comfortable and not get into the mix of things so quickly. This limits the consultant's ability to contribute.

FROM THE FIELD

Interview with Bill Farnsworth

Name: Bill Farnsworth
Title: Senior Partner Strategy Consultant
Company: Microsoft Corporation
Years as an IT project manager: 5

Bill Farnsworth is the Senior Partner Strategy Consultant for Microsoft Consulting Services in Northern California. Bill is a Microsoft Certified Systems Engineer, a Microsoft Certified Trainer, and a Microsoft Solutions Framework Master Trainer. In addition to his Microsoft certifications and experience, Mr. Farnsworth is also a Certified Novell Engineer, a Certified Novell Instructor, and a Certified Internet Architect.

Q: What is the best thing about IT project management?

A: The best thing about IT project management is being able to take a concept to completion. Projects develop for a variety of reasons: to solve a business problem, to address technical issues, to provide proof of concepts, and so on. But all successful IT projects result in a delivered product that, in some way, addresses a need in the company. I like working on the team that delivers that solution.

Q: When you begin to create a team for an IT project, what do you consider first?

A: Ideally, I look for the business problem we are solving by forming the team. This is a critical element in determining the composition of the team. While technical expertise is also critical to the success of an IT project, having representatives on the project team who understand the business problem we are trying to solve is the main consideration.

Q: When a project has been initiated, that is, management has approved it but no formal implementation plans have been created, how soon do you begin to organize a team?

A: Organizing the team as early as possible is very important. Setting an environment where you can best ensure consistency by having the same team evaluate the business problem, define the scope of the project, propose the solution, and then develop and deploy the solution is the best case. By forming the team after some of these steps are already complete, the team may not support or understand some of the underlying justification or may not agree with the scope of the project from the outset. I feel successful projects depend on forming the project team at the earliest point possible.

Q: How does a project manager recruit and motivate team members to be excited about an IT implementation?

A: Project team members like to have a sense of ownership. Owning an identifiable piece of the solution to a problem the company is facing is motivating. Approaching candidates for the team and demonstrating how their contribution will directly affect the team, the project, and the company is an effective way to recruit and motivate team members.

Q: What are characteristics of a successful project manager in regard to creating a project team?

A: A successful project manager needs to be able to motivate, coordinate, and facilitate the activity of the team. No project manager can complete all, or even a significant portion, of the work the team needs to accomplish. The project manager should work to ensure that the project team has what it needs to accomplish its goals. A successful project manager will also seek to prevent herself from being a bottleneck for communication and information with the project team, or within the team itself.

Many failed projects result from a project manager who interacts with team members individually, and then represents team members' needs, concerns, and input to other team members. Similarly, project managers also place themselves between the project team and the project sponsor for the project, reducing the team's exposure to the business requirements, and the impact their project will have on the business. Being a bottleneck in these ways is one of the easiest methods to ensure partial or complete failure of a project. Removing yourself as a bottleneck, and ensuring communication and information sharing within and between the project team and the business, is one of the key contributors to a successful project.

FROM THE FIELD *(continued)*

Q: What are characteristics you look for in IT professionals when you are considering adding them to a project team?

A: The IT professionals' technical knowledge is, of course, very important. However, it is just as important to identify team members who are willing and able to participate on the project team. Having a less experienced, more motivated team member could be better than a more experienced, time-restricted member. Looking at team candidates' time commitments, technical knowledge, organizational understanding, creativity, and ability to work within a team will give project managers some insight into how effective they can be as team members.

Q: What type of questions do you ask potential team members to determine their involvement on the project team?

A: I ask candidates for the project team what their approach to the role will be, what they hope to accomplish, how they deal with ambiguity and conflict, what their contribution to the team would be, and what they see as the perfect team dynamic. These kind of open-ended questions give me a good insight into how they are going to interact with the other team members and if they see their role as contributing to the solution or more as an obligation of the job. Positive answers to these questions, as opposed to stories about how projects have failed in the past, typically show an optimistic and productive approach to the project.

Q: What can a project manager do when his team does not have the technical expertise to implement the project?

A: There are several options for the project manager in this case. Dependent on the timeframe of the project, training the project team to enhance technical expertise is an option. If this is not a viable option, recruiting additional team members from within the organization who do have the required expertise is also an option. If this is not possible, or the organization does not have individuals with that expertise, finding outside resources, such as contractors, or hiring to fill the need are other options. Which of these options is best for any given project depends on the time and money available to the project manager.

Q: When it comes to decision making, what is the best approach: allow the teams to make the decision or should the project manager take charge?

A: Project managers who make the effort to solicit feedback, engender discussion, and promote shared decision making typically deal with less resistance from the project team as the project proceeds. If the team makes a decision together, through consensus, votes, or other methods, and the project manager has created a team environment that supports those decisions, the team will develop a culture of bringing up issues or disagreement before a decision is made, allowing for issues to be addressed before moving to the next phase of a project. The team must, however, agree that, after the team makes such a decision, this becomes the team decision and that any individual disagreement must be minimized in light of the team decision. In some cases, the team may not be able to come to or agree upon a decision. In these cases, the project manager may need to make the final decision with the understanding that the initial disagreement will have to be abandoned to ensure the successful progression of the project.

Q: What is the most difficult part of creating an IT project team?

A: The most difficult part of creating a project team is identifying the skills, both technical and soft, that will be required in future phases of the project. Without knowing the architecture or other details of the solution, knowing which technical skills might be required or which organizational contacts and relationships could best be leveraged in later phases is difficult. It's possible to add team members as the project progresses, but having those team members on board as early in the project as possible helps ensure that their skills and contributions can best be utilized.

Q: What methods do you use to deal with conflicts among team members?

A: Conflicts about the direction of the project can usually be addressed by consensus, as long as the idea of consensus has been positioned and agreed to by the team at the very start of the project. If the team "signs on" to the idea of team agreement at each milestone, and that the team's decision is everyone's decision after that milestone is reached, conflict is easier to address.

While this approach does not, in any way, eliminate disagreement, it does allow the team to make progress as the team members "agree to disagree," as long as the majority of the team agrees on one course of action.

Q: How do you address team members who are less than thrilled being involved with the IT project you are in charge of?

A: In a perfect world, those team members would opt out of the project. In reality, taking the roles of less-than-enthusiastic team members and assigning them to other team members can help persuade difficult team members that they can either change their difficult attitudes, if they want to remain in their roles, or they can easily be replaced if their attitudes become counterproductive to the project. The project manager should make it clear that those who contribute to the project, with a positive attitude, will be encouraged to do so; and that those who insist on maintaining a discouraging mood will have their role, and thus their exposure to the rest of the team, reduced or, if possible, eliminated from the project team.

Q: What has been the most rewarding experience you've had in regard to creating a project team?

A: The most rewarding experience with regard to forming a project team has been the single project I have run in which the team remained intact for the duration of the project. The initial core team remained on the project from start to finish. The feelings of ownership, accomplishment, and impact were extremely rewarding. In addition, each of the other members became great advocates of the approach we took to the project: a team of peers, decision by consensus, equal valuation of contribution, and so on.

Q: What traps can IT project managers fall into when organizing a project team?

A: One of the easiest traps project managers can fall into is selecting team members based on personal relationship or other characteristics that make them more likely to support the decisions of the project manager. There can be a tendency to select team members, for instance, who support the technology to which the company is migrating. However, this usually prevents the selection of team members who know the legacy system very well, and could contribute a great amount of historical, organizational, and operational information to the project team. Similarly, selecting project team members who will support the project manager under any circumstances prevents the team from benefiting from healthy exchanges of disparate viewpoints and approaches.

Q: What advice can you offer for aspiring IT project managers?

A: Observe project teams you work on and the dynamic that project managers create and maintain. See what works and what doesn't and make conscious decisions to use what has worked and avoid what hasn't. Using historically successful techniques borrowed from successful project managers will often help you succeed in projects you manage in the future. Don't be afraid to develop creative approaches, but don't force a creative solution to a problem when you have seen another approach work in the same situation in the past.

CHAPTER SUMMARY

Teamwork is the key to project management success. As a project manager, you must have a team that you can rely on, while at the same time, the team must be able to turn to you for guidance, leadership, and tenacity. When creating a team, evaluate the skills required to complete the project and then determine which individuals have those attributes to offer. Interviewing potential team members allows you to get a sense of their goals, their work ethics, and what skills they may have to offer.

Subteams are a fantastic way to assign particular areas of an IT project to a group of specialists or to a geographically based implementation. When creating subteams, communications from the project manager and the team leaders is essential. Subteams require responsible leaders on each team, and a reliable, confident project manager.

When disagreements flair among team members, you must have a plan in place before the disagreement happens. Document problems with troublesome team members in the event that a team member needs to reprimanded or removed from the team. The project sponsor should be kept abreast of the situation as the project continues.

Should the scope of the project be beyond the abilities of the internal team, the project can be outsourced. When outsourcing the project, you need to use careful consideration in your selection of an integrator. Project managers should rely on references of vendors, their ability to work with the technology, gut feelings, and word of mouth to make a decision.

Building a project team is hard work, but it is also an investment in the success of the project. Once again, the success of any project is only as good as the members on the project team.

CHAPTER QUIZ

1. When creating a project team, why must the project manager know the skills of each of the prospective team members?

   A. It helps the project manager determine the budget of the project.

   B. It helps the project manager determine how long the project will take.

   C. It helps the project manager determine if he wants to lead the project.

   D. It helps the project manager assign tasks.

2. Of the following, which two are methods the project manager can use to assess internal skills?

   A. Prior projects

   B. Reports from other project teams

   C. Recommendation of management

   D. Projects the project manager has worked on

3. When requesting an internal resume to recruit team members, why must the project manager use extreme caution?

   A. Resumes have the connotation of getting, or keeping, a job.

   B. Resumes have the connotation of pay raises.

   C. Resumes have the connotation of relocating users.

   D. It is illegal, within the US, to ask for a resume once the individual has been hired.

4. Of the following, which one is not an example of team development?

   A. Training for the project work

   B. Industry certifications

   C. Team events such as rafting

   D. Forming, storming, norming, and performing

5. When is training considered an expense?

   A. When the cost of training is beyond the budget of an organization

   B. When the time it takes to complete the training increases the length of the project beyond a reasonable deadline

C. When the training experience does not increase the ability of the team to implement the technology

D. When the training experience does not increase the individual's salary

6. The project team is in disagreement over which OS to use on a new server. The project manager tables the issues and says the decision can wait until next week. This is an example of which project management negotiating technique?

A. Confrontive

B. Yielding

C. Coercive

D. Withdrawal

7. What is the best way to create reliable, hard-working teams?

A. Fire the team members who do not perform.

B. Set the example by being reliable and hard working.

C. Promise raises to the hardest working team members.

D. Promise vacation days for all that are hard working.

8. How is camaraderie created on a team?

A. By years of working together

B. By creating an us-against-them mentality

C. By the experiences of the team as a whole

D. By creating friendships on the team

9. Why is the WIIFM principle a good theory to implement with project management?

A. It shows the team how the success of the project is good for the whole company.

B. It shows the team how the success of the project is good for management.

C. It shows the team how the success of the project will make the company more profitable.

D. It shows the team how the success of the project will impact each team member personally.

10. What is a subteam?

A. A specialized team that is assigned to one area of a large project or to a geographical area

B. A specialized team that will be brought into the project as needed

    C. A collection of individuals that can serve as backup to the main project team

    D. A specialized team responsible for any of the manual labor within a project

11. What is the key to working with multiple subteams?

    A. A team leader on each subteam

    B. Multiple project managers

    C. Communication between team leaders and the project manager

    D. Communication between team leaders, the project manager, and the project sponsor

12. Of the following, which is a good team building exercise?

    A. Introductions at the kickoff meeting

    B. A weekly lunch meeting

    C. A team event outside of the office

    D. Team implementation of a new technology over a weekend

13. Why should a project manager conduct interviews for prospective team members?

    A. To determine if a person should be on the team or not

    B. To learn what skills each team member has

    C. To determine if the project should be outsourced

    D. To determine the skills required to complete the project

14. What is the purpose of conducting interviews of existing team members? Choose two:

    A. To determine if the project should be outsourced

    B. To determine the length of the project

    C. To determine the tasks each team member should be responsible for

    D. To determine if additional team members are needed

15. When a project manager asks a vendor for an RFP, what is he asking for?

    A. A Request For Proposal so a decision can be made based on price.

    B. A Request For Proposal so a decision can be made based on the proposed solution to the WBS.

    C. A Request For Proposal so a decision can be made based on the proposed solution for the SOW.

    D. A Request For Proposal so a decision can be made based on the proposed schedule.

CHAPTER EXERCISES

Exercise 1

In this exercise you will create a job description for a web application developer from a project scenario. You will be given prompts to guide you on the creation of the job description.

Scenario: You are the project manager for Cardigan Adhesives Corporation. You have been assigned as the project manager for the development of the new corporate Internet site. The web site should be easy to navigate for all guests. In addition, the web site will have an application that will query a database to report on inventory, cost of goods available, and online ordering.

Answer the following questions to begin creating the job description for a web developer. If you are uncertain of the answers, use the Internet to research web developers and the types of activity they are required to do.

Prompt	Your Answer
What is the primary purpose of this role on the team?	
What type of software will the team member be using to create the application?	
What type of database is being queried?	

Prompt	Your Answer
To whom will the team member report?	
What other activities will the team member be responsible for?	
What are some personal traits that this person should have?	

Based on your answers, create a job description that is appropriate for a web developer on this project. A solution appears at the end of this chapter.

Exercise 2

In this exercise you will create a 12-question interview to assess the skills of a prospective team member using the project scenario provided. Prompts will assist you to create key questions for your interview. On questions that you find relevant, create reactionary questions for the interviewees' expected answers.

Scenario: You are the project manager for Cardigan Adhesives Corporation. You have been assigned as the project manager for the development of the new corporate Internet site. The web site should be easy to navigate for all guests. In addition, the web site will have an application that will query a database to report on inventory, cost of goods available, and online ordering.

Prompt	Your Question for the Prospective Team Member Interview
How important is the level of experience for this job?	
How important is it to you that this person know web development software?	
STAR?	
How important is an industry certification for this role?	
How important is the ability of the individual to work with web design software?	

Prompt	Your Question for the Prospective Team Member Interview
How important is experience with databases for this project?	
What are some web technology requirements and how does this relate to the interviewee?	
How important are security concepts on a web application?	
Will the e-commerce portion of the project be done in-house or outsourced?	
What type of personal traits are you looking for in this role?	

Prompt	Your Question for the Prospective Team Member Interview
Create the next two questions that are relevant to the position on your own:	

QUIZ ANSWERS

1. **D.** The project manager should know in advance of the WBS creation the skills of the team members so that she can assign tasks fairly. A skills assessment also helps the project manager determine what skills are lacking to complete the project.

2. **A, C.** Experience is always one of the best barometers for skills assessment. If the prospective team member has worked on similar projects, that person should be vital for the current implementation. Recommendations from management on team members can aid a project manager in assigning tasks and recruiting new team members.

3. **A.** Resumes can show the skill sets of prospective team members, but they have a tendency to imply getting or keeping a job. In lieu of resumes, project managers can use a listing of accomplishments and skills to determine the talent of recruits.

4. **B.** Industry certifications are a valuable source for proving that individuals are skilled and able to implement the technology. Certifications on their own, however, do not provide team development.

5. **C.** Training is an expense rather than an investment when the result of the training does not increase the team's ability to complete the project. A factor in determining if training should be implemented or not is the time of training and its impact on a project's deadline.

6. **D.** This is an example of withdrawal. While this method often is the failure to effectively come to a decision, it can be effective when a decision is not needed immediately. This approach can allow the team to "cool off" on the decision and move into other pressing matters.

7. **B.** A leader leads best by doing. By setting the example of being hard working, reliable, and available to your team members, you will show them the type of workers you hope they are as well. Leading by fear, or through an iron-fist mentality, should not be an option in today's workplace.

8. **C.** Camaraderie is an element that can't be forced upon a team. Years of working together, friendships, and us-against-them mindsets do not create camaraderie. The experience of the team as a whole is where camaraderie stems from.

9. **D.** WIIFM, the "What's In It For Me" theory, personalizes the benefits of the project for each team member. By demonstrating what the individual will gain from the project, you help increase that team member's sense of ownership and responsibility to the project.

10. **A.** Subteams are not less important than the overall project team. Subteams are collections of specialists who will be responsible for a single unit of the project plan, or a geographical structure.

11. **C.** When working with multiple subteams, the project manager and the team leader of each subteam must have open communications. The subteams should follow the change of command through each team leader, to the project manager, and the project manager to the project sponsor.

12. **C.** A good team building exercise is something out of the ordinary that gels the ability of the team to work together. Luncheons and introductions at meetings are standard fare that don't always bring a team closer together.

13. **A.** Interviews of prospective team members allow the project manager to determine if those people have assets to offer to a project. Because the team members are prospective, the project manager can conduct a typical interview using formal or informal approaches to ascertain the level of skills from each prospect.

14. **A, C.** In some instances, interviews can determine if the project, or more likely portions of the project, should be outsourced because of the skills required or the timeline of the project. Interviews of the existing team members, if they've been assigned to the project manager, can help the project manager determine the tasks each team member can be responsible for.

15. **C.** An RFP is a Request For Proposal to the SOW, or statement of work. The RFP typically means the buyer is open to recommendations and solutions from the seller. The decision to buy is not made on cost alone.

EXERCISE SOLUTIONS

Exercise 1: Possible Solution

Prompt	Answer
What is the primary purpose of this role on the team?	Web developer
What type of software will the team member be using to create the application?	ColdFusion, Java, Visual J++, or any other web development program
What type of database is being queried?	ColdFusion, Oracle, SQL, Lotus Domino, or others

Prompt	Answer
To whom will the team member report?	The project manager
What other activities will the team member be responsible for?	Working with the database designer, the database administrator, the web developer, and other team members
What are some personal traits that this person should have?	Hard working, fast learning, dedicated, focused
Your job description should be something like this:	Web developer: This highly skilled, focused individual will be responsible for creating a commerce-enabled application that communicates with a SQL database. Experience in Visual J++, XML, and SQL Transaction statements are a must. Experience working with SQL or Dreamweaver a plus.

Exercise 2: Possible Solution

Prompt	Your Question for the Prospective Team Member
How important is the level of experience for this job?	How many years have you been working as an application developer?
How important is it to you that this person know web development software?	What type of web development applications do you work with?
STAR?	Can you give an example of a particular web development project where you found a faster or better solution?
How important is an industry certification for this role?	Have you ever taken any classes on the applications you work with? Reactionary question: Have you earned any certifications from the associated vendor?
How important is the ability of the individual to work with web design software?	Have you ever designed any of your own web pages? Reactionary question: What web software did you use to design the site?
How important is experience with databases for this project?	Have you ever worked with SQL (or the database you specified for this job description)?
What are some web technology requirements and how does this relate to the interviewee?	What type of web servers have you worked with? For example, UNIX, IIS, Linux?

Prompt	Your Question for the Prospective Team Member
How important are security concepts on a web application?	What type of security mechanisms have you worked with? For example, how did you address security with other commerce-enabled designs?
Will the e-commerce portion of the project be done in-house or outsourced?	Have you implemented e-commerce applications from the ground up? Reactionary question: If so, what are some examples?
What type of personal traits are you looking for in this role?	What's your average day like? Reactionary question: How often have you worked overtime?
You create the next two questions that are relevant to the position:	What's the best thing about web development?
	If you could change one thing in web design, what would it be?

Chapter 7

Building the
Project Plan

Remember the story of Noah and the ark? When did he build that ship? Aha! He built it before the rain started. That's the same idea with all of this planning you're doing for each of your projects. By effectively planning, analyzing, and examining your plan from different perspectives, you increase your chances to complete your project on time and on budget.

At this point of your project, you've already done a great deal of work. Look back at all you've accomplished: you've created a vision, researched the technology, partnered with management, created a budget, made a WBS, and assembled your team. Phew! That's a ton of progress, and the actual implementation of the project work hasn't started yet. Don't get discouraged— these activities that you've been doing are the building blocks of a strong foundation for the success of your project. Without all of those activities, your project would be doomed.

This chapter focuses on bringing your plan together. If you've done all of the preliminary work described in the earlier chapters, your plan is already coming together—which is grand. However, there are still a few more things that require your attention before you set your plan into motion. Particularly, you need to give some thought to the project schedule and determine if it's reasonable. This is crucial for any project.

Building the Project Plans

Based on the size of your project, your project plans will vary. The project plan is not one big plan, but rather a collection of plans that detail how different conditions, scenarios, and actions will be managed. It is a formal document that is reviewed and, hopefully, approved by management. The project plan is not a novel that tells the story of how the project will move along, but rather a guide that allows for changes to the project plan as more details become available.

While the project plan may evolve, there are some elements within the project that generally do not change—or are protected from change. Of course, the foundation of the project is the project scope. Recall that the project scope is all of the required work—and only the required work—to complete the project objectives. The scope statement defines what the project will and won't accomplish. Once the project scope statement has been agreed upon, your change control system protects it.

Other elements of the project plan that should be immune to change are the project charter and the performance baselines. The project charter authorizes the project. It is a formal document that allows the project manager to manage the project work, resources, and schedule to deliver on the project scope. Performance baselines are time, cost, scope, and quality metrics that the project manager must meet within the project delivery. These baselines rarely change as they reflect the scope of the project. In other words, you're supposed to have enough time, budget, and obtainable quality metrics to meet the requirements of the project.

Project Plan Elements

When you and your project team create the elements of the project plan, you can start from scratch and build your plan or you can rely on historical information to lend a hand. Many times, project managers will find that their projects are similar, or even identical, to past projects they've completed. Rather than reinventing the project management wheel, they'll rely on past project plans to serve as templates for their current projects. There's nothing wrong with this approach at all—it's just working smart, not hard. Of course, when you use older plans as templates you'll update the older plan to reflect your current project.

Regardless of which approach you take to building your project plan, there are some common elements you should have for each one:

- **Project charter** This document comes from someone in a supervisory position that is higher in the organizational flowchart than the immediate management of the project team. This document authorizes the project.

- **Scope statement** This document is written to clearly define the project objectives for scope, schedule, cost, and quality. It also defines what will be delivered and what won't be delivered as part of the project. The project requirements help define the scope statement. This important document is the foundation for all future project decisions as it helps determine if requests, actions, or project work results are in or out of scope.

- **Work Breakdown Structure** The WBS is a deliverables-orientated decomposition of the project. The project components are decomposed to work packages, which are the smallest, most manageable elements within the structure.

- **Time and cost estimates for each work package**   Recall that cost and time estimates reflect the labor and materials needed to deliver the project. This section of the project plan will also detail how the estimate was derived, the degree of confidence in the estimate, and any assumptions associated with the estimates.

- **Performance measurement baselines**   These baselines are boundaries or targets the project manager and the project team are expected to perform within. For example, the cost baseline may predict the amount of budget that should be spent by a given milestone with an allowable variance.

- **Milestones and target dates for the milestones**   Within your project there should be easily identified milestones that signal you are moving toward project completion. Associated with these major milestones are some target dates that you and management agree on. This allows you and management to plan on resource utilization, and adjunct processes within your business, and keeps all stakeholders informed—of where the project should be heading— and when.

- **Required staff and their availability and costs**   There may be portions of your project plan that require procured resources or temporary specialized resources to complete a portion of the project work. The required personnel should be identified, their availability determined, and their associated costs documented.

- **Risk Management Plan**   All projects have some degree of risk. This plan addresses the risks within your project, documents the assumptions and constraints of the project, and details how each risk is managed.

- **Open issues**   There will often be open issues and pending decisions as the plan is first created. This section of the plan identifies and documents the issues to be determined and allows the project to continue. Of course, the decisions and issues in this section of the project plan should be addressed accordingly, which may cause other areas of the project plan to be updated.

- **Supporting details**   The supporting details are any relevant documentation that influenced your project decisions, any technical documentation, and any relevant standards the project will operate under.

Adding Subsidiary Plans

While your project should have all the elements of the preceding section, there are additional plans that your project may warrant or your organization may require. As with the required elements in a project plan, you can use a project template for these subsidiary plans.

- **Scope Management Plan**   This plan details how the project scope will be protected from change, where changes to the scope may be permitted, and how the management of approved changes will be handled.

- **Schedule Management Plan**   Once the schedule has been created, which we'll discuss in a moment, the schedule management plan details how changes to the schedule may be allowed. This plan also details how the actual changes themselves will be managed and how the changes may affect other areas of the project.

- **Cost Management Plan**   This plan details how changes to costs within the project will be managed and the procedure to report and document cost changes.

- **Quality Management Plan**   This plan details the expected level of quality for the project and how the project must map to the quality expectations of the performing organization. This plan addresses any quality program your organization may participate in, such as ISO 9000 or Six Sigma, and how your project must operate within those requirements.

- **Staffing Management Plan**   Your project may not require the project team members to be on the project for the duration of the project schedule. This subsidiary project plan determines how project team members will be brought onto, and released from, the project.

- **Communications Management Plan**   This important plan details the expectations and requirements for communication across the project team, management, and stakeholders. It details the communication processes, forms, standard meetings, and any other pertinent communication management.

- **Risk Management Plan**   This plan identifies the risks within the project, their probability and impact on the project objectives, and how they should be managed. The Risk Response Plan also includes risk owners, their responsibilities as risk owners, and what actions the project team will take if risk events are coming into fruition. This plan also includes contingency and fallback plans.

■ **Procurement Management Plan**   Projects often need to procure resources and materials. This plan details the procurement process and how it is managed according to the organizational policies of your company.

Defining the Project Schedule

Your project must have a definite set of deliverables that mark its end. Projects also require a finish date. Some projects' finish dates are a touch more firm than others. For example, the Y2K bug most companies worried themselves over in 1999 had an inflexible deadline. Or consider a project that management says must be completed before a peak business period. Other projects, such as the release of a new e-mail program within an organization, can have a tendency to go on forever and evolve into runaway projects.

Runaway projects stem from loosely guarded project scope, poor planning, and lack of research. Of course, the longer a project takes to produce its deliverables, the more the project will cost. In addition, to make it personal, a missed deadline can impact bonuses, incentives, and raises for project managers and team members. The best way to reach a target date for completion is to plan, plan, plan. And then analyze the plan. And then adjust and readjust until the plan is acceptable and the team is ready to implement the technology.

Deadline-Orientated Projects

A project schedule should be a reflection of the WBS, the accumulation of all of the work packages within the project, and then the assignment of resources for each task. Most new project managers work around specific target dates for milestones, phases, and a completed project. This makes the most sense, right? IT professionals are used to working from a specific calendar for so much of their lives that this next concept can be a little confusing at first: do not schedule project tasks to happen on a specific date if at all avoidable.

Project managers should not work around specific dates when creating the project plan, but instead should initially work around units of time—for example, one day, two weeks, three months, and so on. Rather than saying a specific work unit will take place next Thursday and Friday, it's better to say that a specific task will take two days to complete. Why? Isn't next Thursday and Friday the same as two days? Yes, and no. Assigning two days to complete a task rather than two *specific* days allows you to move the task around within your project plan. Figure 7-1 demonstrates the concept of working in units of time rather than specific dates. This little trick allows for a process you'll learn more about later in this chapter: project compression.

Working with units of time rather than specific dates for each of the tasks within your project plan allows you to tally your plan to a specific amount of time—regardless of when the actual project is implemented. For example, if tasks within your project were all assigned a deadline based on the project start date of July 9 and end date of November 2, each task is very time constrained and date specific. However, this same project takes 90 workdays (depending on the year and allowing for weekends). When you assign tasks units of time within the span of 90 workdays, regardless of when the actual start date commences, the project can shift 90 days into the future from the start date.

As you learned during the creation of the WBS, certain work units can be tackled simultaneously with others. Rather than assigning dates to specific tasks, assigning time units to tasks allows the project manager to move activities closer to the start or finish of the project. For some tasks that are effort driven, a project manager can assign additional resources to reduce the amount of elapsed time required to complete the task. Of course, the task still takes the same number of work hours to complete, it is just being accomplished faster as more people are working together on the work unit to complete it.

Often, however, project schedules and deadlines are determined before the project even begins. We've all been there, right? You've been handed a project to create an

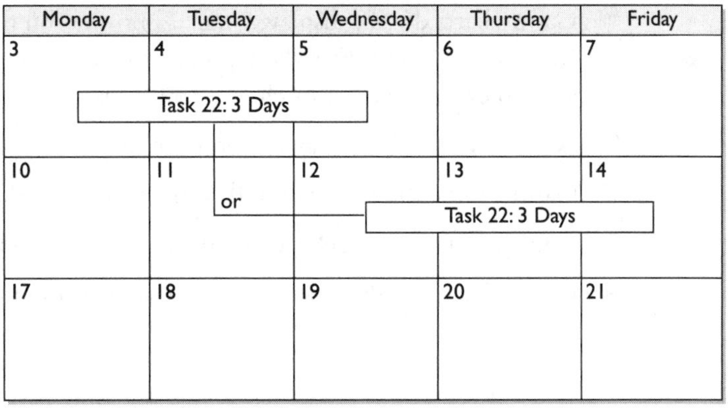

FIGURE 7-1

Assign tasks to be completed in units of time rather than by specific dates.

Monday	Tuesday	Wednesday	Thursday	Friday
3	4	5	6	7
	Task 22: 3 Days			
10	11	12	13	14
	or	Task 22: 3 Days		
17	18	19	20	21

application that must be delivered by April 1. There hasn't been real reflection on the needed time to create a quality application by the given date. In these instances the project manager needs to still address the project, the work decomposition, and the assignment of resources to complete the work just as with a project where the end date is not known.

Once the project manager has determined how long the project will really take, based on accurate time estimates, activity sequencing, and identified resources, he can make realistic decisions about scheduling the work, assigning resources, and, ultimately, negotiating for more time, more resources, or less scope to complete the project by the preset deadline.

Creating a Project Network Diagram

Recall that a WBS is a topology of the project deliverables. A WBS takes the project and breaks the project down into major components. These components can then be broken down again into other components, then again into work packages, and, finally, documented with a task list that is derived from the WBS. Once the WBS has been created, the activity list can then be entered into Microsoft Project, or your favorite Project Management Information Systems (PMIS) software . Once you enter the activities into Microsoft Project, you can create a Gantt chart like the one in Figure 7-2. It shows a mapping of each of the units of work required to complete each phase of the project.

The Gantt chart is ideal for simple, short-term projects. It is a timeline of the events with consideration given to tasks that can be completed concurrently within a project's lifespan. Traditional Gantt charts have some drawbacks:

- Gantt charts do not display detailed information on each work unit. (Microsoft Project does allow project managers to add task information and notes within a Gantt chart on each task.)

- Gantt charts only display the order of tasks.

- Gantt charts do not clearly reflect the order of tasks in multiple phases.

- Gantt charts do not reflect the shortest path to completion.

- Gantt charts do not reflect the best usage of resources.

FIGURE 7-2   A WBS decomposed the project into similar, accessible work units.

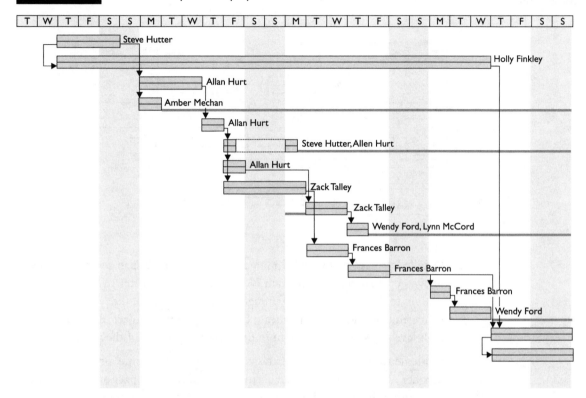

To address these issues, project managers can use a Project Network Diagram (PND). PNDs are a fluid mapping of the work to be completed. Figure 7-3 is a sample of a portion of a network diagram. Incidentally, the terms "PND," "Project Network Diagrams," and "network diagrams" all refer to the same workflow structure—don't let the different names confuse you. Such diagrams allow the project manager and the project team to tinker with the relationships between tasks and create alternative solutions to increase productivity, profitability, and the diligence of a project.

A PND visualizes the flow of work from conception to completion. Network diagrams provide detailed information on work units and allow project managers to analyze tasks, resources, and the allotted time for each task. You can use a PND to determine the flow of work to predict the earliest completion date. Network diagrams are ideal for these situations:

FIGURE 7-3   Network diagrams demonstrate the relationship between tasks.

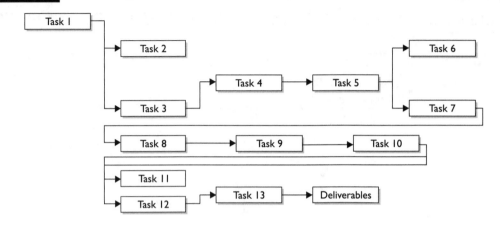

- **Detailed project planning**   In large projects that may span several months, or even years, a network diagram is essential as it can correlate each task in relation to the project scope. Through a network diagram, the project manager, management, and the project team can see the entire project plan from a high-level view, and then zoom in on a specific portion of the project plan.

- **Implementation tracking**   As tasks are completed on time, or over time, the number of time units used can accurately display the impact on dependent tasks within the project. If you use software to track the project implementation, the reflection of the impact is automated for you. Imagine a task that has four dependencies and the task is two weeks late in completion. The failure of the task to be completed on time now pushes the dependent tasks back by two weeks. A network diagram can illustrate this impact and allow the project manager to react to the changes by adjusting resources or other dependent tasks.

- **Contingency plans**   Network diagrams allow a project manager to play out "what if?" scenarios with any work unit within the project plan. A project manager can adjust units of time to see the impact of the work units on the entire project. For example, it may be obvious to see an impact on dependent tasks when a work unit is two weeks late, but what about units that are completed early? Imagine that pay incentives are based on project completion dates—a series of work units that each have one day shaved off their target completion times may have positive impacts on all future tasks.

■ **Resource control** A network diagram shows the flow of work and the impact of the finished tasks on the rest of the project. By utilizing the Gantt chart's assigned resources to a unit of work, a project manager can add or remove resources to a task to complete it faster or delay the completion. Resources can be both workers and physical objects such as a bandwidth, faster computers, and leased equipment.

Utilizing the Precedence Diagramming Method

You could start the PND by mapping out work units on a whiteboard, like you did for the WBS—which is a fine method. However, rather than creating a flat timeline of activity, project managers can use the Precedence Diagramming Method to create a fluid project structure. This sophisticated approach stems from the 1950s, when the original concept was called the *activity-on-the-arrow* (*AOA*) method. As you can see in Figure 7-4, each arrow represents a task in the project. The origin of the arrow is the "begin activity" sign, and the end of the arrow is the "end activity" sign.

As you can imagine, this representation of a project, especially a large project, could prove very cumbersome, as project managers can only have very simple relationships between tasks. What replaced the AOA method is the *activity-on-the-node* (*AON*) method. With the AON method, the focus is on the activities rather than on the start and end of activities.

This methodology of creating a network diagram is also called the *Precedence Diagramming Method* (*PDM*). PDM requires the project manager to evaluate each work unit and determine which tasks are its successors and which tasks are its predecessors. Once this information is obtained, you can begin to snap the pieces of the PDM puzzle together. You must give careful consideration to the placement of each task, as all tasks are connected even if they are scheduled to run concurrently.

Each unit of work in a network diagram using PDM is represented by a rectangle called the *activity node*. Predecessors are linked to successors by arrows, and are always upstream from successors, as Figure 7-5 demonstrates. One work unit can

FIGURE 7-4 The AOA method uses arrows to represent the start and end of activities.

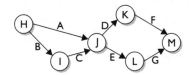

FIGURE 7-5

Arrows link
predecessor and
successor tasks
using AON.

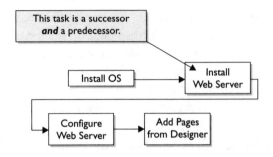

be both a successor and a predecessor; for example, the task to install and configure a web server may first require the installation of an operating system; only after the web server task is complete can the web pages the web server will host be added.

To begin creating the network diagram using PDM, a project manager will have to determine the order of tasks to be completed. Basically, a project manager asks, "What tasks must be completed before the next tasks can begin?" The activity list, which you derived from your WBS work packages, is what you are sequencing. You do not want activities that are too short in length to be useful. Based on your project, you may have work units that last days or weeks—generally not hours.

A rectangular box represents each individual task within the network diagram. As you add tasks to the network diagram, draw an arrow between tasks to connect them in the successor/predecessor relationship. As expected, the network diagram is read left to right, top to bottom. Each task within the diagram must have a successor and predecessor—except for the first and last task in the project. Once the diagram has been completed with successor and predecessor tasks, it is considered a "connected network." A project manager, or anyone involved in the project, can trace any activity through the network.

The relationship between activities is what allows a project to move forward or to wait for other tasks to complete. An accurate description between tasks is required for the project manager to analyze and make adjustments to each task in the network diagram. Figure 7-6 shows the dependency types you may have between tasks. There are four types of dependencies:

- **Finish to start (FS)** This relationship is the most common. It simply requires the predecessor task to complete before the successor task can begin. An example is installing the network cards before connecting PCs to the Internet.

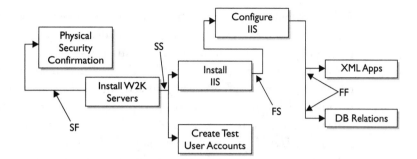

FIGURE 7-6

Dependencies
describe the
relationship
between tasks.

- **Start to start (SS)**   These tasks are usually closely related in nature and should be started but not necessarily completed at the same time. An example is planning for the physical implementation of a network and determining each network's IP addressing configurations. Each are closely related and can be done in tandem.

- **Finish to finish (FF)**   These tasks require that the predecessor task and the successor task be completed at the same time. An example is rolling out a new software package and finishing the user training sessions. While users are in the new training session, the new software should be installed and configured on their workstations by the time the training session ends.

- **Start to finish (SF)**   These rare tasks require that the predecessor doesn't begin until the successor finishes. You won't find yourself using this activity all that often. It's often used with just-in-time scheduling for inventory and manufacturing instances. For example, if you're opening a coffee shop, you'll want your inventory of coffee to be on hand as close as possible to when the construction of your shop is done. The coffee has to be ordered to officially open the shop, and the construction has to be done before you can open the doors. You'll need to time the order of coffee with the completion of the construction in order to open your doors on time without your merchandise spoiling—or tying up your cash flow in inventory that's not being sold.

Working with Project Constraints

A constraint is a boundary or limit based on the project. You've dealt with constraints before: a preset budget for your project, an inflexible deadline, limited availability of computer hardware, locating a resource with a specific skill. Constraints are any factors that can limit your options. They must be documented, their risks examined, and then the project manager must plan on how to meet the project objectives with the identified constraints.

When it comes to scheduling activities, you can also create constraints on the relationships you assign between your activities. For example, an FS relationship is constrained by the completion of the predecessor before the successor can begin. This is a natural constraint. This relationship between activities is sometimes called hard logic. *Hard logic* describes the matter-of-fact order of activities. For example, you must install the operating system before you install the application. On the other hand, *soft logic* is when the project manager decides to do tasks in a particular order based on experience, conditions in the project, time, or other reasons. This logic is also called discretionary logic. For example, it is a good practice to have completed all the coding before beginning the testing phase. It is not mandatory—you can unit test certain modules that are complete before all the coding is done—but it is preferred to have all the coding complete before any testing begins.

Date Constraints

Often in project management, projects have preset deadlines that require project managers to work backward from the assigned completion date. The problem is that the person establishing the deadline may not realize the work required to complete a project by that given date. Unfortunately, this is often the way project management works: you're assigned a deadline and then you have to figure out how to complete the tasks by that date.

Whenever possible, avoid using specific dates for tasks unless it is absolutely required. The reason that you should avoid date constraints is that you are signifying a certain task must happen on a specific date regardless of the completion of tasks before or after it. The best method of assigning tasks is to use a unit of time and then predict when the task may happen based on the best- and worst-case scenario for the predecessor tasks' completion. There are three types of date constraints:

- **No earlier than** This constraint specifies that a task may happen any time after a specific date, but not earlier than the given date.

- **No later than** This constraint is deadline orientated. The task must be completed by this date—or else.

■ **On this date** This constraint is the most time orientated. There is no margin for adjustment, as the task must be completed on this date, no sooner or later.

These constraints can be set on a task using your project management software.

Management Constraints

Management constraints are dependency relationships imposed because of a decision by management—this includes the project manager. For example, a project manager is overseeing the development of a web-based learning management system. The web site will allow students to register for classes, check grades, and pay for their tuition, all online. The e-commerce portion of the project and the database development portion of the project are scheduled to happen concurrently. Because of the unique relationship between the two tasks, the project manager decides to rearrange the work schedule so the database portion of the project must finish first and then the e-commerce portion of the project may begin. The project manager accomplishes this by changing the relationship between the tasks from start-to-start to finish-to-start. Now the database task must be completed before the development of the e-commerce portion. This is another example of soft logic.

Technical Constraints

Technical constraints stem from FS relationships. Most often within an IT project, tasks will be logically sequential to get from the start to the end. These constraints are the simplest and most likely the ones you'll find in a project. The technical constraints you may encounter when building your network diagram fall into two major categories:

■ **Discretionary constraints** These constraints allow the project manager to change the relationship between activities based on educated guesses. Imagine two tasks that are scheduled to run concurrently. Task A, the design on the web interface, must finish, however, before Task B, the development of the web application, is well under development. Because of the cost associated with the programmer, the project manager changes the relationship between the tasks from SS to FS. Now the first task must finish before the second task begins.

■ **Resource constraints**   A project manager may elect to schedule two tasks as FS rather than SS based on a limitation of a particular resource. For example, if you are managing a project that requires a C++ programmer for each task and you only have one programmer, then you will not be able to use SS relationships. The sequential tasks that require the programmer's talents will dictate that the relationship between tasks be FS.

Organizational Constraints

Within your organization there may be multiple projects that are loosely related. The completion of another project may be a key milestone for your own project to continue. Should another project within your organization be lagging, it can impact your own project's success. For example, a manufacturing company is upgrading its software to track the warehouse inventory. Your project is to develop a web application that allows clients to query for specific parts your company manufactures. The success of your project requires the warehouse inventory project be complete before your project can end. These relationships are entered into your network diagram as FS, with the origin activity representing the foreign project.

Building the Network Diagram

Because the network diagram can be a long and detailed map of the project, you probably don't want to enter it into a computer on the first draft. One of the best methods of building and implementing the network diagram is on a whiteboard utilizing sticky notes. A project manager, along with the project team, should begin by defining the origin work unit on a sticky note and then defining the project deliverables on another sticky note. On the left of the whiteboard, place the origin task, and on the right, place the deliverables. Now the project manager and the project team can use the activity list to identify the relationships between the units of work.

You and the team will continue to create the PND by adding activities in the order they should happen based on upstream and downstream activities. This can be a long process but it's necessary in order to complete the PND. Chances are you'll be moving activities around and changing their relationships—that's why the whiteboard and sticky notes are so nice.

Once the network diagram has been roughed out, you'll refer to your time estimates for each activity. You can use the WBS, PERT, and supporting details to reiterate the amount of time allotted for each task. Once the units of time have been recorded, you may then begin to assign the resources to the tasks. Use sticky notes to move and strategize the relationships between the tasks, connecting each task with an arrow and identifying the relationship between the tasks to be implemented. You will have to consider the availability of the resources to determine if tasks can truly run concurrently within a network diagram. In other words, you can't assign Susan the programmer to two activities that are supposed to happen at the same time.

Once the initial diagram is constructed, examine the activity lists and the WBS to determine if tasks or project deliverables have been omitted. If you find omissions, you will want to update the WBS and task list to reflect the work and deliverables you've found. Examine the relationships directly between tasks but also the relationships of tasks upstream and downstream. Review these relationships to see if you can edit any of the tasks to save time or resources. If so, rearrange the necessary tasks to update the diagram. A balance of acceptable risk and predictable outcome is required to discern the type of relationships between each task.

A project manager must also consider business cycles, holidays, and reasonable times for completing each task. For example, a company has sent new cellular modem cards to all of its employees working out of the office on laptops. Part of the deployment requests that the users in the field connect to the corporate LAN as soon as they receive their cellular cards. There must be a reasonable amount of time allotted between the cards being shipped to the users in the field and the confirmation that the cards have been received.

Finally, once the network diagram has been created, break for a day or two to allow the team to ponder any additional tasks or other considerations in the workflow prior to implementing the plan. When you reconvene to finalize the network diagram, consider the amount of risk you've allowed into the project by asking these questions:

- Are there adequate resources to complete the project?
- Are the time estimations accurate?
- Are there too many concurrent tasks?
- Are resources spread too thin?
- Is this a proven plan?
- Is the plan realistic?

Analyzing the Project Network Diagram

One of the most satisfying accomplishments in IT project management is to step back and, looking at the PND, follow the project conception through each task to the final deliverable of the project. Don't get too infatuated—this network diagram will likely change.

Now that the PND has been constructed, you can find the critical path. The *critical path* is the sequence of events that determine the project completion date. The critical path is the longest duration from project start to project completion. For example, imagine that you have created and analyzed your network diagram. Most likely there are multiple paths from project start to completion. One of the project paths will take longer than any of the other paths. This is the critical path. It's called the critical path because if any activities on it are delayed, the project completion date is also going to be late.

Calculating Project Slack

Given you know that activities on the critical path cannot be delayed, what about activities that are not on the critical path? Can these projects be delayed? Yes, usually they can—but there is a limit to the amount of time an activity not on the critical path can be delayed. This limit is called slack. Sometimes you might see slack as "float," but it's the same business. There are three different flavors of slack, or float:

- ■ **Free slack**   This is the total time a single activity can be delayed without delaying the early start of any successor activities.

- ■ **Total slack**   This is the total time an activity can be delayed without delaying project completion.

- ■ **Project slack**   This is the total time the project can be delayed without passing the customer expected completion date.

Most project managers allow their project management software to calculate the available slack on each activity, but it's really not that hard to do manually. To find the slack for each activity, you'll first find the earliest possible start date and the earliest possible finish date for each activity by completing what's called the "forward pass." Once you've got this info, you do just the reverse through the "backward pass"—you'll find the latest possible start and latest possible finish date for each activity. There are a few different methods for calculating project slack. Here's one of the most common approaches.

For this example, we'll be using a simple network diagram as seen in Figure 7-7. (You can print out Figure 7-7 from the CD if you'd like; it's in Adobe Acrobat format.) If you examine the network diagram, you'll see there are two simple paths to completion: ABDF and ACEF. The number over each node represents the duration of the activity. If you add up the duration of each path, you'll find the critical path— the longest path to completion. In this example, it's ACEF because it takes 17 days while ABDF only takes 15 days.

Now let's try the forward pass. (Again, there are different methods of completing this science, so don't be alarmed if you've been exposed to a different one). Follow these steps:

1. Make the Early Start (ES) for Activity A one because you'll start on Day one. Add the duration of the activity to the ES and you'll have three. Now this part trips some folks up: you'll subtract one day from the value of the ES and the task duration to arrive at the Early Finish (EF) of the activity. The reason is that the duration of Activity A is only two days, not three, right? In other words, if you start on Day one, you should have two days of work to get to Day two. The EF for Activity A is two.

2. The next activities are Activity B and Activity C. The ES for both of these will be three. Why? Because Day three is the next day in the schedule, the earliest possible day to begin either activity.

3. Let's finish the ES for activities B, D, and F first. The EF for Activity B is the ES, plus the duration, minus one, for an ES of five. The ES for Activity D is six and the EF for Activity D is eight. The ES for Activity F is 9 and the EF for Activity F is 15.

FIGURE 7-7

The longest path to completion is the critical path.

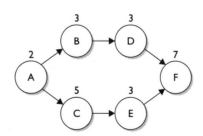

4. Now let's do activities C, E and F. The ES for Activity C is three and the EF is seven. The ES for Activity E is eight and the EF is ten. Activity F is the last activity in the project so you can bet it'll be on the critical path—with no slack. The ES for Activity F is actually 11. It's 11 because Activity F cannot begin until your project team completes Activity E. So, the EF for Activity F is actually 17. Figure 7-8 shows the project updated with all of the ES and EF dates.

Now that the forward pass has been completed, it's time to do the backward pass. It's a cinch; just follow these steps:

1. You'll begin with the last activity in the Network Diagram, Activity F, which has an EF of 17. You'll make the Late Finish (LF) the same as the EF value: 17. This is because Day 17 is the latest day the project can finish without being late.

2. The Late Start (LS) for Activity F is the LF value, minus the duration of the activity, plus one. Yes, plus one. Because you're going backward in the network you'll add one rather than subtract one. This accounts for the full day of work you have completed on the first activity and the last activity. So, Activity F has an LF value of 17, less the duration of seven, plus one, which equals an LS of 11. It's no coincidence that the EF and the LF have the same value of 17. It's also no coincidence that the ES and LS have the same value of 11. It is because this activity is on the critical path.

3. Next let's do activities D, B, and A. The LF for Activity D is ten—one day prior to the ES of Activity F's LS. You get the LS for Activity D by subtracting the duration of the activity, plus one, which equals eight. The LF for Activity B is seven and the LS for Activity is five. The LS for Activity A is, well, it's the first activity in the project. Do you think it'll have any float? Hey! You're right—it's on the critical path so we can skip it for now.

The ES and EF dates are found by completing the forward pass.

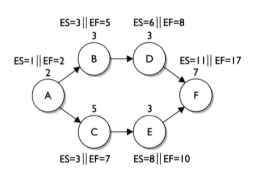

4. Let's go back and complete the backward pass for E, C, and A. The LF for Activity E is ten and the LS for Activity E is eight. The LF for Activity C is seven while its LS is three. The LF for Activity A is two and it's LS is one. Figure 7-9 shows the completed backward pass.

To finalize the process of finding slack, you'll subtract the LF from the EF and the ES from the LS on each activity. Wherever there's a zero, you have a task on the critical path; wherever there's a number, the activity has slack. In this example, activities B and D have two days of slack. Okay, technically they both don't have two days of slack; there's two days of slack on the whole project. Or you could say, Activity B and Activity D can each have one day of slack, or either day can have two days of slack. However you slice it, if either activity goes two days beyond its expected completion time this project is late.

Adjusting the Project Schedule

Once you've found the critical path information, you can then apply this time to a calendar and, after accounting for holidays and weekends, a target completion date can be predicted based on the project start date. Chances are the target completion date your network diagram predicts and the target completion date requested by management or your client won't be the same. The date that you have computed will typically be beyond the date management has requested. (Funny how it always seems to work out that way.)

What you will now have to do is adjust and readjust the critical path. This is known as *schedule compression*. By making adjustments to when tasks begin or by adding additional resources, you can complete the same work in less time.

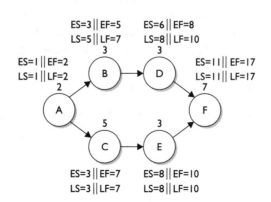

FIGURE 7-9

The backward pass reveals the LF and the LS.

There are four processes you can do to affect the flow of project schedule:

- **Fast tracking** This method allows activities to be done in parallel that would normally be done in sequence. For example, you may allow two phases of the project to overlap slightly where normally you'd have quality control events, walkthroughs, or other events scheduled before the second phase of the project would be allowed to begin. This approach usually increases project risk.

- **Crashing** Crashing allow the project manager to add more resources to effort-driven activities in an attempt to shorten their duration. For example, if you have to physically install 1,000 workstations and you've only eight people assigned to the task, it may take them months to complete. If you crash the project, you might assign 16 more people to this task to complete it in a matter of weeks. Crashing doesn't always work because some activities are a fixed duration and additional labor won't ensure the activities will finish faster. Crashing usually increases project costs because of the expense of the labor.

- **Lead time** Lead time is negative time because it brings activities closer together—even allowing them to overlap. For example, you may have to install a new network cable throughout a campus. Your schedule calls for all of the network cables to run before any PCs plug into the new network. To speed up the schedule, you elect to allow the activity to connect the PCs to the new network as soon as half of the new cables are ready. The first activity, to run the network cables, does not have to be complete for the second activity, connecting to the new network, to begin.

- **Lag time** Lag time is waiting time. It's often applied to activities where there must be an added duration between the tasks. For example, after installing a database, you have to wait four hours for all of the records from other databases in the network to recognize the database and synch with this database server. Lag time adds time to the project schedule.

To begin schedule compression, do the following:

- Analyze the critical path to move tasks earlier in the workflow—where possible.
- Consider relationships between tasks to change FS to SS.

- Identify tasks that require lag time and evaluate the predecessor task to move it earlier in the workflow.

- Consider any tasks and the level of acceptable risks by changing relationship types.

- Consider adding additional resources to tasks to shorten the duration required to complete tasks. (Not all tasks can be shortened with additional resources.)

Management Reserve

You and your project team will no doubt be tempted during the creation of each task to overstate the estimated amount of time for it to be completed. Don't yield to this temptation. Always reflect the accurate amount of time it should take to complete a task. You can use PERT's optimistic, pessimistic, and most likely approach if you'd like, but don't inflate the time required for each task to allow for a mistakes, rework, and late activities within the project.

The reason is explained in Parkinson's Law. Parkinson's Law states that work will expand to the fill amount of time allotted to it. In other words, if your project team says an activity will take them 24 hours to complete, but they know the work will probably only take 16 hours to complete, it'll magically take 24 hours. Really, it's no magic. When people overestimate their time to account for expected troubles, just-in-case scenarios, and other time-munching issues, they rarely take advantage of the time they've created for themselves. They'll find other work to complete or simply wait until the time they've reserved for issues has passed and then hop into the work and hope for perfection.

Think of your own experiences. How many times have you had some small task to complete but spent hours cleaning your desk, organizing your materials, and researching the best mode of attack rather than just hopping in and completing the assignment? But how do you work on the day before your vacation? You are able to complete considerably more work on that particular day because the tasks must be completed before you're able to escape.

The same experience will be transferred to your team if you allow them two generous weeks for a task that should typically only require one. Your team will quickly discover that it will take every moment of the two weeks to complete the task you've assigned them.

FIGURE 7-10

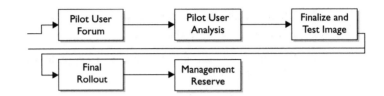

Management
reserve accounts
for task overruns.

Instead, what you should do is use management reserve. *Management reserve* is an artificial task that is added at the end of the project. The time allotted to the reserve is typically 10 to 15 percent of the total amount of time to complete all the tasks in a project. When a task runs over its allotted time, the overrun is applied to the management reserve at the end of the critical path rather than on each lagging task. Figure 7-10 demonstrates the benefit of using management reserve.

Management reserve allows a project manager to use percentages to see how the overall project is coming along. For example, if the project is only 40 percent complete but the management reserve is 65 percent used, then the project is in trouble if the remaining tasks follow the trend of the project thus far. You'll learn more about maintaining management reserve and dealing with late projects in Chapter 8.

Using Microsoft Project

Microsoft Project does have the ability to create a network project diagram. Your best approach, however, is still to create the network diagram as described in this chapter. Then, once the initial creation is complete, transfer the plan to Microsoft Project. As you make adjustments to your network diagram on the whiteboard, you can update the changes in Project to see their impact.

When you enter a task into Microsoft Project, you will assign constraints to the task to signify when its completion should occur. The nature of your project, your units of work, and the urgency of the task will determine the type of constraint you assign. Constraints in Microsoft Project are flexible, semiflexible, or inflexible:

- **Flexible constraints** These constraints do not have dates assigned to their activities and are only bound by their duration, and predecessor and successor activities. Use flexible constraints as much as possible.

- **Semiflexible constraints** These constraints do have date values associated with them but also require that the tasks begin or end by the specified date. Use these constraints sparingly.

- **Inflexible constraints** These constraints also have date values associated with them but are very rigid. Constraints that are inflexible require that activities happen on a specific date. Use these constraints very sparingly.

Here are the eight types of constraints you'll encounter:

- **As Soon As Possible (ASAP)** When you specify a task constraint of ASAP, Microsoft Project will schedule the associated task to occur as soon as it can. This is the default for all new tasks when assigning tasks from the start date. This constraint is flexible.

- **As Late As Possible (ALAP)** When you have a task with this flexible constraint, Microsoft Project will schedule the task to occur as late as possible without delaying dependent tasks. This is the default for all new tasks when scheduling tasks from the end date.

- **Start No Earlier Than (SNET)** A task assigned the SNET constraint will start on or after a specific date. This constraint is semiflexible.

- **Start No Later Than (SNLT)** This semiflexible constraint requires that a task begin by a specific date at the latest.

- **Finish No Earlier Than (FNET)** This constraint requires that a task be completed on or after a specified date. This constraint is semiflexible.

- **Finish No Later Than (FNLT)** This semiflexible constraint requires that a task be completed on or before this date.

- **Must Start On (MSO)** A task with this constraint must begin on a specific date. This constraint is inflexible.

- **Must Finish On (MFO)** This inflexible constraint indicates a deadline-orientated task. The task must be completed by a specific date.

FROM THE FIELD

Interview with Niral Modi

Name: Niral Modi
Title: Senior Project Manager, MBA
Company: Computer Discoveries Inc.
Years as an IT project manager: 5

Niral Modi is a Senior Project Manager for CDI, a software consulting company. He has worked on various consulting assignments with Fortune 1000 companies, like Motorola, Johnson Wax Professional, Sybase, and also small and medium-size companies, like First International Digital and 1internet, and helped them evaluate their IT strategy and manage various projects.

Q: When you are about to create a project schedule, what is the first thing you do?

A: The first thing a project manager should do is understand the functional requirements of the project, the reasons this project is being implemented, and what are the key things that would be a show stopper if not achieved. Prior to requirements validation, it is important to ensure that the project management infrastructure is in place and that all team members understand their roles and responsibilities. It is important that all team members have an understanding of the business case, scope, strategy, estimates, staffing requirements, and schedule in order to successfully complete the project. Activities for this phase include

- **Set up project infrastructure** Establish methods for tracking issues, questions, and assumptions. Document the roles and responsibilities for each of the team members.

- **Develop communication plan** Define communication types, frequency, and responsibilities for all project stakeholders.

- **Conduct kickoff meeting** Communicate the business case, scope, strategy, estimates, staffing requirements, and schedule to the project team. Project roles and responsibilities are also defined at this time.

- **Assess risk** Assess project risk and develop contingency plans to mitigate the identified risks.

FROM THE FIELD *(continued)*

Q: When creating a project schedule, how much room for variance in the schedule do you allow?

A: The amount of variance I allow in the project plan depends upon the kind of project being done. If the project ends before deadline, there will be certain functionalities you can add that will always make the client or your colleagues love the product. If there are only a few unknowns, then you want to include between 12 to 15 percent of variance for unknowns.

Q: How can a project manager know if the schedule she has created is realistic?

A: For experienced project managers, it comes out of their experience to evaluate a project and find out if it is achievable. For new project managers, talk to a few team members and see if the schedule of development is possible. From my experience, the more projects you manage, the easier it is to manage complex projects and develop a realistic project plan. Always use past experience to estimate what is possible for your team to do in the allocated time.

Q: What is the most difficult part of creating the project schedule?

A: The most difficult part of creating a project schedule is to assess the time required to finish each part of the project, and assign the resources to make sure that there is no lead time, and resources are not overallocated on certain days and don't have anything to do on other days. As such, a project schedule needs very close attention. People have historically neglected to spend the necessary time to perform this phase adequately. Regardless of whether you beg, borrow, buy, or build the final system, this is critical.

Q: When creating the project schedule, what method can a project manager use to determine project dependencies?

A: The method for project dependencies changes based on every project deliverable and requirement. I usually break the project into small pieces and write them all on a sheet of paper. I then print the calendar for the next few months. Each part of the project is then entered into the calendar based on the resource and the scheduled delivery. It is of utmost importance that you don't overallocate a resource.

Q: How much input should the project team have during the creation of the project schedule?

A: Once all the requirements are known, the project manager should have a meeting with the project team explaining the project and what is required from the project. The team members should be asked for their input while developing the schedule. I have seen projects fail because the project managers are aggressive when quoting time and then can't deliver.

Q: Do you use project manager software?

A: I usually use Microsoft Project for most of my project management. Every project manager can select different software based on their needs. But out of my own experience, although Project has a few things I don't like, it is by far the easiest tool. Also, many of my clients and colleagues use Project, so it is much easier to share files and export files to Excel for people who don't have Microsoft Project on their computers.

Q: What methods can a project manager use to inspire a team to perform under a tight project deadline?

A: I feel this is the most important skill that a project manager has to learn. You have to learn to inspire the team members to give their best and most to a project. There are different things I have tried and that have worked for me, such as Friday lunches with the team or a big party to celebrate the end of the project. Everyone has personal reasons to need time away from the technology—it may be they are sick of the project, need to go on a vacation, or just have to have some downtime. The trick is to work with the team members and give them the days off, but get them to work a few extra hours every day or work on a weekend to recoup the lost time. This way you improve the morale of the team members and they feel their needs are being understood.

Q: Are there any advantages to allowing teams to determine the tasks that must be completed in a certain order rather than a detailed plan from the project manager?

A: You should take the feedback from your team members on the order of the project tasks, but you have to make sure that you have the final say in the matter. It is key that your team members don't take you for a ride and adjust the project plan to meet their needs. So taking feedback is important, but it will only make sense when it is used in the right way. When you take feedback from your team, they feel good about the whole project, do an excellent job, and enhance the quality of the deliverables.

Q: What is the most difficult part of planning a long-term project?

A: There are a few things you need to be aware of when the project is long term: Make sure the team members are planning to be in the team until the project is over. In case a member has to leave, have at least a few days for knowledge transfer. Even if you are running on a tight schedule, make sure the new member is up to speed with the needs of the project. You should always have leeway for a few surprises to happen. Project managers should also have periodic updates for the client or department the deliverables are designed for. Without the periodic updates, the project may be going the wrong way from what the client envisions and when you realize the error, it may be too late to recover when it comes to time or the budget.

Q: What are the challenges of planning a short-term project?

A: In a short-term project, the project manager has to understand the needs of the client and be a functional as well as a technical resource. I have seen short-term projects go haywire because the project manager thought that the project was a piece of cake and didn't spend enough time to understand the needs of the client.

Q: What are some pitfalls a project manager should be aware of when assigning tasks to the project team members?

A: When assigning tasks for the team members, always make sure that they are familiar with what is required from them and they understand the functional requirements. Also make sure that they accept the time allocated to the finish of those tasks. In addition, ask team members about their schedules to make sure that there are no vacations or other time commitments that can take them away from the project.

Q: How flexible should a project plan be?

A: Project plans should be as flexible as possible. Unexpected things happen, and if you haven't accounted for them, chances are that you will not finish the project on time. Also be flexible to team members' needs, and understand their problems and work with them to resolve them. If you have accounted for the unexpected and have Plan B in place, chances of the project failing go much lower.

FROM THE FIELD *(continued)*

Q: Can you share an experience you had with a difficult project plan and the steps you took to overcome the difficulties?

A: I was working on a project with a client where more than 50 percent of the project deliverables were unknowns, and it was a fixed-fee-and-time project. The project was to develop a mini ERP system in a time span of four months. In case of a lot of unknowns, always try and get a quick-and-dirty prototype done. I worked with the clients to find out if this is what they were looking for. Before I started the project, I let the team members know that this would be a high-pressure project and the schedule would be extremely tight, so they should only join this team if they were ready for a lot of hard work.

Despite the project's tight timeline, I was flexible to the needs of the team. I worked with team members to resolve all the problems. One of them had an unexpected personal problem and had to leave work for four days. I worked with him and empathized with his trouble, but I also had to ask him to work longer hours and even weekends to recover the lost time, as every team member was essential to the project's success. Fortunately, everything worked out fine.

On this project, we also made a project web site for the client to come in and look at the development. We participated in a conference call every day to make sure that the development was going in the right direction. In addition, I met with the client team twice a week to brief them about the developments and the changes. There were certain requirements that changed in the last three weeks of the project completion, so we made a log of all the changes that would be required in the next phase of development. We also kept on testing the product, as each function was ready. This helped us make sure that each function that was developed was ready for delivery. Because of this, we didn't need a long testing period when the final product was ready.

Q: What advice do you have for aspiring project managers?

A: Always understand the needs of the client. Make sure you are flexible in the project plan. Keep on assessing the developments and compare with the plan to make sure everything is in order. Communicate to the team members and the clients about the problems and solutions. Always encourage your team about the developments. Always share the glory and be ready to take the pain. The project manager is the one who is responsible if the project fails.

CHAPTER SUMMARY

Putting together the project plan is a process of combining the creation of the Work Breakdown Structure and the assembly of your project team, and then mapping the project into a detailed structure of the work to be completed. As project manager, you realize the importance of the PND and determine how your project will be implemented. The project schedule will determine if the targeted date is reasonable with the resources available.

By using the Precedence Diagramming Method, you and your project team can map out the entire project from the start to end. Once the project network diagram has been created, schedule compression can be implemented, if needed, by designating tasks that may run concurrently or be completed faster with additional resources.

As the Project Network Diagram morphs from a simple timeline into an advanced diagram of events, you can use Microsoft Project to track changes, resources, and the impact of changes on a project's timeline. Microsoft Project allows a project manager to tweak constraints based on the type of activity involved and the sense of urgency for each task.

Creating the project plan is a type of alchemy. Adequate research, technical skills, and the ability to use logic and reason are required to create a solid, consistent plan for the project team, management, and the project manager to follow. Patience and vision are two attributes of a successful project manager. Just ask Noah.

CHAPTER QUIZ

1. A project schedule is comprised of which of the following? Choose all that apply:

   A. The network of all of the tasks within the project

   B. The assignment of resources

   C. The budget for the project

   D. The reflection of the WBS

2. What two things can a project manager do to reduce the amount of time required to complete a task?

   A. Partition the task into smaller work units.

   B. Increase the resources assigned to the task.

   C. Move the task out of the critical path.

   D. Move the task into the critical path.

3. Which of the following will add time to a project schedule?

   A. Lag

   B. Lead time

   C. Crashing

   D. Fast tracking

4. Of the following, what are two drawbacks of a Gantt chart?

   A. Gantt charts are difficult to create and adjust.

   B. Gantt charts do not display task details.

   C. Gantt charts do not reflect the shortest path to completion.

   D. Gantt charts work well with the WBS creation.

5. What is a Project Network Diagram?

   A. An expansion of the WBS

   B. An expansion of the Gantt chart

   C. A sequential mapping of the project work

   D. A topology of a project phase

6. Of the following, which one is not a true statement about network diagrams?

    A. Network diagrams allow for detailed project planning.

    B. Network diagrams allow for contingency plans.

    C. Network diagrams allow for implementation tracking.

    D. Network diagrams allow for detailed time management.

7. All of the following statements about slack are incorrect except for which one?

    A. Every project will have slack.

    B. Only complex projects will have slack.

    C. Slack is the amount of time an activity can be delayed without increasing the project costs.

    D. Slack is the amount of time an activity can be delayed without causing the project to be late.

8. What is the Precedence Diagramming Method (PDM)?

    A. PDM is a charting method that focuses on the start and end of each activity within a project.

    B. PDM is a charting method that focuses on each activity within a project rather than the start and end of activities.

    C. PDM focuses on only the successors of each task in a project.

    D. PDM starts at the deliverables and maps each dependent task back to the origin predecessor of the project.

9. What law states that work will expand to fill the amount of time allotted to it?

    A. Law of Diminishing Returns

    B. Moore's Law

    C. Parkinson's Law

    D. Murphy's Law

10. You are the project manager of a web server and web site upgrade. You have assigned Mark the task of creating the web pages and Janice the task of developing the web pages. Mark and Janice can work on their assigned tasks concurrently. What type of relationship do these tasks have?

    A. FS

    B. SS

    C. FF

    D. SF

11. Phil is the project manager of a network upgrade. All of the client workstations are to be replaced, and this task has been assigned to Steve, Harry, and Beth. Once the physical workstations are in place, Sam will release an automated script to deploy an operating system to each of the new workstations. What type of relationship best describes these two tasks?

  A. FS

  B. SS

  C. FF

  D. SF

12. When a project manager begins to create the network diagram, what type of relationship between all of the tasks would reduce any risk in the original plan?

  A. FS

  B. SS

  C. FF

  D. SF

13. Why should a project manager avoid assigning specific dates to tasks when at all possible during the creation of the network diagram?

  A. Dates cannot change, tasks can.

  B. Dates require the activity to happen at a specific time.

  C. Tasks assigned to dates do not consider successor tasks.

  D. Tasks assigned to dates do not consider both successor and predecessor tasks.

14. Elizabeth is the project manager for the development of a new database and a web application that will access the database. Originally, the creation of the database and a portion of the application development was scheduled to happen concurrently. Elizabeth felt, however, that the application development phase should not start until most of the database was created. What type of constraint is this?

  A. Discretionary constraint

  B. Experience constraint

  C. Resource constraint

  D. Organizational constraint

15. Why must lag times be scheduled between tasks in a Project Network Diagram?

  A. Lag times allow the team to take a break.

  B. Lag times reflect instances when task overruns are anticipated.

C. Lag times reflect weekends and holidays.

D. Lag times allow other events to be completed before successors tasks can begin.

CHAPTER EXERCISES

Exercise I

In this exercise, you will create a PND for a fictional company named Donaldson Investments and Holdings. You will be given the core information on the project and then create the diagram based on the information supplied. This is based on the WBS you examined in Chapter 5.

As you have learned, the creation of a Project Network Diagram can be a long and tedious process. If during this exercise you need some prompts to create the PND, you can refer to the Network Diagram Worksheet file on the CD-ROM. The worksheet has key tasks completed to help you develop the PND. To access the Network Diagram Worksheet, follow these steps:

1. Insert the IT Project Management CD-ROM into your CD-ROM drive.

2. Navigate to the Exercises and then the Chapter 7 folder.

3. Open the document named Network Diagram Worksheet.

4. Print the document.

The worksheet has key assignments completed to coach you through the creation of the diagram. If you would prefer not to use the worksheet to receive any coaching, you can create your own network diagram.

Scenario: Jennifer is the project manager for Donaldson Investment and Holdings. The project is an implementation of a new mail server and the mail clients on all of the workstations. Here is a WBS of the tasks to date. To organize your PND, begin by mapping out the network diagram by identifying the sequence of tasks and the relationship between tasks.

Task Name
Install Windows 2003 Server
Install Exchange Server
Configure Exchange Server
Link to other servers

Task Name
Create test user accounts in Active Directory
Set mailbox rules
Create client installation packages
Create Windows 2003 policies
Test policies
Develop installation procedures
Test installation procedures
Create CD image for remote access users
Test CD image
Host pilot users class
Create class workbook for training
Host pilot users training class (groups of ten)
Send image to pilot users
Hold pilot users forum to discuss usage
Analyze pilot user feedback
Finalize and test install image
Hold user training classes
Roll out based on attendance

Exercise 2

Now that you have completed the PND for this project on paper, you will now enter the project tasks into your Project Management Information System (PMIS). This exercise uses Microsoft Project as an example, but you can also enter the tasks into your favorite PMIS.

1. Open Microsoft Project and click the Network Diagram icon.

2. To begin generating your network diagram, click and drag your mouse to create a new task in the network diagram. Enter the name of the first task, **Install Windows 2003 Server**, and press TAB to move you through the various fields of the task you've entered. When you reach the duration field, indicate the task lasts two days by typing **2d**. Press ENTER.

3. Draw another task in the network diagram, label it **Create class workbook for training**, and specify the duration as **3w**.

4. Add the task **Install Exchange Server** and specify the duration as **3d**.

5. Add the task **Create Test User Accounts in Active Directory** and specify the duration as **1d**.

6. Now before adding the remainder of the tasks, you will create a link from the predecessor task Install Windows 2003 Server and the secondary tasks. Click the task Install Windows 2003 Server and drag to the task Install Exchange Server before releasing your mouse.

7. An arrow is created between the tasks to represent the relationship. Repeat the process to link from Install Windows 2003 Server to Create test user accounts in Active Directory. Note that the two tasks can be completed in unison after the installation of the Windows 2003 Servers.

8. Complete the network diagram based on the following information and your network diagram from Exercise 1. (If you have not completed Exercise 1 you can use the solution file named Completed Exercise One on the CD-ROM.)

Task Name	Duration
Configure Exchange Server	1d
Link to other servers	1d
Set mailbox rules	1d
Create client installation packages	2d
Create Windows 2003 policies	2d
Test policies	2d
Develop installation procedures	2d
Test installation procedures	2d
Create CD image for remote access users	1d
Test CD image	2d
Host pilot users training class (groups of ten)	3w
Send image to pilot users	1w
10 day lag	10d

Task Name	Duration
Hold pilot users forum to discuss usage	1d
Analyze pilot user feedback	2d
Finalize and test install image	3d
Hold user training classes	12w
Management reserve	12d
Image to users	12w

Exercise 3

In this exercise, you will change the relationships between tasks to reflect the dependency types using a Microsoft Project file named Exercise Three on the CD-ROM. If you have Microsoft Project installed, you can complete this exercise. Follow these directions to complete the exercise:

1. Open the file named Exercise Three in the CH7 folder on the CD-ROM.

2. The file reveals a network diagram for the Exchange upgrade project. On the task labeled Installing Windows 2003 Server, change the date to one month from today's date. Notice how the dates change throughout the entire project as a result.

3. Double-click the line between the task Installing Windows 2003 Server and the task Create class workbook for training. The Task Dependency dialog box opens.

4. Change the dependency type to SS to reflect that these tasks may both occur at once. Choose OK when finished. Notice how the dates of the tasks are updated throughout the project to reflect this change.

5. Double-click the link between the tasks Host pilot users class and Send image to pilot users. The plan is to send the application image to the pilot users as they take the class. These tasks can have an SS relationship to signify they can happen in unison. Change the relation to SS and click OK.

6. On the View bar, click the icon that represents the Gantt chart. As Microsoft Project is integrated through all of the views, the Gantt chart has been built in tandem with the network diagram chart.

7. Close the file. You do not have to save your changes.

QUIZ ANSWERS

1. **A, B, D.** A project schedule is the compilation of all of the tasks to be completed within a project and the assignment of resources, and should reflect the entries of the WBS. If you are using Microsoft Project, then you can streamline your efforts, as Microsoft Project will allow you to create the network diagram and work toward the WBS.

2. **A, B.** By partitioning a task into smaller work units, a project manager can allow the work units to overlap. A project manager can also add more resources, particularly team members, to a task to reduce the amount of time it takes to complete the task. Moving the task into or out of the critical path isn't really an option.

3. **A.** Lag time is waiting time. If a project manager adds lag time, the project schedule will expand.

4. **B, C.** Gantt charts do not display task details like a network diagram does. Gantt charts also do not reflect the short path to project completion. A network diagram is more powerful than a Gantt chart because it allows tasks to be moved and adjusted to participate in schedule compression.

5. **C.** A network diagram is a fluid mapping of the entire project, not just one phase. A network diagram is not an extension of the Gantt chart or the WBS.

6. **D.** Network diagrams do not allow for detailed time management. They do allow for some time planning, but usually only down to days or weeks—not hours and minutes. Network diagrams do allow for contingency plans, detailed planning, and implementation tracking.

7. **D.** Slack is the amount of time an activity's completion can be delayed without delaying the project end date.

8. **B.** PDM, Precedence Diagramming Method, focuses on the activities required within a project rather than the start and end of activities.

9. **C.** When project team members and project managers add time to their time estimates they'll likely succumb to Parkinson's Law: work expands to fill the time allotted to it.

10. **B.** These tasks can use SS dependency, which means "start to start." The FS dependency is the most common, which means "finish to start." The FF means the tasks must be "finish to finish" and the last dependency is "start to finish."

11. **A. FS.** Because the tasks involving the replacement of workstations must be completed before the script can run, the dependency used is FS, or "finish to start."

12. **A. FS.** To reduce practically all risk in the network diagram, all tasks can begin with FS relationships. This means that no task would begin until its predecessor had been completed. Once the diagram has been created, tasks can be rearranged to represent other relationships.

13. **D.** Tasks assigned to dates do not consider successor and predecessor tasks. This becomes a huge problem when upstream tasks are delayed by several days; the task assigned to a specific date does not change to reflect the changes of the tasks upstream. Whenever possible, do not assign tasks to a specific date. Examples include when a particular resource is available or a consultant is scheduled to be present.

14. **A.** Because Elizabeth had a "gut feeling" that the tasks should be changed to FS, it's a discretionary constraint. If the decision had been made on prior experience, it would have been an experience constraint. If the task needed to be delayed because of a resource, it would have been a resource constraint. An organization constraint is typically enforced when another project within the organization is delaying the success of the current project.

15. **D.** Lag times allow other events to be completed before successor tasks can begin. For example, a dependent task is to mail a survey to all of the network users. Before the successor task, analyzing the user surveys, can happen, there must be time allotted for the users to respond to the survey. It's not an actual task, but it still requires times within the diagram.

EXERCISE SOLUTIONS

on the
Cd-rom

Exercise 1
The network diagram solution can be found on the CD-ROM as the file Completed Exercise One in the CH7 folder.

Exercise 2
The solution to Exercise 2 is found on the CD-ROM in the CH7 folder. Open the Project document called Completed Exercise Two.

Exercise 3
The solution to Exercise 3 is found on the CD-ROM as the file Completed Exercise Three in the CH7 folder.

Chapter 8

Implementing the Project Plan

A t this point of your project, things should be getting very exciting. You've researched the project, planned for success, created (and survived) the budget process, and now you're ready to set your plan into action. Your team is eager to get moving on the project, and there is electricity in the air as all of your hard work is about to come to fruition. Don't break out the champagne yet. You can congratulate yourself for successfully completing a solid foundation for your project, but you're going to have to coach your team to follow the project plan through the implementation phase to have a real reason to celebrate.

In this portion of your project, your team will create the components defined in the Work Breakdown Structure (WBS) and follow the sequence of activities in the Project Network Diagram (PND). You will interact with your team members to ensure their successes as they complete the tasks. You'll create a Work Authorization System to allow work to continue based on work results. You'll add quality control mechanisms, and you'll continue to increase your communication among the project team and stakeholders. You'll be deeply involved with tracking the actual costs of the project and comparing them to the budgeted costs. Finally, you'll be tracking the implementation against your PND, cost, and time estimates and then implementing corrective actions as needed to keep the project on track and on budget. Of course, you'll document what's working on the project, what's not working, and other things you've learned in your Lessons Learned documentation.

This part of project management will test and challenge all of your planning, research, and ability to lead and react to situations that may impact your project completion. Keep your cool, analyze problems when they arise, and always remember that this project is yours to control, to complete, to savor.

Reviewing Assignments with the Project Team

An ideal project team will consist of people who are confident in their work, their abilities, and their commitment to the project. They will always complete their tasks on time, without flaw, and happily report to you that everything is perfect and on schedule. "In fact," they'll say, "we're a little ahead of schedule." Now let's step into the real world. Team members will be nervous about their duties. They won't always complete their tasks on time or without flaw. Team members may report to you that everything is fine when, in fact, it's far from that.

One of your responsibilities as the project manager will be to mold this team into a reliable, interdependent collection of professionals who can rely on each other, themselves, and you. Through regular team meetings, outings, and one-to-one conferences, you'll develop a working relationship with each member and learn how to motivate, inspire, and lead each individual. (Chapter 11 discusses leading a team in more detail.)

Focus on the Work

One message all project managers should convey to the project team members, but often don't, is to simply focus on their work, their tasks, and their responsibilities. If team members would ignore the superfluous activities of the project and hone in on what their responsibilities are, the project would scream along with few interruptions. Of course, this depends on the level of detail you have completed in the planning phase.

This is not to say that team members shouldn't be involved in project planning—they should! However, once the plan has been created, the team should just get to work, ignore the gossip and the details that don't involve them, and focus on their duties to complete their tasks. The planning phase is not, however, one that's completed and never returned to. Planning is an iterative process throughout the project. As issues and needs arise, which they will, the project shifts back into planning mode to discover the best response to issues and concerns that have happened within the project.

Part of planning is to find the most appropriate resource for each project task. The assignment of resources to tasks allows the team members to know what they have to do and when they need to do it. If team members could just ignore the activities that are not related to them, the attraction of other technology, and the world of office politics, what a fantastic team they'd make! As a project manager, you should directly encourage your team to focus on their individual tasks. Encourage them to focus on their duties and their commitment to completing their assignments, and ignore what anyone else may or may not be doing.

Like a machine, this team is collectively working toward deliverable results, but within the machine there are many moving parts to make the deliverable happen. Each component of the machine is responsible for only certain tasks; one component cannot do everything—and all components are required to make the machine work. The same is true within your project. The team is a collection of individuals who need to work together, but also have the ability to work independently as their tasks require it.

This doesn't mean that team members should not help each other with tasks because the work may not be assigned to their realm of responsibility. The goal is that team members know their responsibilities, focus on them, take pride in them, and complete them successfully. If other team members need help with tasks, the team should by all means be fluid enough to help a colleague and keep the project moving toward its completion.

Hosting a Project Status Meeting

Within your Communications Management Plan you'll define which people need what information, when they need it, and how they'll get the information. Communication can be both formal, like a report, and informal, like a hallway conversation. In project management, both methods of communication are needed. The type of communication you'll use should be appropriate for the message you send. In other words, communicate major decisions using formal means, such as reports, project plan updates, or memos.

When it comes to informal communications, project managers should be in close proximity to their project team. Managing a project where you and your project team are in separate buildings is not conducive to effective management. If you can be seated physically close to the project team, you should. This allows for informal meetings and conversation to pop up, and it lets you get involved with the team and really lead the work.

Regardless of where your office is, close to the team or in a different building, you will need to create a regular schedule to meet with your project team. Regular meetings, whether weekly, biweekly, or on your own custom schedule, will serve several purposes:

- Allows a team member to report on his activities
- Underscores the project vision
- Allows the team to resolve problems
- Allows the project manager to lead the team without hovering
- Creates a sense of ownership of the project
- Creates a sense of responsibility to the project for team members

To host a team meeting you need one thing: preparation. Create an agenda, even if it's a quick list of what needs to be discussed, and then follow it. Also, set a time limit for these meetings—and make it snappy. Perhaps the number one complaint among project teams is WOT (waste of time) meetings. For every meeting, your agenda should include at least these points:

- The objectives accomplished since the last team meeting
- Discussion of any situations impacting the entire team

- Acknowledgment of major team member accomplishments
- Overall project status—good or bad
- Pending risks, issues, and upcoming activities
- The objectives in queue before the next meeting

By starting with a review of the objectives of the past week, you are allowing team members to report on their activities and update the team on the state of the project. You are also allowing the team members to shine in front of their peers by reporting what tasks they have successfully completed. Don't be surprised if your team applauds when key events are finished.

Another aspect of having your team report what objectives were accomplished creates, again, a sense of responsibility. A team member who knows she'll have to report that an assignment was not completed on time in front of her peers may be inspired to complete the task. The goal is not to embarrass team members; it is a tactic to keep team members on schedule and committed to the project.

Should there be any outstanding issues left unresolved from the last meeting, for example the delivery of hardware, software, or other resources, the project manager, or the responsible party, should quickly update the team on the status. The issues discussed should only be those that affect the entire team.

If team members have completed a major challenge or task within the project plan, call attention to that in front of the entire team. Offering a public acknowledgment to the team members is simply giving credit where credit is due. Always acknowledge major completions and, when necessary, acknowledge team members who may not have major tasks but are doing a great job. This heartfelt thank-you is an excellent way to boost morale and show your team that you do care for them and their success—not just the project's. As Figure 8-1 depicts, team morale has a huge impact on the project's success. Remember, acknowledgments, thank-yous, and kudos are not something you can fake—develop a true sense of care and compassion for your team.

Next on your agenda should be a quick capsule of the overall status of the project. If the project is on target and moving along swimmingly, this is easy. However, if the project is lagging and the team members aren't completing their assignments, you need to let them know. Being a tyrant and reprimanding a group is not the goal. The goal is to make adjustments to get the team back on track and focused on their duties, and to avoid a pile-up of work and a completion date that has to change. Don't be shy in expressing your discontent; just use tact and express your passion for the success of the team.

You'll also want to review risks that have passed, been mitigated, or are pending within the project. Risk management calls for a review of risks and a reminder to

The morale
of the team
can impact
the project's
success.

the risk owners of triggers that may signal a risk is coming into play. You're not micromanaging the project team over pending risks, but rather bringing everyone's attention to the identified risks, making them aware of the risk response plans you've created, and assigning ownership to the project team.

Finally, hold a round-table discussion against your PND to review assignments in the queue for the upcoming week or weeks. Ideally, you should have each team member verify what tasks he is working on before the next scheduled meeting. This does not need to be a long, drawn-out discussion, just a confirmation of duties. It is also a way to ensure this team meeting ends with your team members knowing what tasks are required of them before they meet with you again.

The foundation for successfully implementing an IT project is not the project plan, the technology being implemented, or the speed of the network, processor, or disk. The foundation is the ability of the team to honestly communicate to the project manager how the actual work is going, the challenges the members are facing, and how they've reacted to those challenges. That type of communication is going to come from their ability to trust you. You have to earn that trust, and hopefully, if you've involved your team members in the planning phases and kept them informed of how the project will develop, you will have it.

Tracking Progress

There are several reasons why you must have a formal process for tracking progress. At the top of the list of reasons: tracking project progress will help you make adjustments and tweaks to the implementation plan, should you need to. Imagine a long-term project that has several milestones and teams dispersed throughout the world. A weekly meeting is not going to be a feasible method to get a grasp on the project status.

You will need to develop an internal process for your team to report completed tasks so that you can reflect the project progress in an electronic form and analyze the team's work, the budget, and the days until completion. This also allows you to accurately report to management how the project is moving along.

Creating a Reporting Process

You should create a mechanism that allows your team to report the status on assigned tasks on a regular schedule. In some organizations, this is a formal Work Authorization System. This system requires project team members to report activities completed with given metrics so that downstream activities can begin. A Project Management Information Systems (PMIS) system can streamline this process— so long as the quality and verification of the work actually being completed exists.

Some project managers like team members to report as each milestone is reached, while others prefer weekly status reports on the tasks completed over the last seven days. Whichever method you choose, or develop, it is important that your collection of data be on a consistent schedule. Although it's not well advised, you can start a project and collect status reports weekly one month and then biweekly the next. Develop a schedule that works best for you and fits the timings of the project and stick with it. Of course, you'll document this schedule of status reporting in your Communications Management Plan.

Determine the format for how work should be reported. Ideally, you should base this on the number of hours or days assigned to the task. For example, during the activity duration estimating process, say you allot 56 hours for testing a new application and assign Rick to the task. When Rick reports his progress, he should indicate the number of hours into the testing phase, in addition to a percentage of the total completed work Rick believes is done. As Rick moves closer to 56 hours, he should be moving closer to 100 percent completion of the task. Figure 8-2 shows the impact of exceeded hours on the budget and the overall time of the project duration. The actual collection of work completed will allow you to see how the progress is going and to make adjustments to the project schedule to keep things on track.

When problems arise in the implementation phase, the number of hours assigned to a task will no doubt increase. For example, Rick's testing of the new application is taking longer than the 56 hours assigned to the task because of the discovery of a hardware conflict. Based on your communication with Rick, through your regular meetings, and the hours reported by Rick through your reporting process, you should be able to quickly ascertain if more hours will be required for the testing activity. In other words, it shouldn't be a surprise when Rick reports he'll need some more time to complete his task.

Tasks that exceed their durations impact both the budget and the project.

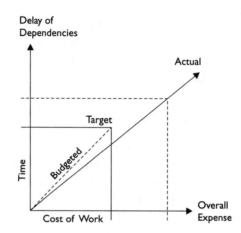

To react to this problem, you need to analyze how additional hours will impact the following:

- Dependent tasks in the PND
- Other, nondependent tasks in the PND that Rick has been assigned to
- The critical path
- The budget
- The project completion date
- The management reserve
- Additional resources
- Risks

To resolve a problem, analyze each of the facets of the project plan impacted by the new requirement for additional time. If dependent tasks are being held up by the problem, you need to find a solution to resolve the problem as quickly as possible. Generally this means you'll have to do one or more of the following:

Assign Additional Resources   When a task is delaying dependencies and needs additional time to resolve an issue, assign additional resources to the task, such as team members or consultants, to reduce the amount of time required. In theory, assigning new resources to a task should reduce the amount of time required for the task to complete. In reality, this is not always the case. For example, when installing an operating system that takes one hour to install, assigning two team

Chapter 8: Implementing the Project Plan **289**

members to the task doesn't mean that the installation procedure will only take 30 minutes. These activities are fixed-duration as opposed to activities that are effort-driven. In some instances, however, assigning an individual who is more experienced in the technology may cost more per hour (as in a consultant), but that person can finish the task in less time, saving overall costs and preventing the delay of dependent tasks.

Invoke Management Reserve   Recall that management reserve is a final task in the critical path of the PND. It is an artificial task that is a generally 10 to 15 percent of the total amount of time allotted for all tasks. When tasks exceed their allotted time, you assign the overrun to the management reserve task. For example, Rick is testing the software and will overrun the allotted time by 24 hours. A project manager could assign the 24 hours toward the completion of the management reserve and allow the critical path to continue as planned—assuming there are not other constraints affected by the delay of the activity.

You can also use a combination of additional resources and management reserve. For example, assigning an additional team member to assist Rick may reduce the time overrun from 24 hours to 16 hours. The 16 hours would then be applied to management reserve.

Reassign the Work Unit   Finally, you can choose to reassign the task to someone more qualified in the procedure. If Rick has exasperated himself and cannot resolve the issue with the software, then you may elect to hire a consultant or assign another team member to the task. The result of this solution is generally less risk of additional hours spent by Rick, but additional financial costs applied to the budget, as Figure 8-3 shows.

Status Collecting Tools

As a project manager, you may not always have the time to chat with each team member each week to get a verbal confirmation on the progress of each task. You will need a process to streamline the collection of hard numbers on the hours and

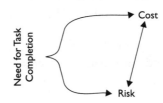

FIGURE 8-3

As risk is reduced, cost may increase.

percentages of the work completed. There are several methods you can use to collect this information from your team:

- **E-mail** A simple solution is to have your team members e-mail the hours on the work they've completed on their assigned task. This simple solution is not very automated, but at a minimum it allows for easy collection and accessible reporting for all team members. Of course, you'd then have to transfer the information into Microsoft Project, Excel, or another project management software program.

- **Spreadsheets** A slightly more advanced method to collect and compute project status is through a weekly spreadsheet each team member would complete to report the tasks that person has been working on. You could create a template that lists the tasks, allotted hours, and hours actually worked on the tasks, and include an area for any comments from the team member. Once you receive the spreadsheet, electronically of course, you can have macros and formulas retrieve the team member's information and dovetail it into a master spreadsheet.

- **Web forms** An aggressive approach is to create a web-based reporting system that would allow team members to report their activities and the hours committed to each via a web page form. The submitted form, via a script or ASP page, would automatically calculate percentages of work, overruns, and impact on the critical path. This would be ideal for a geographically dispersed team.

- **Microsoft Project** Any of the preceding methods can be used in conjunction with Microsoft Project. Microsoft Project supports collaboration via e-mail, web interfaces, and other applications such as Excel. If you are using Microsoft Project from the onset of your project, you will have created the WBS, the Gantt chart, and the PND within the application. Calculating task completions, overruns, and assignments of additional resources is very easy to do with Project.

- **Microsoft Project Server** Microsoft Project Server is a server-based product to Microsoft Project that allows for true collaboration between the project manager and the project team via an intranet. Microsoft Project Server can automate the submission for task reports—and the request of task updates from team members. This solution is ideal for small or large projects.

Whichever method you choose or develop for your project, it is imperative that you create and document a detailed schedule for collecting project status. You must have periodic project updates, or the project will grow stale, you'll miss opportunities to make adjustments to prevent overruns, and team members may lag behind on tasks. A consistent, persistent project manager is needed to keep a project team dedicated to tasks and collect information about the completion of each task.

Tracking Financial Obligations

In addition to collecting information on the status of tasks from your team members, you will also have a responsibility to collect information on the financial aspect of your project. You will need, and generally be required, to meet with your project sponsor to report the status of the cost of the project. When variances exist, you'll likely have to document these variances in a Cost Variance Report. This report explains the variance, the cause of the variance, and the impact on the project's success. You will have to be able to report on a regular schedule the following items:

- The amount of finances spent on the project to date
- Any cost variances
- Actual costs versus the budgeted costs
- Value of work performed
- Cost variances and offset
- Suggestions, when necessary, to reduce the cost of resources

Controlling Finances

Your organization probably already has set processes for how requests for payments, purchase orders, and payment on invoices are handled. If you are not familiar with the internal flow of paperwork, the approval of funds dispersed, or the procedure to supply purchase orders versus payment on invoices, speak with your project sponsor or company comptroller, who'll be happy to give you an education on the process.

In addition to just knowing where to route papers and whom to call when invoices are due, you'll need a formal approach to tracking and analyzing the actual costs. You can use a number of ways to create a system of collecting this information, though Microsoft Excel and Microsoft Project are two of the best tools available to project managers. In addition, you'll need organization and a regular schedule to update the expenses on your project.

Here are some terms you'll need to be familiar with to track and compute your project's finances:

- **Budget at Completion (BAC)**   The amount of money budgeted for your project prior to the start of the project implementation phase. This is the expected cost of the project.

- **Actual Costs (AC)**   The amount of money actually incurred by the project to date.

- **Cost Variance (CV)**   The difference in the amount of budgeted expense and the actual expense. A negative variance means that more money was spent on the service or goods than what was budgeted for it.

- **Earned Value (EV)**   The value of the work performed. Earned value is a dollar amount assigned to the value or worth of the work performed by the project team or vendors. The percentage of the work completed allows the project manager to compute the amount of the Earned Value for the work unit. Earned value can be calculated a few different ways, but the most accessible formula is simply EV=% of work complete BAC. For example, if the project's BAC is $200,000 and the work is 10 percent complete, the EV is $20,000. More on Earned Value in a moment.

- **Qualitative value**   A successful project will produce attributes that are not easily tracked, such as improved customer service, improved quality, and better process to complete tasks within the organization. You'll need metrics in place to measure these nondescript terms.

Tracking Actual Costs

Tracking the actual cost of the project is done by collecting the amount charged on invoices from vendors and consultants, and the dollar amount assigned to the team members' hours or the tasks they are completing. The ongoing sum of this collection is the actual cost of the project. This includes rework due to lack of quality, waste from materials, and purchased time from consultants, subject matter experts, or vendors.

The invoices you receive from vendors will be, obviously, a result of the goods or services rendered. The deliverables (service or goods) stem from a commitment document—which is a generic way of referring to a contract, a purchase order, or letter of intent. This leads to the committed cost. A *committed cost* is the amount of money approved and assigned to a portion, or the entirety, of a project. On a regular schedule, you apply the committed cost to the actual cost. As Figure 8-4 demonstrates, the process of applying the committed cost to the actual cost should result in a balance based on the original budget creation.

The comparison of the actual cost and the committed cost should reflect on the cumulative budget cost for the entire project. If there are inconsistencies, a line item comparison of the goods and services delivered against the cumulative budget may be required. Discrepancies between actual goods and the committed cost may arise from flux in hardware prices, additional services or features added, or an error on behalf of the vendor (at least you can call it an error). Refer to your contract for details on price overruns.

The key to controlling the finances within your project is to safeguard your budget and react to cost variances as soon as they appear. This requires a routine to confirm the cost of goods or services delivered and the cumulative budgeted costs. You can automate this procedure within Microsoft Excel and Microsoft Project.

When cost variances happen, and sooner or later they will, you will need a plan to analyze the costs and see what offsets may be made to control the total actual costs for the project. In other words, spending $5,000 for a consultant's time that was not planned for will leave your budget $5,000 in the red. (*In the red* means a negative balance. *In the black* means a positive balance.) You will either have to find a solution of how costs may be reduced or approach management for additional funding.

Your first approach is to examine the budget to see how the extra expense can be reduced. You can reduce expenses by

■ Using less expensive resources

■ Assigning additional resources to a task to complete it sooner and reduce its overall labor costs.

■ Arranging the PND so tasks are SS rather than FS

■ Reducing the cost value allotted to the management reserve

FIGURE 8-4

The committed cost and actual cost should balance.

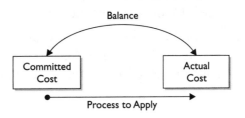

Determining Earned Value

Earned Value is an excellent system to test, in an ongoing process, if the work completed on a project is in alignment with the budgeted costs for a project. Earned Value is a measure for project performance. This approach to financial management is ideal for hourly workers such as consultants, application developers, and resources that have a fixed hourly rate.

Earned value project management evolved from the early 1900s from the factory floors. Industrial engineers created a formula to predict the value of a factory. Their formula has three variables: earned standards (what the factory actually produced), the accumulative costs incurred, and the original budgeted costs. To use the formula, the engineers took the earned standards number and compared it to the actual costs amount. Then they compared the earned standards with their planned goals for the factory output.

The comparison of values allowed the engineers to predict the profitability for a company based on the output and costs of the workers and machines within the factories. Based on these figures, changes could be made to streamline production, address actual costs, or determine a plan of action for a less-than-profitable output.

To apply this formula to today's world, a project manager needs to first have completed all of the planning stages. Specifically, the project manager must have the WBS completed with accurate predictions of the amount of time required for each of the work packages. While some of the time required may be little more than estimates, there must be a serious attack on calculating time for each work unit, as addressed in Chapter 5. Without an accurate account of time for each task within a project, Earned Value is not reliable because it compares the current output with the predicted output.

Earned Value Management (EVM) has a few fundamental values:

- **Planned Value (PV)** Planned Value is how much the project should cost to get to a specific point in the schedule. For example, if a project has a budget of \$100,000 and month six represents 50 percent of the project work, the PV for month six is \$50,000. Planned Value used to be known as the Budgeted Cost of Work Schedule (BCWS).

- **Earned Value (EV)** Earned Value is representative of the work completed to date regardless of how long it took to accomplish it. For example, if a project has a budget of \$100,000 and the work completed to date represents

25 percent of the entire project work, its EV is $25,000. Earned Value used to be known as the Budgeted Cost of Work Performed (BCWP).

■ **Actual Costs (AC)** Actual Costs is the actual amount of monies the project has required to date. For example, if a project has a budget of $100,000 and $35,000 has been spent on the project to date, the AC of the project would be $35,000.

■ **Cost Variance (CV)** A Cost Variance occurs when the actual cost of the project work is more than the EV. For example, your EV is calculated to be $25,000, but you had to spend $35,000 to get there.

■ **Schedule variance (SV)** A Schedule Variance occurs when the EV is less than the PV. For example, the project is supposed to be worth $75,000 in month six; however, at month six your EV is only $45,000. You've got a whopping SV of $30,000.

To implement Earned Value Management, the project manager collects the status of the computed percentage of tasks completed. For example, as team members report their status of hours applied to their assigned duties, your project management software can report a percentage of the task completed. Each work unit that has a predicted number of hours can be assigned a dollar amount as well. For example, if Marcy the programmer needs 36 hours to reach a particular milestone, and her hourly rate is $130, the dollar amount assigned to the work is $4680.

If Marcy has completed 12 hours of the work, and is on schedule now at a third of completion, the earned value is 33.33 percent of $4680 (the total cost of the work unit), which is $1560. However, if Marcy has completed 12 hours of the work, but reports that only 20 percent of the project is completed, the earned value is now out of sync with budgeted costs. The cost of the work unit has just risen to $7800 if Marcy stays on this schedule of production.

The primary benefit of predicting Earned Value is that a project manager can predict if the project is going to be in financial trouble early on in the implementation phase, as Figure 8-5 demonstrates. Unfortunately, many IT project managers simply do not take the time necessary to predict the Earned Value of their project as they implement it. It is not a hard process and should be, quite frankly, mandatory to keep expense in alignment.

Let's take a look at the EV formula in action. This example is of a project that has a budget of $250,00. The project is 15 percent complete, but it should be 20 percent

Earned Value
can predict if
a project will
be financially
strapped.

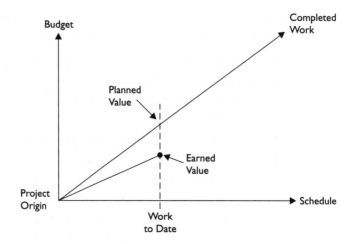

complete by this point in the calendar. In addition, the project manager has had to spend $43,000 of his budget just to get to this point in the project:

Term	Value	Definition
Budget at Completion (BAC)	$250,000	This is the expected cost of the project.
Percent complete	15 percent	The actual percentage of the work completed as reported by the project team.
Earned Value (EV)	$37,500	This is simply 15 percent of the BAC.
Planned Value (PV)	$50,000	The Planned Value is what the project work should be worth by this point in the project.
Actual Costs (AC)	$43,000	The Actual Costs reflect the amount of funds the project manager had to spend to get to this point in the project.
Cost Variance (CV)	$5,500	This is found by subtracting the AC from the EV. This project is off budget.
Schedule Variance (SV)	$12,500	This is found by subtracting the PV from the EV. This project is off schedule.

On the CD-ROM, in the CH8 folder you will find an Excel file named EVWorksheet that you can use to calculate your own earned averages for your projects. You will be working more with computing Earned Values in an upcoming exercise.

Calculating the Cost Performance Index

The Cost Performance Index (CPI) is a reflection of the amount of actual cumulative dollars spent on a project's work and how close that value is to the predicted budgeted amount.

For example, as Figure 8-6 depicts, a total network upgrade project has a budget at completion of $209,300 , and to date the project has spent $34,500 on Actual Costs. Based on the percentage of the completed project, which is 15 percent, the EV is $31,395. The Planned Value, however, is $ 36,000. The project also has a CV of $3,105.

To compute the CPI for this project, the Earned Value, $31,395, is divided by the Actual Costs, $34,500. This results in .91, which means the project is 9 percent off the target rate of spending for this stage in the project. The project manager can use this information to reschedule resources, adjust schedules, reassign tasks, and, if worse comes to worse, ask for additional funding.

Calculating the Scheduled Performance Index

The Scheduled Performance Index (SPI) is a formula to calculate the ratio of the actual work performed versus the work planned. The SPI is an efficiency rating of the work completed over a given amount of time. It is not a dollar amount, but rather a percentage of how closely the completed work is to the predicted work. The formula to calculate the SPI is fairly simple, as Figure 8-7 shows.

FIGURE 8-6

CPI reflects how closely the project is following the budget.

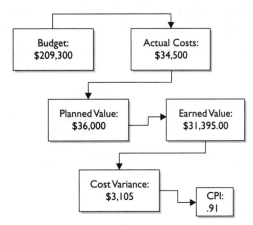

FIGURE 8-7

$$\text{SPI}= \frac{\text{Earned Value}}{\text{Planned Value}}$$

SPI is the ratio of the work planned and actual work performed.

If the result of your formula is 1, you are on schedule. If the result is less than 1, you are behind schedule. Of course, if the result is greater than 1, you are ahead of schedule. For example, if the EV is $18,887 and the PV is $20,875, the SPI is .90, which is less than one, so this project is not on schedule.

Calculating the To-Complete Performance Index

Once you've calculated the SPI, and you realize your project may be late, your first thought is, "How can we get back on schedule?" Okay, that's not your first thought, but pretend it is.

To predict how much harder you and your project team will need to work to finish the project on time and on schedule, you'll need to calculate the TCPI, which stands for *To-Complete Performance Index*. At the end of the formula, which is shown in Figure 8-8, if the number is greater than 1, you'll have to buckle down and work harder. If the result is 1 or less, breath a sigh of relief, you can make it on your current schedule.

To put the formula in action, assume the BAC is $75,000 and the EV is $5000. The Estimated at Completion (EAC) is $75,000 and the AC is $7500. This formula would read TCPI=(75000-5000)/(75000-7500) and equate to 103.7 percent. Which means, in English, you and your team will have to work 3.7 percent harder than originally planned to finish on time and on budget; basically, you're in a little bit of trouble, but not much. You'll likely need a little bit more time, more money, or both.

FIGURE 8-8

Numerator is how much is left in the budget.

$$\text{TCPI}= \frac{\text{Budget} - \text{Earned Value}}{\text{EAC-AC}}$$

TCPI is a formula to predict the ability of a project to stay on track.

EAC is the Estimated Cost at Completion.

FROM THE FIELD

Interview with Jason Duigou

Name: Jason D. Duigou

Title and certifications: IT Administration Team Leader; Lotus Notes Principle CLP Administration; Lotus Notes Principle CLP Development; MCSE

Years as an IT project manager: 4

Jason Duigou is a project manager for a leading Fortune 500 company. During his 12 years of experience in information technology, his previous positions included director of operations for a consulting firm; manager of information systems at a graphics company; senior systems analyst; and freelance consultant. Jason stays actively involved with local, national, and international IT groups by participating in shared learning conferences, seminars, and trade shows. Jason also volunteers his time teaching the youth and single parents in his community by demystifying technology and helping them understand how it can apply to their everyday lives.

Q: What is the most important thing a project manager can do when starting the project implementation phase?

A: Review the implementation plan with all teams, internal and external, to ensure alignment, and provide a clear understanding of the objectives, roles, and responsibilities of all resources during the project. Verify that all questions regarding the plan have been addressed before the implementation.

Q: How much supervision should a project team require from the project manager on any given project?

A: It is the project manager's responsibility to ensure that continual communication throughout the project is achieved. The project manager needs to drive the project by requiring each team's representatives to meet at regular intervals to monitor progress, timelines, costs, and dependencies. Lack of supervision by a project manager can cause the teams to jeopardize the overall success of the project.

Q: Do projects always go perfectly to plan?

A: No. There are always unknown variables that may come into play. Resources are subject to change during the project, company priorities may change, and so on. One example: a component of a project was awarded to an outside contract firm. Midway through the project, the vendor ran into financial difficulty, resulting in a loss of those resources. As a result, resources had to be reassigned to the team from other sources, causing a delay during this phase of the project.

Q: What is the most difficult part of implementing a project?

A: Aligning all the resources to achieve effective results within the time specified for the project. The project manager needs to be fully aware of the progress of each team at any given time in order to be completely effective.

Q: What processes should be in place for the team members to report their successes, or failures, on project tasks?

A: Many processes and tools may be used. It comes down to what works most effectively for the team members and their relationship to one another. A close-knit group can simply gather and give regular reports. Large, virtual teams separated by geography and radically different time zones can present communication challenges. In this case, shared electronic project management is most practical. Tools that are accessible via browser over secure connections provide the greatest flexibility, since they do not require specific software to reside on the local PC. Such tools need to have "digital dashboards" to quickly display and monitor the progress of all units and dependencies at any given time. Often the tools include collaborative discussion, shared information repositories, and all project details including timelines. Other enhanced features such as auto-notification and alerts based on roles and assignments are beneficial as well.

Q: Do you use a software program to track team progress?

A: For small-scale projects, I use the commercially available products such as MS Project. For larger collaborative initiatives, I use a series of customized tools that are accessible via browser over a secure extranet connection. This provides the greatest flexibility since it does not require specific software to reside on the local PC.

Q: How can a project manager successfully track the budget and expenses in a large, multiphased implementation?

A: The project manager must have the right tools for the job to provide dynamic data at any given point in time. This enables the project manager to proactively monitor the project including budget and expenses as they are reported. This offers the option to throttle resources forward or backward as necessary.

Continual communication and commitment on the part of each unit or resource is absolutely necessary in order for the data to be current and accurate. Without such tools and communication, the project manager risks being blindsided at some point during the project by resource deficiencies.

Q: What methods can a project manager use to inspire a team to perform under a tight project implementation?

A: Ongoing reward and recognition is crucial in order to motivate a team, especially when faced with common challenges such as time, resources, or money. First of all, it is important to share lessons learned from previous project implementations to help guide the team in approaching tasks in the most efficient manner to avoid common pitfalls. Next, you need to recognize or offer praise when teams exceed expectations. Speed, quality, and value should always be rewarded via peer or formal recognition methods. This can happen when a time-saving or money-saving event has occurred. It is important to highlight these events whenever possible. The project manager should not overlook recognition, whether formal or informal. Recognition drives motivation and the project, and everyone involved can reap the rewards as well.

Q: What methods do you use to resolve team disagreements once the project is in the implementation phase?

A: It is important to capture the rationale around each decision point made during a project. You need to also continually elicit feedback from each member on the team during this process and provide continual updates and communication to assure everyone is aligned and focused on the same goal. Disagreements are often caused by miscommunication or lack of input from a particular unit on the team, or even at the introduction of a new resource. At that point, you need to evaluate the feedback by placing it into the proper perspective, which is done by referring to the decision point at a high level. This enables the team to measure the input against a baseline of information. The expectation should be set that the team needs to present alternate ideas with their arguments that allow the team to focus on possible solutions instead of stalling on an unfocused debate.

Q: What is the most difficult part of implementing a long-term project?

A: A team can lack focus, motivation, and direction if active participation and communication wanes.

Q: What are the challenges of implementing a short-term project?

A: Short-term projects require a team to work effectively together in order to achieve optimum results in a short time. Well-defined project management processes along with the necessary project tools need to be readily available in order to jumpstart a project as quickly as possible.

Q: What are the advantages, or disadvantages, to contracting the project implementation out to an IT integrator?

A: If you have limited resources, contracting a project is the ideal way to achieve the desired results. There can be disadvantages if this type of relationship is new or the IT integrator or its resources are not reputable.

Q: What are some pitfalls new project managers may encounter when they start to implement a new project?

A: New project managers need to thoroughly plan and elicit input from other project managers, subject matter experts, or "lessons learned" documentation before diving head first into a project. Project managers need to stay actively engaged in all phases of the project and provide clear, continual communication. They must also keep their finger on the pulse of the project at all times. Without clear direction, communication, and feedback, a team can waver, resulting in an inefficient project and a frustrated project manager.

Q: Can you share an experience with a difficult project implementation and how you finished the project?

A: One particular project involved a high-impact deployment of a software package that had to be delivered to every employee in a global enterprise. The project was severely hampered when significant issues were uncovered with the software package. Steps were taken to prioritize and triage these issues with the vendor. The project was modified to allow for the extended timeline and resources as necessary. By proactively monitoring the progress of the project, we were able to identify, diagnose, and report the issues in a timely and efficient manner. Following the partnership with the vendor, the product issues were corrected, and the project was completed successfully.

FROM THE FIELD (*continued*)

Q: What advice do you have for aspiring project managers?

A: Learn from the successes and failures of other projects. Peers and mentors can provide a wealth of information, often highlighting issues not taken into consideration. Communication is the key! Begin building your project manager network. Learn all you can, and then share what you have learned with others. Your learning point may help another project manager avoid pitfalls and costly mistakes.

CHAPTER SUMMARY

As the project manager, you are responsible for all facets of the project planning and implementation. If you've built a solid foundation, and surely you have, the implementation will follow your Work Breakdown Structure and the Project Network Diagram.

On a regular schedule you'll meet with your team members to review their work, congratulate them on successful milestones, and prep them for the following week's activities. A regular, efficient meeting keeps the team focused on the project vision and accountable for the tasks to be completed.

Part of keeping the project on track will be to create a process to collect work information from your team. You'll need a regularly scheduled method to request and retrieve information on the team members' progress for assigned tasks. Microsoft Project and Microsoft Project Server are two of the ideal tools to use to track progress.

Just as you hold your team members accountable for their actions, management will hold you accountable for yours. Specifically, management is interested in your ability to control the finances and deliver expected results on time. You will need an education on how your organization processes payments, creates purchase orders, and reviews budget adjustments. You will also need a process to keep tabs on the finances and hours committed to a project, and a method to track the value of work.

Project management is a long process that requires dedication from you and the project team. Your job is to ensure that the team stays dedicated to the project, finances are always in order, and you are always ready to react to any situation. Sounds easy, right?

CHAPTER QUIZ

1. Of the following, which factor most likely determines the speed of a project's implementation?

    A. The project sponsor

    B. The project manager

    C. Dedication of the project team

    D. Effective planning

2. What should be the goal of the individuals on the project team?

    A. To make the company more profitable

    B. To help each team member finish their tasks

    C. To focus on completing their own tasks

    D. To finish their work as quickly as possible

3. Why should a project manager host a regularly scheduled team meeting? Choose two:

    A. A meeting allows team members to report on their activities.

    B. A meeting allows the project manager to make changes to the project scope.

    C. A meeting allows team members to air grievances about other team members.

    D. A meeting allows the team to resolve problems.

4. What is the key to hosting a successful project team meeting?

    A. Preparation

    B. Attendance of all team members

    C. Collection of project status

    D. Reviewing assignments for the upcoming week

5. What is a Work Authorization System?

    A. A method to approve work that's been completed

    B. A method for the project stakeholders to approve the project work

    C. A method to allow successor work to begin based on the completion of predecessor work

    D. A method to allow the project manager to track uncompleted milestones

6. Why should a project manager allow team members to report on completed milestones in a team meeting? Choose two:

    A. To ensure the tasks are being completed

    B. To create a sense of pride on the work accomplished

   C. To create internal competition on the project

   D. To create peer pressure to outdo the other team members

7. Why should you review the upcoming assignments in a project team meeting?

   A. To remind the team members of the work they must complete

   B. To remind the team you are in charge of the project

   C. To confirm the team members know their duties for the week

   D. To confirm the project is moving and on track

8. Your project has a budget of $280,000 and is 30 percent complete. You have spent $90,000 on your project, however, due to some rework and additional time from a vendor. Your project is supposed to be 50 percent complete by this time. What is your earned value for this project?

   A. $56,000

   B. $84,000

   C. $140,000

   D. .93

9. Your project has a budget of $280,000 and is 30 percent complete. You have spent $90,000 on your project, however, due to some rework and additional time from a vendor. Your project is supposed to be 50 percent complete by this time. What is your CPI for this project?:

   A. .93

   B. 93

   C. .60

   D. $6,000

10. Your project has a budget of $280,000 and is 30 percent complete. You have spent $90,000 on your project, however, due to some rework and additional time from a vendor. Your project is supposed to be 50 percent complete by this time. What is your SPI for this project?

   A. .93

   B. .60

   C. .77

   D. 1.01

11. What element should be on an assignment status report from team members?

   A. Hours completed on the assignments

   B. Cost of work to date

    C. Earned value of the work

    D. Percentage of work completed

12. Heather is working on an operating system rollout to 1256 workstations. The rollout is completed through imaging software, but there are scripts that have to be run at each workstation to complete the installation. The task has been assigned 400 hours to complete. Heather reports that she has committed 200 hours to date, but is only 30 percent complete on the assignment because the process is taking longer than originally planned. What should a project manager do in this instance?

    A. Remove Heather from the assignment and reassign another team member.

    B. Add resources to the assignment to decrease the length of time to completion.

    C. Add additional time to the critical path.

    D. Remove all of the time from the management reserve and apply it to this assignment.

13. When a work package is taking more hours to complete than originally planned, which of the following is not a viable solution to reduce the hours required while maintaining costs? Choose two:

    A. Use less expensive materials.

    B. Hire contractors to complete the job.

    C. Assign additional resources.

    D. Apply management reserve.

14. True or False: Assigning additional resources to a task will always reduce the amount of time required to complete the task.

    A. True

    B. False

15. What is the risk in reassigning a lagging task to a consultant you've hired to complete the task?

    A. Additional time

    B. Additional costs

    C. Demoralization of the project team

    D. Decrease in management reserve

CHAPTER EXERCISES

Exercise 1

In this exercise you will use a Microsoft Project feature called resource leveling. *Resource leveling* is a process to suppress overallocation of a resource, typically a team member. Microsoft Project tracks resources and creates reports based on the resources that are overallocated. This process is helpful in balancing the implementation of your project to reduce expenses, time wasted, and project burnout.

To complete this exercise, you will need Microsoft Project installed on your computer and the CD-ROM included with this book. Follow these directions to complete the exercise:

1. Open Microsoft Project and then select File | Open.

2. Navigate to the Exercises folder and then to the CH8 folder on the CD-ROM and choose the Microsoft Project named Exercise One.

3. This project is based on the PND you created in Chapter 7. Click the Resource Sheet on the View menu. Notice how the team members have been added to the project.

4. Note how Allan Hurt and Zack Talley are listed in red. In the Indicators column, note how there is a yellow exclamation next to their names. Hover your mouse over the yellow exclamations. The pop-up message reports the resource should be leveled as it is overallocated.

5. Click the Resource Graph. Double-click anywhere under the calendar (on the right side of the screen). The Bar Styles dialog box opens. In the Overallocated resources section, set the Show As option to Step Line and then click OK.

6. Scroll through the calendar and you will see the resources that are overallocated and the days they are overallocated. On the left of your screen, you can also scroll to the right and left to toggle through each team member and see their allocation.

7. From the View menu, select Gantt Chart to see the tasks the team members are responsible for. You will now invoke resource leveling to see the impact on the overallocated resources and the project.

8. From the View menu, select Resource Sheet.

9. From the View menu, confirm that Table: Entry is selected. If not, choose Table and then choose Entry from the pop-up menu.

10. From the Tools menu, select the Resource Leveling command to open the Resource Leveling dialog box.

11. In the Leveling Calculations field, choose Manual and in the Look for overallocations drop-down menu, choose Day by Day.

12. Confirm that the Clear Leveling Values check box does have a check mark in it.

13. In the Leveling range for Exercise One, confirm that Level Entire Project is selected.

14. In the Leveling Order box, confirm that Standard is selected.

15. Confirm that there isn't a check mark beside the option Level Only Within Available Slack. (This option will only allow Microsoft Project to allocate resources within available lag times. By not checking this option, the project end date can be moved to resolve the overallocation problem.)

16. Confirm that there is check mark beside the options Leveling can adjust individual assignments on a task and Leveling can create splits in remaining work.

17. Click Level Now.

18. Confirm that Entire Pool is selected and click OK. Microsoft Project will level the resources.

19. Notice that the yellow indicators are now gone. You have leveled the resources on a day-by-day process.

20. From the View menu, choose More Views | Leveling Gantt | Apply. Within the Leveling Gantt view, the Gantt chart demonstrates the difference before the leveling and after. The green bar on top of the task duration represents the preleveled task, while the blue represents the task after leveling.

21. Close the file. It is not necessary to save your work unless you would like to examine the file in more detail at a later time.

Exercise 2

In this exercise you will enter hours and percentages of work completed from your team members into Microsoft Project. This exercise requires that you have Microsoft Project installed on your computer; you also need the CD-ROM that accompanies this book.

1. Open Microsoft Project and select File | Open.

2. Within the CH8 folder on the CD-ROM, choose the Microsoft Project file named Exercise Two.

3. From the View menu, choose More Views | Task Sheet | Apply.

4. From the View menu, choose Table | Tracking.

5. Notice the actual start date is set as NA. Until work is actually reported, this setting remains "Not Available"; once work is entered, the start date is reflected.

6. In the first task, Installing W2K Server, navigate to the cell under %Comp. Type **100** and press ENTER to advance to the next cell in the %Comp

column. Notice how the remaining columns are updated to reflect the work completed.

7. For the second task, Create Workbook, type **10** and press ENTER to advance to the next cell in the %Comp. Again the remaining columns are updated.

8. For the third task, Install Exchange, type **50** and press ENTER.

9. For the fourth task, type **40** and press ENTER.

10. To finish, close the file.

Exercise 3

In this exercise you will compute the Earned Value Management for a project and review the EVM formulas. If you have Microsoft Excel installed, you will be able to use a template to complete the exercise. If you do not have Microsoft Excel, you will be able to complete the exercise, but will need a calculator to finish.

Exercise 3a: Follow these directions if you have Microsoft Excel installed:

1. From your CD-ROM, in the CH8 folder, open the Microsoft Excel document named EVWorksheet. The document is a spreadsheet that will automatically calculate the Earned Value Management values based on the information you supply.

2. To begin, confirm that you're on the worksheet named EVM formulas. This worksheet lists all of the EVM formulas and how they operate. You can hop back to this worksheet as you move through the exercise.

3. Move to the worksheet named EVM Actions by clicking on the worksheet name at the bottom of the workspace.

4. You'll enter values into the green highlighted area at the top of the worksheet. You won't need to edit any of the values that are highlighted in yellow.

5. Here's your scenario: You are the project manager of the APPDEV Project. Your project has a BAC of $550,000 and is expected to last one year. As of now, your project is 25 percent complete, but you should actually be 40 percent complete. Due to some incidents early on, you've already spent $225,000 of your project budget. Enter the appropriate values from this scenario into the appropriate cells in the green highlighted area in the worksheet.

6. What is your Earned Value?

7. What is your SV?

8. What is your CPI? What does this value mean?

9. What is your SPI? What does this value mean?

10. Good news! You've just learned that your project is actually 40 percent complete, not 25 percent. What does this do to your project's EVM values?

Exercise 3b: Follow these directions if you do not have Microsoft Excel installed:

1. Here's your scenario: You are the project manager of the APPDEV Project. Your project has a BAC of $550,000 and is expected to last one year. As of now, your project is 25 percent complete, but you should actually be 40 percent complete. Due to some incidents early on, you've already spent $225,000 of your project budget. Enter the appropriate values from this scenario into the appropriate cells in the following table. Grab your calculator and complete the table:

Term	Formula	Result
Earned Value	%Complete * BAC	
Cost Variance	EV–AC	
Schedule Variance	EV–PV	
Cost Performance Index	EV/PV	
Estimate at Completion	BAC/CPI	
Estimate to Complete	EAC–AC	
Variance at Completion	BAC–EAC	
Planned Value	Where the project should be at this point.	
To Complete Performance Index	(BAC–EV)/(EAC–AC)	

QUIZ ANSWERS

1. **D.** Effective planning led by the project manager will ensure an effective implementation of the project. Dedication of the project team is required, but if there is no plan to be dedicated to, there's not much for the team to accomplish.

2. **C.** The goal of project team members should be to focus on completing their own tasks. If each team member would focus on completing the assignments as planned, the project would flow smoothly. This is not to say the team members should not help each other, it's just that they should focus on completing their own assignments without meddling. Team members should not focus on completing their work as quickly as possible, as "haste makes waste."

3. **A, D.** Regular team meetings accomplish many different tasks—including allowing a team member to report on his activities and allowing the team to solve project problems as a group. A project team meeting is not the place to discuss grievances among team members.

4. **A.** As the project manager, preparation will ensure an efficient, successful meeting.

5. **C.** A Work Authorization System is a formal process where project team members report the completion of their tasks so that downstream activities may begin.

6. **A, B.** By requiring team members to verbally report on the status of their assignments, they are held accountable for their activities. In addition, this practice creates a sense of pride for the team members who have accomplished major milestones in the project.

7. **D.** By reviewing the assignments with the project team, you are ensuring that the project is moving and on track. At the same time you are confirming that the team members know their duties for the week and reminding them what their assignments are, but, overall, the purpose is to keep the project moving.

8. **B.** The project's EV is found by multiplying the budget at completion by the percent of the project that is complete. In this instance, the EV is $84,000.

9. **A.** Your CPI found by dividing the EV by the AC. In this instance the CPI is .93.

10. **B.** Your SPI can be found by dividing the EV by the PV. In this instance, the SPI is .60.

11. **A.** Team members should report their hours involved in a project If you supply the hours committed to the assignment, Microsoft Project can predict the percentage of the task completed.

12. **B.** The project manager should assign additional resources to the project if at all possible. By adding additional resources to the project, Heather and another individual can launch the installation process on more workstations throughout the network simultaneously. The length of the actual installation process will still take the same amount of time, but the number of workstations involved can increase.

13. **A, D.** Using less expensive material will reduce the overall cost of the project, but it will not have an impact on the hours required to complete the installation. Hiring contractors and adding additional resources to complete the tasks will reduce the hours required to complete the assignment, but it will also increase the cost of the assignment as more resources are used. Applying management reserve does not reduce the number of hours required, it just compensates for the extra hours the work unit requires.

14. **B.** False. Simply adding resources to all tasks will not always decrease the amount of time a task requires. For example, when installing an application, the time of the application installation can be streamlined through policies or scripts, but the installation time is limited by the speed of the workstation, not the number of team members installing the application.

15. **B.** When reducing risk, project managers usually increase cost. By hiring an expert consultant to complete a lagging task, the project manager will most likely have to pay a higher hourly rate for the consultant to be involved in the project.

EXERCISE SOLUTIONS

Exercise 1
The solution to Exercise 1 can be found in the file Completed Exercise One, which appears on the CD-ROM in the CH8 folder.

Exercise 2
The solution to Exercise 2 can be found in the file Completed Exercise Two, which appears on the CD-ROM in the CH8 folder.

Exercise 3
The solution to Exercise 3a can be found in the file Completed Exercise Three, which appears on the CD-ROM in the CH8 folder.

The solution to Exercise 3b is as follows:

Term	Value
Budget at Completion	$550,000.00
Percent Complete	40%
Planned Value	$220,000.00
Actual Costs	$225,000.00

Term	Value
Earned Value	$220,000.00
Cost Variance	$ (5,000.00)
Schedule Variance	$ -
Cost Performance Index	0.98
Schedule Performance Index	1.00
Estimate at Completion	$562,500.00
Estimate to Complete	$337,500.00
To Complete Performance Index	0.98

Chapter 9

Revising the Project Plan

Have you ever taken a wrong turn? One minute you're cruising along listening to your favorite radio station, windows open, and you're enjoying a perfect summer drive. The next thing you know, you're on I-90 when you should really be on I-94. You've cruised along for 20 minutes and now you're frantic. Not only are you now 20 minutes out of your way, you've got to drive those 20 minutes again in the opposite direction just to get back to where you should have been to start with. So what do you do? Forget the radio station, put the windows up, and grit your teeth as you pretend you meant to screw up all along.

IT project management can be like that unfortunate summer drive. No matter how much research you do, how many times you test a process, or how detailed your plan, no one can predict the future. Project managers can, and often do, start in one direction and, by chance or design, realize they've been going in the wrong direction. In some instances, they discover a better method or product in the early stages of the implementation. In others, a request from management or the customers to change the deliverables of the product can alter a project's direction. And still in some cases, the cause for change rests on the shoulders of the project manager.

In this chapter, you'll examine the process a project manager can use to decide if a change in a project is feasible—and which system to put in place to review, approve, or decline change requests. You'll also see how the project manager can incorporate change, react to difficult situations, and try to keep her project, and her wits, together. Pull the car over, turn off the radio; it's time to get to work.

Defining the Need for Revision

The English writer Arnold Bennett said, "Any change, even a change for the better, is always accompanied by drawbacks and discomforts." How true that is!

In the world of IT project management, change is not, and generally should not be, an easy process to incorporate. Every project, as you know, needs a scope statement. The *scope statement* defines what will and will not be delivered as part of the project. The scope is a point of reference for all future project decisions. Recall that the project scope is all of the required work—and only the required work—to complete the project. Once the scope has been created and agreed upon by the stakeholders, it must be protected from superfluous changes.

IT projects, however, are particularly subject to change due to the nature of the industry. Patches, service packs, new releases of software, bugs, threats, security issues, and new wishes from stakeholders can all task an IT project on a daily basis. Each change request must be documented, and be evaluated for cost, time, risk, and repercussions. In addition, each change request must be documented, tracked, and implemented in the plan or denied.

But what happens in many projects? Change is forced into the project scope, even if it's a complete redesign on the deliverables, and then a project manager tries to shoehorn the project plan into the new and improved requirements. This rarely works. Instead what happens is that team morale declines, frustration ensures the deliverables aren't met, and the project manager loses control. To prevent this, you must have a process to control change and implement change when it is needed.

Establishing Change Control

Change control is an internal process an organization can use to block anyone, including management, from changing the deliverables of a project without proper justification. Change control requires the requestor to have an excellent reason to attempt a change, and then the proposed changes are evaluated in regard to their impact on all facets of the project.

The change control system (CCS) is a documented, formal process for proposing, reviewing, and allowing changes within a project. The CCS presents the process of how changes are reviewed for their value, costs, schedule impact, risks, and feasibility. The CCS also has a method to enter, track, and record the approval or denial of proposed changes.

In many organizations, the change control system includes a Change Control Board (CCB). This board completes the review and analysis of the proposed changes to determine their worthiness and justification. Your organization may call the Change Control Board an Engineering Review Board, Technical Review Board, or even the Technical Assessment Board.

There are dozens of reasons why management or the project customer may want to change a project's deliverables. The worst is when the recipient of the project deliverables drops by your office one day deep into the implementation plan and says, "Hey, I forgot to mention that this project thingie you're working on also needs…."

Another situation, equally painful, is a change that stems from your project team. In these instances, someone on your team will discover that the technology you are implementing really doesn't fit the bill. The technology won't actually deliver, the new technology will conflict with existing technology, or it becomes outdated during the course of installation. When this happens, you can almost hear your plan being sent through a paper shredder.

Or it could be your team is pulled in so many directions that it's impossible for them to keep the project on schedule. In organizations that are short on IT staffers, 60- to 80-hour workweeks are not uncommon. They'll be working on so many different implementations, development projects, and their daily duties to put out fires that it is physically impossible for them to keep pace with your project. In these situations, nothing short of additional resources will help.

As a general rule, it's easier to change the project deliverables in the beginning of the project than at the end. In other words, as the project moves closer to completion, the willingness to change the project deliverables wanes. The best method to avert serious change is prevention through serious planning. Again, like most aspects of project management, a solid preproduction of research, planning, and interviews with the users impacted by the project is crucial. You can avoid the preceding situations using these methods:

- Interviewing the client (or end user) of the product, in detail, as part of the initiation and planning phases, will ensure the requirements are well defined.

- Researching and testing the technology thoroughly before the implementation phase. A testing lab or project simulation that emulates the working environment is a must in many IT projects.

- Examining the required resources prior to the implementation. A reality check is needed to see if the existing staff has the time or knowledge to implement the proposed technology.

Impacts of Change

The one thing that always stays the same in project management is change. Sooner or later something will happen that will blindside your plan of attack and force you to change your plans.

A formal change to the project plan, regardless of who's responsible for the change, is serious business—no matter how seemingly small or innocent it might seem. At this point of the project life, your Project Network Diagram (PND) is tight and solid. Recall that your PND is a visual representation of the flow of the work. It defines the paths to completion of the project and when tasks begin, and identifies the critical path. The critical path is the longest path of tasks within the PND. There should be little room for additional deliverables without expanding the project finish date—not something that is always acceptable.

In addition, new deliverables cost money. A change in the project scope may mean additional resources—internal or external—and your budget may not be able to afford them. The changes can mean additional hardware and software expenses. Typically, additional funds will be required if the project scope is to change.

Team morale may plummet. Facing your team and telling them that all of the planning, research, and work so far is about to get additional criteria for completion is not good news. You'll need to handle the news with grace and tact.

Project Change Request

As you can imagine, you want to control and restrict changes to the project scope. When changes are inevitable, you need a formal process to incorporate these changes into the project plan. This formal process begins with something called the *Project Change Request form.*

As you can see in Figure 9-1, the Project Change Request form formalizes requests from anyone to the project manager. The form can be electronic or paper based. The requestor, the project manager, and even the CCB will contribute to the form as they consider the change. The Project Change Request requires the requestor to not only describe the change, but also supply a reason why this change is appropriate and needed. Once the requestor has completed this form, the project manager, project sponsor, and other relevant stakeholders can determine if the change is indeed needed, should be rejected, or should be delayed until the completion of the current project.

Change requests must follow a certain process to determine if they should be incorporated into the current plan. Figure 9-2 follows the path of the change request from start to conclusion.   For example, a sample IT CCS goes through these steps (refer to Figure 9-2):

1. Integrated change control is a project-wide method of tracking change throughout all areas of the project. First, the project manager works with the stakeholders to determine if the proposed changes are really needed, funding changes within the project, and then managing them when they are inserted into the project.

Change Request Form
Submitted by:
Phone:
Date submitted:
Request ID:
Summary of desired change:
Purpose of change:
Cost:
Time:
Risk assessment:
Recommendation:

2. Ideally, the organization has a documented, working CCS in place and
   the project manager has a certain amount of autonomy to approve or
   decline changes based on the nature of the submitted change request.

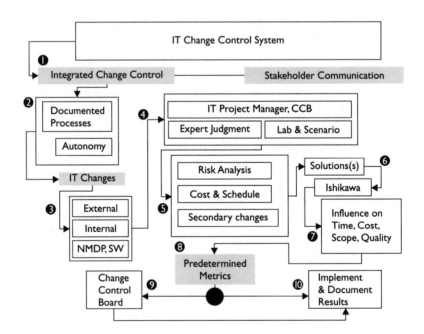

3. Next, the change request is filtered into one of several categories. This example focuses on three broad categories. External changes are changes from outside the project, such as service packs and technical advances. Internal changes are changes from the organization's stakeholders, project team, or (sigh) even the project manager. The last category of change presented deals with the hardware and software. (NMDP means network, memory, disk, and processor.)

4. The change request then moves to the project manager and possibly the CCB who rely on expert judgment regarding the proposed change. Expert judgment comes from those experienced with the technical nature of the change, such as subject matter experts, other project managers, and the project team. If needed, the change should be worked through in a lab or scenario environment to determine the actual impact on the project if it is approved.

5. The change request is then evaluated for risks, costs, schedule requirements, and any secondary changes the change may need if approved. A secondary change is simply the effect the change will have on other work within the project. For example, upgrading a workstation to a new operating system (OS) may consequently require upgrading older applications to work on the new OS as well.

6. The change solutions are evaluated. An Ishikawa diagram is one method of determining the cause and effect of the work, deliverables, and conditions within the change. An Ishikawa diagram is also called a cause-and-effect diagram or a fishbone diagram.

7. This step illustrates that the change, if it is to be approved, must be thoroughly evaluated—especially with regard to its impact on time, cost, scope, and quality.

8. Predetermined metrics are values that would eliminate a change or allow it to continue in the CCS. For example, any change that affects the project budget by more than 10 percent is not allowed. Or any change that adds more than 14 days to the project is not allowed.

9. Should the change seem valuable, questionable, or prove to be worthy even though it does not necessarily meet the predefined metrics (such as providing a high return on investment), the results should be presented to the CCB for their approval or denial.

10. If the results of the change request are not worthy of moving to the CCB because of the predefined metrics, the change is automatically denied, and documented, and the requestor is informed of the status of his request.

Consider a project to release a new OS to hundreds of users based on a common image. One department, however, needs additional software installed that other departments do not. An OS image is an exact replica of an entire disk, generated using an imaging application like Ghost. Such applications allow an administrator to capture the entire image of a disk and then disperse it to multiple machines quickly and easily. Because the one department needs a slightly different image than the others, it's really outside of the predetermined project scope.

In this example, the department that needs additional software installed would basically require a different image of the disk to complete the job quickly and easily. While the request for the installation is valid, it does not fit within the current project scope. This request, as innocent as it sounds, may be better served as a separate project dependent on the completion of the current project. As Figure 9-3 demonstrates, project managers rejecting changes to a current project prevent runaway projects and advance change requests into the process to determine if a new project is warranted.

FIGURE 9-3

Change control can spur new projects.

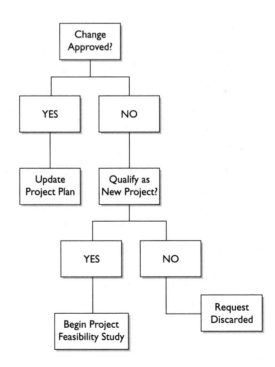

If the research of the change does not prove that the change can or should happen, the change should be rejected. Reasons for rejection could be lack of time, technology, funds, or resources, or the complexity of the request qualifies it for a separate project.

Finally, if the change is approved for project incorporation, the project manager must begin a plan to incorporate the change into the project schedule. The project manager, the project sponsor, and the project team must address the incorporated change. An examination of the PND and a review of the resources and budget will be most helpful when determining where, when, and how the change will fit into the current project.

Change Impact Statement

A *Change Impact Statement* is a formal response to the Project Change Request form. It summarizes the proposed actions to incorporate the changes. Usually this is a listing of the paths and trade-offs the project manager is willing to implement. In some instances, the Change Impact Statement is given back to the customer with several responses the requestor can choose from. There are seven different responses a project manager can use on the Change Impact Statement:

- The proposed change is not approved. Sorry! The change cannot be incorporated into the project scope. These add-on wishes cause runaway projects, scope creeps, and a waste of funds, time, and resources.

- The proposed change can happen within the current timeline, with the current resources. Good news! The change is simple and won't require additional resources or time. This can be something as simple as changing the name of a domain, server, or another variable.

- The proposed change can happen with the current resources, but will require an extended timeline. The change request will take additional time to finish the project, but the current resources are able to complete the additional activities.

- The proposed change can happen within the current timeline, but additional resources are required. Based on the change and the project, the deadline may not be movable. Therefore, in order to complete the change on time, additional resources will be needed to incorporate the additional work.

- The proposed change can be completed, but the timeline will need to be extended and additional resources are required. Phew! Based on the change request, the timeline is no longer realistic nor is it achievable for the current project team to complete the change. This stems from adding an additional component that requires skills beyond those of the current project team.

■ The proposed change can be completed, but the deliverables will be produced in a tiered strategy. This reaction to the change accepts the proposal, but the deliverables will be released in priority sequence according to the customer. For example, if an OS rollout was to be just for a few departments, but the rest of the company was added to the plan, this solution could address the change. Management could choose the department order in which the OS rollout would occur.

■ The proposed change cannot occur without considerable changes to the project plan. Bad news! The proposed change to the project is so significant it would render the current plan obsolete. The changes must have an excellent justification for scrapping all of the hard work, time, and funds committed to the project to date. An example could be a shift in business cycles, a company buyout, a new technology, or change in management.

Internal Project Trouble

The most difficult changes to the project plan, unfortunately, happen from within. These changes are not always changes brought about by discovery of a new technology, a flaw in the project plan, or a conflict with the implementation. These changes are brought about by the one variable in any project that remains constant: the human element.

The human element is the predictable problem that arises from team members who fail to complete their assignments, fail to communicate troubles or flaws, or lose interest in their work. These blunders are the epitome of leadership failure. You, the project manager, must have such an active role in the implementation phase that you can sense trouble brewing like a fireman can smell smoke. You need to spring into action, address the issue at its conception, and squelch it before it erupts into a full-fledged delay!

On long-term projects, it is easy for everyone, including the project manager, to get burned out on the implementation. As Figure 9-4 shows, the longer a project, the easier it is for the project team and the project manager to lose interest and focus. Once a team member gets burned out on a project, he loses interest, care,

FIGURE 9-4

Long-term
projects require
dedication to
avoid burnout.

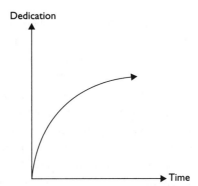

and motivation. It's difficult to spark a team member's drive once he's reached this point. A project manager should sense a team member's dedication waning long before it actually happens.

Another problem IT project managers are often faced with is turnover. As you may know, within the IT industry, professionals are constantly climbing their own ladder of personal achievement. Workers come and go as they shift from company to company, and move up within their own organizations.

When a team member leaves the team because she resigns from the company (or moves within the company), you must act immediately to find a replacement. This is no easy task. If you're lucky, someone within the organization can join the project team and begin where the original team member left off.

As Figure 9-5 depicts, the longer a project team position is vacant during the implementation phase, the longer the project's delay. In addition, costs may rise on the overall project as hours increase and IT consultants/contractors may be brought in to fulfill the duties of the missing team member.

FIGURE 9-5

Vacant team
member positions
cause delays.

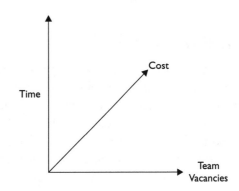

What's likely is that a new team member will join the team, and you'll be faced with assessing that person's skills and then rearranging the resources to complete the project on schedule. For example, if you're involved with an application development team and your SQL guru leaves the company, you may not have to hire a new SQL pro. Instead, you may have to move one team member who knows SQL into the role of the SQL pro, and promote a new team member into the now vacant app developer role—assuming that the person's skill sets match your requirements.

You may also have no other choice but to hire an independent contractor, a consultant, or an integrator to help the team finish the project. This independent contractor will most likely cost more than the hourly wage and benefit costs of the team member who has left the company. Additional funds may be required to complete the project.

Implementing Project Changes

Your project is always in a state of flux. Changes are called for from management, team members come and go, and new technology sprouts up along the way to completion. All around you are temptations to shift the focus of the project, to change your vision, and to broaden the scope just a bit at a time.

You must resist these temptations. Little, innocent changes pile up and result in scope creep. Changes to the project, no matter how small they may seem at first glance, are always major changes! Stay firm and require management, the customers, and the project team to stay focused on the original vision. Scope creep is when your project scope is defined and then it grows a little at a time. If a change to the project scope must happen, because of internal or external forces, you will need to enter the proposed changes into the CCS.

Changes from Internal Forces

When delays caused internally by the project team happen—due to the team's inventive changes, a lack of quality in the product, or a failure to complete assignments—and inevitably they will, the project manager can do several things to resolve the problem and keep on schedule. While these are not changes to the project deliverables, they are changes that jeopardize the project from being completed on time, on budget, and with the expected level of quality. The project manager must take corrective actions to get the project back on track, including

- Hiring additional resources to complete the project on schedule
- Changing FS (finish to start) tasks within the PND to be SS (start to start) so tasks can happen in tandem rather than in sequence
- Reassigning highly skilled resources to the critical path to speed the completion
- Reassigning tasks evenly among the remaining project team to keep on schedule
- Applying management reserve to lagging tasks
- Removing a portion of lag times to take up slack within the project

Changes from External Forces

When delays to the project are caused from external forces, such as the customer, management, or business cycles, the project manager can do all that he can to ensure the project will finish on schedule and on budget, but often delays or expenses are unavoidable. In these instances, the project manager must rely upon his negotiating skills to use leverage to secure additional finances, time, or both.

The Iron Triangle of project management comes to mind. The Iron Triangle is an equilateral triangle. The sides of the triangle (time, cost, and scope) must all be in balance with one another for the project to be successful. If a new deliverable is added to the project, there will likely be a need for more time, more money, or both. For a project to be successful, all three sides must remain in balance. You can't expect a $500,000 project scope to be met with a $300,000 budget.

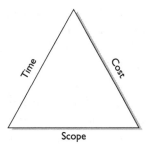

If the deadline of the project cannot be moved, but the newly incorporated deliverables have put an unforeseen strain on the project team, new resources may be required. There are only so many hours in a day, and it is not reasonable for a project manager to ask, or require, the project team to work all of them. In these instances, the most direct route to satisfying the demands of the project change are additional resources.

This means, usually, additional funding. The new resource may be a consultant, an independent contractor, or an internal resource that the project team absorbs. Whatever the solution, the project manager must work to quickly educate the resources on the project plan, their requirements for the plan, and when their assignments are due.

The project manager should make an effort to make the resource feel comfortable and welcome to the project. Poor project managers add team members, show them their assignments, and leave them to figure things out for themselves. You must welcome the new team member, introduce that person to the team, and explain why she was brought on board. A comfortable, happy team member will be more productive than one who is confused, misinformed, and uncertain of why she is on the team.

In some instances, changes to the project will not require additional resources, but just more money. For example, the new project deliverable may change the number of workstations, servers, or application licenses that are needed to complete the plan. These all will require additional funds. In such cases, if the deliverable must be met, then additional funds will have to be assigned to the project. There is no negotiation—it's simple arithmetic: additional technology equals additional funds.

Negotiate for Tiered Structures

A tiered structure allows the IT project manager to agree to meet the new requirements of the project scope, but the deliverables are released over multiple dates. For example, if the project deliverables have changed to be a database-driven web site with e-commerce support, the IT project manager can bargain to meet the new scope but with multiple release dates. First, the web site can be released, then the tie-ins to the database, and finally the hooks into the e-commerce solution. Of course, the web site would be updated on each release to reflect each new add-in.

With this type of approach the project manager wins, as he's given more time to ramp up his team to deliver the project. And the organization wins, as there are usable resources at each delivery.

Extension of Time for Delivery

At the very least, when a project scope has undergone serious changes, and no additional resources are available for the project, a delay is likely. What else can you do when significant deliverables have been added to your project? At first, you should examine the PND to determine if any slack exists or whether some tasks can begin SS rather than FS.

After those adjustments, the project manager must take a serious look at the project delivery date. If the date is not feasible, then additional time must be added. Neither you nor management should consider the project late—additional deliverables were added to the scope and additional time is required to meet those changes.

Issue Management Meetings

An *issue management meeting*, as its name suggests, is a meeting to resolve problems and issues as they arise on a project. Every project, no matter who planned it, will encounter troubles—they just always do. A delay in the critical path is a delay you cannot afford. For example, if a critical task is delayed because of a software compatibility problem, that's a delay for all dependent tasks in the project lifeline. Pushing your project timeline beyond the targeted completion date, as in Figure 9-6, will cost additional funds because of the hours required to complete the project.

An issue management meeting allows you to address problems with your team, the vendor, technology, or key personnel to find solutions. You can address an issue, brainstorm for different ideas, and drop in plans of variance in your PND.

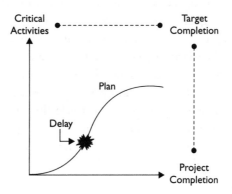

Delays will ultimately result in budget overruns.

An issue management meeting is a serious piece of business that allows you to quickly and accurately get your project back on track.

At the end of your issue management meeting, which may run over days or weeks, you should have a resolution to the issues and a plan on how to attack. This plan allows you to address the problem with a solution, and address how the solution will impact the remaining tasks in the project. Meet and discuss with the entire project team the solution you've arrived at and explain the justification for the plan. And then assign the task to the appropriate team members to implement.

Delaying a Project

There will come a time in every organization when someone proposes that a project, specifically your project, be cut. Your hands will get sweaty, your gut will develop a sinking feeling, and you won't sleep well at night. Your poor, poor, project! The one you've invested months of your life in, the one you've inspired your project team to work so hard for, and the one you've sold management on how valuable it will be to the company. Sooner or later, one of your projects may face its demise.

There is, however, a tactic that you can try to save your project from being cut from the company's plans altogether: convince the company to delay, not cut. Delaying a project is different from cutting a project. A delay is a nod from management that your plan is still active, still worthy, and will be resurrected at some point in the future.

The typical cause of healthy projects being cut is a lack of funds. Is your business experiencing a downturn? Are layoffs imminent? How's your stock doing? These are all signals that a project cut may be visiting your team in the near future. Management has a responsibility of managing their project portfolio. If your project is low in priority, it's not difficult for management to give it the axe. Some project managers, when they sense these changes coming, will commit as many funds available to the project immediately to secure the implementation of the technology. For example, a project manager is leading a project to upgrade servers over the next eight months when he senses cuts may be looming. Rather than being stuck with a project without servers, he immediately orders all of the hardware necessary to finish his plan.

If this sounds sneaky to you, that's because it is. This is not a good project management technique because

- It does not follow the project plan or the project budget.
- The hardware may be present, but the team may not be available to implement it.
- It is a waste of the company's money as the technology purchased today may drop in prices over the upcoming months.
- If management wanted to rescind approval of the plan, they have final say.
- It is a reaction to gossip, and not to facts.

You should continue on your project until you are told the project has been halted. There is nothing wrong with talking to your project sponsor about the possibility of your project being cut if you two have a strong working relationship. When the word comes that your project is to be halted, first find out the reason the project must be stopped. If the reason is financial, and usually it is, make a request to change the project status to inactive rather than retired. Make a request to revisit the project in three to six months or after certain conditions are met to reactive the project implementation.

Once the project has been officially delayed, edit the project to formalize the three-to-six month delay. You will then have to break the news to the project team. Share with the project team the same reasons you were given, if you're allowed, as to why the project has been delayed and when the project will reconvene. Make backup copies of any current work done on the project and store them for safekeeping.

Coping with Vendor Delays

If you have outsourced all or a portion of your project, you may be faced with a vendor that cannot complete tasks according to the original schedule. In these instances, you will have to be stern, diplomatic, and reasonable all at once. Some methods you can use to work with vendors:

- Review your contract with the vendor to determine what repercussions you may have.
- Review their practices and recommend methods they can implement to improve the lagging schedule.

- Clearly identify to vendors the impact of the delay on the project scope and the completion date.

- Once a compromise has been reached, share this news with management and the project's customers.

Rebuilding Management Support

Here you are in front of management. Your project is a month off schedule and your budget is nearly gone. You need more time and you need more money to finish. Gulp. If you've blown the opportunity to complete the project, don't be surprised if you are removed from the project. Sorry. But wait a minute, is this really your fault? Well, there is that whole poor planning results in poor implementation argument, but let's take the benefit of the doubt. Has the project scope changed? Have crucial members of your team left the project? Did you ever really have enough money to begin with?

If you are not to blame, things can be a little easier. Of course, management doesn't want to hear the bad news about your late project and the lack of cash to finish it, but someone has to tell them. The best method is to cut to the chase and tell management what the problem is. Prepare this ahead of time and document your needs. You do not want to go before the company board, the partners, or an executive committee without some plan to present to them. Never go to management with a problem unless you also have a solution. Management is looking for value and solutions in their day—not your project problems.

Tell management what the problem is in clear, direct terms. Then, in equally clear terms, explain why the problem has occurred. If it was your fault, say so—honesty is always the best policy. If the problem has presented itself because of the project scope being changed, or other circumstances clearly outside of your control, let management know—with your supporting evidence.

Once you've broken the harsh news and presented the honest, direct reason why the problem has arisen, present a plan to resolve the issue. You are now selling management the sizzle of the project once again. Remind management of the value of this project, the investment it means for the organization, and of the time and dollars already committed to progress the project to this point. While the monies that have been invested are sunk costs, it's hard to ignore the commitment invested into a project.

If these executives agree to continue to support your project, you will now have to rebuild their trust. To rebuild their support, you will have to prove to them that you are capable of leading the project team to the conclusion of the project. You'll have to prove to them that you are capable of managing their investment. And finally, you'll have to prove to yourself that you are capable of finishing this project after all you've been through thus far.

To begin once more, meet with your project team and discuss why and how things got off track. Look for reasons why you let down the team, or the team members let each other down. Address these issues and then promise they won't happen again. You'll need to return to your WBS and the PND to determine what tasks are lagging and how the team can regroup and attack the plan with gusto once again.

Focus and Refocus

Okay, your project has changed either through internal or external forces. You've made changes to the project plan, worked out details of the change, and are ready to move forward with the project. Put the frustration of the project change process behind you, rally your troops, and charge ahead into the project plan.

You now have to take on the role of an even more active project manager and ensure that the team is not discouraged with the change of the project plan. You will need to speak with the team members that the change has the most impact on to ensure their commitment and ongoing support.

You will also need to increase your level of communication between the team members and management. You want to keep all parties informed of the process of the project and your continued dedication to it. Some project managers are tempted to keep a low profile after the change process—either out of embarrassment or frustration. Hiding it is not a good decision, as now you need to be seen and heard.

Renewal of Commitment

A change in the project plan, whether your fault or not, requires a change in you as well. After one of the most frustrating aspects of project management, changing the plan, you need to rekindle your excitement for the original project vision. Often, especially on long-term projects, it's easy to drift away from the excitement that surrounded the first few team meetings, the kickoff meeting, and reaching the first milestone.

The fact is, the business of project management is not always the most exciting business. But, the day-in, day-out tasks and review of work completed and work that needs completing are what gets the project from an elaborate plan on a whiteboard to a living portion of a business. Rekindle the excitement, renew your commitment to the project, and lead your team to victory!

FROM THE FIELD

Interview with Anne Walker

Name: Anne Walker
Title and certifications: Enterprise Project Manager, MCSE, PM Certified
Company: Convergent Computing
Years as an IT project manager: 7

Anne Walker is an Enterprise Project Manager for Convergent Computing, a nationally recognized consulting, technical services, and IT staffing organization. For the past seven years, Anne has managed simple and complex technical projects, which include a 30-site, 7000+ users, enterprise-wide migration of all equipment, e-mail, data, and applications. Anne has been largely involved with developing internal project management processes for Convergent and past employers.

Q: When does a project manager know that a project plan has to be revised?

A: The project environment is dynamic by nature. It is practically impossible to prepare for all aspects of any one given project, and inevitably things do not always go as you had planned. Any good project plan should have objectives that are clearly defined prior to getting started on the actual work so that when things do go awry, everyone knows what the objectives are and can make decisions around them. If those objectives are in risk of not being met, the project plan needs to be revised. In essence, you need a road map that has concrete objectives that can easily be followed to get to some destination. If, during the project that destination changes or the project, is going in the wrong direction, you go back to the road map and make modifications.

Q: How can a project manager guard against scope creep while still allowing for some flexibility in a project plan?

A: When developing the project plan, project managers should strive to identify not only the work that is to be done within the project, but also what is *not* to be included. By having what is not to be done defined, the project manager can ensure those tasks do not get included in the project. The project manager should also work with the project sponsor and stakeholders to get this identified early on and in doing so will find out what parts of the project can and cannot be flexible. For example, a project may have a timeline where there is absolutely no flexibility; however, there may be flexibility in the budget. In this instance, you would have flexibility in adding more people to the project to meet the timelines or paying a premium for expedited deliveries to meet an inflexible schedule.

Q: What process should be in place to control proposed project changes?

A: First, project managers should plan on project changes; they happen no matter how well project plans are defined. Any changes should be tracked as you work toward successful completion of the project. As you track changes, you will be building a historical record that will be invaluable if any disputes arise as the project is finishing or completes.

On a recent project, the customer wanted all changes tracked and entered into a database. A change request form was developed and policies were put in place so that any changes had to be submitted via this form and then approved prior to an actual change occurring. Each change request form had to be approved by the key stakeholders of the project via a weekly meeting where each request was reviewed.

Q: What is the most difficult part of changing a project plan during the implementation phase?

A: During implementation, most people involved in the project have their "heads down" and are focused on completing the project plan. Communicating any changes to the plan can be difficult because you have all kinds of work happening and probably people working in different areas. Overcommunicating is the key to making this work, so utilize all means of communication you have.

Q: How does a project manager address budgetary concerns, such as a budget increase, once the project has been approved for implementation?

A: This truly depends on how much budget flexibility has been incorporated into the project plan. Good project managers will incorporate a percentage of flexibility into the budget depending on the complexity of the project. For simple, noncomplex projects, the percentage may be 5 percent; whereas for large, complex projects, the percentage may be 15 percent.

If the budget is fixed and the project manager sees that an increase will be needed to successfully complete the project objectives, the project manager needs to identify where the increase in budget is needed and work with the stakeholders to rectify the problem. The stakeholders may decide to cut costs on one level of the project to meet the budget increase needed, or they may work to get the increased budget improved.

Q: What is the most difficult portion of revising a project plan?

A: It is to have everyone buy into a necessary change and have everyone impacted understand what necessitated the need for the change. In order for projects to be successful, the people who are out there doing the work need to understand and get behind any plan changes that are necessary.

I was working on a large migration project where our customer was swapping out all hardware and had ordered new hardware to replace the old. In order to keep to our schedule, the new hardware had to be onsite and installed prior to the actual migration date. Even with contingency and risk plans in place, we had to change a couple of planned migrations due to hardware either not arriving or hardware failures that even the manufacturer could not overcome.

Think through your schedule, remember the defined objectives of the project, and work to meet those, rather than only focusing on one piece of the project, which in this example would have been just "fixing" the schedule. Had we done that, we may have not had a successful migration for those sites because we would have had to use people who did not understand the technology or the migration process. One of our project objectives was to not impact business users, and utilizing new people would have set us up to not reach that objective.

Q: Have you ever experienced a dangerous change in the project plan?

A: Yes. In one instance, we had a site of 700+ users, workstations, laptops, servers, applications, mail, and data to be migrated over a weekend. A team of 10 engineers in various roles was already on site and prepping for the migration. Over 100 volunteers would be arriving in a couple of days to assist over the weekend. I won't go into detail, but you can imagine the amount of prep work that goes on even prior to the team arriving, and then it really kicks into gear once the team is onsite.

A storm hit and we lost power for one full day during that weekend. We were in contact with the site management and always presented them with options and what the results of choosing those options would be. A point came where we had to decide to keep moving forward or to roll back so as not to impact the day-to-day business that needed to get done. With that many people onsite, everyone just wanted to keep going forward and looked for ways to do that. People lost sight of the higher-level project objectives and only focused on the short-term goal—getting the work done over the weekend. Bringing that large of a group to the realization that we were going to have to reschedule that site's migration was like getting a freight train to stop on a dime.

Q: What can a project manager do when a project has to be delayed due to circumstances outside of the project?

A: The best a project manager can do is to be calm and get people to focus on options for moving forward rather than focusing on circumstances outside of their control. People will look to the project manager and will mirror what emotions are coming from that person.

You have three options: the first is whether or not you can do anything about whatever is delaying the project. If you can't, you need to realize there is nothing you can do to change what is happening and look at what options you have. The second piece to consider is if you have influence over what is occurring. If you can influence what is happening, maybe you can change the circumstances.

The third thought is that you do have control over what is happening and should exercise that control. When this opportunity presents itself, project managers should use good judgment and practical sense.

Q: How does the project manager regain the trust and respect of management and the project team should a project plan have to be revised?

A: Honesty and open communication with management and the project team is key. Also, deliver what you say you are going to deliver and build the reputation of being reliable and on top of issues. Always be looking ahead and planning for what may be lurking as the next problem and be proactive rather than reactive.

FROM THE FIELD (continued)

Q: When working with an IT integrator, how can a project manager ensure that the vendor is on schedule and that changes to the project plan are limited?

A: Project managers need to know up front that much of their time will be devoted to ensuring that all integrators, whether they are hardware vendors, software resellers, or staffing agencies, get on board with the project and understand deliverables and deadlines. The earlier the integrators are involved, the better they will understand the project deliverables and can get behind them. The integrators can also better understand what they are to deliver and what is expected, and it gives integrators an opportunity to let the project manager know what they can and cannot accommodate. Setting up regular meetings throughout the life of the project with key integrators is a great way to communicate any changes or updates to keep them on board. It also gives the project manager an opportunity to get status updates from the integrators. If meetings are not possible, request weekly status updates from the integrators.

Q: What advice do you have for aspiring project managers?

A: Project managers need to have problem solving, administration, and interpersonal abilities in general. Aspiring project managers should look at their own personalities and understand what drives them and how other people interact with them. Being a "people person" is not necessary; however, you will need to understand how to motivate and influence people. Along those same lines, you may be asked to develop team members and facilitate teamwork and cooperation. You may have to deal with conflict and should be skilled in conflict resolution. In order to handle many of the pressures, you should be emotionally stable and open to change. If you don't enjoy working with people and would rather be behind a desk, project management is probably not for you. You also need to be organized and able to balance or multitask many activities.

Also, aspiring project managers should get some training. There are classes available at universities, certificate programs, and also vendor training. If your goal is to manage technical projects, get some technical training around your product interests. Having technical knowledge goes a long way when you are working with technical experts.

CHAPTER SUMMARY

Whoever said "The more things change the more they stay the same" never worked in IT project management. No matter how much planning, preparing, and strategizing you invest in a project, change can happen. A change in deliverables can happen from management or the customer receiving the deliverables. Business cycles, new requirements from the customers, or new management can all lead to changes in a project plan.

As the project manager, you must implement a change control system to formalize a change request and then react to the change in a formal statement as well. A request to change the project deliverables, no matter how seemingly small, is a significant one that requires a business justification to begin implementation.

A change in the project deliverables may require additional resources, additional funding, additional time, or all three to complete the project. Management or the customers must be willing to comply with your requests to complete the project. Solid research of the change will provide evidence of the new requirements to produce the deliverables.

Should change come about because of internal forces—such as lack of focus, change in resources, work units not being completed, or improper funding—you must take the lead on rectifying the problem. You have to face management and explain the problem and offer a solution to correct the problem and get the project back on track.

Once the project scope has been modified, you and your project team must renew your dedication to the vision of the project. A new sense of responsibility, dedication, and channels of communication must emerge to keep the project moving to completion.

CHAPTER QUIZ

1. What is a change control system?

   A. A formal process to review and then decline changes to a project

   B. A formal process to decline a project without management interaction

   C. A formal process to manage, review, approve or decline changes to a project without proper justification

   D. A formal process to decline all change to a project without additional funds committed to the project

2. Pierre is the project manager of a project to upgrade all of the print servers and printers within his company. The deliverables require that each floor have a pool of print devices, with the exception of the graphics department. They will have several different types of printers, including two high-end color printers. Marty, the sales manager, requests that his department receive a color printer as well. What is the first process Marty should follow?

   A. Submit funding for the color printer.

   B. Submit a Project Change Request form.

   C. Submit a Change Impact Statement.

   D. Submit a proposal on how the new printer will help his department be more productive.

3. Of the following reasons to change a project's deliverables, which is a result of lack of planning?

   A. A discovery that the technology is not compatible with the workstations' OS

   B. A request from the client for additional features within an application

   C. A request from management to finish the project earlier than the set date

   D. A request from the project team to delay the project by a week

4. What is the best method to prevent change in a project plan?

   A. Adequate funding

   B. Adequate resources

   C. Proper planning

   D. Tasks that are SS rather than FS

5. Finish this statement: A change to the project plan, no matter how seemingly minor, is
   _____.

   A. Easy to implement

   B. Hard to implement

C. Significant

D. A lack of planning

6. What is one of the most dangerous things that can happen when the project scope is changed due to a request from the customer?

A. The project cannot be completed on time.

B. The project team's morale may plummet.

C. The project manager loses interest.

D. Management takes over the project.

7. What is the purpose of the Project Change Request form?

A. It allows changes to be easily melded into the project.

B. It allows the project team to request changes to the project based on discoveries in the field.

C. It allows the project sponsor to formalize and control change from external sources.

D. It allows the project manager to determine if proposed changes are valid or not.

8. If a proposed change to a project does have merit, what must the project manager do in the change control process?

A. Implement the change.

B. Update the PND.

C. Research the proposed change.

D. Assign the change to a new resource.

9. True or false: Rejected changes should be made into separate projects.

A. True

B. False

10. What is a Change Impact Statement?

A. A formal request to change the project scope

B. A formal response to a request to change the project scope

C. A formal response to a request to change the project deliverables

D. A formal rejection of a request to change the project scope

11. Of the following, which two are valid responses to a project change request?

    A. The proposed change can happen with the current resources, but will require an extended timeline.

    B. The proposed change can happen with the current resources, but will require additional funding if the original deadline is to be met.

    C. The proposed change can happen with the current resource and with the current financial obligations, but a change incorporation processing fee must be applied.

    D. The proposed change can be completed, but the timeline will need to be extended and an additional project manager is required.

12. What is a Change Control Board?

    A. A committee that reviews the project looking for value-added changes to insert into the project scope

    B. A committee that must approve all changes for a project

    C. A committee that approves or declines proposed changes to a project

    D. A committee that studies the change impact a proposed project will have on an organization

13. What is an Ishikawa diagram?

    A. A diagram to study the cost-benefit ratio of a proposed change

    B. A diagram to study the cause and effect of a proposed change

    C. A diagram to rank the most common problems caused by a proposed change

    D. A diagram that shows the flow of a change request from concept to implementation

14. Of the following, which is a serious problem to a project team, but is not a lack of commitment to the project?

    A. Burnout

    B. Staff turnover

    C. Lack of focus

    D. Reassignment of the project manager

15. When a new team member joins the project, what is the most important thing a project manager can do?

    A. Get the team member to work immediately.

    B. Introduce the team member to the team and allow them to assign him tasks.

C. Have the team member research the project to get to know the project plan.

D. Spend time with the team member to get her caught up on the implementation and to make her feel welcome.

CHAPTER EXERCISES

Exercise 1

In this exercise, you will complete a Project Change Request form as if you were the customer of a project.

Scenario: You are the sales manager for Carlington Enterprises. You are working with Carla, an IT project manager, on a new sales automation application. The highlights of the requirements for the project that the software her team is developing are as follows:

- Contact management features
- Database searchable by any property of the client (sales, birth date, last contact, city, and so on)
- Ability to block salespeople from viewing records they did not enter
- Ability for the sales manager to reallocate leads to sales reps
- Ability for the contact information to be downloaded to a PDA
- Fax and e-mail ability
- Ability to log sales calls activity to the contacts by the sales staff

The project is moving along when you suddenly realize that the software requirements are missing a major feature. You would like the software to have the ability to retrieve a contact's record through caller ID when a contact calls into the center.

Complete the following Project Change Request form based on the new request:

Project Change Request Form	
Name of Project:	
Your Name:	

Project Change Request Form	
Date:	
Summary of Desired Change:	
Reason for Desired Change:	

Exercise 2

In this exercise you will approve or disapprove a Project Change Request form.

Scenario: You are the project manager for an operating system upgrade of all workstations throughout the company. The key points of your rollout plan are as follows:

■ All workstations will be configured with Microsoft Windows XP Professional.

- The workstations will be deployed through a disk imaging software.
- The workstations will be configured through scripts and Windows 2003 policies.
- The OS upgrade will be released to employees after they complete a four-hour training session.

Based on the following Project Change Request form, determine if the change is valid and should be approved. Complete the answers after the form to justify your decision.

Project Change Request Form	
Name of Project:	Workstation OS Upgrade
Your Name:	Mark Turner
Date:	December 30
Summary of Desired Change:	I would really appreciate it if you could release Windows XP Professional to my department (marketing) ASAP. If you could bypass any other departments en route to us in your rollout plan, that'd be great.
Reason for Desired Change:	We've added new software that we must use in the new year, and it is not compatible with our current operating system. If you want to chat about this give me a call at x232. Thanks!
Question	**Your Response**
What risks could this change have on your project?	

Project Change Request Form	
Should this change be incorporated into your project plan?	
Why or why not?	
Will any aspect of the change request require additional resources? (If so, what aspect?)	

Project Change Request Form	
Will any aspect of the change request require additional funding? (If so, what aspect?)	
Will any aspect of the change request require additional time? (If so, what aspect?)	
What areas of the change request have the most impact on your project?	

QUIZ ANSWERS

1. **C.** A change control system is a formal process to prevent change to a project without proper justification. Change control is not a method to decline all change to a project, rather it formalizes the approach and allows the project manager to fully understand the proposed change and then determine if the change is necessary.

2. **B.** Marty should submit a Project Change Request form. The Project Change Request form allows Marty to explain the change to the project manager and to offer justification for the proposed change. A Change Impact Statement is a response from the project manager to Marty's request.

3. **A.** As part of the research phase, the project manager should ensure the proposed technology is compatible with the existing OS. A request from the client for additional features is not necessarily a result of lack of planning, as the client can be fickle. Management's request to finish the project early is outside of the project manager's control, as is the request from the project team.

4. **C.** Planning is the foundation of a project. Proper planning will help the project manager determine the amount of required funds and resources needed to complete the project. Planning will also help the project manager determine the order in which tasks begin.

5. **C.** A change in the project plan is always significant and must be treated as such—anything less is flirting with trouble. Once a change has been easily approved, additional change requests may follow.

6. **B.** Changes to the project plan can cause the project team's morale to plummet. Team members may view the change as bad news and become disgruntled about the project and the new required work to complete the plan. A project manager must get behind the team members, support them, and encourage them to complete the project even with the new deliverables.

7. **D.** A Project Change Request form allows the IT project manager to determine the proposed change and if the change is valid. The project manager may have to research the change and determine its impact on the overall project to make a decision.

8. **C.** Once a proposed change proves to have some merit, the project manager has to research the change to determine its impact on the project. He doesn't have to immediately implement the change, but he is required to determine if the change should be inserted into the PND and assigned new resources.

9. **B.** False. Often, proposed changes to a project are valid, good ideas—but are well beyond the scope of the current project. In these instances, the rejected change should enter the first phase of project management to determine the need for a project. However, not every change deserves to be its own project.

10. **C.** It is a formal response from the project manager to the requestor of a change. It is a summary of the decision to implement or reject the proposed change.

11. **A, B.** When responding to a Project Change Request form, the project manager can approve the change with one of seven options. In this instance, the project manager can approve the change with additional time or with additional funding. C, a change incorporation processing fee, is not typical in project management. Finally, answer D is not valid as there is only one project manager per project.

12. **A.** A tiered structure project is one that produces several deliverables over time. For example, a change in an application may spur multiple deliverables such as the original interface, then the request for database tie-ins, and finally, a web portal.

13. **B.** An Ishikawa diagram illustrates the relationship between the cause and effect of a problem. When used in change management, the method can be applied to see what effect the change will have on the project.

14. **B.** Staff turnover can seriously hamper a project's implementation phase. Each team member is needed to implement the project plan; if a team member leaves the team, then some tasks are delayed, and the project may miss the targeted completion date.

15. **D.** Of course, the project manager needs the new team member to get to work as soon as possible, but some time must be invested in the new team member to ensure her focus on what her responsibilities are. The project manager and the project team must welcome the new team member and help ramp her up on the project implementation.

EXERCISE SOLUTIONS

Exercise 1: Possible Solution

Project Change Request Form	
Name of Project:	Sales automation software
Your Name:	Your name

Project Change Request Form	
Date:	Today's date
Summary of Desired Change:	I would like the software to have the ability to use caller ID to retrieve the contact's information before a saleperson answers the phone.
Reason for Desired Change:	This feature would eliminate the delay it takes for the salesperson to look up the client's record. Not all of the salespeople can type very fast, and it's embarrassing for the sales rep and rude to clients to have them spell out their last names. An automated feature like this would increase sales and help the sales team develop better relationships with our clients.

Exercise 2: Possible Solution

Question	Your Response
What risks could this change have on your project?	The marketing department will need to be upgraded as part of the rollout. There's no real risk in moving the department to an earlier time in the project implementation. This is with the assumption that all of the marketing laptops are available on the day of the rollout.
Should this change be incorporated into your project plan?	Yes
Why or why not?	It is essential that the marketing department use the new software in the new year. The OS upgrade will allow them to get to work on their software.
Will any aspect of the change request require additional resources? (If so what aspect?)	The one drawback of the change is that the OS upgrade is dependent on the training sessions. The users in the marketing department will need to complete the training first before the OS upgrade will be released. No additional resources are required.
Will any aspect of the change request require additional funding? (If so what aspect?)	No additional funding is needed, just a shift in the release.
Will any aspect of the change request require additional time? (If so what aspect?)	No additional time will be required.
What areas of the change request have the most impact on your project?	The users in marketing will need to complete the training sessions before other users in the company. The class dates are still the same, only the users in this department will complete the training sessions first in order to receive the OS rollout first.

Chapter 10

Enforcing Quality

Picture this: you and your lover are dining out at a wonderful Italian restaurant. You're seated at an elegant table with a white tablecloth, shining utensils, and crystal glasses. The warm glow of the candlelight makes everyone look great. There's Puccini on a distant speaker, and the scents of sizzling vegetables, steamy pasta, and crushed garlic drift from some hidden kitchen.

Everything is perfect: the waiter attentive, but not overbearing. Warm bread, followed by a crisp salad, and a delicious dinner that looks as good as it tastes. All in all, it's a magnificent evening out. You're feeling swell, so you order two cappuccinos and Italy's best dessert: tiramisu.

Dessert arrives and you and your date each take a bite—and oh! It tastes like wet cardboard! Just awful! The worst taste you've ever had in your life. Now no matter how excellent the evening had been, this one bite has ruined it all. Your entire evening has been ruined by this bite.

Hopefully this will never happen to you, at least the dessert part. But what happened? How did such a wonderful experience go from excellent to horrible? Someone, likely the pastry chef, didn't do his job. Now the hard work of the chef, the wait staff, and the proprietors is all ruined, or at least tainted, by a letdown in quality management.

Quality management is the process of ensuring the entire experience, the entire process for the management and for the customers, is excellent.

Defining Quality

Quality. How many times a day do you hear that word? Reports of it come from all around you: upper management, television commercials, salespeople, and the news. At every turn, someone is spouting off about their quality carwashes, the process of quality management, or the benefits of purchasing their quality products.

But what is quality and how does it relate to project management? Quality, according to the Guide to Project Management Body of Knowledge, is the "totality of characteristics of an entity that bear on its ability to satisfy stated or implied needs." Quality, according to *Webster's New World Dictionary*, is "the degree of excellence of a thing." Hmm… to a project manager then, quality could mean many things—and it does. Quality to a project manager falls into two areas:

- The quality of the deliverable
- The quality of the process to produce the deliverable

In this chapter, both areas will be examined, though the focus will be on the process to produce the deliverable. Arguably, to produce a quality product, there must be a controlled, organized process to get to the end result. Not often can a project full of chaos, disorganization, and pandemonium create an excellent deliverable.

Quality of the Deliverables

Every project must produce a deliverable to finish. A project to create a new application must, obviously, produce the application. A project to create a Windows 2003 domain must result in planning, designing, and producing the expected environment. No project manager would set out to create a new application and end with a print server—it just doesn't make sense. Every project must have a clearly stated objective as to what the project will produce.

Producing a Service

Imagine a project that is designed to establish Routing and Remote Access Service (RRAS). The goal of the project is to allow users from the field to connect to resources on the LAN. Resources could include e-mail, printers, file servers, and databases. To end users, the experience must be just like it is when they are on the local LAN.

The project manager and his team complete the research, create a plan of action, and implement the new service. Of course, it's all a bit more complex than this, but you see the big picture: conceive, plan, and achieve. The users, from home or anywhere in the world, connect to the resources within the LAN through a Virtual Private Network (VPN), as in Figure 10-1. A VPN allows users to connect to company resources through an Internet connection.

FIGURE 10-1

A project can deliver goods or a service such as a VPN.

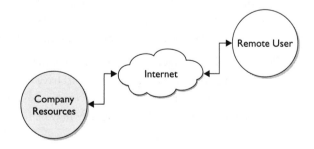

To produce this service, the project manager had to see, and know, what the end results should be. The project manager worked with the project team and the project stakeholders to determine the exact requirements of the project deliverable. Research allows the project manager to create the vision of the project, leadership allows the project manager to transfer the vision, and dedication to the project allows the project team to implement the plan.

The good of the service is measured in value by several factors:

- **Value of the implementation**   What did it cost the company to create the RRAS solution and what are the measurable results? There is a cost-benefit ratio for the project. The cost of the project, let's say it was $75,000, is in ratio to the benefits of secure, remote access. An ongoing process, as described in Chapter 8, must be executed to see the true costs and benefits of the implementation.

- **Value of the service**   After the project, there must be a process to measure the value of the service. Metrics are needed to measure the value of the organization before and after the project. The measurement of the service can be accomplished through tools to log the service's usage. From the logged data, calculations can be enforced to see the amount of activity over a set period and the cost of each session. For example, the number of users accessing the LAN through the RRAS connection over a six-month period will reveal the usability while an increase in productivity through the RRAS connection can show the profitability of the implementation.

- **Value of the experience**   How well do the deliverables work? If the project manager has over promised the deliverables and the speed, reliability, or convenience of the service, then the value of the experience will diminish. For example, if the project manager has stated that the RRAS connections will be just as fast as if the user were on the LAN and this does not prove true, users will consider the service less than excellent. People may use the new ability to connect to LAN and access resources and retrieve their e-mail, but their focus will be on the slight delay through the Internet connection.

- **Value of the longevity**   How long will the service stay implemented? If the project manager and the project team have failed to adequately research the service and it is replaced within a year by faster, more reliable, and less expensive methods, the value of the longevity may be slim. In some instances, the service may be adequate for the time it is in place; in others, the service may offer little or no ROI. For example, if the project manager had offered the RRAS service through analog dial-up connections and offered no support for broadband connectivity, the thrill of RRAS would be diminished by the availability of broadband connections versus analog dial-up connections.

■ **Value of the reliability** How reliable is the implemented service? If the project is declared finished, but the service consistently fails or is unavailable, the quality of the deliverable is lacking. The service implemented must be reliable, and the underlying process of the service, whether it is hardware-related or depends on the skill sets of the individuals operating the service, must be reliable and able to fulfill the demands the service requires. For example, if the RRAS server is consistently unavailable because the hardware the RRAS software is installed on is weak and cannot handle the workload, then the hardware was not addressed properly in the planning phase and must be upgraded. The upgrade in hardware may cause delays in the service availability and additional costs to the organization.

Projects that produce services must be planned and implemented toward the end result of the service. A service deliverable must live up to the promises of the project manager, and the project team must have the skill sets and funding available to install the service for reliability and availability, and in proportion to the expected longevity of the service. As Figure 10-2 illustrates, a balance between the reliability and the cost of the implementation must be obtained.

Project managers must work to ensure that the proposed service is not going to be replaced with faster, stronger, and better services within a timeframe that would squelch any ROI on the service. This is derived from the research and planning phases of the project manager versus the demand from management for an immediate solution.

FIGURE 10-2

Project managers must balance cost and reliability to obtain quality.

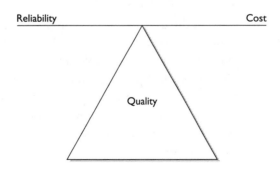

Producing Goods

A project that requires deliverables be a tangible object, such as network, an application, a database, or an application server, has traits similar to those of a project creating a service. A project that creates a thing, however, has different measurements to gauge the quality of the product.

For example, imagine a project that involves creating software to allow customers to design a landscaping scheme. The application will walk users through a wizard that will build an ideal garden based on their area of the country, the amount of sunlight their lawns receive, the amount of color they'd like, the care of the plants, and other factors.

The software will be sold and used online. The interface of the software is not a typical web browser, but it does take advantage of the Internet connection to retrieve plant names, photos, and nursery information in the customer's ZIP code. This application's quality will be judged differently from that of a service, though it may have similar attributes.

Values used to judge a product are dependent on what the product is. For example, an application will have some characteristics of a service, whereas a laptop, a physical piece of hardware, will have different attributes of quality. For any goods, however, there are measurable values:

- **Value of the product**   Is the product worth the cost? A product that must be created, such as an application, has to allow the customer to get some level of satisfaction, enjoyment, or benefit from the product that has a perceived or measurable level of worth. For example, a computer game that sells for $39 must be, to the consumer, worth that money in enjoyment. The $39 investment is measured in the ability of the application to create fun, in this instance. In other words, does the product deliver on its promises in relation to the cost of the product?

- **Value of the usability**   Is the product usable? A product must deliver on its promises to be usable. The usability factor stems from the need for the product to exist. For example, a laptop is expected to complete certain duties. The need of the laptop is mobile computing. A project manager who manages a project to install and configure laptops for the sales team must know the level of usability the sales team anticipates from the hardware. The product itself is not the deliverable of the project—the satisfaction of the usability is the deliverable.

■ **Value of the reliability**   Is the product reliable? A product must be reliable, functioning, and usable by the customer. A project manager who implements a device, such as a Personal Digital Assistant (PDA), is responsible for the quality of the device implemented. A PDA with batteries that burn up too quickly, doesn't synch properly with a workstation's software, or is difficult to use is not a reliable product. The project failed not because of the hardware— but because either the requirements of the stakeholders were not established or there was inadequate planning to meet the stated requirements.

■ **Value of the longevity**   What is the product's life cycle? Like the process of delivering a service, a product must also have a life cycle in proportion to its cost. A project manager who is installing web cameras for all workstations throughout a company does not want to learn after he's purchased 2,546 web cams with moderate resolution that a new high-resolution camera has been released for less than the model he has just purchased. Today's technology, or so it seems, is always outdated as soon as it's purchased. A project manager, however, must be able to judge the life cycle of a product in relation to the ROI of the product. The project manager must calculate the cost of the product and how long the product must be used before the product becomes profitable.

Quality Versus Grade

Quality, within a project, is the capability of the project to meet the requirements of the project customer. Grade, however, is the ranking or classification of a thing or service. For example, you're managing a project for the art department within your organization. The project requires six new printers for the artists. Two of the printers are inexpensive color inkjet printers, two of the printers are moderate color laser printers, and the remaining two printers are high-end image setters that print directly to film.

You have six different printers ranging in price and capability. All of the printers deliver on what they promise, but do they differ in quality? No. The printers differ in grade. Each printer is capable of printing under the specifications its manufacturer says it can. While the inexpensive inkjet printers are of a lower grade, they can still deliver on what they promise.

Consider also the grade of paper you may use with the printers. You can buy slick, photo-ready paper or cheap copy paper. Paper is paper, but the grade of paper can differ.

Low grade may not be a problem, but low quality is always a problem. Say one of your new printers consistently jams the paper, fails to print, smokes, or has other defects—that's a quality problem.

Quality of the Process

Whether you are creating a product or a service, you will follow a process to arrive at the deliverables. As you've read in all of the earlier chapters, there is a set process, a logical and discrete order of getting a project from start to finish. The project management framework from initiation, planning, execution, control, and closure of each phase is guarded and led by the demand for quality.

No doubt, a project manager who is unorganized, lacks leadership abilities, and fails to motivate the project team will most likely create a project deliverable that is short of excellent. As Figure 10-3 demonstrates, a project manager who is organized, follows a proven process of getting to the deliverables, has established the project requirements, and inspires the team to success will most likely create a deliverable that is solid, efficient, and valuable to the organization.

The quality of the management process is measured by several factors:

■ **Results** The deliverables are a reflection of the ability of the project manager to manage and complete a project. The project team may be doing the actual implementation, but it is the responsibility of the project manager to coach and lead the project team throughout the entire process, not just at the beginning and the end. A deliverable that does not meet the expectations of the project's scope represents a project manager who failed to do his job.

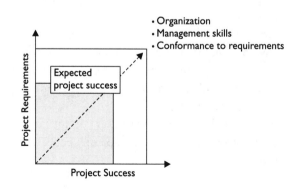

- **Experience** The experience of completing the research, the planning, and the implementation of the project should be rewarding and educational for the project manager, management, and the project team. Not all projects are exciting and thrilling, but the experience of working with an excited project manager who is dedicated to the success of the project is contagious. At the end of the project, all parties involved should possess a sense of pride and satisfaction with the experience of being a part of and contributing to a successful project. The quarterback of the team, the project manager, has to call plays from the line, analyze defense, and discipline the team when it's necessary. Organization, communication, and a desire to achieve are all factors in the sense of accomplishment.

- **Project team** The project team members will measure you by your ability to lead them to finish. They will look to you from day one to inspire, lead, and encourage them. They need you to be decisive, fair, and responsive to their needs. How you work with, talk to, and interact with the individuals on the team will determine their opinion of you. They won't keep their opinion of you a secret, either; news of your ability, or lack thereof, will be shared with their peers and their supervisors throughout your organization.

Managing the Quality

An IT project manager must have the keen sense to manage both the expectations of the deliverable and his own process to obtain the deliverables. The quality of the process is directly related to the quality of the deliverables. Simply put, the greater the project manager's ability to lead the process, the greater the quality of the project deliverables (see Figure 10-4).

FIGURE 10-4

A project manager's ability to lead impacts the project quality.

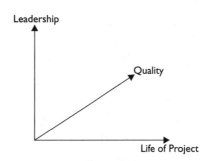

A project manager can use numerous tactics to ensure that the project management process is excellent and superior to projects that may be anchored with delays and cost overruns. There are several key managerial skills a project manager needs to have to successfully manage a project:

■ **Finance and accounting skills** While the project manager doesn't have to be a Certified Public Accountant, he should have some fundamental accounting experience or training.

■ **Planning skills** The project manager must know how to plan for the project implementation. A clear understanding of the project requirements is a fundamental precursor to project planning.

■ **Leadership skills** Leadership is the ability to establish direction, align people, motivate, and inspire.

■ **Management skills** A project manager must have the management skills to produce the results the project stakeholders are expecting from the project team.

■ **Communication skills** Ninety percent of a project manager's time is spent communicating. It's a fundamental skill for a quality project manager.

■ **Problem solving skills** It's key a project manager has the ability to "figure stuff out." He recognizes the problem, finds a way to solve it, and then makes the decisions necessary to implement the solution.

■ **Negotiating skills** A project manager must balance stakeholders' interests, keep peace and harmony on the project team, and use the appropriate give and take when it's needed.

■ **Achievement orientation** A good project manager has to have a drive to get things done.

■ **Agility** A project manager must be able to see the big picture, coordinate all of the moving parts of the project, and decompose the project end results into manageable components.

■ **Service-orientated** A project manager works for his manager and the project customers. For projects to be successful, the project manager must serve the project—this includes serving customers, stakeholders, management, and even the project team.

■ **Personal management** A project manager won't successfully manage projects if he can't manage himself. This includes control, temper, flexibility, time management, and so on. A project manager must be personally well organized and forward thinking.

- ■ **Organization**   This trait is probably the talent all successful IT project managers have in common. If you are not an organized person, learn how to become organized. Not only will your ability to manage projects increase, but also your quality of life will improve.

Project Information Center

One approach to project organization is to create a Project Information Center (also called the War Room). The size of your project and the available real estate within your office building will determine your ability to create a Project Information Center. This centralized room is a collection of all materials related to the project.

From here, the project manager, the project team, vendors, consultants, and whoever else is involved in the project can drop by to retrieve information, learn the project status, and review work related to the project. In your Project Information Center, you can, and should, create a map of the entire PND on a wall to gauge where the project is at any time.

Resources needed by the team can be centrally stored here, along with books, videos, and magazines related to the technology being implemented. Tools and equipment connected to the implementation are stored here. Finally, the Project Information Center is an excellent location to hold team meetings, as resources are a footstep away.

Web Solutions

Another excellent resource, especially for long-term projects and geographically dispersed teams, is the creation of an intranet solution for the project team. A central web page should be secured for the project team, the project manager, and relevant management. The web solution should offer the same features as the Project Information Center and can be designed to allow for milestone completion, project updates, and a method to communicate with other team members.

A web solution for your project may be applicable to the entire organization. Some companies have a central Project Management Office that coordinates all activities of projects through a web solution. In other words, the process is uniform, with some flexibility, across all projects through the web solution. Projects are kept separated, but costs are streamlined as resources may be used across projects. A web solution allows projects that are dependent on each other to interact, and allows project managers to see the status of a successor or dependent project to judge the completion of tasks.

Software Solutions

There are many different Project Management Information Systems (PMIS) available to assist a project manager. With a PMIS, a project manager can organize, track, complete estimates, and schedule events to happen. A project manager can use traditional project manager techniques with his PMIS as the catalyst for reaching the project's end. PMIS applications all have features that can be designed to track tasks, project flow, and the surge of e-mails, documents, and information. Whichever method you choose, a solid foundation on how to use the application is required to gain the full benefits.

Quality Management as a Process

Quality project management is an activity you need to perform from the concept of the deliverable to the release of the deliverable to ensure quality in all your activities. It is a belief that the process a project manager follows to ensure quality from the start of a project will propagate to the activities of the project team throughout the life span of the project.

Several concepts claim to be the "secret potion" for guaranteed successful projects every time. However, the one weakness, and common theme, in all project management processes is the reliability and willingness of the project manager and the project team to participate. This situation is comparable to joining a gym to get in shape— you have to actually go to the gym and work out to get the desired results. The same holds true with these concepts: you have to use and follow their principles for them to work.

Quality Phases of Project Management

There are five phases within a project as Figure 10-5 demonstrates. Each phase keeps an eye toward the quality of the deliverable or ensures that quality exists within the creation of the deliverable. Within each of the following areas, a project manager must work to implement quality and quality management checkpoints:

- **Initiating**   The origin of the project results from a reaction to a need or an opportunity. This realization of the need or opportunity is the concept of the project. The business needs of the organization are addressed to ensure that

FIGURE 10-5

Quality is an issue
in each of the five
phases of project
management.

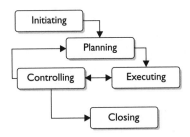

the project will satisfy these needs first. Once the project charter has been
written to authorize the project manager, the project can move into planning.
Quality is affected from the start. If the expectations of the quality aren't set,
aren't planned for, or aren't quantified, the project's success is doomed.

■ **Planning**   The cornerstone of a successful project is the planning phase.
The project manager and project team must identify the required activities
and estimate the time necessary to complete the activities in order to reach
the project goal. Through the research, project managers can identify the
necessary resources, funding, and skills required to achieve success. Armed
with this information, the project manager can create the project plan. Quality
doesn't happen by accident. During the planning process group, the project
management and the project team must plan how the quality demands will
be met.

■ **Executing**   Once the project plan has been approved, the project work can
begin. The project manager will rely on the work authorization system to
record task completion and allow new projects to begin. Quality must be
executed as part of the work. The project team must follow the specifics to
meet quality demands as defined in the project plan.

■ **Controlling**   This phase of project management is a continuous cycle to
oversee the project. In this phase, more than any other, the project manager
ensures quality through quality control. Scope verification is also done here to
ensure that the project is delivering what was promised. Project managers also
control projects through cost control, schedule control, and risk management.
The process of managing the project must be of quality as well. Quality control
is inspection-driven.

■ **Closing**   This phase of project management is the sigh of relief. It requires
proof of the project deliverables, approval from management, and satisfaction
from the customers or end users. This final stage moves the project from

a work in progress to a component of the business. The final reports are submitted, archived, and the Lessons Learned is completed. Quality also happens in the closing phase. A complete and final review of the project, its ability to meet the quality objectives, and the quality of the project management experience is required.

These five phases of project management all contribute not only to the success or failure of the project, but also to the quality of the deliverables. A dedication to doing the required activities properly and with confidence in each phase is what leads to quality. Any one phase that is lacking a commitment to the success of the project can cause the entire project to be off balance, and ultimately fail.

Ensuring Quality Throughout the Project

As your project moves along through each process group, over hurdles, and through barriers, you'll need a proven system to check the quality of your progress. You may subscribe to any one of multiple theories in the world of project management to test the quality of your project. All of these theories, however, have one common thread: work completed must be proven to be in alignment with the project deliverables. This is scope verification—the process of ensuring that the project is creating what the customer has asked for.

For example, a project to create a new application for an organization will have several milestones in its path to completion. The desired deliverable of this project is that the application will allow users to submit HR forms through a company web site. The project manager can check the work in progress to verify that it is in alignment with the project deliverable. Should the work be out of alignment, the project manager must take immediate corrective actions to nudge the work back on track.

Planning for Quality

Quality planning is a process to determine which quality standards are relevant to the project, and how they can be implemented. Planning for quality is a fundamental exercise in the planning phase—each deliverable must have metrics that prove its quality. In IT, this can be bandwidth, latency, database accuracy, the speed of an application, and more.

Your organization may have a quality policy that dictates the expectations of a project in regard to quality, how the expectations are measured, and what the outcomes of those measurements should be. This quality policy is considered and applied to the project scope, which is important because the project scope contains all of the work your project will undertake. What good is a quality policy if it's not implemented with the project work?

Depending on your organization, you may also have relevant standards and regulations that will serve as input to your quality planning. A regulation is a law or practice that is not optional in your industry. For example, the health care industry has the Health Insurance Portability and Accountability Act (HIPAA) regulations as well as other regulations it has to be abide by. A standard, on the other hand, is a rule or generally accepted practice within an industry. For example, most software application windows close using some button in the upper-right hand corner. While there's no law that says this is a must, it's a generally accepted standard regardless of the application or operating system.

When you're planning for quality, there are five major approaches you can rely on:

- **Benefit-cost analysis** Within every project, there will be a demand for quality—and a cost to reach that demand. A benefit-cost analysis considers the cost to reach the level of quality in relation to the benefits of obtaining the quality. For example, a customer may demand that a series of databases provide 100-percent accuracy 24/7. While this seems good, the synchronization of multiple databases after each change may result in a very costly solution. Instead of the expensive 100-percent solution, a better solution, for example, may be a less costly approach that ensures 98-percent accuracy.

- **Benchmarking** This approach uses other projects as a measure of performance on your current project. It examines the deliverables, the project management processes, and the successes and failures within each project to measure how the current project is performing. The problem with the approach, especially in IT projects, is that unless the nature of the IT projects is the same, it's difficult to use. You can't measure the performance metrics of a project to develop an application against the metrics of a project to create a new network. Additionally, because technology is changing so rapidly, benchmarks that were applicable 18 months ago are very likely outdated and inappropriate.

- **Flowcharting** Flowcharting shows how the components within a system are related as shown in Figure 10-6. This is an ideal approach within IT. Consider an application that follows a client-server model. The front end and the back end application must communicate over a network or series of networks.

FIGURE 10-6

Flowcharting shows how the components within a system are related.

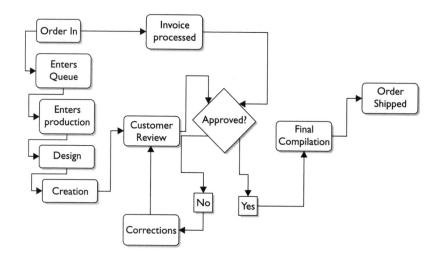

A flowchart can illustrate the various components, how they interact, and their effect on quality. Another example of a flowchart is a cause-and-effect diagram to illustrate the causes that are contributing to the quality defect within the project. These diagrams are also Ishikawa, or fishbone, diagrams.

- **Design of experiments** This approach relies on statistical what-if scenarios to determine which variables within a project will result in the best outcome. The design of experiments approach is most often used on the product of the project, rather than the process of the project itself. For example, a project team creating a new network may experiment with the capacity of the network cable, the network switches, the routers, and the number of the network cards on the servers to determine which is the best combination for the best price. Design of experiments is also used as a method to identify which variables within a project, or product, are causing failures or unacceptable results.

- **Cost of quality analysis** Cost of quality is the sum of all the costs to achieve the expected quality the customer demands in the project deliverables. This includes all of the work to conform to the quality requirements and the expense incurred from nonconformance to the quality requirements. The cost of nonconformance is most evident when work needs to be redone and there's wasted materials. Technically, the cost of quality has three costs: prevention costs, appraisal costs, and failure costs. Failure costs are associated with what could happen if the project fails: the lack of sales, loss of customers, product returns, fines and fees, downtime, and so on.

Traditional Quality Assurance

Quality assurance (QA) is a series of actions and requirements to assure the organization that each project will meet the relevant quality standards. QA is typically mandated on an organization-wide, or departmental-wide program or quality system. For example, if your company uses Six Sigma or is ISO 9000 certified, your project will have quality standards that it will have to map to under these guidelines and regulations. QA is concerned with the systematic activities that are applied to each individual project to ensure that quality exists.

To implement quality assurance, you'll first follow parent organizational procedures that may be established for your projects. These can include reports, forms, audits, and other quality-assuring activities. Quality assurance is prevention-driven, in that the goal is to prevent a lack of quality. The same tools a project manager uses for quality planning can also be applied as part of the QA process:

- Benefit/cost analysis
- Benchmarking
- Flowcharting
- Design of experiments
- Cost of quality analysis

Depending on the nature of your project and organization, your project may also undergo quality audits. A quality audit is a formal review of the quality management activities you have in place within your project. Quality audits can be completed in-house by QA professionals your organization employs or by third-party experts.

Traditional Quality Control

As you now know, quality is measured by the end result of a project. Obviously you cannot wait until the end of a project to determine if quality exists. Quality control (QC) is concerned with the quality of the actions and deliverables within a project. QC is inspection-driven; QC reviews the deliverables to establish that the quality expected by the project stakeholders is present.

QC is also concerned with the root cause of results that are below the quality standards, and with eliminating the issues that are causing quality to slip so that quality issues are not repetitive. It focuses not only on the product of a project, but also on the project management process itself. For example, QC is used to determine why cost and schedule variances have occurred and what corrective actions can be enforced to ensure the same mistakes don't happen again.

QC requires the project manager to have some understanding of statistical analysis, sampling, and probability to track trends, predict quality results, and determine root causes in quality issues. Trend analysis is especially useful in IT projects as most work within an organization is cyclic. For example, the network servers take a processor hit every morning as users log on to the network, check their e-mail, and open files. In the afternoon, the proxy servers may have an increase in Internet traffic as users check the news, the weather, or the traffic for their commutes home. In an IT project, trend analysis can allow the project team to make educated decisions on how to react to conditions within the project.

QC must be managed throughout the project. It's unacceptable to wait until the project is ended to see if the deliverables are of quality. The project management must get out, look, listen, and inspect. Throughout the project there are four fundamental facts about quality control:

- Prevention keeps quality errors out of the project. Inspection keeps quality errors away from the customer.

- Attribute sampling means the results meet the expected quality standards or they don't. Variables sampling tracks the level of acceptability of the results over time.

- Within a project you have special causes where quality excels or diminishes due to anomalies within the project. Otherwise you expect the results to vary as part of the project; this typical variance is simply called random causes.

- A tolerance is an acceptable range of quality for the project or deliverable. Control limits are the outer and upper limits that the quality results must fall within. If results are within the limits, the project is in control. If the results are out of the limits, it's considered to be out of control.

Implementing Quality Control

Know this: quality is planned into a project, never inspected in. A goal for any project is to achieve quality by planning for quality—and then following the plan. But how will you know if quality exists on a project unless there is accountability? Sure, you could wait until your project is complete and then test out the deliverables, but that's a little late. Quality control must happen throughout the project to ensure that quality exists.

The most accessible method to ensure quality is inspection. Once you inspect the work, you can measure and react to the evidence you and your project team have found. There are many different approaches to inspecting the project deliverables. Here are four of the most common:

Peer Review

One approach to QC throughout an IT project is to use peer review. Peer review, as its name implies, is the process of allowing team members to review each other's work. It is an excellent method to ensure that each team member is completing her work and doing an excellent job. Peer review provides for many things, including

- Ensuring that each task is checked for quality
- Allowing a team member to show others her work
- Allowing a team member to learn about other areas of the project
- Allowing the project manager to ensure the work is being completed
- Holding the team responsible for the quality of the work completed

The risk involved with peer review QA is that not all team members are up to the challenge of reviewing another's work or having their work reviewed by an equal. If you use this approach, your team members must have confidence in each other's ability to fairly review other members' work, and confidence in their own abilities to complete the assigned tasks.

Statistical Sampling

Statistical sampling is the process of choosing a percentage of results at random. For example, a project creating a database and web site to sell concert tickets may require a measurement of database accuracy, the speed of the web site, and the functionality of the overall program. This testing must be completed on a consistent basis throughout the project, rather than on a hit-and-miss basis.

Statistical sampling can reduce the costs of QC, but mixed results can follow if an adequate testing plan and schedule are not followed. The science of statistical sampling, and its requirements to be effective, is an involved process. There are many books, seminars, and professionals devoted to the process.

Management by Walking Around

One of the most successful methods for managing quality is to allow yourself to be seen. Get out of your office and get into the working environment. You don't have to hover around your team, but let them know you are available, present, and interested in their work.

So many IT project managers have a fear of being disliked, or seen as typical management, or consider themselves too important to speak with their team. These less-than-successful project managers alienate themselves by hiding in their offices, ignoring the opportunity to work with the project team to ensure quality from the get-go. Don't let this happen to you! Get involved with the project team members and make yourself visible.

Reviews by Outside Experts

Hire an outside expert to review the project as it progresses. This approach allows the project manager, who may not be as skilled as his team on the project's technology, to ensure the team is completing the assigned work with care and precision. A consultant can be brought into the project at key milestones to make an unbiased review of the work done to date. The consultant can accomplish many things for a project's success. This practice

- Ensures quality and accuracy
- Allows for an unbiased review by a third party
- Creates accountability for the team completing the work
- Allows the project manager to know the true status of the work
- Allows the project manager to make any needed adjustments

Analyzing Quality

Once you've completed the inspection of the project and the product deliverables, now what? Of course, you'll be doing QC inspections on a regular basis, so you'll need to track and analyze the results. You'll want to complete root cause analysis to determine why quality issues may be random or repetitive. There are five major approaches to tracking and analyzing quality:

Using Control Charts

A control chart displays the results of your inspections over time. The results of inspections are plotted out against a mean, and an upper and a lower control limit. As you can see in Figure 10-7, the results of inspections are measured and then added to the control chart. When results are over the control limit, they're out of control; otherwise, the project is acceptable. However, this approach can be a little tricky in many IT projects. Control charts are best when you have projects that are extremely repetitive, such as manufacturing and construction projects. That's not to say that you still can't use these charts within IT projects—just be aware that the results of your measurements may fluctuate as the nature of the work within the project changes. You can use control charts to track server usage, update, network throughput, and more.

When results of a measurement fall out of control, this is called an assignable cause. An assignable cause means there is some reason for this event to occur. It could be a hardware error, a different developer, or some other reason. It's a signal that root cause analysis is needed. In addition, whenever seven results of your testing all fall on one side of the control chart's mean, it's called the "Rule of Seven" and is also an assignable cause. There will always be some reason why the quality has stymied on one side of the mean or the other. Again, time for root cause analysis.

Using Pareto Diagrams

A Pareto diagram is somewhat related to Pareto's Law: 80 percent of the problems come from 20 percent of the issues. This is also known as the "80/20 rule." A Pareto diagram illustrates the problems by assigned cause from smallest to largest as Figure 10-8 shows. The project team should first work on the largest problems and then move onto the smaller problems.

FIGURE 10-7

Control charts measure results over time.

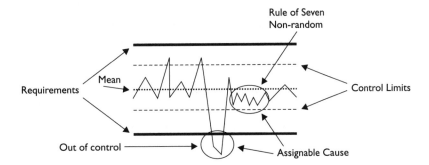

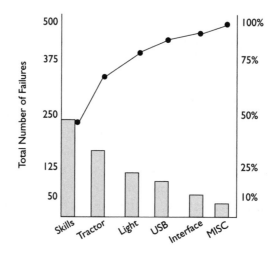

FIGURE 10-8

A Pareto diagram is a histogram ranking the issues from largest to smallest.

Revisiting Flowcharting

Remember flowcharts? Flowcharting is a method to chart how the different parts of a system operate. Flowcharting is valuable in QC because the process can be evaluated and tested to determine where in the process quality begins to break down. Corrective actions can then be applied to the system to ensure quality continues as planned—and expected.

Applying Trend Analysis

Trend analysis is the science of taking past results to predict future performance. Sports announcers use trend analysis all the time: "The Cubs have never won in Saint Louis, on a Tuesday night, in the month of July, when the temperature at the top of the third inning is above 80 degrees."

The results of trend analysis allow the project manager to apply corrective action to intervene and prevent unacceptable outcomes. Trend analysis on a project requires adequate records to predict results and set current expectations. Trend analysis can monitor

- **Technical performance**   Trend analysis can ask, "How many errors have been experienced by this point in the project schedule, and how many additional errors were encountered?"

- **Cost and schedule performance**   Trend analysis can ask, "If we are $4,000 over budget now, what is our final cost likely to be?"

Total Quality Management

No book on project management would be complete without at least a nod to *Total Quality Management* (TQM). Total Quality Management is a process that involves all employees within an organization working to fulfill their customers' needs while also working to increase productivity. TQM stems from Dr. W. Edward Deming and his management principles, which the Japanese adopted after WWII. In the U.S., these principles were readily adopted in the 1980s after proof of their success in Japan.

The leading drive of TQM is a theory called *Continuous Quality Improvement.* According to this theory, all practices within an organization are processes, and these processes can be infinitely improved, which results in better productivity and ultimately higher profitability.

Here's how this relates to IT project management: the processes a project manager utilizes to communicate, schedule, and assign resources can be streamlined, improved, and modernized to make the project easier to implement and more profitable as a whole. Examples include Microsoft Project Server and other web solutions for project teams.

In project management, the customer is the end user of the deliverable, and the concept of streamlining processes is dependent on the project manager and the project team. Scores of books have been written about Total Quality Management, though one of the best books, *Out of the Crisis*, is from the concept's originator, Dr. W. Edwards Deming.

Quality project management as a process is not a magical formula, an equation you can map out in Excel, or a dissertation from a business professor at Harvard. It is a simple thing to describe, but fairly difficult to implement. Quality project management comes from the dedication of the project manager and the project team to completing with gusto the required activities in each phase to produce an excellent deliverable. Anything less should be unacceptable.

Creating a Strategy for Quality

As with any area of project management, you won't be successful without a plan. Quality control requires a plan, a process, and a strategy to implement and enforce it. You can attack quality enforcement many ways; the best, however, is to lead by example. You should be the focal point of quality for your team, as Figure 10-9 depicts, in all that you do. Leading by example shows your team your own level of dedication to the project and that you expect your team to follow.

FIGURE 10-9

Project managers are the foundation for quality.

Revisiting the Iron Triangle

The second best method of implementing quality, regardless of the project, is a balance of time, cost, and scope. As you can see in Figure 10-10, the quality of the project is dependent on your management of the allotted time, the assigned budget, and the expected scope. Of course, there's leadership, managerial skills, and more—but without balance, the project will fail.

The one element that you should already have a strong handle on is time. Some projects will have more freedom with time than others. During the planning phase

FIGURE 10-10

Quality can be achieved with a realistic balance of time, cost, and scope.

of your project, you should be able to predict what the required time is to complete the project and meet the assigned objectives. Projects that are constrained on time will, no doubt, require you and the team to work diligently and quickly to achieve the objectives. When time becomes an issue, the quality of the project will as well.

The budget for the project is approved by management and will be yours to manage—most likely under management's watchful eye. Your planning and implementation of the plan will help determine the budget of the project. Should your plan be full of holes, underdeveloped, and not comprehensive enough to counter foreseeable problems, your budget will be blown and the quality will suffer.

Finally, the scope of the project must be protected from unnecessary change. A change control system must be in place, backed by management, and used. When the scope begins to creep, the project's time and budget must match the changes to the scope. Most often, however, when unapproved changes come into the project, quality begins to diminish because time and funds that should be allotted to complete approved project activities are spent on unapproved activities.

Progress Reports

One method to implement quality is to use progress reports. A progress report is simply a formal, informative method of summarizing the status of work completed. Typically, on longer projects, progress reports are essential for keeping a record of the work completed, and they make for handy references in the end phase of the project.

In regard to quality, the process of creating progress reports allows the project manager and the project team to ascertain where the team is on the project and the amount of work yet to do. It's a great way to visualize the progress the team has made so far and determine if the project is on track with the project vision.

Project sponsors and your project team's functional managers will typically want to see the progress reports, as it allows them to keep in tune with your ability to lead the team and manage the project. Upper management may not want to see these reports, as their time may be limited. These reports can be based on templates that allow you and the project team to quickly and accurately complete the progress report. There are four types of progress reports you'll use as a project manager:

Current Status Reports These reports are quick news on the work completed, or not, since the last status report. For example, you may determine that status reports should be completed every two weeks. Within each two-week window are tasks that must be completed. This report will focus on the scheduled tasks and their status over the last two weeks.

If scheduled tasks were not completed, the report should clearly state why the work has lagged behind and what solution is offered to get the work back on schedule. Distribute this report to the project team and the project sponsor, and keep a hard copy in the project binder. These reports are excellent for record keeping and nudging the project team back on track.

Cumulative Reports   As its name implies, this report focuses on the work from the beginning of the project until the current date. Cumulative reports are excellent in long-term projects and should be created based on management's requests, at milestones within the project, or on a regular schedule such as every three months. Use these reports for looking back on the progress accomplished so far on the project. Information in this report should include:

- Work completed
- Lagging tasks and plans for recovering lost time
- Significant accomplishments
- Variances
- Budget information

Management Summary Reports   Management summary reports detail the overall status of the project, changes from the original plan, change in execution, or cost variances within the budget. These reports are created on an as-needed basis and are ideal for upper management, as upper management does not have the time to read detailed reports to discover that everything on the project is going as planned. These reports are quick and to the point—effective when sharing bad news. The purpose of these reports is a fast, honest way to summarize the project status so that management may keep the project in check.

Variance Reports   Variance reports are summaries of any variances within the project, mainly time and cost, but they can also be reports on scope variances. They require the project manager to evaluate the cumulative work against the original project implementation plan. The comparison of the two should indicate where the project is and where it is heading. These detailed, number-orientated reports are an ideal way of enforcing quality and keeping the project on track.

FROM THE FIELD

Interview with Greg Zimmerman

Name: Greg Zimmerman
Title and Certifications: Network Administrator, CCNA, CompTIA Network+
Organization: Minnesota Department of Transportation
Years as an IT project manager: 4

Greg Zimmerman is the systems administrator for the Office of Materials and Road Research, a division of the Minnesota Department of Transportation. Greg is solely responsible for all aspects of technical projects at the Office of Materials and Road Research. Greg has a bachelor's degree from the University of Wisconsin, Lacrosse. He previously worked as an IT consultant.

Q: As a project manager, what is your definition of quality?

A: From my perspective, which is working on network projects, I define quality as reliability.

Q: How can a project manager work with each team member to ensure quality throughout the project?

A: To ensure quality throughout the project, there must be clear, decisive goals. Each member must understand what it takes to reach his goal and how his responsibilities within the project affect the project as a whole. The project manager must track and evaluate the process to see if the goals that each member has been assigned are being met. In other words, the project manger must manage the project and the people working on it.

Q: How can a project manager inspire the project team to impact quality on each phase of a long-term project?

A: By establishing clear, decisive goals and enforcing their establishment. Most projects that fail do so because there were never clear and decisive goals set in the beginning.

Q: What is most difficult part of enforcing quality?

A: The most difficult part of enforcing quality is scalability—the ability to grow and evolve the project either during the project management process or after. The reason being is that so often a project manager's concentration is on the completed product, not what the product will be after it is completed. Poor project managers do not look beyond the constraints at hand nor do they look to the future and try to forecast future expectations or requirements.

Q: What processes should be in place so that a project manager may take a sampling of the work completed to ensure an ongoing commitment to quality?

A: There should be major goals set at the beginning of the project, and each of those major goals should be broken into subgoals.

Q: How does a project manager address a situation where a team member is lackadaisical about his duties?

A: The project manager should immediately address the team member to rectify the problem. If the problems persist, then the team member should be excused from the project.

Q: What are attributes of a project manager who is committed to quality on each IT project she's involved with?

A: Good leadership, follow-through, determination, and resourcefulness.

Q: When a project manager is working with an IT integrator to complete an implementation, how does he address and ensure quality control issues?

A: By establishing expectations ahead of time. Enforcing preagreed expectations is simple. Trying to enforce uncommunicated expectations is an uphill battle.

Q: What role does the team play in quality control issues?

A: The team plays the biggest role in quality control issues. Their overall importance is the leading factor when it comes to quality control.

Q: If a project plan needs to be delayed, how does the project manager address this issue in regard to quality control?

A: Quality should never suffer to meet a deadline. I often have an agreement in place that states the deadline is always extended by the number of days that a project is delayed by forces not stemming from the project manager or team members.

Q: Can you share an experience of a project you've managed that required quality control and dedication to the project?

A: We did a hot swap of an entire 750-node network from hubs to switches with zero down time. The key ingredient was planning, planning, and more planning. Each new switch and router was thoroughly tested before it was implemented. This project took approximately 1000 man hours and four months to implement. The project was completely successful due to the planning and the establishment of goals at the beginning.

Q: Can you share an experience where a lack of quality severely impacted an organization?

A: I was running several projects when I was asked to take one more "small one" on. The project involved recabling a building with Category 5 cable and establishing new access points and patch panels. The vendor was very established, one I had worked with before. When the project was approximately fifty percent done (and on a Friday), I realized the vendor had not established the access points or the patch panels in the correct location. I stopped all work and stated that I needed it done as originally specified. The contractor stated that the only way to get the project done on time was to work all weekend long, including nights. Since it was my responsibility to see it through, I stayed with the contractor all weekend until the errors were corrected.

Q: What advice do you have for aspiring project managers?

A: Work for as many project managers as you can. You can learn from the bad ones as well as from the good ones. As a team member, look at situations the project manager is dealing with and ask yourself if you would handle the situations the same way the project manager did. If you wouldn't, ask yourself why not. If you would, ask yourself why.

CHAPTER SUMMARY

Quality, quality, quality. Everyone talks about quality, but what is it? Quality is the capability of the project to meet the expected requirements of the project customer. Quality is the good, the worth, the profitability gained from and during the implementation. Quality is also the level of excellence within the project process. An IT project that produces quality results will have quality at its core—which is accomplished through planning, guidance, and leadership.

The trick to ensuring quality deliverables is to make sure that quality is designed into the project itself. Quality management is a process that ensures quality is a central point of each work unit of a project. As the project moves through its different phases, you must sample and readjust the work to be in alignment with the project deliverables to ensure quality.

Progress reports allow the project team, the project manager, and management to be aware of the status of the project at any given time. The reports can be simple one-page summaries or lengthy detailed accounts of problems encountered and solutions discovered. Reports designed for management typically are quick and to the point—good news or bad. Management doesn't have the time, or desire, to read a lengthy report only to discover everything is great.

As the project progresses, you must implement a process to ensure quality through each phase of the work. You can use leverage with your team members to ensure quality within their work by implementing peer review, sampling the project, and hiring an outside consultant to review the work.

Ultimately, the quality of a project is measured not by the project manager, the project team, or management, but by the end users of the project. Their experience and the productivity gained by the technology will be the true measure of the worth of the project.

CHAPTER QUIZ

1. Quality comprises what two things to a project manager?

    A. The quality of the deliverable

    B. The commitment of the project team

    C. The commitment of management

    D. The quality of the process to produce the deliverable

2. What must every project have to ensure the work in the project sticks to a standard of quality?

    A. A commitment from management

    B. A project manager experienced with the technology

    C. Clearly defined requirements

    D. A budget with plenty of cash reserve

3. Complete the sentence: Research allows the project manager to create the vision of the project. _____ allows the project manager to transfer the vision.

    A. Dedication

    B. Inspiration

    C. Commitment

    D. Leadership

4. What is the difference between quality and grade?

    A. Quality is the conformance to requirements, while grade is the ranking of the quality.

    B. Quality is the conformance to requirements, while grade is a ranking assigned to a material or service.

    C. There is essentially no difference between quality and grade when it comes to project management.

    D. Quality is the end result of the project, while grade is the ranking of the quality as the project moves toward completion.

5. How are the value of a service and the value of a product measured?

    A. A service is measured by the initial usage.

    B. A product is measured by the initial usage, and then its worth declines with each usage.

    C. A service is measured with each usage; goods are measured only on the first usage.

    D. A service and goods are measured with each usage. The more often each is used for productivity, the more worthy the deliverable.

6. What is QA?

    A. It is the measured value of the goods or service over a set period of time.

    B. It is the measured value of the goods or service for the duration of its usage.

    C. It is an organization-wide approach to preventing quality defects.

    D. It is an organization-wide approach to ensure that the project managers are applying corrective actions on a regular basis.

7. What is the purpose of quality planning?

    A. It determines which quality standards are relevant to the project.

    B. It is not needed on every project, because smaller projects are easier to manage.

    C. It ensures that the project manager and the project team are completing the work.

    D. It is only needed if the organization is using Six Sigma, TQM, or ISO certified programs.

8. Of the following, which is a factor that measures the quality of the management process?

    A. Project plan

    B. Results

    C. Project team

    D. Budget management

9. All of the following do not describe QC except for which one?

    A. Prevention

    B. Assurance

    C. Inspection

    D. Quality standards

10. What is the purpose of a Project Information Center?

    A. To centrally organize the resources, planning, and research phases of a project

    B. To centrally organize the resources, planning, research, and implementation phases of a project

    C. To centrally organize the project team, resolve disputes, and provide additional resources for all projects within an organization

    D. To centrally organize all projects within an organization

11. What value determines that when seven consecutive results of testing are on one side of the mean, this is an assignable cause?

    A. Six Sigma

B. Control Limits

C. Rule of Seven

D. Pareto's Law

12. What is the purpose of a Pareto Chart?

    A. It tracks trends over time.

    B. It plots out the results of sampling to determine the root cause of each problem.

    C. It ranks the quality of each component within a project.

    D. It ranks the quality problems within a project from highest frequency to lowest frequency.

13. Of the following, which is not one of the five areas of the project management process?

    A. Project genesis

    B. Planning

    C. Executing

    D. Controlling

14. What is the definition of Total Quality Management?

    A. It is a belief that all employees within an organization work to fulfill customers' needs while also working to improve profitability.

    B. It is a belief that all employees within an organization work to fulfill customers' needs while also working to improve productivity.

    C. It is a belief that upper management leads by enforcing quality in all of their work. The quality implementation will trickle down through the organization.

    D. It is a belief that a project manager must implement quality by leadership and a series of risk/reward principles.

15. What is Continuous Quality Improvement?

    A. It is the theory that all practices within an organization are a process and that processes can be infinitely improved.

    B. It is the theory that all practices within an organization can be infinitely improved.

    C. It is the theory that all practices within an organization are projects and that all projects can be infinitely improved throughout the life span of the implementation.

    D. It is the theory that all organizations provide services and that these services can be infinitely improved.

CHAPTER EXERCISES

In these exercises, you will evaluate three different IT projects that are experiencing problems with quality. For each scenario, you will offer a solution to ensure quality.

Exercise 1

Michelle is the IT project manager for an implementation of seven Windows 2003 Servers. The scope of the project is to install and configure a Windows 2003 domain with Active Directory. Three of the servers are to be located in the company headquarters in Atlanta. Two are to be installed in the Tampa office, and the remaining two are to be installed in the Nashville office.

The servers in Atlanta and in Nashville have been installed successfully, but Jerry, the network administrator, has yet to install the servers in Tampa. Jerry reports that he is leery of moving from his NetWare environment to the Windows 2003 Servers. Michelle, the project manager, insists that Jerry install the servers as planned to complete the project. A week passes and Jerry still has not completed the installation. What steps can Michelle take to ensure that the installation is completed?

Your proposed solution:

_____

_____

_____

_____

Exercise 2

You are the IT project manager for a software development project. Customers of your company, RWE Architects, should be able to use the Internet to check on the status of the building plans, review the work draftsman and architects have completed, and communicate with their account managers.

The plan to complete the project calls for a central database that can be queried by customers and the internal staff. The architects will also use a web portal to report the progress of each building plan they are working on so that customers will see the progress of the work.

The timeline for the project development and implementation is four months. At the end of the second month, you want to sample the work to date. You first evaluate the internal web portal that the architects will use to report the status of customers' work. You discover that this application has actually been designed to track hours worked on the project for billing purposes and not to report the overall progression of the building plans. This is not what the project scope called for. What steps should you take to correct the problem?

Your proposed solution:

_____

_____

_____

_____

Exercise 3

Mike is the IT project manager for an installation of four SQL Servers. The servers are all clustered for fault tolerance and are installed on multiple-processor machines, with 2GB of RAM for optimal performance. A server will be located in each network within the company.

The scope of the project requires a persistent, fast connection between each of the sites as the databases will synchronize on a regular, frequent schedule. Currently, the connection between Tempe and Phoenix is restricted to an ISDN line, well below optimal speed for fast updates. What are two recommendations you can make to ensure quality for the users in the Tempe office?

Your proposed solution:

_____

_____

_____

_____

QUIZ ANSWERS

1. **A, D.** Quality for a project manager comprises two factors: the quality of the deliverable and the quality of the experience to produce the deliverable. Commitment of the project team and of management will certainly aid in creating a good deliverable, but those factors are part of the quality of the experience to create the deliverable.

2. **C.** Clearly defined requirements are required for the project manager to check the status of the project's work. Should the project be moving away from the project's objective, the project manager must take corrective actions to nudge the project back on track.

3. **D.** Leadership allows the project manager to transfer the vision of the project from a personal concept to a goal for the project team.

4. **B.** Quality is the capability of a project to conform to the requirements as expected by the customer. Quality is planned into a project, not inspected into it. Grade is the ranking of a material or service, such as paper, metal, or first-class versus coach.

5. **D.** Goods and services are measured with each usage. The more often the goods and services are used productively, the greater their value. An expensive project that creates a deliverable that is rarely used has a small ROI.

6. **C.** QA is an organization-wide approach to ensuring the prevention of defects within the project. QA is prevention-driven while QC is inspection-driven.

7. **A.** Quality planning is the process determining which quality standards are relevant to a project and then how the project work will achieve these quality requirements.

8. **B.** The results of a project are always the ultimate barometer of quality for a project. The project plan may be beautifully written, but if it is not implemented properly, poor quality ensues. The project team must be dedicated to the project, but dedication without leadership and a focus on the deliverables will not ensure quality. Finally, budget management is essential in every project, but it will not ensure quality. The planning, the project team, and budget management, among other attributes, must all work in harmony to create quality results.

9. **C.** All of the answers, except for C, describe QA. Inspection is a key activity within QC.

10. **B.** A Project Information Center is useful for organizing all facets of a project. It is typically a room dedicated to the project where resources, testing, and documentation can take place.

11. **C.** The Rule of Seven is a guideline that states when seven consecutive results of testing fall on one side of the mean in a control chart there is some purpose for the event. This is an assignable cause.

12. **A.** Quality management is a top-down approach to project management. The project manager implements quality in every facet of the project as part of the project plan. The project team members will then absorb the dedication to quality in their implementation processes.

13. **C.** Project organization is not one of the five phases of the project management. The five areas are initiating, planning, executing, controlling, and closing.

14. **B.** TQM is the belief that all employees within an organization are consistently working to fulfill customers' needs and at the same time working toward improving productivity by refining processes.

15. **A.** Continuous Quality Improvement is the theory that all practices within an organization are processes. These processes then can be infinitely improved to streamline the business cycle and better the quality of the organization regardless of its deliverable.

EXERCISE SOLUTIONS

Exercise 1: Possible Solution

Your proposed solution may be something to this effect: As the project manager, Michelle should first reason with Jerry that this is the plan approved by management and the servers are to be replaced by Windows 2003. Michelle should then let Jerry know that the servers in Nashville and Atlanta have been moved onto Windows 2003. If there were any difficulties in installing the servers, Michelle should pass that information along to Jerry.

Another approach may be to interview Jerry as to why he's hesitant to move onto Windows 2003. It may be that Jerry does not understand the technology and feels threatened by it. A solution could be to work with Jerry through the installation and then provide training for Jerry through a Microsoft training provider. Tasks that need to be completed on Jerry's server can be done remotely until Jerry is comfortable with the solution.

Exercise 2: Possible Solution

Your proposed solution may be something to this effect: You should immediately speak with the application designer to discuss the issue. It may be that the designer is aware of the application status, and the hours worked on the project is a portion of the overall formula to communicate the customer's plans and billing information.

Of course, it may also be that the application developer does not have a clear understanding of the project's requirements. A meeting with the designer is needed to ensure the project is on track or to move the project back in alignment with the expected deliverables.

Exercise 3: Possible Solution

Your proposed solution may be something to this effect: Depending on the available funds, a faster connection should be implemented between Phoenix and Tempe. This would allow the database to replicate its information to all of the sites through the WAN connections. If funds are lacking, you may elect to edit the frequency of updates from Tempe to Phoenix. This second solution, while cost effective, may not be the best, however, because the working data in Tempe may be out of sync with the rest of the organization.

Chapter 11

Managing Teams

V ince Lombardi, arguably one of the greatest football coaches of all time, said, "The achievements of an organization are the results of the combined effort of each individual."

What a powerful idea!

Imagine any technology project you've been a part of. What made the project a success? Was it the technology? Was it all because of your efforts? Was the success all because of the project manager? Probably not. Most likely what made the project a success was the "combined effort" of the project team, as in Lombardi's quote. The team collectively worked toward the project vision, and got the job done.

IT projects often require a wide range of skills and talent. As a project manager, you'll have to lead and inspire your team to work together towards the common goal of the project. Your team members will have to learn to rely on and trust each other. The individuals on your team will need you to help them complete their tasks, challenge their abilities, and provide opportunity for growth and achievement.

The collection of the individual skills working toward a common goal is a powerful force.

Leading the Team

To lead the team, a project manager must first act like a leader. Think of any of your favorite leaders from politics, sports, or history. What are some of the attributes they possessed to lead and inspire? Chances are, all of the leaders will have one common trait: an ability to motivate people to achieve and aspire. Now this is not to say you have to be the next motivational circuit speaker, but it does mean you'll need to develop a method to connect with your team members to inspire them to work toward the vision of your project.

The easiest and most direct path to making others develop a passion for your project is for you yourself to develop a passion for the project. Passion for the deliverable, excitement and zeal for the success of the project is contagious. A project manager who wants to lead the project team has to care not only for the success of the project, but also for the success of the individuals on the team. Take time to get to know the team members, learn what their passions are, and develop a relationship with them to work with them, not over or around them.

Establishing the Project Authority

With any project, regardless of the size, the project manager must establish his authority over that project. Authority over the project is not the same as authority over the project team members. You, the project manager, will be responsible for the success of the project, so you need to take charge of the activities to finish the project. In other words, responsibility for the success of the project must have an equal level of authority over the actions to create the deliverables.

Authority and responsibility are bound together in project management. The success of the project rests on the shoulders of the project manager. The project manager's career, opportunity for advancement, and reputation all rest on the ability of the project team to finish the project and create the deliverables. As Figure 11-1 demonstrates, if the project manager does not have the authority to assign tasks to the project team members, how can she ever reach the objectives of the project? The level of authority is relative to the autonomy assigned within your organizational structure. It's not impossible for a project manager to successfully lead a project in a functional or weak matrix environment. The authority of a project manager, in any organizational structure, must be leveraged with the respect of the project team.

Team members, of course, also have a level of responsibility for completing the work, and they have risks involved in the project as well. For example, a team member may be dedicated to the project because he can perceive the personal benefits of working on a successful project. A successful relationship between the team members and the project manager should be symbiotic, as Figure 11-2 depicts.

FIGURE 11-1

A project manager must have authority in proportion to responsibility.

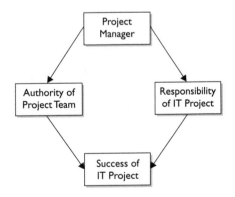

FIGURE 11-2

The relationship between the project team and project manager is symbiotic.

Team members must agree that you are the leader of the project and that they will support your decisions, your management of the resources, and your leadership to the deliverables. The project manager, though not the manager of the individual team members, still must exude a level of confidence and authority over the project team to gain their respect and desire to work on the project.

Many IT project managers stem from IT backgrounds. For these individuals to be successful, they must possess the following attributes:

- Organizational skills
- Passion for the team's success
- Passion for the project's success
- Ability to work with people
- Good listening skills
- Ability to be decent and civil
- Ability to act professionally
- Commitment to quality
- Dedication to finish the project

Mechanics of Leading a Team

There is no magic formula to leading a team. It is one of the unique qualities that some people have naturally and others must learn. One of the best methods you can use to lead a team is to emulate the leaders you admire. By mimicking the actions of successful leaders, you will be on your way to being successful too. Much of your ability to lead will come from experience and maturity. There are, however, certain procedures and protocols of project management that you must know to be successful.

Decision Making

Many new project managers are afraid to make decisions. They do not want to offend team members, make a mistake, or look bad in front of management. The fact is, your job as a project manager will require you to make decisions that may not always be popular with the project team. Figure 11-3 demonstrates the balance between acceptable risk and the safeguards of using experienced staff. The decisions you make will need to be in the best interest of fulfilling the project requirement, in alignment with the project budget, and in consideration of the project timeline.

Some decisions you will not have to make entirely on your own. The project team can make many decisions. For example, a company that is upgrading all of the workstation operating systems from Windows 98 to Windows XP will have many obstacles to pass. One of the primary questions that will need to be answered in the planning stage is how the operating system will be deployed to the workstations.

Some on the project team may be in favor of using disk imaging software. Others may want to use scripts to deploy the image. Still other members may want to visit each machine and install from a CD-ROM. Obviously, many different approaches exist for installing this operating system, but there needs to be a clear decision on what the best method is for the project—and why that method is preferred.

A project manager can lead the team through these decisions utilizing the talents, experience, and education of each team member to come to a conclusion. To facilitate the discussion, the project manager may use three types of decision-making processes to arrive at a solution:

- **Directive**   The project manager makes the decision with little or no input from the project team. Can you see the danger here? The project manager may be aware of the technology to be implemented, but he may not be the most qualified to make the entire decision. Directive decision making is acceptable, and needed, in some instances, but it isolates the project manager from the project team.

- **Participative**   Participative decision making is what you should aim for. In this model, all team members contribute to the discussion and decision

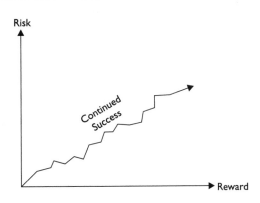

FIGURE 11-3

Project managers must balance risk and reward to be successful.

process. This method is ideal for major decisions such as the process to roll out an operating system, design a new application, or develop a web solution for an organization. Through compromise, experience, and brainstorming, the project team and the project manager can create a buzz of energy, excitement, and synergy to arrive at the best possible solution for a decision.

■ **Consultative**   This approach combines the best of both preceding decision-making processes. The project team meets with the project manager, and together they may arrive at several viable solutions. The project manager can then take the proposed solutions and make a decision based on what she thinks is best for the project. This approach is ideal when dealing with projects under tight deadlines, restrictive budgets, and complex technology. When there are many variables that can cause the project to stall, the project manager must assume more of the responsibility to safeguard the project.

Working with Team Members

During the process of arriving at a solution or after a solution has been made, some team members may simply disagree with you. Disagreements are fine and are encouraged, as it will show team members are thinking and looking for the best solution to a project. In some instances, though, team members may create conflicts among themselves over differences of opinion. These internal conflicts can cause a team to break into cliques, uncooperative partners, and ultimately a nemesis to the success of the project.

You will have to learn how to be diplomatic among the team members to keep the project moving toward its completion. You will encounter four types of team members in your role as a project manager:

■ **Evaders**   These team members don't like confrontation on any level. They would just as soon nod their heads, smile, and scream internally, "No, no, no!" These team members may be new to the company, shy, or intimidated by outspoken team members—including the project manager. When using the participative method to arrive at a decision, everyone's input is needed—including from these people. You will learn very quickly who these people are on your project team, as they'll never or rarely offer a differing opinion or disagree with any suggestions made. To get these individuals involved, try these techniques:

■ Have each team member offer an opinion on the topic, then write the suggestion on a whiteboard.

- If possible, allow team members to think about the problem and then e-mail their proposed solution to you.

- Call directly on the evader team members first when asking for suggestions.

- **Aggressive**   These team members love to argue. Their opinions are usually in opposition of the popular opinion, they are brash in their comments, and they are typically smarter than anyone else on the project team—at least they think they are. These folks may be very intelligent and educated on the technology, but they play devil's advocate out of habit rather than trying to help the team arrive at the best solution. You'll know who these individuals are rather quickly—as will everyone on the project team. To deal with these folks, try the following methods:

  - Allow these team members to make their recommendation first before taking suggestions from other team members.

  - Ask them to explain their position in clear, precise reasoning.

  - If necessary, speak with them in private and ask for their cooperation when searching for a solution.

- **Thinkers**   These team members are sages. They are usually quiet through much of the decision-making process and then they offer their opinion based on what's been discussed. These team members are excellent to have on the project team, though sometimes their suggestions stem from other team members' input. Try to work these thinkers into the discussion by asking them questions or calling for their opinions early on if you think they should contribute early on in the process.

- **Idealists**   These team members, while their intentions are good, may see the project as a simple, straight path to completion. They may ignore, or not be aware of, the process to arrive at the proper conclusion. Often, idealists are well trained in the technology but have little practical experience in the implementation. These team members are usually open to learning and eager to offer solutions to the project.

Dealing with each of these personas takes patience, insight into their personalities, and knowing what their motivations are. You have to spend time with your team members, develop a relationship with them, and lead by example. You won't be effective leading your project team if your only time invested with them is talking about the project, their assigned work, and your review of how they're doing on the project.

Team Meetings

A project manager who wants to lead an effective team must be organized, prepared, and committed to a strict timetable. When you meet with your team members, they will be looking to you to lead the meeting in an organized, efficient manner. It is not necessary, or advised, to ramble on about the project and discuss issues that are not pertinent. Simply put, call the meeting to order, address the objectives of the meeting, and then finish the meeting. Time in meetings is time not spent completing the project.

Meeting Frequency

Decide at the onset of the project how often the team should meet to discuss the project. Depending on your project, a weekly meeting may be required; in other circumstances, a biweekly meeting is acceptable. The point is to decide how often the team needs to meet as a group to discuss the project as a whole and then stick to that schedule. The project' meeting schedule should be documented in the Communications Plan.

It is acceptable, (and wise) to meet with some members of the project team if the agenda of a meeting is geared toward just those individuals. Project managers often feel the need to involve the entire team in every discussion related to the project—this is a waste of time. While an effort should be made to keep the team informed and moving forward as a whole, there will often be instances when the objectives of a meeting are geared to just a few individuals. These meetings should be separate and in addition to the regularly scheduled team meetings.

Meeting Purpose

Once you have decided to meet on a regular basis for the duration of the project, you must also decide why you are meeting at all. In other words, what is the purpose of the meeting? Typically, you will want to meet regularly with your project team to discuss the status of the work and concerns that may have evolved. Other ongoing issues include

- Review of tasks completed
- Review of upcoming tasks
- Risks and pending risks
- Recognition of team members' achievements
- Review of outstanding issues on the project
- News about the project

A project manager should create an agenda of topics that need to be discussed and then stick to the schedule. These regular meetings with the staff should usually consist of the same order of business, the same length of time, and the same participants. In a geographically dispersed project with subteams, teleconferences or videoconferences are ideal.

Using a Meeting Coordinator

A meeting coordinator runs the business of a meeting to keep the topics on schedule and according to the agenda. The project manager does not have to be the meeting coordinator. If you have a very eager team member who is excited about the technology and is ambitious, she may be an excellent meeting coordinator. This individual, like the project manager, must be organized, timely, and able to lead a team meeting. The meeting coordinator will work with the project manager to be certain key points are covered in the meeting and that the agenda is followed.

When sensitive issues are discussed, the project manager may intervene for the meeting coordinator. If you decide to use a meeting coordinator, you must be certain she has certain attributes:

- Agreement to maintain the position throughout the project
- Willingness to learn and speak before the project team
- Organization skills
- Time management abilities
- Commitment to gathering resources needed for the meeting

A meeting coordinator can be a great help to the project manager, and the associated responsibilities allow the designated meeting coordinator to gain some experience hosting meetings. You should, however, respect the position and not interrupt as she leads the meeting or take over the meeting. If the meeting coordinator needs help, then step into the role or meet with her outside the meeting to offer advice.

Meeting Minutes

IT projects require documentation on all activities; meetings are not an exception. Determine prior to the meeting who will keep the minutes of the meeting. This does not have to be the same person each time, but it would be helpful if it's someone who can type and distribute the minutes to the team members.

You need meeting minutes because they provide a record of the meeting, the problems and situations that were discussed, and documentation of the project's progress. Meeting minutes are an excellent method for keeping the team aware of what has already been discussed and settled, resolutions of problems, and proof of the attendees.

Maintaining Team Leadership

Once the project has been launched, the meeting schedule established, and the project team has developed a routine for completing, reporting, and finishing assignments, it's tempting to relax and let the project take care of itself. Unfortunately, as Figure 11-4 shows, projects won't lead themselves to the finish line—the project manager has to.

A constant flux of problems, scenarios, lagging tasks, and technology challenges will be lurking just beneath the surface no matter how calm things may appear. The project manager must lead the team around the pitfalls, past the traps, and over the hurdles to finish the project. This requires a project manager with many talents, abilities, and experience. So what is the ideal project manager as a leader?

Background and Experience

When it comes to information technology, experience means practically everything. An IT project manager may see project management as a logical segue into a management position with a company—and certainly it can be. But to be a great IT project manager, experience within the technology sector is needed. By relating personally to the technology, a level of respect is gained not only by the project team but also by management. Your experience in the IT field will allow your guiding hand to nudge the project back in alignment with the project's goals. Some IT

FIGURE 11-4

Projects require the project manager's constant attention.

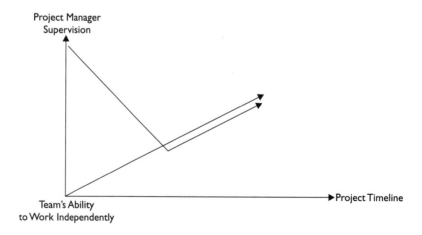

professionals, however, may be lacking in the interpersonal skills, tact, and charm that is sometimes required to motivate and lead a group of individuals.

For other IT professionals, it may be difficult to surrender the workload to the project team. They may discover it's difficult to assert their authority and to rely on someone else to complete the implementation. It may behoove these professionals to take a management course such as Dale Carnegie Training to enhance their ability as a manager.

But what of project managers who come from other industries? Perhaps they've joined a company to become a project manager within the IT field, but their experience is based on a traditional managerial background. How can these individuals relate to the technology and the type of people who excel with technology?

These individuals will have to rely on their skills as managers to relate to and lead a project team. They will need to rely heavily on the subject matter experts on their team to give them accurate information. They are also going to have to work with the project team to learn about the technology they are implementing to gain technology experience. It may be helpful for these professionals to enroll in a course on the technology being implemented to understand the process of the implementation from a technician's point of view.

Of course, the best project managers, which there is always a demand for, are the rare individuals who have years of technology experience but also have the keen ability to work and lead the project team. Figure 11-5 demonstrates the ideal balance of managerial experience and technical background for any IT project manager. You can become one of these professionals regardless of where you are in your career right now. The secret is to identify the areas of your career where you may be lacking and then seek out projects and opportunities to gain experience with the technology or the management position.

FIGURE 11-5

Managerial and technical experience is necessary for IT project managers.

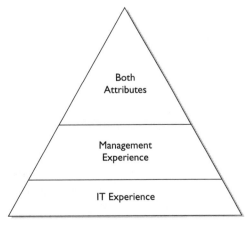

Industry Certifications

Regardless of where you are in your career, experienced or still striving to achieve, industry certifications can underscore your commitment to your field. When it comes to technology certifications, you have many choices: Microsoft, Novell, CompTIA, Cisco, Lotus, and many more are offered. Technical certifications are usually earned from years of experience and the passing of one or several exams, depending on the vendor sponsoring the exam.

Certifications related to project management are also available, such as CompTIA's IT Project+, and the Project Management Institute's Project Management Professional certifications. These certifications show a dedication to the career path of project management. A combination of technical certifications and the project management certifications is ideal for any IT project manager. (The exam objectives for CompTIA's IT Project+ can be found in Appendix A.)

Web Sites for Certification Information

Here are just a few of the many web sites that can provide additional information on technology and project management certifications:

- **Cisco** www.cisco.com/warp/public/10/wwtraining/
- **Microsoft** www.microsoft.com/traincert/default.asp
- **Novell** www.novell.com/education/certinfo
- **Oracle** www.oracle.com/education/certification
- **Lotus** www.lotus.com/home.nsf/welcome/certification
- **Project Management Institute** www.pmi.org/certification
- **CompTIA** www.comptia.com/certification/index.htm

Working Toward the Finish

A project requires many things: finances, hardware, time, and other resources. Chief among the required resources is a commitment from all parties involved in the project. This includes the project manager, management, the project sponsor, and the project team. You will need to create and maintain a relationship with each of these parties to ensure their continued support of the project and their commitment to seeing the project through. Project managers who isolate parties that are not actively involved with the implementation are doing their project and career a disservice. Management, project sponsors, and departments that are impacted by the technology implementation want to hear from the project manager on a regular basis, as Figure 11-6 shows. They want, and need, to be kept informed.

Commitment from the Project Team's Managers

If you are working in a functional or matrix environment, managing a project team is a complex process that requires a commitment from the team members' managers. The managers of the team members may be from several different departments within the organization, or they could all be directly within the IT department. The structure of your organization will have a huge impact on the attitude and outlook of the project team on the technology project.

For example, if all of the team members have the same manager, as is the case in a functional organization, it will be easier to coordinate activities and participation from all of the team members and the one manager. This scenario is typical in smaller companies or organizations with a very tightly structured IT department. In these instances, a relationship between you and the manager is easier to create than a project that has team members from several departments with different managers.

Typically, your project team will be comprised of team members who come from various departments and have an interest in the development and implementation of the technology. In these instances, you'll need to develop a relationship with each of the managers to relay to them what their employees are contributing to the project. A relationship is also needed so the manager can see the importance of the project and the team member's dedication to it.

FIGURE 11-6

Project managers must keep many people informed on the project status.

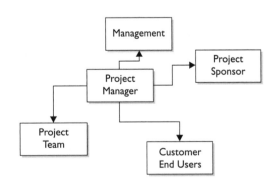

Project Completion and Team Members' Growth

As a project manager, your obvious goal is to complete the project as planned, on time, and on budget. As you begin to assign your team members to the tasks, you'll have a serious challenge to conquer. Team members will look to you to assign tasks that allow them to grow and learn new skills. You, on the other hand, will be looking toward the project deliverables and will want to use the resources available to get there the best and fastest way you can. The paradox is your desire to assign the strongest resources to the critical path and the desire of the team members to learn new skills and improve their abilities. This is the concept of acceptable risk in regard to team development, as Figure 11-7 demonstrates.

The managers of the team members will want you to assign tasks to their employees fairly and according to their skill, but also allow them to stretch their abilities. The team members, using the WIIFM principle, will have a desire to complete the exciting parts of the project to gain valuable experience for their own career growth. You, of course, have a desire to complete the project smoothly and accurately from the start.

A project manager who never allows team members to attempt tasks that may be slightly beyond their grasp will not win the support of the project team. A project manager must give team members a chance to learn from the work and glean new skills and abilities. If you always assign the critical path tasks to the same technically advanced team members, they may become bored with the same type of work, just as the less technically astute team members may be bored with their perceived menial duties.

Team members' growth must be balanced with the project's health.

A solution that you should try to incorporate is mentoring. Allow the inexperienced (but willing to learn) team member to work with the more advanced team member on the critical path assignments. By coupling these two team members on assignments through the critical path, you are accomplishing several things:

- Allowing the inexperienced team member to gain new experience
- Allowing the technical team member to share his knowledge
- Providing a degree of on-the-job training
- Ensuring the critical path will be completed accurately
- Satisfying the needs of management to allow team members to grow
- Allowing your resources to become more savvy for future projects

Motivating the Team

Your team looks to you for more than just directions on what tasks should be completed next, settlements of issues, and updates on the project. Your team also looks to you for motivation. Motivation is more than a pep speech and a positive quote in your outgoing e-mails. Motivation, in project management, is the ability to transfer your excitement to your team members and have them act on that excitement.

No matter how wonderful your smile, your ability to talk with your project team, and your passion for the project, not everyone will be motivated. Much of the motivation of the project doesn't even stem from the project manager! The motivation and level of excitement will come from the company itself, the working atmosphere, and the overall commitment to the organization of each project team member.

Fred Herzberg, a management consultant and business theorist, conducted a study in 1959 that resulted in his *Motivation-Hygiene Theory*. This study arrived at the conclusion that workers are impacted by nontangible factors that are called *motivating agents* and *hygiene agents*. Hygiene agents are elements we expect in employment: a paycheck, insurance, a safe working environment, vacation time, and a sense of community. Motivating agents are elements such as opportunities to learn new skills, promotions, and rewards for our hard work. The presence of hygiene agents does nothing to motivate employees—only motivating agents motivate them. However, the absence of hygiene agents will demotivate workers.

Herzberg theory also believes people are either motivation-seekers or hygiene-seekers. Hygiene seekers take comfort

- Company policy and administration
- Supervision
- Salary
- Interpersonal relationships
- Working conditions

These employees like to feel safe, guarded, and secure in their job and their organization. They are not overly excited by opportunity, growth, or the challenge of the work. Inversely, there are five factors that motivation seekers take comfort in:

- Achievement
- Recognition
- The work itself
- Responsibility
- Advancement

The contrast between the two workers is startling. The hygiene seekers take comfort in, for example, the health insurance policies, sick day allowance, and the number of vacation days allowed per year. While motivation seekers appreciate the company policies, they find more comfort in the challenge of achievement, growth, and opportunity for advancement.

Which would you rather have on your project team? Chances are you'll encounter both types of workers, so the actual motivation for each type of employee will vary. Perhaps for the hygiene seekers, time off for work, a bonus, or the opportunity to travel on the project will be their reward. Motivation seekers will look for more long-term rewards than a free day from work and will be motivated by their achievements, their opportunity for advancement, and public recognition of the work they've completed.

In all of us, there is likely a mixture of both the hygiene seeker and the motivation seeker. The trick for you is to determine which personality type is predominant in your project team members and then act accordingly.

FROM THE FIELD

Interview with Tom Robinette

Name: Tom Robinette
Title: Project Manager, Director of Infrastructure
Company: Paragon Consulting Service
Years as an IT project manager: 6

Tom Robinette is the owner of Paragon Consulting Services, a Houston, Texas–based firm. Paragon's clients include Cummins Engine, Eaton Corporation, Dana Corporation, ArvinMeritor, and others. Mr. Robinette specializes in the design and implementation of large, complex infrastructure–based UNIX servers, storage array implementations, and high-demand technology centered on Oracle solutions. You may contact him at Twrobin@aol.com or at 713-703-8658.

Q: What is the key to successfully managing a team?

A: I think it's imperative that you have functional control of the team members; the project that you are managing must be their number one priority. A critical success factor for project managers in general is to understand the real business problem that you are trying to solve and then provide a solution for it.

You have to do a sales job with management to ensure that whatever time you've determined is needed to meet the scope is the time you get. One of the most difficult things you'll face as a project manager is when a team member's manager assigns the team member additional tasks outside of the project. The team member's manager takes away time from a resource that you needed.

Q: What must a project manager do to ensure that his team is committed to the project?

A: You have to work with the team member's manager to ensure that part of the team member's performance evaluation includes a reflection of the milestones and deliverables that are part of your project. Cash is always a great motivator. All others not withstanding, performance reviews can directly touch a team member's pocketbook. It is a great motivator to reward based upon the quality and speed of the deliverable.

Q: How can a project manager inspire the project team?

A: I think you have to lead by example. A project manager has to be in the trenches helping the team to get the work done, helping them solve problems. One of the things that has made me successful is that this is how I manage: I am a resource for the team members. My job as a project manager is to make their jobs as smooth as possible. Not only do I manage the project, but I also attempt to do everything I can to support the people on the project team. When you do that, people will do everything they can to support you, people will die to finish their objectives for you. It behooves you to develop a personal relationship with every member of the project team. If you are friends with your team members, then they will go a lot further than if you were rude and unapproachable.

Q: What is the most difficult part of managing a project team?

A: It's not as difficult managing a project as some might think. For me, it's plan your work, work your plan. The most difficult part of the project isn't the execution of the plan at all; it's the conflicting priorities business sends your way. It's always a squeeze between the budget, the project scope, and the timeline. Management must understand that those things equal a triangle, and if one side is increased, then all of the sides must increase as well. You can't nickel and dime the project and expect the project to get done on time and with the same deliverables—just like the sky is blue and the grass is green, and there's no changing it.

Q: How does a project manager lead a team when team members are geographically dispersed?

A: I've found it to be fairly easy; the key to doing that is to provide a clear structure of the way you communicate. You need a clear plan of how you'll have meetings, and how you will include each of virtual teams as part of the entire team. Don't let remote teams feel as if they're off on their own swinging in the breeze without support or communication. Most of the projects I've worked on have been in manufacturing throughout the U.S. and Mexico. We would always very early on in the process define set meeting schedules and work on practically overcommunicating to get people used to the communication channels through e-mails, memos, meeting schedules—stressing the importance to be on time and committed to the project. We would do things to periodically get people collated. We'd offer day-long work sessions that were planned early on in the project so everyone could meet and focus on the project's goals. Once you set the lines of communication, they become very efficient.

Q: How do you handle team members who are disgruntled and unpleasant?

A: Every project I've worked on has had some disgruntled folks to deal with. Almost invariably people who are assigned to a project team but are not happy with the assignment are not going to be happy in general. Disgruntled team members require you to invoke anthropology, dig at the problem, and find a solution. Project managers have to understand where these folks are coming from, and to accomplish that you have to develop a personal relationship. The project manager's job is to act as a counselor, a father, and a confessor to turn the situation around and make it a win for everybody. The reality is that you can't have someone sabotaging your success. You have to find a way to hook that person into the project, even if it takes something personal such as a relationship with the project manager, career advancement, or being able to show the management that gave them the assignment what they are capable of doing. And sometimes there are just situations where you eventually have to have someone reassigned.

Q: What are attributes of a good project manager in regard to leading a team?

A: First off, she has to be able to keep a lot of balls in the air at the same time. I think the key for a good project manager is to understand the subject matter in the scope of the project. The greater the project manager's experience and knowledge in the discipline being implemented, the greater the degree of her success. The project manager is a direct contributor in the success or failure of a project. The more you understand the skill set involved, the better you are at dealing with the problems that arise. Personal knowledge of the subject matter is key, not from a traditional business and project management standpoint, but from a technical standpoint. Another key to success is being a salesperson, being an advocate for your project, and effectively talking to multiple layers of the organization. Having some sales savvy and flexibility in the way you communicate is key.

   Just doing the work and selling the project is important. So often projects get bogged down in meetings, and politics, and personal goals to gain consensus. Eventually you just have to start kicking ass and taking names. People respect that, as it is just how things get done. Regardless of how that is perceived, unless you are abrasive, that's how the project is brought in on time, on scope, and on budget.

Q: How does a project manager lead a team when a project is consistently going awry?

A: I think if you are a good project manager, your project won't go awry. I know that sounds conceited, but you will always have difficulty on the project. You have to plan and explain to people what's going on, what the plan is, and how to execute it. Actions in the face of adversity are what separate the excellent project managers from the mediocre. You have to think on your feet and evaluate a variance's impact on the scope and the timeline. Should things need to change, let people know that day—that moment. It's one thing to say there's drama and the sky's falling. Management doesn't like to hear that. Management does, however, like to hear there's drama and the sky's falling—but here's how we're going to fix it. Most of project management is just common sense kind of stuff.

Q: What must a project manager do when new team members come aboard when a project is already in the integration phase?

A: What I usually do is figure what their most solid skill set is. What do they bring to the table? I'll pair them up with someone on the project team on an objective that both team members are qualified to complete. I'll give them tasks and activities to co-deliver for some period of time, perhaps for a few months on a year-long project, or weeks on a project that lasts a few months. While they are working with other team members, I'll try to figure out how to get the full-time equivalent (FTE) out of the new team members, given that they're coming into the project late.

Project managers must interview new team members and figure what they want to do and can do. You may have to shuffle resources around to maximize the amount of resources you have. Typically, though, you can't always do that and keep everyone happy and the project moving forward.

Q: What methods do you use to resolve disagreements among team members?

A: They are many and varied. Copious quantities of alcohol can go a long way toward conflict resolution (*laughs*). I say that in jest, but it's always easiest to resolve conflict when parties are actually looking for resolutions. Usually, conflicts arise when people are emotionality tied to an area of the project. They are so attached to that area it is to a fault. Generally, people don't like confrontation; they'll scream and cry in private, but they won't approach the people they have a conflict with—usually.

I think conflict creates a better work environment; overall, it creates a better project, a better deliverable. What is productive is to get people in a room, and work as adults. I'll say, "You guys hash this out and we'll meet in the middle." Ultimately, the project manager has to settle them down and say, "This is my call."

Q: What types of rewards have you used for your team members to keep them motivated?

A: We've used cash payment, additional vacation time, comp time; we've used tickets to the opera and sporting events, and the real incentive is to deliver rewards right as they're earned.

I tend to shy from public recognition because someone may feel left out. If you personalize the reward and recognition and get it out of the business stage, it's less emotional and more personal.

An official recognition requires that you have to be very upfront on the award. It can cause some jealousies. For example, you've got a big plaque in your office and I don't. But I worked just as hard on this project as you, and so on.

Public recognition in team meetings is fine. I slip them in as kudos and a round of applause to team members who have accomplished milestones that will make the whole project team's life easier. I tie it in so everyone benefits from recognition.

Q: Can you share an experience of a project you've managed that required you to go the extra mile to lead a team to a project's conclusion?

A: Which ones don't? On the Dana implementation project, we had a very lean project team, we were scrambling at the 11th hour to finish some things that seemed to be more on the project plan than what they were. We were in the process of rolling out the first plan, and in a five-day period myself and five other guys worked around the clock to complete the project. We were all covering five different bases at once.

Q: What are some pitfalls a new project manager may face in regard to leading a project team?

A: Not knowing which battles he should fight and which battles are worth losing. New project managers should be careful of how to use "tell-assertive" assignments versus "ask-assertive" assignments with project team members. And the converse is true for a new project manager—he needs to know when to be firm and aggressive to solve issues on a project. It's all wisdom he has to gain over time. To get it, he has to learn from his mistakes. The more mistakes you make early in your career as a project manager, the more effective you are down the road.

Q: What advice do you have for aspiring project managers?

A: If you want to be effective as a project manager, you need to start doing the math on how technology really impacts your business. Start putting your name in the hat for technical projects that affect the business. Start small on projects that have a smaller scope, and get your feet wet. Implement some project manager 101 basics, set communication channels, and learn how to expect deadlines to hit on target while not being lax about the quality of work. Go through the motions on the smaller scale and work your way up. If you jump into something too big, it will eat you up. If you don't have the skill set, you will fail.

CHAPTER SUMMARY

As the project manager, you will find yourself managing things, but leading people. Through your actions, your example, and your excitement for the project, you will find solutions to motivate, inspire, and urge your team to complete the project according to plan.

You can nearly always succeed by emulating the activities, processes, and solutions of other successful project managers and leaders they admire. By mimicking the abilities of successful leaders, you can begin to absorb and implement the same talents with your team.

IT project managers who come from a technical background may need to learn interpersonal skills, organizational abilities, and management techniques to best lead the team and benefit the company. On the other hand, project managers who come from a more traditional management background will need to gain experience and an education in the technology being implemented to be most effective.

You must allow the team to make decisions as a group. Discussion from each team member's perspective is required and will contribute to the overall good of the project. You'll also need a method for dealing with team members who don't want to contribute, or become confrontational when others conflict with their suggestions. There must be a balance of input, compromise, and some disagreement in discussions by the project team.

Managers of the project team must be as committed to the project as the project manager and the project team. To be a successful project manager, you have to make an effort to create relationships with management and share the news of the project status. The team members must also be given an opportunity to increase their value and their skills by working on critical path assignments. This can be accomplished by partnering less-experienced team members with a more advanced professional.

Finally, you need to recognize the two primary personality types—hygiene seekers and motivation seekers—and learn to use what excites them to move them forward on the project. Motivation seekers are likely to be the more exciting personality. These folks are achievers, entrepreneurial in nature, and excited by learning.

Leading a project team is one of the toughest assignments a project manager has. Developing a personal relationship with each team member, establishing mutual respect, and motivating each person to succeed will not only help you complete the project, it will make you a better person.

CHAPTER QUIZ

1. What is the best path to make others develop a passion for the project?

    A. Offer bonuses if the project is completed on time.

    B. Remind the team members the project is essential to their careers.

    C. Become passionate about the project yourself.

    D. Remind the team members that mistakes they make on the project will be documented.

2. Why must the project manager have authority over a project?

    A. To ensure the team will complete the work as dictated

    B. To ensure the actions required to complete the project will be enforced

    C. To ensure the budget required to complete the project is available

    D. To ensure the organization realizes your potential as an effective manager

3. What is the relationship between authority and responsibility?

    A. Authority is the ability to control the team. Responsibility is the ability to do it well.

    B. Authority is the ability to assign resources to tasks. Responsibility is the commitment to the project.

    C. Authority is the ability to ensure the project team respects the project manager. Responsibility is the commitment to the project.

    D. Authority is the ability to assign resources to tasks. Responsibility is the ownership of the success or failure of the project.

4. Complete this sentence: A successful relationship between the team members and the project manager should be _____.

    A. Orderly

    B. Symbiotic

    C. Symbolic

    D. Relaxed

5. Of the following, which are two skills that a project manager must have to be successful?

    A. Public speaking abilities

    B. Organizational skills

    C. Ambition for a successful career

    D. Passion for the project

6. True or False: A project manager must make all of the decisions on a project.

   A. True

   B. False

7. Of the following, which decision-making process is reflective of the directive decision?

   A. A project manager who makes the decision with no team input

   B. A project manager who makes a decision based on team members' counsel and advice

   C. A project manager who allows the team members to arrive at their own decision

   D. A project manager who allows the team members to arrive at their own decision with his approval

8. Of the following, which decision-making process is reflective of the consultative decision?

   A. A project manager who makes the decision with no team input

   B. A project manager who makes a decision based on team members' counsel and advice

   C. A project manager who allows the team members to arrive at their own decision

   D. A project manager who allows the team members to arrive at their own decision with her approval

9. Why are disagreements considered to be an effective part of team discussions?

   A. It keeps the team competitive among itself.

   B. It allows the project manager to "pit" team members against each other to keep the project moving.

   C. It shows that the project team is thinking and considering alternative solutions.

   D. It allows team members to become passionate about their decisions.

10. Of the following, which is not a method you should employ when working with "evaders" during a team discussion?

    A. Have each team member offer her opinion on the topic, then write the suggestion on the whiteboard.

    B. If possible, allow team members to think about the problem and then e-mail their proposed solution to you.

    C. Have the evader listen to all of the comments and then make his decision.

    D. Call directly on the evader team members first when asking for suggestions.

11. You are a project manager for an application development project. You have eight team members who are all adding opinions about the web connectivity feature of the application. Of the

following statements, which most likely came from a team member with the aggressive personality type?

A. I've done this before so I know it works.

B. We could model our application after a project we've made before.

C. I agree with Susan.

D. I think we should make two different approaches and let the users decide which is most effective.

12. How often should a project manager meet with the entire project team?

A. On a regular basis, as warranted by the size and duration of the project

B. As directed by management

C. At least weekly

D. At least monthly

13. Of the following, which is the best choice for conducting meetings when the project team is dispersed geographically?

A. Have the entire project team travel to a central location to discuss the project.

B. Have the team leaders from each subteam travel to a central location to conduct the project. Team leaders would then report the results to the team when they return from the trip.

C. Have the project manager travel to each location and meet with the project team there.

D. Use videoconference software to link to all of the different teams to discuss the project.

14. Why should project team meetings have minutes recorded?

A. It allows management to have a record of each meeting.

B. It allows the project sponsor to have a record of the meeting without having to attend.

C. It allows the project manager to maintain a record of what was discussed.

D. It allows subteams to have details on what is happening in the other subteams' meetings.

15. Of the following, which two are attributes of a successful project manager?

A. Experience working with technology

B. Experience working with the project team

C. Experience working with the project sponsor

D. Experience as a traditional manager

CHAPTER EXERCISES

Exercise 1

In this exercise, you will be presented with a project management scenario. You will then be asked a series of questions based on the scenario.

You are the project manager for the rollout of 1200 Windows XP Professional workstations. Of the workstations, 730 will be new, while the remaining 470 computers will be operating systems upgrades. You have decided that all of the workstations, regardless of the new equipment or the upgraded operating system, will need a uniform installation. Domain names, installed software, and the security policies should be the same across all of these workstations.

Your team has discussed the various methods that could be used to install the operating system image. Here is a quick record of their recommendations:

Team Member	Recommendation
John	I think that we should deliver and place all of the workstations first and then configure the workstations according to guidelines. Applications can be installed via Windows 2003's policies capability.
Susan	I think the machines should all be configured prior to delivery to the clients. We could use imaging software to deploy the images to the workstations and then deliver them once all of the workstations have been configured.
Henry	Imaging software is definitely the way to go. But I think we should map out the physical departments where the machines are to be delivered. Once we've identified all of the machines in each area, we can put the image on the PC and then move it to each department.
Shelly	What we need is a combination of solutions. Let's take Susan's imaging idea and combine it with Henry's mapping of the physical placements of the machines. We should take the machines and physically place them on the network. Then, over the network, push the image to the machines through the imaging software. This way we can be delivering the PCs, installing the PCs, and installing multiple PCs over the network all at once.
Fred	Okay, that's a good idea. The only problem is it's going to be hard to deliver 730 workstations during the workday—or even over a weekend. We're going to have to do this after hours and in sections. Let's take Shelly's idea and combine it with Henry's idea to deploy the workstations over several weekends.

Complete the following questions to finish the exercise:

1. What type of decision-making process was your team participating in?

2. What are advantages to using this process?

3. Are there any disadvantages? If so, what are they?

4. Which team member may feel that his contribution was not valuable?

5. How could you respond to this team member to encourage that individual to continue to participate?

6. Which team member could be considered the sage personality type?

7. Now that you've heard what the team members have to say, what method would you recommend for this installation process?

8. Why would you deploy the workstations in the method you just described?

Exercise 2

In this scenario, you will be presented with three descriptions of team members on your project. To complete the exercise, answer the questions after each team member description.

Scenario: You are the project manager for a Lotus Notes installation. The software will need to be customized to fit your environment and will be installed on 1700 workstations throughout your company's network. Here are your team members:

John Umprheys   John is a Certified Lotus Professional. He has worked with Lotus Notes for several years and is generally considered to be the lead technician on Lotus Notes development. John is getting bored with Lotus Notes and would like to move into management, networking, or Visual Basic development after this project.

1. What methods can you use to motivate John on this project?

2. What personality type do you think John is, a hygiene seeker or a motivation seeker?

3. Why do you think that John is this type of personality?

4. How does this information help you in motivating John on the project?

Sarah Williams   Sarah is the new member of the IT department. She graduated last year from the University of Illinois with a degree in computer science. She does not have much experience in Lotus Notes, but is very eager to learn. She considers herself a quick learner, but likes to experiment with the technology before she is willing to try anything in production. She feels she must master the entire product before her contributions will be of value.

1. What methods can you use to motivate Sarah on this project?

2. What personality type do you think Sarah is, a hygiene seeker or a motivation seeker?

3. Why do you think that Sarah is this type of personality?

4. How does this information help you in motivating her on the project?

Sean Young   Sean is an experienced network administrator. He has his MCSE, and has worked with Lotus Domino Servers. He has limited experience with Lotus Notes development work. Sean is not very interested in learning the development side of Notes, as he'd rather stay in his comfort zone with network administration. His biggest concern is that the project will not go smoothly and his job as a network admin will be compromised.

1. What methods can you use to motivate Sean on this project?

2. What personality type do you think Sean is, a hygiene seeker or a motivation seeker?

3. Why do you think that Sean is this type of personality?

4. How does this information help you in motivating Sean on the project?

QUIZ ANSWERS

1. **C.** The best method you can use to make others become passionate about a project is to become passionate about it yourself. Your excitement and desire for success is contagious. Bonuses for completing a project on time are a fine tool, but it may result in rushed work. Implying threats of job loss is no way of inspiring passion for your project team; in fact, it may have the inverse effect.

2. **B.** A project manager needs authority over a project to ensure that the team will complete the tasks to finish the project. As a project manager is responsible for the success or failure of a project, she should also be given a level of authority to ensure her success.

3. **D.** Authority and responsibility are intertwined. A project manager cannot be effective if he does not have the authority to assign resources to tasks and have ownership over the success of the project.

4. **B.** The relationship between the project team and the project manager should be mutually beneficial.

5. **B, D.** A successful project manager does not have to be an effective public speaker, though it may help. Ambition for a successful career is not necessarily an asset required of the project manager. Organizational skills and a real passion for the project, however, are two attributes every project manager requires.

6. **B.** False. The project manager does not have to make every decision on a project. The team can make decisions, as can project sponsors and management.

7. **A.** When a project manager makes a decision with no team input, but on his own experience, research, or intuition, he is making a directive decision.

8. **B.** A consultative decision allows the project manager and the project team to work together to make a decision. This is ideal for situations where the project manager may not be well versed in the technology, but she must make a decision to safeguard the project.

9. **C.** Some disagreements in a team meeting are healthy as it shows the team is working toward the best solutions. Compromise and openness to different ideas is a fantastic component to any project.

10. **C.** Evaders are team members who avoid confrontations and do not want to contradict any other team member. By allowing the team member to wait until he's heard all of the other team member's suggestions, his true opinion may be masked by the desire to agree with the majority of opinions.

11. **A.** Aggressive team members are typically experienced, but have no qualms about stressing their ability to always be right.

12. **A.** Project managers should determine a schedule that is appropriate for the project. A team that meets too often will waste valuable work time. A team that meets infrequently is missing an opportunity to discuss and resolve issues on the project.

13. **D.** Videoconference software is an excellent solution for all of the team members to participate in a discussion of the project without losing days to and incurring expenses for travel.

14. **C.** Minutes need to be kept in team meetings so that the project manager has a record of the discussion of the meeting. It allows the project manager another avenue to document the details of the meetings.

15. **A, D.** A project manager who has experience either in working with technology or in the role as a traditional manager has an advantage over unproven project managers. Technical experience and a traditional management background is a great combination for any IT project manager.

EXERCISE SOLUTIONS

Exercise I

1. Your team was using the participative decision-making process. This is evident as each team member contributed to the discussion and offered solutions.

2. It allows team members to brainstorm for a solution and interact with different solutions to create an ideal resolution to the implementation challenge.

3. The disadvantages are that team members may not be comfortable offering their opinions on the technology; some may be confrontational, while others may evade confrontation and side with the majority.

4. John's opinion on the installation was immediately dismissed and never referred to again in the discussion, so he may feel his opinion isn't valuable.

5. You could invite John back into the discussion by asking what his opinion of the other solutions is. John may need some encouragement to participate in the discussion after his suggestion had been eliminated.

6. Fred did a good job listening to the other solutions and then offering a combination of all the proposals. Team members who fall into the sage category are often great at analyzing problems and then creating a solution from what others have proposed.

7. Fred's solution is probably the wisest as it addresses the bulk of the machines to be delivered, the process of installing and configuring the operating systems, and the desire to use imaging software.

8. A tiered deliverable is ideal in this situation due to the number of PCs involved. It would be practically impossible to deliver all of the workstations in one step. By delivering the PCs over several weekends or after hours, production is not interrupted and the network traffic will be minimal for the network push of the disk image.

Exercise 2

Answers for John Umprheys

1. John is likely a motivation seeker. His desire to move into management after this project may be an excellent motivational tool. By assigning John more responsibility on this project, he can learn new skills to aid his career.

2. John is a motivation seeker.

3. John is a motivation seeker due to his desire to achieve and his apparent boredom with his talents with Notes.

4. Knowing what excites John allows the project manager to assign him to tasks that John will find interesting and challenging.

Answers for Sarah Williams

1. First allow Sarah to get comfortable in the project by assigning her to tasks that are not in the early stages of the critical path. By assigning her to tasks that she will be able to successfully complete, her confidence will grow. Once she is comfortable, she can be grafted into tasks on the critical path to underscore and test her abilities.

2. Sarah may be either a hygiene seeker or a motivation seeker.

3. From the information provided, she has a desire to learn and to achieve, but also seeks comfort in having a complete understanding of the product before completing any tasks.

4. One method a project manager could use with Sarah is to assign her to tasks not in the critical path. Upon successful completion of the tasks, she could enroll in a technical course on the product. A reward of learning may excite Sarah and enable her to accomplish more later in the project.

Answers for Sean Young

1. Assign Sean to projects that you and he feel he is comfortable completing. His forte is likely in the server side of the project, so tasks within that path would be best for Sean and the good of the project.

2. Sean is likely a hygiene seeker.

3. Sean is likely a hygiene seeker because of his desire to stay put in his current role and his fear of risk in the new project.

4. A project manager can use Sean's fear of failure to assign him to tasks that are closely related to his own area of expertise. By assigning these tasks to Sean, he will likely do his best to complete the assignments correctly and efficiently not only because he is qualified and talented to do so, but also because of his apparent fear of failure on the project.

Chapter 12
Completing the Project

Congratulations! You've made it to the end of your project. The critical path is nearly completed, your team is happy, but exhausted, and management is all smiles. You've been sampling the project as you move along through production for quality and scope verification, and you can reminisce about events that tried to shove your project off schedule and how you and the team recovered and pushed it back on track.

Already there's a buzz of excitement among the end users of the technology. As you walk through the halls of the company, you feel a couple inches taller, and it's hard not smile like a big, goofy kid.

But hold off on putting that cocktail umbrella in your favorite frosty drink. There's still plenty of work that has to be completed to get the project out the door and to finalize the entire process. In this final chapter, you'll not only learn how to finish the project, but also how to formalize the project closure. It's okay to smile and feel a sense of pride at this point of the project—just don't let it get in the way of finalizing a job well done.

Whether you are working on a short-term project that lasted just a few months, or a large, complex implementation that has taken over a year, the principles behind completing the project are the same: to complete any project, you and your team have to continue the momentum and supply the final surge to get the project to the finish line.

Completing the Final Tasks

When you begin to see the final tasks coming into focus, it is not a signal to ease off of the project team and the project. Some project managers make the costly mistake of allowing the project to finish under the guidance of a team leader or have too much faith in the project team to complete the tasks. These project managers allow themselves to relax, begin looking for new projects to lead, or begin their efforts to prove that Microsoft's FreeCell game 11982 can be won.

The problem with relaxing as the project is nearly completed is that the project team will follow your lead and relax as well. Project managers have an ownership of the project that sometimes leads them to believe they are superior to the project team and have permission to put their feet up. As the project team sees the project manager ease out of meetings, out of sight, and out of focus, they'll follow suit and do the same, as Figure 12-1 demonstrates.

In the final stages of project, a project manager must actually do more to motivate and communicate with the project team. A project manager must attend every meeting as she's done throughout the project. She needs to get into the trenches and work

FIGURE 12-1

The project team
will follow the
project manager's
actions.

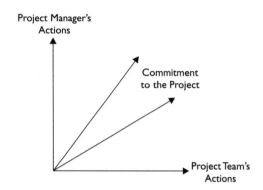

with the team members to help them complete the work and keep them moving
to complete the project on time. A project manager needs to discuss any final issues
with the team, with the client, and with management. A project manager's presence
is obviously required throughout the project, but even more than usual during the
final chunk of the implementation.

Going the Distance

What is, unfortunately, more typical of project managers than easing off an on-track
project is working in a frenzy to complete a project that's gone awry. For example,
consider a project that has had six months to complete the implementation of a new
e-mail client, develop workflow forms, and convert the existing e-mail servers. In
this scenario, the final tasks are the most critical in the entire project. All of the prep
work, research, and design has led the project team to this moment. The switch from
old to new is when the curtain comes up and everyone in the company will see your
work, your design, and your implementation. As Figure 12-2 demonstrates, these
tasks, close to the finish, are the revelation of your ability as a project manager.

FIGURE 12-2

The final tasks in
a project require
the project
manager's full
attention.

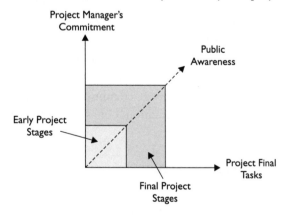

That fact becomes quite evident when the project team and the project manager realize they are not prepared to complete the project on schedule. Now the project manager looks for ways to speed up the process to complete the job on time. This usually means additional hours, nights, and weekends. Be prepared to work the hardest in the final days of a project's implementation if the project is off schedule even by just a few days.

The secret here is to control your emotions, the project team, and any other parties who have volunteered to help with the final tasks. If the folks looking to you to complete the work see you losing control, getting angry, and cutting corners, they'll do the same. Cool heads always prevail.

When you find yourself with a huge amount of work to complete in just a few hours, here are a few guidelines to being successful:

- Remain cool, calm, and collected. Set the example for your team; think clearly, but quickly.

- Get organized and treat the final work as a mini-project. Analyze the work to be completed, break down the tasks, and set the plan into action. Create a map of the final implementation in a central war room and color code the completed tasks.

- Communicate with the team members, but don't get in the way of their completing tasks.

- If you're visiting multiple workstations, organize a method to visually represent the completed work. For example, if a workstation has been prepped for a new installation, put a red sticky note on the monitor. Once the workstation has been completed, put a green sticky note on the monitor. At a glance, anyone can see the status.

- Check for quality. Periodically take a sampling of the work to confirm that what you are attempting to deliver on time is the quality you and the end user will expect.

- Work in shifts. If your team must work around the clock, which is not unheard of, break up the team in shifts so that the team can get some rest and be refreshed. It's tempting to have the entire team on the final phases of an implementation, but as the entire team wears down, the quality of the work suffers.

Examine the Critical Path

As the project begins to wind down, take a close look at the critical path to determine that the tasks to completion are in order, and confirm that the team members who are assigned to the tasks are still motivated. In your team meetings, review the upcoming final tasks to reinforce the importance of their completion. Team members will likely be as excited to complete the project as you, so offer a little urging to continue the momentum to finish.

Within the network diagram, trace the history of the successor paths and determine if there has been a history of tasks being late or lagging. If there is, address this issue to the project team and challenge them to complete the remaining tasks on schedule. You must do all that you can to ensure that the project team is committed, moving, and excited to complete the project.

A source of motivation can be a review of all the work the project team has completed. You can show the team the number of hours committed to the project, and how healthy the project is. Also, remind the team members of the rewards awaiting them once the project has been completed.

At the end of the critical path should be the management reserve. Recall that management reserve is a percentage of the total time allotted for all of the work within a project, usually 10 to 15 percent. Examine the management reserve to see how much time is still left for slippage. For example, a six-month project would likely have 14 to 20 days in management reserve for tasks that are lagging. In the final stages of the project, examine the balance of time in management reserve; if things have gone well, you should have a few days left in reserve. If there have been serious mistakes in the project, then all of the available days in the reserve have been used. Figure 12-3 demonstrates the application of management reserve to early tasks in the critical path, which can impact any delays in the final task of a project.

The point is, an examination of the management reserve will give you an idea of the overall health of the project and will predict how much time you truly have to complete the work. Hopefully, you've got a sliver of time left over to complete the

FIGURE 12-3

A depleted management reserve can impact final tasks.

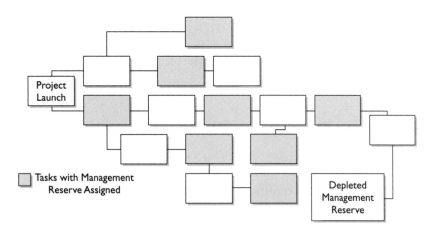

project and allotted for any unforeseen troubles. In some instances, management reserve doesn't matter—for example, when a network switch must take place over one weekend. A management reserve with two extra days won't help at all if the network has to be switched when the production is not in place.

98 Percent Done Is Not Complete

When dealing with third parties that will complete the implementation phase of your project, you really need to convey to them that 98 percent done is not complete. Far too often, integrators begin a project with gusto, but lag in the final implementation. Vendors sometimes need to be reminded a project is not complete until it is 100 percent done. You can motivate these folks with these techniques:

- Final payment is held until the project is completed.

- Specify the project deliverables as 105 percent to get them to aim for 100 percent completion.

- Commit them to specific times and dates to work on the project in the final phases of the implementation.

- Assign a task in the critical path that is a walk-through and sampling of the work they have completed. The critical path is not complete until you approve their work.

The Project Postmortem

The final task has been completed, and there's a collective sigh of relief from all of the parties. But, sorry, you've still got a touch of work left to go on the project. Once all of the implementation tasks in the critical path have been completed, a project manager and the project team must do a few chores to inspect their own work. This time should be worked into the PND and shouldn't take very long at all, maybe 1 to 3 percent of the total project time.

Reviewing for Quality

The primary task that you personally must be involved with is to inspect the quality of the project. Of course, throughout the implementation you will be sampling the project and confirming the quality, but at completion you need to experience or test the project deliverables and confirm that they are the required deliverables to complete the project. You want to perform a final inspection before the project customer sees the deliverable. The point of this inspection is to correct the mistakes that may be present before the customer sees the deliverables during its scope verification process.

To do this, re-create the experience that a typical user would have when using the deliverables. If your project produced an application, use it. If the project was to implement a network, log into a workstation and test connections, print to a few printers, and access some network resources. Evaluate the product from the end user's point of view and review the results to determine if the project deliverables are acceptable, as seen in Figure 12-4.

If you encounter problems, address them immediately so that the responsible parties can react to them and find a solution. At this point of the project, if you've done your job, there shouldn't be any major surprises. You may encounter a quirk that can be quickly addressed and solved, but overall, things should be smooth and the customer happy.

Assessing the Project Deliverables

Once you've completed the final inspection and the quality of the work is acceptable and in alignment with the expected project deliverables, you can enjoy the sense of satisfaction that comes from the success of completing a project. There is a wonderful feeling that comes with taking a project from start to finish. The project is now part of the company's life, and you helped get it there.

FIGURE 12-4

The process must be in place to test the quality of the project deliverables.

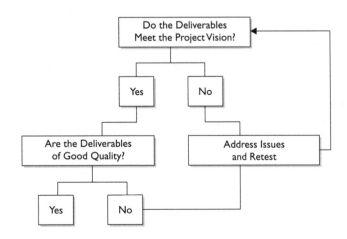

Examining the Project's Worth

Now that the project is complete, you may want to calculate the worth of the project. This activity involves a bit of math magic, but it allows you to predict the overall usefulness and profitability of your implementation. You calculate the time saved, the new sales earned, and the productivity gained to create a gross value of the project. The expense of the project, the total cost of the implementation, is subtracted from the gross value of the project to learn the project's net value. From here you can create formulas to predict the value of the project over the next six months, the next year, or beyond.

Don't get too excited by the math, however, because eventually the infrastructure processes of the company will absorb your deliverables as a matter of doing business. What happens is that your project's deliverables, the wonderful things that they are, will fall victim to the *Law of Diminishing Returns*. In other words, the twenty minutes you take out of a process will be consumed by some other activity.

The *Law of Diminishing Returns*, sometimes called the *Law of Variable Proportions*, is a rule of economics that grew from Thomas Malthus' "Essay on the Principle of Population," written in 1798. The law states that if one factor of production is increased while other factors remain constant, the overall returns will eventually decrease after a certain point, as demonstrated in Figure 12-5. When that point is reached is difficult to say without serious analysis given to the process of a company.

Another way of viewing the Law of Diminishing Returns is to imagine a cornfield that needs to be harvested. If you were to continue to add workers to the field, each new worker you added would have less to do than the worker added before him because there is less and less corn to harvest as additional labor is added.

To apply this law to a technical implementation, imagine a new application that allows workers to be more productive when entering human resource forms and typical paperwork. Before the application, the workers had to manually enter the forms into Microsoft Excel, save the file, and e-mail it to the human resources

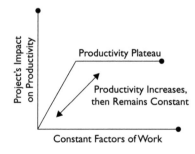

FIGURE 12-5

The Law of Diminishing Returns prevents exponential productivity.

department. The wonderful folks in human resources would open the e-mail, open the file, and merge it into some master file.

Your application streamlines the process through an ASP web page and pumps the information into a database. Now when users within the company need to complete insurance forms, request days off work, request new ID badges, or deal with any other HR-related issue, they can complete the process through your company's intranet.

The productivity of this application allows the processes to be faster, better, and easier to complete. However, this level of productivity will not affect other areas of the workers' roles in the organization exponentially. It will allow for additional time to complete other work, but the additional time gained does not continue to grow on, and on, and on. Eventually the productivity reaches a plateau, and the Law of Diminishing Returns reigns.

All of the project's worth may not be measured in immediate finances. The success of the project may create a feeling of satisfaction, new pride in the company, and general happiness throughout the company driven by the benefit of the new technology. For example, a project that replaces an outdated and lagging technology with a new, proven technology can ease headaches and spur productivity.

Third-Party Review

A final method to measuring the worth of a project's deliverables to an organization is to call upon a third party to analyze the before-and-after processes of a company. For example, imagine an implementation of a wireless Personal Digital Assistant (PDA) in a manufacturing environment. The goal of this project is to shorten the process a forklift operator must use to deliver a palette of the product to a delivery truck.

In the before example, workers pick up palettes of the goods the company manufactures and then move the palettes to the trucks that will deliver the product to the stores and merchandisers. The problem this project resolves is that workers, after dropping off their palettes in the delivery trucks, would have to drive the forklift back to a central base to get their next assignment of the product to be loaded on the trucks.

The project created a wireless PDA device that will send a message to the forklift operator on the floor to instruct him on the next product he is to pick up and deliver to a specific truck. The process has been improved; the worker does not have to return to the central base. Additionally, the palettes, which are wrapped in plastic, have a bar code that the worker can scan from the forklift to log the goods that are actually placed onto the delivery truck. All steps within the process are logged and can be analyzed from the start of the process to the end of a workshift.

A third party could evaluate the productivity before the implementation and after. The process analysis would allow the consultants to track the amount of product moved per workshift to predict the average amount of productivity before and after the implementation. That information can then be analyzed and tweaked, and the original project deliverables can be adjusted in a new project to streamline the process again.

To complete the project, the information gathered by the completed process would be analyzed and reviewed internally or externally. The review would allow the company to see a true ROI and productivity gained on the implementation. Far too often, organizations don't invest in the time to validate the promised benefits of the project. The verification of the benefits is needed not only to show the return on investment for the current project, but to afford success in future projects.

Obtaining Final Sign-Off

Once you're satisfied with the project deliverables, you will need to move into the transfer of ownership of the project. You, the owner of the project, will release it to the organization so that the deliverables may go into production.

Obtaining Client Approval

The client, whether that be the end user on a workstation or an administrator in a behind-the-scenes release such as a new server installation, will accept the project using one of two methods:

Informal Acceptance   The informal acceptance does not include a sign-off of the completion or even the acknowledgment of the deliverables. An example of the informal acceptance is a project that ends on deadline whether or not the deliverables are finished—for example, a project to organize and build an application for a tradeshow demo. The tradeshow will happen regardless of the completion of the project.

Another example is a project that creates a deliverable that doesn't require additional testing to prove the implementation. Imagine a short-term project to replace all of the printers in the organization with newer models. The implementation of the new printers is obvious. You've configured a script to install the printer driver on all of the workstations in the network to automate the end-user installation. All of the print jobs are controlled through a central printer server so the end users experience little impact from the implementation other than their print jobs come out of a new print device.

Formal Acceptance   The formal acceptance of a project's deliverables is a process that is completed by the client of the project and the appropriate members of the project team. This is the preferred method of client acceptance. These acceptances are contingent on a project acceptance agreement. The project acceptance agreement is typically written very early in the project timeline and in alignment with the defined project deliverables. The document clearly explains what qualifies for an acceptance of the deliverables. These are typical of application development projects and often consist of a checklist of the required features of the project.

The client and the team members will test the deliverables against the acceptance agreement to confirm that the deliverables exist. The sidebar "Application Development Acceptance Agreement" shows an example.

Application Development Acceptance Agreement

The purpose of the project "Learning Management System" is to create a web-based reporting system to log the hours an employee completes in the corporate continuing education department. The application must provide for the items in the following checklist to be accepted:

- An intranet-based portal that allows the corporate training department to submit completed classes via a form.

- An intranet-based portal that allows human resources, trainers, and management to view the classes completed by each employee. Managers should only be allowed to see the classes completed by the employees within their supervision.

- An intranet-based portal that allows employees to view completed classes.

- An intranet-based portal that allows employees to view the available classes and to register for upcoming classes.

- Registration requests must be automatically forwarded to the registering employee's managers for approval and to the continuing education registrant.

- Upon approval of the class by the employee's manager, the class enrollment should increase by one to reflect the new class participant.

- Should the class become full during the approval process, the student and the manager should receive an offering of the next available class, for which the student will have a priority over new attendees.

- The registration feature should also allow management and participants to cancel their participation or trade enrollment with another employee.

- When a student enrolls for a class, the corporate calendar should indicate that the student is busy during class hours. Should the student cancel his attendance, his calendar should be updated to indicate the time is available.

- The application should send an e-mail to class participants reminding them of their enrollment and the class hours one day before the class is to start.

The application created in this project meets the preceding criteria and the project is accepted as whole and complete.

_____   _____
Project Manager   Project Client

_____
Date

Post-Project Audit

At the conclusion of the project and before the final project report is submitted, a project manager should complete an audit of the success of the project. The purpose of the audit is to analyze the completed project, the effectiveness of the project team, the success of the project, the value of the deliverables, and the overall approval from the clients. The audit can become part of your Lessons Learned documentation.

This audit must answer the following questions:

Was the Project Vision Achieved?   Remember when you first created the vision of the project? That vision may have changed as the project evolved. The first question should answer whether the project accomplished what its original intent was. If the project did not, explain why. Projects have a tendency to change and develop from the concept to the creation—sometimes for the better.

Was the Project on Track from Start to Finish?   Hopefully, the project was able to stay on plan, on time, and within the allotted budget. If the project wasn't able to stay within the bounds of any of these areas, explain why. Sometimes the scope changed, the resources flexed, or the expenses of the project were not predicted as accurately as they should have been. This should be an honest reflection of each side of the project triangle (scope, time, and budget).

Did the Project Create a Recognizable Business Value?   The deliverable of the project should be to make a company more profitable in its streamlined process, attract more sales, or gain productivity. This business value needs to be identified and proven to show the ROI of the project.

Can You Share the Knowledge?   Some organizations have a project management system in place that requires project managers to report on their methodology and how it worked for them, or what they may have done during the project to improve the process. These adjustments that you make during the implementation need to be shared so that other project managers within the organization may benefit from your insights.

The post-project audit is an activity that far too many project managers skip. Don't ever skip it. It is an extremely valuable process that will help you become a better project manager. In addition, it is an excellent method for reporting on the work you've completed and the value you've added to a company. You may choose to use this report as leverage in negotiations for future projects.

Creating the Final Report

As with every other phase of the project, documentation is required. The good news is that the final documentation of the project does not have to be an in-depth novel of all of the work completed. If you have completed cumulative progress reports throughout the project, consider the final report one last cumulative record with a few extra ingredients. The collection of all of the cumulative reports may serve as a final record of each phase's work with a few extra parts. You will need

- The project vision statement that introduced the project
- The project proposal that you may have used to sell management on the idea of the technical implementation—or the supporting information for the project that was assigned to you
- The scope statement
- The statement of work
- The project schedule
- The WBS and the PND
- The minutes from each team meeting
- Any Project Change Requests forms that were approved (Some project managers may choose to include the denied Project Change Request forms to verify why the request was not included in the deliverables.)

- Variance reports
- All communication relevant to the project deliverables. (Some project managers include all memos, letters, and e-mail in the report.)
- Total cost of the project and the calculated value of the implementation
- Scope verification agreement
- Post-project audit report

Evaluating Team Members' Performance

In many organizations, a project manager is called upon to review the work of the team members who were involved with the project. This evaluation is a serious process that may impact their salary, their job, or opportunities to advance within the company. Your organization may have you complete a form on your own, conduct an interview with the team member and his immediate manager, or hold a private meeting with the team member's immediate manager to discuss the work.

Whatever method is invoked, use caution to be accurate, fair, and professional. This is another reason why the project manager requires the amount of documentation he does throughout the project. The evaluation process, formal or informal, accomplishes three goals, as seen in Figure 12-6.

Declaring Victory

At the end of the project, you'll have a fairly good idea whether the project is a victory or a failure. A project is a victory if you have completed the project on time, on scope, and within budget, and the project has resulted in the quality deliverable that was expected. A project manager and the project team should take measures throughout

FIGURE 12-6

Team member evaluations are serious reviews of their contributions.

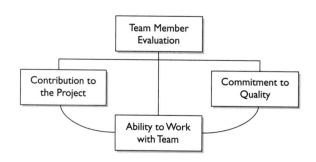

the project to ensure that the vision of the project is being worked toward and achieved. Think of the pyramids in Egypt. However those were built, it's doubtful the Egyptians started building a condo and then midway through decided they were really after a pyramid instead. The same is true in your project management skills: by knowing and recognizing the vision of the project, you constantly check that the work being completed is moving closer to the desired results.

Declaring Failure

No one likes to be called a loser. Unfortunately, some projects can make the project manager, the project team, and all associated parties feel like failures. How many projects are started, stopped, and rearranged, only to complete the cycle again and again without ever getting anywhere near the projected deliverables?

For a project to be a success, it must include these things:

- A vision of the project's deliverables
- Adequate skills by the project manager
- Adequate skills by the project team
- Enough finances to provide for the resources to complete the implementation
- Time to complete the work to produce the deliverables
- Change management to protect the project scope
- Commitment from the project manager, project sponsor, the project team, and management

Without these elements, a project will have a very tough, if not impossible, time succeeding. At some point in a doomed project, the team, the project manager, and management may become so disgusted by the lack of progress that the project needs to be written off and put out of its misery.

In these instances, the project ceases to exist. The attempted implementation is a failure, and it's a general unhappiness for everyone. If you find yourself in this situation, and hopefully you will not, look for an understanding of why the project failed. Evaluate the project requirements, the finances, the talents of the team, and the available time. Evaluate your own performance and the performance of your team. Learn from the mistake and become a better person because of it. As Thomas Edison said, "I know that I will succeed sooner or later because I am running out of things that won't work."

In other instances, the project may be canceled not because of a lack of leadership, finances, or time, but because of a new influence on the project. Examples include the following:

- A better, cheaper technology is released.
- A better solution is discovered within the current project.
- The need for the deliverables has been eliminated by the client.
- The organization has changed its focus.
- The organization is experiencing financial strains.
- The organization has been absorbed by another organization.

Regardless of the project status as success or failure, the project manager must create a final project report so that management may review the work of the project. Scope verification and an audit of the project up to the point of the project's cancellation is needed.

Cheers! Celebrating Victory

At the end of the project, congratulations and kudos to the project team, the project manager, the project sponsor, and anyone else who helped make the project a success. It is necessary to celebrate the victory of a project and reward the team members for their commitment and hard work. Hopefully, especially if you want future projects to be a success, your organization will spring for something elaborate and in proportion to the project you've completed and the success of the victory.

The team members that you've coached along have formed friendships and trust among themselves and hopefully with you. This group of individuals has worked hard day and night for you to make you look good and make the project a success. Reward them! Offer tickets to an event, take the team to a fancy dinner, go out dancing, or offer individual rewards that the team members can enjoy on their own such as videos, gift certificates, or cold, hard cash. The point is, reward them, love them, and they'll come back to work with you again and again.

FROM THE FIELD

Interview with Rob Adams

Name: Rob Adams
Title: Corporate Skills Lead, Project Management, PMP
Company: Online Business Systems
Years as an IT project manager: 5

Robert Adams is the Project Management Corporate Skills Lead for Online Business Systems, a North American IT/e-commerce consulting firm, as well as a project manager.

Q: What is the best thing about completing a project?

A: The best thing about completing a project is stepping back and measuring the success. There are two aspects you are measuring. First, while completing an IT project is one measure of success, it is really only a small part of the whole picture. Ask yourself these questions:

- Were you on time?
- Was the project on budget?
- How was quality?
- Are you comparing against a baseline only or are you considering change request?
- From a business perspective, was it successful?

Second, as a team how did you perform? Was it successful on that front? We are sometimes constrained in our approach and need to deliver under less-than-ideal circumstances. Perhaps there are numerous risks or constraints we are asked to deliver under. While one goal should be to eliminate unnecessary risks and constraints, you rarely eliminate them all.

Q: What are some activities that you do in the completion stage of an IT project?

A: Always review lessons learned by the project manager and by the project team. You need to include the client as well. Forms are easy to use for lessons learned activities; however, it is significantly more valuable to conduct a lessons-learned session with the client or have a face-to-face debriefing. We all know how the team's process affects the outcome of the project. One of the shortfalls I have seen in the IT industry is the lack of emphasis on the impact of how the business process works for projects. Two of the top reasons cited for project failure are lack of sponsor support and lack of end-user involvement.

There is little value to be gained from lessons learned if they are not used in future projects. Additionally, all deliverables, metrics, and pertinent information should be archived in a central repository. My favorites for reference on future projects are project plans, estimation, and risk management. Archiving will also lead to faster development of best practices.

Q: How important is it to create a report on the project's success or failure at the conclusion of a project?

A: This is related to lessons learned and is critical to future improvement in delivering successful projects. Additionally, the report or information must be disseminated. Lessons learned in a nutshell are asking, "How do we repeat the positive and avoid the negative?" If one of your problems was changing business priorities, then this must be communicated to upper management. Perhaps they are not aware of the impact.

Q: What is the most difficult part of completing a project?

A: A lesson learned from a troubled project is the most difficult part. Tension can be high and people can be defensive. Ignoring the problem will not make it go away. It will be a good chance to test your conflict resolution and your communications skills. You may need to communicate unpleasant information to management and team members.

Q: What methods do you use to confirm that the project has reached its conclusion?

A: While the absolute end of the project is administrative closure, the key milestone will be the acceptance of the performed work. This goal begins back in planning. You need to define an end point through a series of deliverables. For many IT project managers, the end is usually recognized by the result of testing the project deliverables.

The quality plan, in concert with the test plan, marks the major end point. The test cases should map directly back to the signed off requirements. We can meet requirements! Therefore, the signed off tests by the client set the marker as to when you are done. The quality plan describes the level of quality attained by the performance of the testing. If you keep the testing phase simple and direct, and there are no serious bugs, the deliverable will be accepted.

Q: What method do you use to evaluate team members' performance at the end of a project?

A: I ask two questions when reviewing each team member:

- How did she perform relative to her skill and experience?
- Did she progress as the project went along?

We gather this through feedback, from my experience with the team member, from the client, and from the team member herself. The timing of the feedback is important as well. If the person rolls off the project, gather feedback. If the project is long, then evaluate progress on a quarterly basis. Waiting to year end makes everyone's memory fuzzy and does not allow the person to act upon the feedback. For long projects, you do not want someone to underperform for eight months when constructive criticism can result in five months of improved productivity.

Q: What methods do you use to assess the deliverables of a long-term project that may have spanned geographical areas?

A: I would start with the standard matching of project deliverables with business objectives, risk management, and a strong communication plan. I ask the following questions:

- Are the business objectives bound to change?
- Is there time-to-market pressure?
- Is funding set for the duration or do you grab funding as you go?

The answers will affect how you assess the project deliverables. If there is a good chance business objectives could change, then deliverables need to be more frequent. Long-term and geographically diverse projects can carry significant risks. A solid plan, including risk management, is the only sure way to have a shot at being on time and on budget. Projects spanning geographical areas scream for communication—which is the key throughout the project. A long-term project can see a change in the players and even stakeholders. A solid communication plan allows new participants to get up to speed quickly.

Q: How does a project manager know if a project should be declared a failure and raise the white flag?

A: There are a couple of ways. First and foremost, the charter or project plan defines the conditions under which you will consider canceling a project—at a more detailed level, earned value. If the Cost Performance Index is off significantly in the first 15 to 20 percent of the project, in the best scenario you're most likely looking at the same performance for the rest of the project. The worst case is that the project will just get worse! You can predict that you will not recover cost. You may be able to recover schedule, but at an even higher cost. You need to be forecasting! It is not where you are, but where you are going that is important. More subtle signs of a failing project could be resources getting pulled, lack of involvement from key end users or stakeholders, major technical hurdles, or severity of unidentified risks.

Q: Can you share an experience of a project you've managed that reached its conclusion and some of the challenges you faced therein?

A: Sure. An intranet application to be used by ten offices across the country comes to mind. The challenges were numerous:

- All four developers were just out of school, but they were quite skilled for their experience.
- We had to use a data model that was being modified by five different projects simultaneously.
- Of course, there was no program manager for the five projects.
- There was no significant project manager authority.
- The IT department lacked development methodology and project manager discipline.
- The project was IT driven with no business sponsor.
- The deadline was tight.
- Our question-and-answer resources from the client were constantly unavailable.
- The client accepted all the risks.

Through long nights and longer days, we made the date as per requirements. The only problem was the requirements were assumed by the IT staff and did not fit the business unit's objective. I'm sure you saw that coming.

Q: What are some pitfalls a new project manager may face in regard to finishing a project?

A: I have seen two common pitfalls. One, knowing when you are finished. This criterion should be defined in the project scope. Two, not conducting a proper lessons-learned session and communication of the findings to the appropriate people. Lessons learned can be a delicate task depending on what needs to be communicated.

FROM THE FIELD *(continued)*

Q: What advice do you have for aspiring project managers?

A: Set expectations. Garner an understanding of the expectations of you and the project. In addition, set standards for what you expect from the team, end users, and the project sponsor. Never stop communicating, and document everything. At the end of the day, it is the people that make the project, not the technology.

CHAPTER SUMMARY

A successful project manager has to complete many tasks to finish any technical project. As the project is winding down, an analysis of the critical path and the resources assigned to the path is required to ensure that the work is completed and resources are committed. You have to be seen, available, and in the trenches with the project team to keep the project momentum moving toward the deliverables.

Once the project work has been completed, the project manager, the project sponsor, and the project team need to review the work for quality, snags, or technical issues that may have popped up in the final tasks. Any issues need to be immediately addressed and resolved. You can evaluate the project's worth to predict the ROI of the product; of course, you'll need to consider the Law of Diminishing Returns as the calculations are made.

Once the work is to your satisfaction, the client accepts the project either formally or informally, depending on the type of work completed. Some projects may require you and members of your team to work with the client to ensure the client acceptance agreement criteria are met as defined in the early stages of the project.

Once the client has approved the work, you must create a final project report that includes all documentation and facts from the project lifespan. An audit of the work and the success of the project need to be included in the plan. Ultimately, the final project report must answer if the project vision was met, and if the overall health of the project is excellent or otherwise.

At the project's finale, you may determine from the evidence of the goods produced if the project was a success or a failure. Regardless of the project evaluation, you should create a lessons-learned document for your own future success, but also for the success of others.

You should review the project together with the project sponsor and focus on the quality of the work, a review of the budget at completion, and the success of the effort. The project sponsor may want to work with you on how you can manage your next project better, or what you did successfully on this implementation.

Finally, once the project is officially finished, then the team is relieved, the client is satisfied, and recognition is given. A celebration is in order for the project team, the support of management, and the hard work and commitment poured into the project vision by you, the successful project manager.

CHAPTER QUIZ

1. Of the following, which is one of the dangers a project manager encounters as a project finishes?

   A. The project scope changes.

   B. The project manager eases off the project.

   C. The budget has a surplus and the project manager doesn't know what to spend it on.

   D. The project sponsor eases off the project.

2. What method should a project manager use to ensure that a project maintains momentum in the final stages?

   A. Host a celebration for the project team.

   B. Discipline any team members who stray from the project.

   C. Become available to the project team.

   D. Get in the trenches and work with the project team.

3. Of the following, which is a reflection of the project manager's ability to lead?

   A. A project manager who attends regular meetings

   B. A project manager who speaks with team members weekly

   C. A project manager who leads by example

   D. A project manager who speaks with management on a regular basis

4. Of the following, which method is a likely solution to successfully finish a project that is near to completion, but may be lagging?

   A. Ask for additional time to produce the deliverables.

   B. Ask for additional funds to hire outside help.

   C. Ask the project team to work additional hours.

   D. Remove parts of the project deliverable for delivery at a later date.

5. Of the following, which is not a suggestion to quickly and accurately complete a project on schedule?

   A. Think clearly, but quickly.

   B. Create a visual marker to represent completed work on the workstations.

   C. Check for quality as applicable within the final phases.

   D. Ask for volunteers to work through the night and into the next day on an implementation.

6. What information can an IT project manager learn from completed tasks in the project?

    A. If the tasks have been lagging, it is a sign that the future tasks may lag as well.

    B. If the same group of team members has completed the tasks, they may be bored with the work.

    C. If the same group of team members has completed the tasks, they may need to be replaced by other team members to keep the team excited.

    D. If the critical path has had tasks that can begin in unison (SS), the remaining work units may have SS tasks as well.

7. Why should management reserve be examined near the end of a project?

    A. To determine the cost of the errors on the project

    B. To determine the additional revenues that are left in place

    C. To determine the amount of time that may actually be used, if necessary, for the implementation

    D. To determine the amount of time that may be used in addition to the allotted time for the remaining work units

8. True or False: Time left in management reserve will always be applicable to any project in the final stages of the work.

    A. True

    B. False

9. What must the project manager do before the customer accepts the project deliverables?

    A. Inspect the project deliverables for quality.

    B. Inspect the project deliverables for missing components.

    C. Present the invoice for the project completion.

    D. Assign the project team to new projects.

10. What method can an IT project manager invoke to ensure that third parties will reach 100 percent completion on a project?

    A. Retain payment until the integrator reports the project is finished.

    B. Retain payment until the project manager approves the deliverables.

    C. Ask the vendor to add a few extra tasks to complete the project.

    D. Assign the final tasks in the critical path to an internal project to ensure the project is finished as planned.

11. When should a project manager inspect the project for quality?

    A. Throughout the implementation phase

    B. During the final task

    C. In the last 1 to 3 percent of the implementation phase

    D. When the project is complete

12. What should a project manager do when evaluating the finished deliverables of a project and she encounters a flaw?

    A. Note the flaw and add it to a to-do list.

    B. Reassign the project to another team member.

    C. Address the flaw immediately to have it resolved.

    D. Complete a Project Change Request form.

13. What is the purpose of calculating a project's worth?

    A. To determine if the project was worth doing

    B. To determine if the project manager did his job properly

    C. To determine if the project was an expense or an investment

    D. To determine the ROI of the project

14. What is the Law of Diminishing Returns?

    A. It is a law of economics that states all processes cannot be improved infinitely.

    B. It is a law of economics that states if one area of profitability increases, the other areas of an organization must increase also to produce higher profits.

    C. It is a law of economics that states if one area of production is increased while other factors remain constant, the overall returns will eventually increase as well.

    D. It is a law of economics that states if one area of production is increased while other factors remain constant, the overall returns will eventually diminish.

15. What is the purpose of having a third party review the completed project?

    A. To ensure the deliverables were worthy of the budget and time required to produce them

    B. To ensure the deliverables are of quality and to second-guess the project team

    C. To ensure the deliverables are of quality and in alignment with the project scope

    D. To ensure the project manager did her job as defined in the project plan

CHAPTER EXERCISES

In these exercises, you will be presented with a scenario of a project for a fictitious company. You will then be asked a series of questions about the project.

Exercise 1

Marcy is the project manager for the All Boots Company. Her project is to lead a team to develop a web-based application that allows customers to visit the corporate web site and search for boots based on several factors such as size, style, color, heel, and toe of the boot. Throughout the project, Marcy has periodically tested the cumulative work to see how the project is progressing. With just a few days to spare, the application developers report that the project is complete and the web site ready for users.

Of course, Marcy wants to experience the application before management and others see the results. Marcy opens the web site and successfully completes a few searches. She then discovers that she cannot search for a combination of factors such as a red boot in a size 10.

Please answer the following questions to complete the exercise:

1. What should Marcy do first to rectify the problem?

2. What could Marcy have done earlier in the project to avoid this problem?

3. What should Marcy do if the developers report that the work can be done but it may take two weeks to complete her request?

4. What can Marcy tell management about the project?

Exercise 2

Robert is the project manager for Margo's Jams and Jellies. The project he has been managing is a rollout of new laptops and operating systems to 720 office workers throughout North America. His plan calls for the laptops to be shipped to his central office in Tampa, Florida, where his team would configure the PCs and then drop ship them to each of the sites throughout the country.

The project itself is designed for tiered delivery of the workstations and addresses just one of the seven North American sites at a time. Unfortunately, the manufacturer of the laptops has been very late in shipping them to Robert. In fact, the rollout has been successfully deployed at only one site in the company, and the project is to end in one week.

Suddenly, a huge delivery from the manufacturer arrives at Robert's office and he now has 480 laptops; his team needs to verify the hardware, push the approved disk image to the PC, pack, and drop ship the laptops to each of the remaining cities.

1. What should Robert do first?

2. What should Robert tell management?

3. Is there anything that Robert could have done earlier in the project to avoid this situation?

4. What are the steps you would take to complete this project?

QUIZ ANSWERS

1. **B.** Some project managers make the mistake of easing off a project as it concludes. The inverse is what is really needed, as project team members have a tendency to ease off the project as well. The project scope rarely changes at this point of the project. A surplus in the budget shows that the project manager did not accurately predict the cost of the goods in the project. Management most likely will not allow the project manager to spend the surplus.

2. **D.** A project manager should always be available to the project team, but getting in the trenches and helping the project team as much as possible to complete the project inspires a team to work harder and commit to the conclusion of a project.

3. **C.** A project manager who sits behind a desk and manages the team through memos is not as effective as a project manager who gets involved with the team members and helps them succeed. Leading by example is never a bad idea.

4. **C.** When a project is lagging behind on tasks in the final stages of a project, a project manager may need to ask the project team to work extra hours to complete the project on time. Additional funds to hire outside help may be attractive, but the time to ramp up the additional help may be counterproductive.

5. **D.** Asking team members to work an excessive number of hours without rest can be wasteful. Team members need a break from the project to be productive and useful.

6. **A.** History of performance is a good indicator of what future tasks may bring. If the project manager can see that prior tasks have been lagging, he can predict that the remaining tasks may also lag. This can allow the project manager to stress the urgency that these final tasks must be completed on time. The project manager may also elect to reassign resources, add resources, or join the effort himself.

7. **C.** A project manager should evaluate the remaining time in management reserve near the end of the project to determine the whole amount of time available for the project. Just because there is additional time in reserve does not mean that the project manager should assign the time to remaining tasks; it means the project manager can calculate the room for error.

8. **B.** False. Management reserve should not be immediately assigned to the remaining tasks at the end of the project. In some instances, such as when the project must end on a specific date, time in the management reserve will not help lagging tasks.

9. **A.** Before the customers accept the deliverables of the project, the project manager must inspect the final product for quality. This inspection keeps mistakes out of the hands of the customers.

10. **B.** A project manager can withhold payment until she has approved all of the work that the vendor was assigned to complete. The project manager should, however, take time to review

the work as soon as the vendor reports that the work is done. It is unprofessional to use this leverage and then take weeks to review the submitted work.

11.   **A.** A project manager should not wait until the end of the project to determine the quality of the work. A project manager should work throughout the project to ensure quality in each phase of the implementation.

12.   **C.** When a project manager discovers a flaw in the implementation during the review, that flaw must be addressed immediately to rectify the problem.

13.   **D.** The project manager and management should calculate the ROI of the project to determine if the budgeted cost and the actual cost outweigh the benefits of the project's deliverables. Hopefully, if everyone has done the proper research and preproject calculations, the ROI will be excellent.

14.   **D.** The Law of Diminishing Returns predicts if one area of production increases, but the other areas remain the same, the overall returns will eventually diminish. For an IT project manager, that means the productivity and the profitability gained by the implementation will eventually reach a plateau because the remaining factors in production have not been improved.

15.   **C.** In some instances, an organization should hire a third-party consultant to review the work of the project to determine the deliverables are of quality and in alignment with the project scope. Third parties that are to review the completed project don't need to analyze the budget and worth of the project unless they are to examine the process of creating the deliverables, rather than the actual deliverables the project produced.

EXERCISE SOLUTIONS

Exercise 1: Possible Solutions

Your answers may be slightly different than the ones presented here, but generally should be similar.

1.   Marcy should verify that the flaw exists and contact the developers immediately to address the problem.

2.   There are many things that Marcy should have done earlier in the project. She should have made certain that the multiple search capability was part of the project requirements. She should have reviewed the work throughout the project to confirm the existence of the search ability. She should have asked her developers for their input and advice on what could make the application better.

3. In this situation, as the work is due in a very short matter of time, Marcy should speak with management about the flaw and assure them it is being addressed. As the web site is currently functional to an extent, it should be released in a tiered manner. The current web site should go live and then be replaced with the updated application as soon as it is finished and approved.

   Marcy may also elect to assign additional developers to the work to shorten the time frame to include the multiple search capability. It may be that the developers are able to complete the request quickly, but they are currently bogged down with other assignments.

4. Marcy can report to management that overall the project is very healthy. She should also emphasize that with a few tweaks, the application will be excellent.

Exercise 2: Possible Solutions

Your answers may be slightly different than the ones presented here, but generally should be similar.

1. Obviously the shock of 480 laptops being delivered at once was not in the project plan, so Robert should first calm himself and his staff down. The volume of computers will make completing the project on time impossible.

2. Robert should report to management the good news and the bad news about all of the laptops having arrived. The good news is that the hardware is finally in place; the bad news is that they are late and there are 480 workstations to configure and drop ship.

3. Robert should have created a closer relationship with the manufacturer to ensure the laptops were delivered earlier in the project, or not paid for the laptops until they were delivered. Robert could also have considered ordering laptops from other vendors.

4. First, consider if it is possible to complete the project on time, given all of the hardware is in place. If not, then a plan to place an image on the hard drives and ship the laptops to the cities must be drafted. Hardware security needs to be addressed so none of the laptops are compromised.

Appendix A

IT Project+
Exam Objectives

T
he IT Project+ examination is designed for information technology (IT) and business professionals involved with IT projects and business projects with a technology component. The examination is designed for candidates possessing at least 12 months of cumulative experience in leading, managing, and directing small- to medium-scale IT projects. IT Project+ examines the business, interpersonal, and technical project management skills required to successfully manage IT projects and business initiatives with a technology component.

The skills and knowledge measured by this examination are derived from an industry-wide job task analysis and validated through an industry-wide survey. The results of this survey were used in weighing the domains and ensuring that the weighting is representative of the relative importance of the content. The exam is in a conventional linear format. There are 80 questions on the exam and candidates have 90 minutes to complete them. The exam is available in English only.

The objectives in this appendix are current at the time of this publication, but you should always refer to the Computer Technology Industry Association web site at www.comptia.org to obtain the most current version of the exam objectives as they are subject to change. The following table lists the domains measured by this examination and the extent to which they are represented.

Domain	Percent of Examination
1.0 IT Project Initiation and Scope Definition	20 percent
2.0 IT Project Planning	30 percent
3.0 IT Project Execution, Control, and Coordination	43 percent
4.0 IT Project Closure, Acceptance, and Support	7 percent

Response Limits

The candidate selects the option(s) that best completes the statement or answers the question from four or more response options. Distracters, or wrong answers, are response options that a candidate with incomplete knowledge or skills is likely to choose given these choices are generally plausible responses for the content area. Test item formats used in this examination are

- **Multiple choice**   The candidate selects one option that best answers the question or completes a statement.
- **Multiple response**   The candidate selects more than one option that best answers the question or completes a statement.
- **Drag and drop items**   The candidate drags a graphic or text to the correct destination.

Domain 1.0 IT Project Initiation and Scope Definition

This domain requires that the candidate possess the knowledge to:

- Identify stakeholder objectives for an IT project and prepare a high-level scope statement that correctly defines the work required to achieve those objectives
- Define high-level business and technical requirements, outcomes, criteria for success, and stakeholders' low-level needs and expectations, including boundaries for project budget, duration, and risk
- Identify the project roles of stakeholders including the project manager, project sponsor, and project team members
- Secure stakeholder/client consensus and obtain approval of the project charter and preliminary scope documents

1.1. Given a vague or poorly worded customer request or business need, determine the appropriate course of action in order to 1) understand a business case scenario and create a project proposal, 2) understand or analyze a Request for Proposal (RFP) and create a project proposal:

- Generate and refine a preliminary project concept definition or statement of work
- Informally determine the business need and feasibility of the project
- Identify project sponsors who will help obtain resources
- Understand the concept of cost-benefit analysis to justify the project
- Obtain formal approval from the project sponsor
- Confirm management support

1.2. Given the set of criteria that outlines an enterprise's minimal requirements for a project charter, together with stakeholder input, synthesize a project charter, including:

- Project title and description
- Project manager
- Key roles and responsibilities
- Project objectives and success criteria
- High-level cost benefit analysis
- Business case/mission
- Product/deliverable description, performance criteria, and enhancement opportunities
- High-level risk assessment
- Consensus building

1.3. Identify strategies for building consensus among project stakeholders. Select an appropriate course of action involving negotiation or interviewing strategies, meetings, memos, etc.

1.4. Recognize and explain the need to obtain formal approval (sign-off) by the project sponsor(s) and confirm other relevant management support to consume organization resources as the project charter is refined and expanded.

1.5. Given a scope definition scenario, demonstrate awareness of the need to secure written confirmation of customer expectations in the following areas:

- The background of the project (for example, a problem/opportunity statement, strategic alignment with organizational goals and other initiatives, why the project is being initiated at this time, etc.)
- The deliverable from the project (that is, what the product will look like, be able to do, who will use it, etc.)

- The strategy for creating the deliverable

- Targeted completion date and rationale behind that date

- Budget dollars available and basis upon which that budget was determined

- Areas of risks which the project client is or is not willing to accept

- The priority of this project as it relates to all the other projects being done within the organization

- The sponsor of the project (that is, who will provide direction and decisions)

- Any predetermined tools or resources

- Assumptions that resources will be available as needed.

1.6. Given a project initiation document (a project charter or contract), including a confirmed high-level scope definition and project justification, demonstrate the ability to identify and define the following elements:

1. The stakeholders, including the primary project client, the ultimate end users, and any other impacted parties (internal or external to the organization), their roles and special needs

2. An all-inclusive set of requirements presented in specific, definitive terms which include:

   - Differentiation of mandatory versus optional requirements

   - Success criteria upon which the deliverable will be measured

   - Completion criteria (for example, what needs to be delivered, such as a fully tested system or a system that's been live for three months)

   - Requirements that are excluded from the project

3. Targeted completion date, including:

   - Relative to a specified start date,

   - Expressed as a specific date (that is, mm/dd/yy), a range of dates, or a specific quarter and year (3rd quarter 2004)

   - The consequences if that date is not met

   - A milestone chart including any phase reviews, if appropriate

4. Anticipated budget, including any or all of the following:

   ■ Plus or minus tolerance

   ■ Contingency funds and/or any management reserves, if negotiated

   ■ The consequences if that budget is not met

5. Which of the above three criteria—for example, technical performance (quality), completion date (schedule), or anticipated budget—is the highest priority to the project client

6. All assumptions made relative to A through E

1.7. Given a project initiation document (a project charter or contract), including the client's highest priority between quality, time, and budget, estimate any or all of the following:

■ The potential impact of satisfying the client's highest priority at the expense of the other two

■ The impact of the project on business operations

■ Worse-case scenario targeted completion date, budget, and quality level

■ Your confidence level in the projected completion date, budget and prospects for a high-quality deliverable

1.8. Given a project charter or contract including a statement of work (SOW), recognize and explain the need to investigate specific industry regulations requirements and contractual/legal considerations for their impact on the project scope definition and project plan.

1.9. Given a proposed scope definition and based on the scope components, assess the feasibility of the project and the viability of a given project component against a predetermined list of constraints, including:

■ A clearly defined project end date

■ A clearly defined set of monetary resources or allocations

■ A clearly defined set of product requirements, based on a thorough decomposition of the system's hardware and software components

- Clearly defined completion criteria
- Clearly defined priorities
- The relative priority of cost, schedule, and scope
- Project ownership
- Mandated tools, personnel, and other resources
- The requirement that scope will change only per change control
- Vendor terms and conditions
- Company terms and conditions
- A "best practices" life cycle for this type of project
- Required reviews of deliverables by stakeholders and approvals by sponsors
- RFP procedures, selection criteria, evaluation criteria, and standards

1.10. Recognize and explain the need to obtain formal approval (sign-off) by the project sponsor(s) and confirm other relevant management support to consume organizational resources as the project scope statement is being developed.

1.11. Given an incomplete project scope definition, complete or rewrite the definition to 1) reflect all necessary scope components or 2) explicitly state what is included in the project and what is not included. Necessary components include:

- Project size
- Project cost
- Projected schedule and window of opportunity
- Stakeholders, their roles, and their authorities
- The project manager's role and authority
- Completion criteria
- Methodologies to be followed
- The scope change control process

■ Mandated tools, personnel, and other resources

■ Industry or government regulations that apply

1.12. Identify the following as possible elements of a final project scope definition and the circumstances in which they would be appropriate:

■ A requirements change control process, including how to request a change, how to analyze the impact of the change, and how to obtain approval for the additional funds and/or time to implement the change

1.13. Recognize and explain the need to build management buy-in and approval into the structure of the project, and describe strategies for doing so, including:

■ Involving management in up-front definitions of project concept and charter

■ Involving management in defining and approving project scope

■ Involving management in reviewing and approving all key project deliverables as they evolve

■ Providing a role for management as a spokesperson-advocate for the project, for team member participation, and for the deliverables

1.14. Recognize the need to obtain a consensus among stakeholders and to obtain buy-in from the team to proceed to the planning stage of the project given a high-level estimate of scope, schedule, budget, and resources.

1.15. Recognize the need to conduct a review meeting as the project transitions from the initiation phase to the planning phase. The review would include an assessment of the following:

■ Completion of the project initiation documentation

■ Viability of the business case

■ Achievement of stakeholder consensus

Domain 2.0: IT Project Planning

This domain requires the knowledge and skills to:

- Define in adequate depth the project deliverable(s)/product(s) and associated requirements
- Create a Work Breakdown Structure (WBS)
- Identify a project strategy and life-cycle
- Create a schedule
- Create a list of required resources
- Perform project cost estimation and create a budget
- Perform risk analysis and create a risk
- Create a Communications Management Plan
- Create a Quality Management Plan
- Organize a comprehensive, detailed project plan
- Validate stakeholder expectations
- Establish change control over the project plan and develop procedures for updating and/or changing the plan
- Close out the planning phase

Project Strategy Development and Preliminary Planning

2.1. Demonstrate knowledge of the typical IT project life cycle and its application to IT projects, including:

- Phases (requirements, design, build/unit test, integration test, deploy)
- The reason for the phases
- The common deliverables from the phases
- Target phase transition dates

2.2. Given an approved project charter, high-level scope documents, and schedule/budget objectives, demonstrate the ability to create a project management plan that illustrates the following:

- Understanding of the roles of stakeholders, what reporting information each needs, and when it is needed
- Understanding the risks incurred by not including key participants during the planning process
- Knowledge of how to establish a project tracking mechanism
- Awareness that a training plan may be necessary
- Awareness that a procurement plan may be necessary

2.3. Demonstrate an understanding of the following estimating concepts, techniques, and issues, including:

- The concept of bottom-up cost estimates, their purpose, and the conditions under which they are necessary
- Standard estimating techniques that can be used to solicit initial financial budget inputs based on mutual agreeable high-level requirements

2.4. Given a team-building scenario, including a scope definition and WBS, identify selection criteria for particular team members. Demonstrate the ability to ask interview questions that will assist the team selection process. Assume project organization includes:

- Business
- Leadership
- Administration
- Technical
- Stakeholders

2.5. Identify methods for resolving disagreements among team members when evaluating the suitability of deliverables at each point in their evolution.

Requirements Analysis

2.6. Given a project description/overview and a list of the project business and technical requirements, do the following:

- Decide if the project is defined well enough to achieve a measurable outcome and metrics for success

- Determine if the requirements include the necessary range of inputs (assumptions, expectations, technical issues, industry issues, etc.) in order to validate the input given and gaps related to scope

- Distinguish any input provided which does not relate to the project at hand in order to achieve greater focus

- Recognize whether the list of requirements is complete, accurate, and valid enough to move on to the planning step

- Give a situation where the project outcomes are not possible to verify

- Recognize the role poorly detailed requirements, assumptions, and expectations play

- Identify the high-level value of the project to the sponsor and end users

- Describe the role of project value and its importance to individual and team effectiveness

2.7. Describe the goals of a useful project requirements review with the client (for example, verify a mutual understanding of client's product delivery, product performance, and budget requirements, etc.) and describe when it is important to have such reviews.

2.8. Given the client's approved project requirements and the input of stakeholders, decompose these requirements into business and functional requirements while maintaining traceability within strict configuration control.

Create WBS

2.9. Given a project planning scenario, demonstrate an understanding of and the ability to develop a phase-oriented WBS with high detail for an early phase and with low detail for later phases by:

- Identifying elements (phases) likely to require iterative planning
- Explicitly deciding to provide for iteration in the project plan (for example, scope approval, plan approval, project design, final deliverable turnover, etc.)

2.10. Given a scenario involving tasks, resources (fixed or variable), and dependencies for a multiphase IT project, demonstrate knowledge of the standards for creating a workable WBS by:

- Recognizing and explaining the need to creatively visualize all deliverables (interim and finished)
- Decomposing the system into all potential hardware and software components thoroughly

2.11. Recognize and explain the need to obtain:

- Consensus among all stakeholders regarding project deliverables and other elements of the WBS
- Formal approval (sign-off) of project sponsor(s) regarding project deliverables and other elements of the WBS.

2.12. Given a project scenario with many phases and activities, set realistic, measurable milestones, and demonstrate an understanding that measurable targets are required to determine if the project is proceeding on time and within budget.

2.13. Given a set of specific milestones and their descriptions, specify entry and exit criteria for each.

Perform an Estimation

2.14. Demonstrate the ability to create an activity cost estimate given:

- An activity scope of work
- Required resources
- Level of effort
- Resource availability
- Resource rate

2.15. Demonstrate the ability to create an activity time estimate (in units of time) given:

- An activity scope of work
- Required resources
- Level of effort
- Resource availability

2.16. Recognize and explain the difference between a project cost estimate, effort estimate, and time estimate.

Create a Schedule

2.17. Identify and list the components needed to generate a workable project schedule. Demonstrate the ability to create appropriate project schedules, which meet the approved project start and finish dates, given the following information:

- A detailed list of project deliverables (both interim and finished)
- A detailed estimate of project tasks
- A list of activities and phases

■ A detailed estimate of the time and resources required to complete all project tasks

■ Information about the preferences of the project team regarding schedule formats

2.18. Given a scenario with necessary project documents, and given enterprise holiday and individual resource calendars, demonstrate the ability to develop a project schedule by doing the following:

■ Define and sequence project tasks, activities, and phases that are needed to bring about the completion of a given interim or finished project deliverables

■ Estimate durations for project tasks, activities, and phases

■ Estimate work effort for project tasks and assignments

■ Specify resources required for the completion of each phase

■ Identify the project critical path

2.19. Demonstrate the ability to identify project team organization roles and responsibilities required for the execution of the project, including:

■ The role of the customer (sponsor) of the project as it relates to the project manager's role

■ The major skills required in the project team

■ The type of team structure; for example, part-time matrix, full-time matrix

■ Confirm the role of the project manager, including any or all of the following:

   ■ Responsibilities, accountability

   ■ Authority: formal and informal

   ■ Percentage of time available to this project

   ■ Performance appraisal process relative to this project

2.20. Demonstrate the ability to assign resources to the schedule by:

■ Creating a list of resources needed and their availabilities

■ Assigning responsibilities to tasks

Create a Budget

2.21. Given a project scope, timeline, cost, project team, and dependencies, demonstrate the ability to:

■ Create and manage a high-level (top-down) budget based on assumptions/estimates

■ Identify and budget the level, cost, and duration of resources and dependencies (internal and external)

■ Create and manage a detailed bottom-up budget containing actual/ scheduled expenses

■ Identify, implement, and budget all project trade-offs while understanding their implications and impact

■ Install and maintain systems for tracking budgetary expenses against the plan based on the existing enterprise systems

■ Align the budget with the spending plan of the organization

Create a Quality Management Plan

2.22. Demonstrate an understanding of the components of a project quality management plan (for example, measured quality checkpoints, assignments for architectural control, systems test, and unit tests, user sign-off, etc.)

2.23. Demonstrate the skills to develop a quality plan that assures:

■ Awareness of the need to develop a test plan and defect tracking procedure that ensure appropriate testing steps, defect resolution, and documentation steps occur during the project life cycle.

■ A configuration management exists that ensures:

■ Phase deliverables are reviewed and inspected for completion, defects are removed, and issues are resolved prior to acceptance

- Documented sufficiency criteria exist for the exiting of each phase
- A change control process exists for all technical environments
- A requirements management process exists
- Formal customer acceptance and sign-off is obtained at appropriate points

Create a Risk Management Plan

2.24. Demonstrate the ability to perform risk assessment and mitigation by doing the following (given a scenario including the appropriate project documentation):

- Identify and prioritize the most important risks that will impact the project
- Evaluate the severity of the risks to successful completion of the project
- Identify risks contained on a project's critical path and identify procedures to reduce potential impacts on schedule

Create a Communication Plan

2.25. Demonstrate the ability to create a project communication plan that clearly indicates what needs to be communicated during a project, to whom, when, and how (using formal, informal approaches).

Organize a Comprehensive Project Plan and Close Out the Planning Phase

2.26. Identify the components/documents of an adequate project plan and explain the function of each. Components include:

- Table of contents
- Overview/executive summary
- Sponsors
- Team members
- Requirements

- Scheduled tasks (WBS)
- Expected resources
- Environmental issues
- Business and technical requirements
- Implementation plans
- Support plans
- Training plans
- Document (plan) location and revision control

2.27. Identify the steps involved in organizing a comprehensive project plan and using it to close out the planning phase of a project, including:

- Assembling all project planning elements (estimates of deliverables, time, costs, etc.)
- Creating an outline or table of contents for the comprehensive project plan
- Reviewing the outline of the comprehensive project plan with sponsor and key stakeholders, obtaining feedback and concurrence, and revising as needed
- Writing the comprehensive project plan by integrating all planning elements according to the outline and creating a full document with transitions, introductions, graphics, exhibits, appendices, etc., as appropriate
- Circulating the comprehensive project plan to all stakeholders
- Obtaining top management support of the comprehensive project plan by making certain it reflects their concerns and that they have had an opportunity to provide input
- Conducting a formal review of the comprehensive project plan in which stakeholders have an opportunity to provide feedback
- Adjusting the comprehensive project plan based on stakeholder feedback
- Obtaining formal approval (sign-off) of the comprehensive project plan by sponsor(s)

2.28. Demonstrate knowledge of how to set performance baselines for:

- Project scope and deliverable performance requirements
- Schedule
- Budget
- Resources

2.29. Demonstrate knowledge of the need to create change management procedures for the project plan.

2.30 Be able to identify project performance indicators that will be used to monitor and control performance during execution.

2.31. Be able to secure staffing commitments and resolve staffing issues.

2.32. Recognize the need to conduct a review meeting as the project transitions from the planning phase to the execution and coordination phases. The review includes an assessment of the following:

- Completion of the project planning documentation
- Resolution of all planning issues
- Continued viability of the business case
- Alignment of stakeholder expectations with the plan

Domain 3.0: IT Project Execution, Control and Coordination

This domain requires the candidate to demonstrate knowledge and skills in:

- Project monitoring, tracking, and performance reporting
- Interpreting project performance indicators and identifying variances from plan
- Taking corrective action
- Updating the plan and replanning by project phase

- Issue tracking and issue resolution
- Risk tracking and risk removal/mitigation
- Change control
- Quality management
- Team management, coordination, and communications
- Resource management

3.1 Identify the following as tasks that should be accomplished on a weekly basis in the course of tracking an "up and running" project.

- Explain the rationale for performing these tasks and explain how to adapt these tasks to different situations:
    - Check the project's scope status to determine "in scope" versus "out of scope" status of project elements.
    - Check the evolution and status of project deliverables.
    - Check the project schedule.
    - Analyze variances (deviations from plan) by comparing "estimated" to "actual" resource time expenditures, dollar expenditures, milestones, and elapsed duration of activities.
    - Handle scope changes, if needed.
    - List, track, and try to resolve open issues.
    - Report project status.
    - Look for opportunities to, and "push" for, close out of activities and sign-off of deliverables.
    - Decide whether it is appropriate to continue the project. Discontinue the project if appropriate.

3.2 Given a scenario with a set of project performance indicators, demonstrate the ability to recognize when performance problems are occurring on the project and determine if/when corrective action/recovery needs to occur.

3.3 Given a scenario with updates/changes made to the project plan, demonstrate the need to check for impact on:

- The project critical path/schedule/WBS
- Project performance indicators
- Resource availability
- Budget
- Risks
- Project objectives

3.4 Given a scenario involving a project with a schedule delay, choose an appropriate course of action.

3.5 Given an approved project and a status report scenario containing a significant variance from plan (for example, excessive overtime, purchased items more expensive than a anticipated, etc.), do the following:

- Clearly identify the reason for the variance
- Determine the impact on the schedule and budget and the effect on stakeholders
- Determine if scope creep is occurring
- Identify options for corrective action
- Identify options for absorbing part or all of the increase in the overall budget (if any)
- Identify stakeholders who must be notified or must give approval to a change of schedule or budget and develop a plan for advising them of the change, the rationale for the change, and the consequences if not approved

3.6 Given a scenario in which a vendor requests a two-week delay in delivering its product, explain how to do the following:

- Negotiate a lesser delay by identifying things the vendor might do to improve its schedule

- Clearly identify the impact of the negotiated delivery on the project scope and critical path

- Present this impact to the appropriate stakeholders

3.7 Given a scenario in which there is a disagreement between a vendor and your project team, identify methods for resolving the problem.

3.8 Identify issues to consider when trying to rebuild active project support from a wavering executive (for example, the need to identify the source of doubts, interpersonal communications skills that might be employed, the need to act without creating negative impact, the need to identify and utilize various allies and influences, etc.). Given a scenario involving a wavering executive, choose an appropriate course of action.

3.9 Identify issues to consider when trying to obtain approval of a changed project plan that is still within expected budget, but has a schedule that extends outside of the original baseline end date.

3.10 Define and explain Estimate to Complete (ETC), Estimate at Complete (EAC), and Budget at Completion (BAC).

3.11 Demonstrate the ability to track the financial performance of a project given the financial management baseline and data on the actual performance of the project. Demonstrate:

- The need to identify and understand proposed changes from plan

- The need to be able to justify and sell the changes

- The need for alternative courses of action if the plan isn't accepted, etc.

Change Control

3.12 Given an approved project plan and a specific scope deviation (for example, design, schedule, or cost change, etc.), demonstrate your ability to:

- Identify the cause(s)
- Prepare a status report for the user identifying problems and corrective action
- Determine the impact of the deviation on the scope of the project
- Quantify the deviation in terms of time, cost, and resources
- Distinguish between variances that will affect the budget and duration and those that will not
- Determine and quantify at least one possible alternative solution that has less impact but requires some scope compromise
- Distinguish between those variances that should be elevated to the sponsor and those that should be handled by the project manager and team
- Develop a plan to gain stakeholder approval
- Use a change order

3.13 Identify and justify the following as conditions for initiating a change control process:

- Resource changes
- Schedule changes
- Cost changes
- Requirements changes (or changes in expectations)
- Infrastructure changes
- As a response to scope creep

3.14 Given scenarios involving requests for changes from sponsors, team members, or third parties, recognize and explain how to prevent scope creep.

3.15 Recognize and explain the importance of communicating significant proposed changes in project scope, and their impacts, to management, and getting management review and formal approval.

Quality Management

3.16 Identify and explain strategies and requirements for maintaining qualified deliverables given a large project with many team members at multiple locations (for example, communication standards work standards, etc.).

3.17 Recognize and explain the importance of testing in situations where tasks are being performed by both project team members and third parties.

3.18 Identify and explain strategies and requirements for assuring quality during the turnover phase (for example, user docs, user training, helpdesk training, support structure, etc.).

3.19 Identify and explain strategies and requirements for assuring quality of deliverables and meeting sufficiency standards during each phase.

3.20 Recognize the need for controlling changes on the configuration of the project deliverable and explain its importance.

3.21 Recognize the relevance of the organization's Quality Policy to project quality.

Team Management

3.22 Identify effective strategies for providing timely performance feedback to team members.

3.23 Demonstrate an understanding of how to effectively manage disgruntled team members so that team performance is not adversely affected.

3.24 Demonstrate an understanding of how to recognize individual team member performance issues and to identify effective strategies for corrective action.

Resource Management

3.25 Given an initial high-level scope, budget, and resource allocation, demonstrate an understanding of the need to investigate the aspects of the project that could be modified to improve outcomes (that is, find out what is negotiable, prepare to negotiate). Provide evidence of the following competencies:

- The ability to recognize that individual project team member's needs must be addressed to the extent that project activities can be modified without significant impact on final scope, budget, quality, or schedule

- The ability to evaluate alternatives to a scope change request that stakeholders may find acceptable

- The ability to recognize which aspects (schedule, budget, quality) of the project are most important to the stakeholders and be able to propose trade-offs during the project that can be made to meet or exceed those aspects

- The ability to identify all of the individuals and groups with which you will need to negotiate during the life of the project (sponsors, vendors, users, internal and external service organizations, other project teams, project team members, finance/accounting, etc.)

3.26 Given a project scenario, demonstrate the ability to resolve a resource availability (staffing) issue requiring escalation to the project sponsor and senior level stakeholders.

Coordination

3.27 Given a project scenario during the implementation phases, demonstrate the understanding of the need to organize and effectively run meetings.

3.28 Given a project team meeting scenario in which a decision must be made with imperfect information, demonstrate the knowledge of problem solving techniques to help the team through a decision making process.

3.29 Given a project team meeting scenario, demonstrate an awareness of the need to provide direction and clarify work instructions to team members.

3.30 Given a project team meeting scenario where the project is behind plan, demonstrate an awareness of the need to:

- Identify an accountable team member
- Clarify the root cause of the problem causing the delay
- Develop a strategy for corrective action
- Implement the corrective action strategy
- Follow up to check on results

3.31 Given a project scenario where intra-team communication is inadequate, demonstrate the ability to improve communication to an appropriate level.

Risk and Issue Management

3.32 Given a project team meeting scenario, demonstrate the knowledge to review an issue log with team members and secure closure of issues.

3.33 Demonstrate the ability to prioritize issues by severity and impact on quality.

3.34 Demonstrate an understanding of how to determine if/when planned risks have materialized and how to implement planned risk mitigation and removal strategies.

3.35 Demonstrate the ability to prioritize risks by severity and impact on quality.

3.36 Demonstrate the ability to remove/mitigate a project risk.

3.37 Demonstrate an understanding of how to report to the project sponsor that a project is in jeopardy and how to report corrective action strategies that are underway.

3.38 Demonstrate an understanding of how to determine when a project should be prematurely terminated.

Relationship Management with Business (Client) Organization

3.39 Recognize potential organizational and political barriers inhibiting an effective working relationship between the IT organization and the client/business organization.

3.40 Demonstrate an understanding of methods to develop and maintain an effective working relationship during projects between the IT organization and the client/business organization.

- Frequent communications
- Team building
- Managing by fact
- Issue management and problem solving
- Timely decision making

- Importance of written communication
- Gaining consensus
- Managing expectations

Domain 4.0: Project Closure, Acceptance, and Support

4.1 Recognize and explain the value of conducting a comprehensive review process that identifies the lessons learned and evaluates the planning, organizing, directing, controlling, execution, and budget phases of the project, identifying both the positive and negative aspects in a written report.

4.2 Recognize the need to plan to transfer the project deliverable to support and maintenance and to budget for these resources, including help desk.

4.3 Recognize the need for acceptance testing (user acceptance testing, factory acceptance testing, site acceptance testing) of the project deliverable.

4.4 Recognize the need to obtain formal customer sign-off on the project deliverable and hand-off to the customer.

- Close out meeting with customer/sign-off on statement of work
- Begin support/maintenance
- Change control to additional scope
- Formally turn over deliverable to the customer

4.5 Recognize the need to complete project documentation, secure approvals, and archive/store documentation appropriately.

4.6 Recognize the need to close out contracts and sign-off for vendors.

Appendix B

Critical Exam Information

Overview

Many readers of this book are prepping are for their IT Project+ examination. Good for you! While the intent of this book is really more to explain a practical approach to IT project management than to serve as just a study guide, you'll find exam-relevant information throughout the book. However, if you're looking for exam-specific information, this is place for you. You will not pass the exam if you're unfamiliar with the specifics in this appendix.

Test-Passing Tips

For starters don't think of this process as preparing to take an exam; think of it as "preparing to pass an exam." Anyone can prepare to take an exam: just show up. Preparing to pass any exam, especially the IT Project+ exam, requires project management experience, diligence, and a commitment to study.

Days Before the Exam

In the days leading up to your scheduled exam, you should do these basics to prepare yourself for success:

- *Get some moderate exercise.* Find time to go for a jog, lift weights, take a swim, or do whatever workout routine works best for you.

- *Eat healthfully and wisely.* If you eat healthful food you'll feel good—and feel better about yourself. Be certain to drink plenty of water and don't overdo the caffeine.

- *Get your sleep.* A well-rested brain is a sharp brain. You don't want to sit for your exam feeling tired, sluggish, and worn-out.

- *Time your study sessions.* Don't overdo your study sessions—long, crash study sessions aren't that profitable. In addition, try to study at the same time every day for the same amount of time your exam will last.

Practice the Testing Process

If you could take one page of notes into the exam, what information would you like on this one-page document? Of course, you absolutely cannot take any notes or reference materials into the exam area. However, if you can create and memorize one sheet of notes, you're legally allowed to re-create it once you're seated in the exam area.

You'll be supplied with several sheets of blank paper and a couple of pencils. Once your exam process begins, immediately re-create your reference sheet. The following are key pieces of information you'd be wise to include on this sheet (you'll find all of this key information in this appendix):

- Activities within each process group
- Estimating formulas
- Communication formula
- Normal distribution values
- Earned Value Management (EVM) formulas
- Project management theories

Testing Tips

The questions on the IT Project+ exam are fairly direct, not too verbose, but may include a few red herrings. For example, you may face questions that state: "All of the following are correct options expect for which one?" The question wants you to find the incorrect option, or the option that is not be appropriate for the scenario described. Use caution when reading what the question is asking for. It's easy to read a question and then see a suitable option for the scenario in the answer. The trouble is if the question is asking you to identify an option that is not suitable, you just missed the question. Carefully read the question to understand what type of answer fits.

A tip that can work with many of the questions is to identify which answer matches the question and then look for an option that doesn't fit with the other possible choices. In other words find the answer that doesn't fit with the other three options. Find the "odd man out." Here's an example: EVM is used during the

_____.

A. Controlling

B. Executing

C. Closing

D. Entire project

Notice how options A, B, and C are now exclusive? If you choose A, controlling, it eliminates EVM from being used anywhere else in the project. The odd man out here is D, the entire project; it's considered the odd choice because it, by itself, is not an actual process group. Of course, this tip won't work with every question—but it's handy to know.

Some answer choices may appear to have two of the four options as possibly correct answers. However, because you may only choose only one answer, you must discern which one is the best choice. Within the question there will usually be some hint describing the progress of the project, the requirements of the stakeholders, or some other clue that can help you determine which answer is the best for the question.

Answer Every Question–Once

The IT Project+ exam has 80 questions and you need to score at least 499 to pass. You'll have 90 minutes to complete the exam. Do not leave any question blank— even if you don't know the answer. A blank question is the same as a wrong answer. As you move through the exam and find questions that may stump you, use the "mark question" option in the exam software: choose an answer you suspect may be correct and then move on. When you have answered all of the questions, you are given the option to review your marked answers.

Some questions in the exam may reveal, or prompt your memory, answers to questions you have marked for review. However, resist the temptation to review questions you've already answered with confidence. More often than not your first instinct is the correct. When you completed the exams at the end of each chapter, did you change correct answers to wrong answers? If you do it in practice, you'll do it on the actual exam.

Use the Process of Elimination

When you're stumped on a question, use the process of elimination. For each question there'll be four choices. On your scratch paper write down "ABCD." If you can safely rule out a, mark it out of the ABCD you've written on your paper. Now focus on which other answer won't work. If you determine C won't work cross it off your list. Now you've got a fifty-fifty chance of selecting the correct choice.

If you cannot determine which answer is best, B or D in this instance, here's the best approach:

1. Choose an answer in the exam (no blank answers, remember?)

2. Mark the question in the exam software for later review.

3. Circle the ABCD on your scratch paper, jot any relevant notes, and then record the question number next to the notes.

4. When you do your review, or answer questions further on in the exam, you may realize which choice is the better of the two. Return to the question and select the best answer.

Everything You Must Know

As promised, this section now covers all of the information you must know going into the exam. It's highly recommended you create a method to recall this information.

The 39 Project Management Processes

Table B-1 shows the 39 project management processes. The intersection of the Knowledge Area and each stage (Initiating, Planning, Executing, Controlling, and Closing) describes the activity that happens at that point in the project. For example, follow the Project Scope Management row and the Controlling column to find *Scope verification and change control.*

Magic Project Management Formulas

Figure B-1 shows the major formulas you should know for the exam.

EVM Formulas

Figure B-2 shows the EVM formulas you should know for the exam.

Quick Exam Facts

This section has some quick facts you should be know at a glance. Hold on, this moves pretty fast.

Organization Structures   Organizational structures are relevant to the project manager's authority. A project manager's authority will vary depending on the organizational structure he's operating within. The structures that offer the least power to the highest amount of power for the project manager are in the following order:

- Functional
- Weak matrix
- Balanced matrix
- Strong matrix
- Projectized

Knowledge Area	Initiating	Planning	Executing	Controlling	Closing
Project Integration Management		Developing the project plan.	Project plan execution.	Integrated change control.	
Project Scope Management	Project Initiation	Creating and defining the project scope.		Scope verification and change control.	
Project Time Management		Defining activities, their sequence, and their estimated duration. Developing the project schedule.		Schedule control.	
Project Cost Management		Determining the required resources, their estimated costs, and completing cost budgeting.		Enforcing cost control.	
Project Quality Management		Planning for quality.	Adhering to the performing organization's quality assurance (QA) requirements.	Enforcing quality control (QC) on the project.	
Project Human Resources Management		Completing organizational planning and staff acquisition.	Ensuring team development.		
Project Communications Management		Creating the Communications Management Plan.	Distributing the required information to the appropriate parties.	Reporting on project performance.	Completing administrative closure.
Project Risk Management		Completing risk management planning, risk identification, qualitative and quantitative risk analysis, and risk responses.		Monitoring and controlling risk.	
Project Procurement Management		Completing the procurement and solicitation planning.	Soliciting vendors to participate on the project. Completing source selection based on defined criterion, and then following-through with contract administration.		Completing the contract closeout.

Table B-1 The 39 Project Management Processes

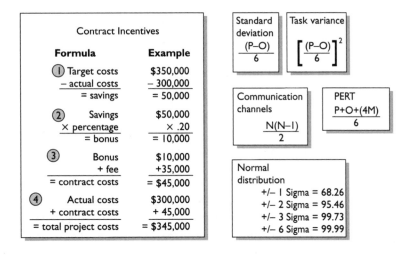

FIGURE B-1

IT Project+ candidates should know these fundamental formulas.

WBS Facts   The Work Breakdown Structure (WBS) is the big picture of the project deliverables. It is not the activities that occur to create the project, but the components the project will create. The WBS helps the project team and the project manager create accurate cost and time estimates. The WBS also helps the project team and the project manager create an accurate activity list. The WBS is an input to five planning processes:

- Cost estimating
- Cost budgeting
- Resource planning
- Risk Management Planning
- Activity definition

FIGURE B-2

IT Project+ candidates will be tested on Earned Value Management fundamentals.

Earned Value Management formulas

VAR = BAC − AC
EV = %COMP × BAC
CV = EV − AC
SV = EV − PV
CPI = EV/AC
SPI = EV/PV
EAC = BAC/CPI
ETC = EAC − AC
VAC = BAC − EAC
TCPI = (BAC − EV) / (EAC − AC)

Older names:
BCWS = PV
BCWP = EV
ACWP = AC

Project Scope Facts   Projects are temporary endeavors to create a unique product of service. Projects are selected by one of two methods:

- **Benefit measurement methods**   These include scoring models, cost-benefit ratios, and economic models.

- **Constrained optimization**   Mathematical models based on linear, integer, and dynamic programming models. (You probably won't see this one on the IT Project+ exam as a viable answer.)

The project scope defines all of the required work, and only the required work, to complete the project. Scope management is the process of ensuring the project work is within scope and protects the project from scope creep. The scope statement is the baseline for all future project decisions as it justifies the business need of the project. There are two types of scope:

- Product scope defines the attributes of the product or service the project is creating.

- Project scope defines the required work of the project to create the product.

Scope verification is the process completed at the end of each phase and project to confirm the project has met the requirements. It leads to the formal acceptance of the project deliverable.

Project Time Facts   Time can be a project constraint. Effective time management is the scheduling and sequencing of activities in the best order to ensure the project completes successfully—and in a reasonable amount of time. There are some key terms for time management:

- **Lag**   Waiting between activities.
- **Lead**   Activities come closer together and even overlap.
- **Free float**   The amount of time an activity can be delayed without delaying the next scheduled activity's start date.
- **Total float**   The amount of time an activity can be delayed without delaying the project finish date.
- **Slack and float**   These are synonymous; duration may be abbreviated as "du."

There are three types of dependencies between activities:

- **Mandatory**   This hard logic requires a specific sequence between activities.
- **Discretionary**   This soft logic prefers a sequence between activities.
- **External**   Due to reasons outside of the project, such as vendors, the sequence must happen in a given order.

Project Cost Facts   There are several methods for providing project estimates:

- **Bottom-up**   Project costs start at zero and each component in the WBS is estimated for costs and then the "grand total" is calculated. This is the longest method to complete, but it provides the most accurate estimate.
- **Analogous**   Project costs are based on a similar project. This is a form of expert judgment, but it is also a top-down estimating approach so it less accurate than a bottom-up estimate.
- **Parametric Modeling**   Price is based on cost per unit; examples include cost per metric ton, cost per yard, cost per hour.

There are four types of costs attributed to a project:

- **Variable costs**   The costs depend on other variables. For example, the cost of a food-catered event depends on how many people register to attend the event.
- **Fixed costs**   The cost remains constant throughout the project. For example, a rented piece of equipment is the same fee each month even if it is used more in some months than others.
- **Direct costs**   The cost is directly attributed to an individual project and cannot be shared with other projects; for example, airfare to attend project meetings, hotel expenses, and leased equipment that is used only on the current project.
- **Indirect costs**   These are the cost of doing business; examples include rent, phone, and utilities.

Quality Management Facts   The cost of quality is the money spent investing in training, requirements for safety, laws and regulations, and steps added to ensure quality acceptance. The cost of nonconformance is the cost associated with rework, downtime, lost sales, and waste of materials.

Some common quality management charts and methods include:

- **Ishikawa diagrams**   These diagrams are also called fishbone diagrams. They are used to find causes and effects that contribute to a problem.

- **Flow charts**   These charts show the relationship between components and the flow of a process through a system.

- **Pareto Diagrams**   These diagrams identify project problems and their frequencies. These are based on the 80/20 Rule: 80 percent of project problems stem from 20 percent of the work.

- **Control Charts**   These charts plot out the result of samplings to determine if projects are "in control" or "out of control."

- **Kaizen technologies**   These technologies make small improvements in an effort to reduce costs and consistency.

- **Just-in-time ordering**   This method reduces the cost of inventory but requires additional quality because materials are not readily available should mistakes occur.

Human Resource Facts   There are several human resource theories you should be familiar with on the IT Project+ exam. They are:

- **Maslow's Hierarchy of Needs**   There are five layers of needs for all humans: physiological, safety, social, esteem, and the crowning jewel—self-actualization.

- **Herzberg's Theory of Motivation**   There are two catalysts for workers: hygiene agents and motivating agents.

  - **Hygiene agents**   These do nothing to motivate workers, but their absence demotivates them. Hygiene agents are the expectations all workers have: job security, a paycheck, clean and safe working conditions, a sense of belonging, civil working relationships, and other basic attributes associated with employment.

  - **Motivating agents**   These are the elements that motivate people to excel. They include responsibility, appreciation of work, recognition, the opportunity to excel, education, and other opportunities associated with work other than just financial rewards.

- **McGregory's Theory of X and Y**   This theory states "X" people are lazy, don't want to work, and need to be micromanaged. "Y" people are self-led, motivated, and can accomplish tasks.

- **Ouchi's Theory Z**   This theory believes the workers are motivated by a sense of commitment, opportunity, and advancement. Workers will work if they are challenged and motivated. Think participative management.

- **Expectancy Theory**   People will behave based on what they expect as a result of their behavior. In other words, people will work in relation to the expected reward of the work.

Communication Facts   Communicating is the most important skill for the project manager. With that in mind, here are some key facts on communications:

- The communication channels formula is $N(N - 1)/2$. N represents the number of stakeholders. For example, if you have 10 stakeholders, the formula would read $10(10 - 1)/2$ for 45 communication channels. Pay special attention to questions wanting to know how many additional communication channels you have based on added stakeholders. For example, you have 25 stakeholders on your project and have recently added 5 team members. How many additional communications do you now have? You'll have to calculate the original number of communication channels, $25(25-1)/2 = 300$, and then calculate the new number with the added team members, $30(30-1)/2 = 435$, and, finally, subtract the difference between the two: $435 - 300 = 135$ additional communication channels.

- Fifty-five percent of communication is nonverbal.

- Effective listening is the ability to watch the speaker's body language, interpret para lingual clues, and decipher facial expressions for insight. The next step is to follow these messages with questions for clarity and to offer feedback. Active listening requires the receiver of the message to offer clues, such as nodding the head to indicate he is listening. It also requires the receiver to repeat the message, ask questions, and continue the discussion if clarification is needed.

- Communication can be hindered by trendy phrases, jargon, and extremely pessimistic comments. In addition, communication can be blocked by noise, hostility, cultural differences, and static among other communication barriers.

Risk Management Facts   Risks are unplanned events that can affect the project for good or bad. Risks should be identified as early as possible in the planning process. A person's willingness to accept risk is the Utility Function (also called the Utility Theory). The Delphi Technique can be used to build consensus on project risks.

The only output of the risk planning is the Risk Management Plan. There are two broad types of risks:

- **Business risk**   The loss of time and finances; a downside and an upside may exist.
- **Pure risk**   The loss of life, injury, and theft. Only a down side exists.

Risks can be responded to in one of four methods:

- **Avoidance**   Avoid the risk by planning a different technique to remove the risk from the project.
- **Mitigation**   Reduce the probability or impact of a risk.
- **Acceptance**   The risk's probability or impact may be small enough that it can be accepted.
- **Transference**   The risk is not eliminated but the responsibility and ownership of the risk is transferred to another party; for example, it's transferred to insurance.

Procurement Facts   A Statement of Work (SOW) is provided to the potential sellers so they can create accurate bids, quotes, and proposals for the buyer. A bidders' conference may be held so sellers can query the buyer on the product or service to be procured.

A contract is a formal agreement, preferably written, between a buyer and seller. On the exam, procurement questions are usually from the buyer's point of view. All requirements the seller is to complete should be clearly written in the contract. Requirements of both parties must be met or legal proceedings may follow. Contract types include:

- Cost-reimbursable contracts require the buyer to assume the risk of cost overruns.
- Fixed-price contracts require the seller to assume the risk of cost overruns.
- Time-and-material contracts are good for smaller assignments but can impose cost overrun risks to the buyer if the time by the seller is not monitored.
- A purchase order is a unilateral form of contract.
- A letter of intent is not a contract, but it shows the intent of the buyer to purchase from a specific seller.

Appendix C

Working as an Independent Contractor

O ver the last few years, IT professionals have left their cubicles and sought the Great American Dream. They've traded the corporate life for the life of an entrepreneur. Is that you? If it is, congratulations!

It is possible to earn a respectable income as an independent IT project manager. You will, however, encounter some issues that a project manager inside the ranks of the corporate world won't.

Getting (and Keeping) the Deal

First and foremost is getting the deal. This isn't a lesson in marketing, sales, and negotiations—there are hundreds of books on those topics. The point to learn here is to deliver on what you promise. As a contractor, it's tempting to grind into the PND and sell yourself short on time to get the gig your calendar so badly needs. Don't heed that temptation. The company you are selling yourself to will hold you to the completion date, the skills, and the price you promise.

If you overpromise but underdeliver, you may find yourself with one less client. Clients will expect you to provide cumulative reports to them just as a staff project manager would do. If your cumulative reports show your project is lacking because of your abilities, your clients may exercise their right to escort you from the building.

One great thing in favor of independent project managers, however, is they aren't part of the company. Imagine a project manager tied to meetings all day long, bogged down in office politics, and stressed over the upcoming holiday party. You don't have to worry about any of that nonsense. You're free to focus on one thing: the success of the project. Take advantage of your ability to work— and get some serious work done before someone around there notices you and tries to suck you into a few extra meetings and their world of corporate politics.

Making Yourself at Home

All eyes are on you, the new guy. Being an independent project manager can be a stressful way to start a project. You've got a project team of strangers to work with. They most likely know each other, but don't know you. You need to immediately get to work learning about the team members, their likes and motivations, and, most important, which team member has what abilities.

You'll have team members tugging on your sleeves for quite awhile trying to whisper in your ear about what they think is best for this and who the best person is for that. Some of their ideas may be great, and sometimes they may be right, but you've got to make the decisions based on what's best for the project, not the latest rumor. As an independent project manager, you've got to focus on the immediate talents of the team members and assume each is as dedicated to the project as you are.

Then, based on their actions (or lack thereof), you can determine their real level of commitment. Team members do, however, have a fantastic way of respecting the requests of an independent contractor, as they see this individual for the specialist she is. The perception is that you are a quality, skilled expert in the project you are managing. It's true—perception is reality. Use that savvy to lead the team to complete the tasks they are capable of completing.

You'll need to also get to know the end users of the anticipated technology, the project sponsor (most likely the person who hired you), and the documentation of the project, if any exists yet. Study the impacted technology, the current technology, and, if needed, brush up on the technology the project is implementing.

Depending on the company you work for, you may not be privy to all of the financial information on the project that a full-time employee would be. For example, the company may not feel it is relevant for you to know the hourly wages of different team members to calculate the CPI or assign tasks based on wages.

On a practical note, create a reference card of the company's terminology for server names and application names, and get the names and contact information of people you should know, as you'll need these throughout the project. You have to do the mechanical, down-to-earth business that will allow you to absorb the project, the company outlook, and the project vision as quickly as possible.

Becoming a Leader

Becoming a leader to your project team is the goal of any project manager. By doing such a thorough, complete job of leading the team, inspiring the individuals you'll be working with, and seeing every task through to completion, the people on the project team will wonder what they ever did without you.

One aspect of becoming a leader as an independent project manager that may be a challenge for you is communication. You need to stress to the project team that communication to management in regard to the project needs to flow through you. Often what happens is the project team finds it very easy to bypass the project manager and report trouble directly to management. Ultimately, this usurps the authority of the project manager, and the project team fails to see the project manager as the leader.

To circumvent this disaster, the project manager must stress from day one the channel of communication about issues on the project. If at all possible, you should speak with the project sponsor about the flow of communication and secure his support. When the project sponsor introduces you to the team, he should also indicate that you are running the show. Everything about the project should flow through you.

Successful independent project managers generally make great leaders because they have a natural ability to get things done. They are not afraid of working extra hours, helping a team member with any task necessary, or meeting with immediate management or the CEO. Great leaders lead by doing.

Delivering More Than What You Promise

One sure way to be a success as an independent project manager is to promise to finish the project. Then look for opportunities to deliver more than what was promised. Always give more than what is expected of you and do it happily.

This doesn't mean you have to reinvent the project, add a few more layers to an application, or create routing tables from scratch. It means you should look for opportunities to make the project process better, such as the following:

- Help a team member with a tough assignment.
- Complete a weekly project update e-mail.
- Guard the management reserve and the budget.
- Motivate and reward team members early and often.
- Write thank-you cards.
- Develop a care and concern for the people you are working with.

As you progress through the project, remind yourself that you are only as good as your last project. When this stint is completed (and that is your job, to get the project to completion), how will you look back on your work and on the project deliverables? Will you be pleased with your work? Will you wish you could change some elements? Answer those questions as you move through the project, and you'll be satisfied with the work you produce.

More important, the organization that hired you will be pleased with the work you completed, and, hopefully, ask you back for more.

Appendix D

About the CD

The CD-ROM included with this book comes complete with a full MasterExam and a collection of templates and forms useful for analyzing and managing projects. The software is easy to install on any Windows 98/NT/2000/XP computer and must be installed to access the MasterExam. You may, however, browse the templates and forms directly from the CD without installation. To register for a second bonus MasterExam (another 250 study questions!), simply click the Online Training link on the Main Page and follow the directions to the free online registration.

System Requirements

Software requires Windows 98 or higher and Internet Explorer 5.0 or above and 20 MB of hard disk space for full installation.

Installing and Running MasterExam

If your computer CD-ROM drive is configured to auto run, the CD-ROM will automatically start up upon inserting the disk. From the opening screen you may install MasterExam by pressing the *MasterExam* button. This will begin the installation process and create a program group named "LearnKey." To run MasterExam use START | PROGRAMS | LEARNKEY. If the auto run feature did not launch your CD, browse to the CD and Click on the "RunInstall" icon.

MasterExam

MasterExam provides you with a simulation of the IT Project + exam. You may take an open book exam, which provides the option of receiving hints, references, and answers; a closed book exam; or the timed MasterExam simulation.

When you launch MasterExam, a digital clock display will appear in the upper left-hand corner of your screen. The clock will continue to count down to zero unless you choose to end the exam before the time expires.

Help

A help file is provided through the help button on the main menu page in the lower left hand corner. Individual help features are also available within the MasterExam application.

Removing Installation(s)

MasterExam installs to your hard drive. For BEST results for removal of programs use the START | PROGRAMS | LEARNKEY| UNINSTALL options to remove MasterExam.

Technical Support

For questions regarding the content of the electronic book, MasterExam, or CertCams, please visit www.osborne.com or email customer.service@mcgraw-hill.com. For customers outside the 50 United States, email: international_cs@mcgraw-hill.com.

LearnKey Technical Support

For technical problems with the software (installation, operation, removing installations), please visit www.learnkey.com or email techsupport@learnkey.com.

Glossary

activity-on-the-arrow PND   This sophisticated approach stems from the 1950s, when the original concept was called the activity-on-the-arrow (AOA) method. The origin of the arrow is the "begin activity" sign, and the end of the arrow is the "end activity" sign.

activity-on-the-node PND   A network diagramming method that allows the project manager to map relationships between activities. With the AON method, the focus is on the activities rather than on the start and end of activities.

actual costs (AC)   Actual costs are used in Earned Value Management and represent the actual cost of the work performed.

administrative closure   This is when the customer or project sponsor documents and accepts the project results. Administrative closure is also needed if a project is terminated.

analogous estimating   This relies on historical information to predict estimates for current projects. Analogous estimating is also known as top-down estimating and is a form of expert judgment.

As Late As Possible (ALAP) constraints   When you specify a task as ALAP, Microsoft Project will schedule the task to occur as late as possible without delaying dependent tasks. This is the default for all new tasks when scheduling tasks from the end date. This constraint is flexible.

As Soon As Possible (ASAP) constraints   When you specify a task as ASAP, Microsoft Project will schedule the task to occur as soon as it can. This is the default for all new tasks when assigning tasks from the start date. This constraint is flexible.

assumptions   Beliefs considered to be true, real, or certain for the sake of planning.

avoidance   This is one response to a risk event. The risk is avoided by planning a different technique to remove the risk from the project.

benchmarking   The process of using prior projects within, or external to, the performing organization to compare and set quality standards for processes and results.

benefit/cost analysis   The process of determining the pros and cons of any project, process, product, or activity.

benefit measurement methods   This method is used when comparing the value of one project against the value, or benefits, of another. It's often used in project selection models.

bid   A document from the seller to the buyer. A bid is used when price is the determining factor in the decision-making process.

bidder conference (also called a contractor or vendor conference)   A meeting with prospective sellers to ensure all sellers have a clear understanding of the product or service to be procured. Bidder conferences allow sellers to query the buyer on the details of the product to help ensure that the proposal the seller creates is adequate and appropriate for the proposed agreement.

bottom-up cost estimating The process of creating a detailed estimate for each work component (labor and materials) and accounting for each varying cost burden.

budget The finances allotted for the completion of an IT technical project.

Budget at Completion (BAC) The sum of the budget for each phase of your project. This is the estimated grand total of your project.

business cycles A time of the business productivity where activities are very high or low. For example, an accounting firm may experience a busy business cycle during tax season.

cause-and-effect diagrams (also called Ishikawa diagrams and fishbone diagrams) These diagrams are used for root cause analysis of what factors are creating the risks within the project. The goal is to identify and treat the root of the problem, not the symptom.

centralized contracting All contracts for all projects need to be approved through a central contracting unit within the performing organization.

Change Control Board (CCB) This board determines the validity and need for project change requests and approves or denies them.

Change Control System (CCS) An internal process the project manager can use to block anyone, including management, from changing the deliverables of a project without proper justification. Change control requires the requestor to have an excellent reason to attempt a change and then it evaluates the proposed change's impact on all facets of the project.

Change Impact Statement A formal response from the project manager to the originator of a Project Change Request form. It is summary of the project manager's proposed plan to incorporate the changes. Usually this is a listing of the paths and trade-offs the project manager is willing to implement.

chart of accounts A coding system used by the performing organization's accounting system to account for the project work.

checklists A list of activities that workers check to ensure the work has been completed consistently. Checklists are used in quality control.

closing The period when a project or phase moves through formal acceptance to bring the project or phase to an orderly conclusion.

coercive power The type of power that comes with the authority to discipline the project team members. This is also known as "penalty power." It is generally used to describe the power structure when the team is afraid of the project manager.

collective bargaining agreements These are contractual agreements initiated by employee groups, unions, or other labor organizations. They may act as a constraint on the project.

communication channel formula   A formula to predict the number of communication channels within a project; the formula is $N(N - 1)/2$, where N represents the number of stakeholders.

Communications Management Plan   A plan that documents and organizes stakeholder needs for communication. This plan covers the communications system, its documentation, the flow of communication, modalities of communication, schedules for communications, information retrieval, and any other stakeholder requirements for communications.

compromising   A conflict resolution method that requires both parties to give up something. The decision ultimately made is a blend of both sides of the argument. Because neither party completely wins, it is considered a lose-lose solution.

configuration management   Activities focusing on controlling the characteristics of a product or service. A documented process of controlling the features, attributes, and technical configuration of any product or service. It is sometimes considered a rigorous CCS.

constrained optimization methods   These are complex mathematical formulas and algorithms that are used to predict the success of projects, variables within projects, and tendencies to move forward with selected project investments. Examples include linear programming, integer algorithms, and multi-objective programming.

constraint   A boundary or limit based on the relationship between tasks.

consultative decision-making process   The project team meets with the project manager and together they may arrive at several viable solutions. The project manager then can take the proposed solutions and make a decision based on what she thinks is best for the project.

contingency plan   A predetermined decision that will be enacted should the project go awry.

contingency reserve   A time or dollar amount allotted as a response to risk events that may occur within a project.

Continuous Quality Improvement   The theory that all practices within an organization are processes and that processes can be infinitely improved.

contract   A legal, binding agreement, preferably written, between a buyer and seller detailing the requirements and obligations of both parties. It must include an offer, an acceptance, and a consideration.

contract administration   The process of ensuring that the buyer and the seller both perform to the specifications within the contract.

contract Change Control System   A system that defines the procedures for how contracts may be changed. Includes the paperwork, tracking, conditions, dispute resolution procedures, and the procedures for getting the changes approved within the performing organization.

contract closeout   A process for confirming that the obligations of the contract have been met as expected. The project manager, customer, key stakeholder, and, in some instances, seller complete the product verification together to confirm the contract has been completed.

contract file   A complete indexed set of records of the procurement process incorporated into the administrative closure process. These records include financial information as well as information on the performance and acceptance of the procured work.

control account plans   A control tool within the project that represents the integration of the project scope, project schedule, and budget. It allows management to measure the progress of a project.

control charts   These illustrate the performance of a project over time. They map the results of inspections against a chart. Control charts are typically used in projects or operations that have repetitive activities such as manufacturing, test series, or help desk functions. Upper and lower control limits indicate if values are within control or out of control.

controlling   The project is controlled and managed. The project manager controls the project scope and changes, and monitors changes to the project budget, schedule, and scope by comparing plans to actual results and taking corrective action as necessary.

core processes   These processes are common to all projects. The core processes are scope planning, scope definition, activity definition, resource planning, activity sequencing, activity duration estimation, cost estimating, risk management planning, schedule development, cost budgeting, and project plan development.

cost baseline   This shows what the project is expected to spend. It's usually shown in an *S*-Curve and allows the project manager and management to predict when the project will be spending monies and over what duration. The purpose of the cost baseline is to measure and predict project performance.

cost budgeting   A process of assigning a cost to an individual work package. This process shows costs over time. The cost budget results in an *S*-Curve that becomes the cost baseline for the project.

Cost Change Control   This is part of the Integrated Change Control System and documents the procedures to request, approve, and incorporate changes to project costs.

cost control   An active process to control causes of cost change, document cost changes, and monitor cost fluctuations within the project. When changes occur, the cost baseline must be updated.

cost estimating   The process of calculating the costs, by category, of the identified resources to complete the project work.

Cost of conformance   The cost of completing the project work to satisfy the project scope and the expected level of quality. Examples include training, safety measures, and quality management activities.

cost of nonconformance   The cost of completing the project work without meeting the quality standards. The biggest issue here is the money lost by having to redo the project work; it's always more cost-effective to do the work right the first time. Other nonconformance costs are loss of sales, loss of customers, downtime, and corrective actions to fix problems caused by the incorrect work.

Cost Performance Index (CPI)   This is a reflection of the amount of actual cumulative dollars spent on a project's work and how closely that value is to the predicted budgeted amount. The formula for the CPI is as follows: CPI = EV/AC.

cost variance   The difference in the amount of budgeted expense and the actual expense. A negative variance means that more money was spent on the service or goods than what was budgeted for it.

crashing   This is the addition of more resources to activities on the critical path in order to complete the project earlier. Crashing results in higher project costs.

critical path   The sequence of events that determine the project completion date.

Critical Path Method (CPM)   The CPM is the most common approach to calculating when a project may finish. It uses a "forward" and "backward" path to reveal which activities are considered critical, and which contain float. If activities on the critical path are delayed, the project end date will be delayed.

date constraints   There are three types of date constraints:

- **No earlier than**   This constraint specifies that a task may happen any time after a specific date, but not earlier than the given date.
- **No later than**   This constraint is deadline orientated. The task must be completed by this date or else.
- **On this date**   This constraint is the most time orientated. There is no margin for adjustment as the task must be completed on this date, no sooner or later.

decision tree analysis   A type of analysis that determines which of two decisions is best. The decision tree assists in calculating the value of the decision and determining which decision costs the least.

decoder   This is a part of the communications model; it is the inverse of the encoder. If a message is encoded, a decoder translates it back to a usable format.

Delphi Technique   A method to query experts anonymously on foreseeable risks within the project, phase, or component of the project. The results of the survey are analyzed and organized and then circulated to the experts. There can be several rounds of anonymous discussions with the Delphi Technique The goal is to gain consensus on project risks, and the anonymous nature of the process ensures that no one expert's advice overtly influences the opinion of another participant.

demotivators   An element of Herzberg's theory that employees are motivated or demotivated by effects within an organization. The demotivators are actually the expected benefits a company has to offer, such as insurance, vacation time, and other benefits. The presence of these elements is expected by the motivation seekers and only their absence has a negative impact.

design of experiments   This relies on statistical "what-if" scenarios to determine which variables within a project will result in the best outcome. It can also be used to eliminate a defect. The design of experiments approach is most often used on the product of the project, rather than the project itself.

detailed variance reports   A summary of any variances within the project.

directive decision-making process   The project manager makes the decision with little or no input from the project team. Directive decision making is acceptable, and needed, in some instances, but it isolates the project manager from the project team.

discretionary dependencies   The preferred order of activities. Project managers should adhere to the order at their "discretion" and should document the logic behind the ordering. Discretionary dependencies have activities happen in a preferred order because of best practices, conditions unique to the project work, or external events. This is also known as soft logic.

earned value (EV)   The value of the work that has been completed and the budget for that work: EV = %Complete * BAC.

Earned Value Management (EVM)   Earned Value Management integrates scope, schedule, and cost to give an objective, scalable point-in-time assessment of the project. EVM calculates the performance of the project and compares current performance against the plan. EVM can also be a harbinger of things to come. Results early in the project can predict the likelihood of the project's success or failure.

effective listening   The receiver is involved in the listening experience by paying attention to the speaker's visual clues and paralingual intentions and by asking relevant questions.

encoder   Part of the communications model, an encoder is the device or technology that packages the message to travel over the medium.

Estimate at Completion (EAC)   A hypothesis of what the total cost of the project will be. Before the project begins, the project manager completes an estimate for the project deliverables based on the WBS. As the project progresses, there will likely be some variances between what the cost estimate was and what the actual cost is. The EAC is calculated to predict what the new estimate at completion will be. The formula for the EAC is as follows: EAC = BAC/CPI.

Estimate to Complete (ETC)   Represents how much more money is needed to complete the project work: ETC = EAC – AC. This value can also be found through BAC-AC.

evaluation criteria   This criteria is used to rate and score proposals from sellers. In some instances, such as a bid or quote, the evaluation criterion is focused just on the price the seller offers. In other instances, such as a proposal, the evaluation criteria can be multiple values: experience, references, certifications, and more.

executing   The project plans are carried out, or executed; the project manager coordinates people and other resources to complete the plan.

expectancy theory   People will behave on the basis of what they expect as a result of their behavior. In other words, people will work in relation to the expected reward for the work.

expert power   A type of power where the authority of the project manager comes from experience with the area that the project focuses on.

fast tracking   Doing activities in parallel that are normally done sequentially.

feasibility plan   A documented expression of what your research has told you. This plan is written to help determine the validity of a proposed project, a section of a project, or the scope of a given project.

final project report   The collection of all of the cumulative reports may serve as a final record of each phase's work, with a few additions. It includes the project vision statement, the project proposal, project plan, the WBS, the PND, meeting minutes, any Project Change Requests forms, all written notices relevant to the project deliverables, client acceptance agreement, and the post-project audit.

Finish No Earlier Than (FNET) constraints   This semiflexible constraint requires that a task be completed on or after a specified date.

Finish No Later Than (FNLT) constraints   This semiflexible constraint requires that a task be completed on or before this date.

finish-to-finish (FF) tasks   These tasks require that the predecessor task and the successor task be completed on the exact date. An example is rolling out a new software package and finishing the user training sessions. While users are in the new training session, the new software should be installed and configured on their workstations by the time the training session ends.

finish-to-start (FS) tasks   These tasks are successors and cannot begin until the predecessor task is completed. An example is installing network cards before connecting PCs to the Internet.

flexible constraints   These constraints do not have dates assigned to their activities and are only bound by their predecessor and successor activities. Use flexible constraints as much as possible.

flexible deadline   A deadline that doesn't assign an exact time for completion.

float   The amount of time a task can be delayed without delaying the project completion. Technically, there are three different types of float: *Free float* is the total time a single activity can be delayed without delaying the early start of any successor activities. *Total float* is the total time an activity can be delayed without delaying project completion. *Project float* is the total time the project can be delayed without passing the customer's expected completion date.

flowchart   A chart that illustrates how the parts of a system occur in sequence.

focus group   A collection of users from all of the departments impacted by the proposed technology of an IT project.

force majeure   A powerful and unexpected event, such as a hurricane or other disaster.

forcing   A conflict resolution method where one person dominates or forces her point of view or solution to a conflict.

forecasting   An educated estimate of how long the project will take to complete. It can also refer to how much the project may cost to complete.

formal acceptance   The formal acceptance of a project's deliverables is a process that is completed by the client of the project and the appropriate members of the project team. These acceptances are contingent on a project acceptance agreement.

formal power   The type of power where the project manager has been assigned by senior management to be in charge of the project.

fully burdened workload   The amount of work, in hours, required by the staff to complete each phase of the project.

functional structure   An organizational structure that groups staff members according to their area of expertise (sales, marketing, construction, and so on). Functional structures require the project team members to report directly to the functional manager. In this type of structure, the project manager's authority and decision-making ability is less than the functional manager's.

future value   A formula to calculate the future value of present money.

Gantt chart   A Gantt chart allows a project manager to see the intersection of dates until completion and the tasks within a project. Henry Gantt, an engineer and social scientist, invented this method of tracking deliverables in 1917.

Graphical Evaluation and Review Technique (GERT)   Conditional advancement, branching, and looping of activities based on probabilistic estimates. Activities within GERT are dependent on the results of other upstream activities.

hard logic   The logical relationship between activities based on the type of work. For example, the foundation of a house must be created before the frame of the house can be built. This is also known as mandatory dependency.

Herzberg's Theory of Motivation   Posits that there are two catalysts for workers: hygiene agents and motivating agents. Hygiene agents do nothing to motivate workers, but their absence demotivates them. Hygiene agents are the expectations all workers have: job security, paychecks, clean and safe working conditions, a sense of belonging, civil working relationships, and other basic attributes associated with employment. Motivating agents are components such as rewards, recognition, promotions, and other values that encourage individuals to succeed.

historical information   Information the project may use from previous projects.

hygiene seekers   An element of Herzberg's theory that employees are motivated or demotivated by effects within an organization. The effects a hygiene seeker takes comfort in are salary, management, and job security.

implementation tracking   As tasks are completed on time or over time, the number of time units used can accurately display the impact on dependent tasks within the project.

indirect costs   Costs attributed to the cost of doing business. Examples include utilities, office space, and other overhead costs.

inflexible constraints   These constraints have date values associated with them but are very rigid. Constraints that are inflexible require that activities happen on a specific date. Use these constraints very sparingly.

influence diagram   An influence diagram charts out a decision problem. It identifies all of the elements, variables, decisions, and objectives and how each factor may influence another.

informal acceptance   The informal acceptance does not include a sign-off of the completion or even the acknowledgement of the deliverables. An example of the informal acceptance is a project that ends on deadline whether or not the deliverables are finished—for example, a project to organize and build an application for a tradeshow demo. The tradeshow will happen regardless of the completion of the project.

initiating   This process group begins the project. The business needs are identified, and a product description is created. The project charter is written, and the project manager is selected.

interviewing   Interviewing subject matter experts and project stakeholders is an approach to identify risks on the current project based on the interviewees' experience.

integration phase   The phase of the project where the project plan is put into action.

interview questions, closed   These questions must be answered with a yes or no. For example: "Have you ever created a batch file before?"

interview questions, essay   These questions allow the candidate to tell you information, and they allow you to listen and observe. For example: "Why are you interested in working on this project?"

interview questions, experience   These questions allow you to see how a candidate has acted in past situations to predict how he may act in future situations that are similar. For example: "How did you react when a teammate did not complete a task on a past project and you had to do his work for him to complete your own? How was the situation resolved?"

interview questions, reactionary   These questions evolve from the candidate's answers. When you notice a gap or an inconsistency in an answer, use a follow-up question that focuses on the inconsistency without directly calling it a lie. This gives the candidate the opportunity to explain himself better or flounder for an explanation. Reactionary questions also allow you to learn more information that may be helpful on your project. For example: "You mentioned you had experienced with Visual Basic. Do you also have a grasp on VBScript?"

Invitation for Bid (IFB)   A document from the buyer to the seller that requests the seller provide a price for the procured product or service.

ISO 9000   An international standard that helps organizations follow their own quality procedures. ISO 9000 is not a quality system, but a method of following procedures created by an organization.

IT project management   IT project management is the ability to balance the love and implementation of technology while leading and inspiring your team members.

job description   A job description details the activities of a team role, the scope of the position, the responsibilities, and the working requirements of the team member who fills the role. A job description should be clear, concise, and easily summed up.

lag   The scheduled time between project tasks, or the amount of time a project task is falling off the schedule.

Law of Diminishing Returns, The   A law of economics, sometimes called the Law of Variable Proportions, which grew from Thomas Malthus' "Essay on the Principle of Population," written in 1798. The law states that if one factor of production is increased while other factors remain constant, the overall returns will eventually decrease after a certain point.

lead   The negative time added to a task to bring it closer to the project start date. The lead is calculated by subtracting time between activities.

Lessons Learned   An ongoing documentation of things the project manager and project team have learned throughout the project. Lessons Learned are supplied to other project teams and project managers to apply to their ongoing projects. Lessons Learned are documented throughout the project, not just at the end of the project.

licensing, per connection   A license is required for each workstation-to-server connection. This scheme allows a maximum number of connections to a server.

licensing, per station   A license that covers the software application at the workstation where it is installed. Think of Microsoft Office installed on each workstation within an organization.

licensing, per station (server-based)   This licensing method allows an unlimited number of connections to a server covered by the licensing plan. Each additional server would require its own licensing to allow connections to that server.

licensing, per usage   This licensing plan allows a user to run an application for a preset number of days or a preset number of times, or charges the user a fee for each instance that the application is used.

management by projects   This approach characterizes organizations that manage their operations as projects. These project-centric entities can manage any level of their work as a project. They apply general business skills to each project to determine its value, efficiency, and, ultimately, return on investment.

management by walking around   A method to manage quality and to allow yourself to be seen. Get out of your office and get into the working environment. You don't have to hover around your team members, but let them know you are available, present, and interested in their work.

management reserve   An artificial task that is added at the end of the project. The time allotted to the reserve is typically 10 to 15 percent of the total amount of time to complete all the tasks in a project. When a task runs over its allotted time, the overrun is applied to the management reserve at the end of the critical path rather than on each lagging task.

management summary reports   Management summary reports detail the overall status of the project, changes from the original plan, change in execution, or cost variances within the budget. These reports are created on an as-needed basis and are ideal for upper management.

managerial constraints   Dependency relationships imposed because of a decision by management, which includes the project manager.

mandatory dependencies   This refers to the logical relationship between activities based on the type of work. For example, the foundation of a house must be created before the frame of the house can be built. This is also known as hard logic.

Maslow's Hierarchy of Needs   A theory that states that there are five layers of needs for all humans: physiological, safety, social, esteem, and, the crowning jewel, self-actualization.

Matrix Structures   An organizational structure. There are three matrix structures: weak, balanced, and strong. The different structures are reflective of the project manager's authority in relation to the functional manager's authority.

McGregor's Theory of X and Y   This theory states that "X" people are lazy, don't want to work, and need to be micromanaged. "Y" people are self-led, motivated, and strive to succeed.

medium   Part of the communications model, this is the path the message takes from the sender to the receiver. The modality in which the communication travels typically refers to an electronic model, such as e-mail or the telephone.

meeting coordinator   An individual who runs the business of a meeting to keep the topics on schedule and according to the agenda.

meeting minutes   A document that represents a record of a meeting, the problems and situations that were discussed, and documentation of the project as it progresses. Meeting minutes are an excellent method for keeping the team aware of what has already been discussed and settled, resolutions of problems, and proof of the attendees in the meeting.

metrics   A standard of project measurement; often applied to cost, schedule, scope, quality, and performance.

micromanage   The negative approach to managing a subordinate's work in a meddlesome, counterproductive manner.

Microsoft Project   A software tool that allows a project manager to create and manage an entire project from start to finish.

Microsoft Project Server   A companion software to Microsoft Project, it is installed on your company's Internet or intranet server. Microsoft Project Server allows the entire project team to work together to report tasks, schedule updates, and track time spent on each project. Using this software, a project manager can enable multiproject tracking, share and track resources among multiple projects, and work with dependent projects.

milestones   Milestones represent the completion of significant tasks within a project's schedule.

mitigation   Reducing the probability or impact of a risk.

Monte Carlo Analysis   This process predicts how scenarios may work out given any number of variables. It doesn't actually create a specific answer, but offers a range of possible ones. When Monte Carlo is applied to a schedule, it can present, for example, the optimistic completion date, the pessimistic completion date, and the most likely completion date for each activity in the project.

Motivation-Hygiene Theory   Invented by Fred Herzberg, a management consultant and business theorist in 1959. Herzberg's study arrived at the conclusion that workers are impacted by nontangible factors called motivators, and hygiene effects called demotivators.

motivation seekers   An element of Herzberg's theory that employees are motivated or demotivated by effects within an organization. The effects a motivation seeker takes comfort in are achievement, recognition, the work, responsibility, and advancement.

Must Finish On (MFO) constraints   This inflexible constraint is a deadline-orientated task. The task must be completed by a specific date.

Must Start On (MSO) constraints   This inflexible constraint requires that a task begin on a specific date.

nonverbal communication   Approximately 55 percent of oral communication is nonverbal. Facial expressions, hand gestures, and body language contribute to the message.

operational definitions   The quantifiable terms and values used to measure a process, activity, or work result. Operational definitions are also known as metrics.

organizational constraints   Within your organization there may be multiple projects that are loosely related. The completion of another project may be a key milestone for your own project to continue.

Ouchi's Theory Z   This theory posits that workers are motivated by a sense of commitment, opportunity, and advancement. Workers will work if they are challenged and motivated.

paralingual   The pitch, tone, and inflections in the sender's voice that affect the message being sent.

Parametric Modeling   A mathematical model based on known parameters used to predict the cost of a project. The parameters in the model can vary based on the type of work being done. A parameter can be the cost per cubic yard, cost per unit, and so on.

Pareto diagram   A Pareto diagram is related to Pareto's Law: 80 percent of the problems come from 20 percent of the issues (this is also known as the "80/20 rule"). A Pareto diagram illustrates problems by assigned cause, from smallest to largest.

Parkinson's Law   Parkinson's Law states that work expands so as to fill the time available for its completion.

participative decision-making process   In this ideal model, all team members contribute to the discussion and decision process. Through compromise, experience, and brainstorming, the project team and the project manager can create a buzz of energy, excitement, and synergy to arrive at the best possible solution for a decision.

peer review   Peer review, as its name implies, is the process of allowing team members to review each other's work.

PERT chart   PERT is short for Program Evaluation and Review Technique. In plain language, this means a PERT chart can graphically illustrate tasks, their durations, and dependency of other tasks in the work unit.

phase   A portion of the project that typically must be completed before the next phase can begin. Each phase has a set deadline.

pilot team   A collection of users who agree to test the project deliverables before the rest of the organization sees the implementation. Their input to the project allows the project manager to realize if the project deliverables are on target or not.

Planned Value (PV)   The worth of the work that should be completed by a specific time in the project schedule.

planning group   This process group is iterative. All planning throughout the project is handled within the planning process group.

PMBOK® Guide   The book, *A Guide to the Project Management Body of Knowledge*, which includes all knowledge and practices within the endeavor of project management.

postmortem   Also referred to as post-project audit.

post-project audit   The purpose of this audit is to analyze the completed project, the effectiveness of the project team, the success of the project, the value of the deliverables, and the overall approval from the clients.

Precedence Diagramming Method (PDM)   This method requires the project manager to evaluate each work unit and determine which tasks are its successors and which tasks are its predecessors to create the PND.

problem management meeting   A meeting to resolve problems as they arise on a project.

process groups   The five process groups, initiating, planning, executing, controlling, and closing, comprise projects and project phases. These five process groups have sets of actions that move the project forward toward completion.

procurement   The process of a seller soliciting, selecting, and paying for products or services from a buyer.

procurement audits   The successes and failures within the procurement process are reviewed from procurement planning through contract administration. The intent of the audit is to learn from what worked and what did not work during the procurement processes.

Procurement Management Plan   This subsidiary project plan documents the decisions made in the procurement planning processes. It specifies how the remaining procurement activities will be managed.

product scope   The attributes and characteristics of the deliverables the project is creating.

Program Evaluation and Review Technique (PERT)   A scheduling tool that uses a weighted average formula to predict the length of activities and the project. Specifically, the PERT formula is $(O + 4ML + P)/6$.

programs   A collection of related projects working in alignment toward a common cause.

progress reports   These reports provide current information on the project work completed to date.

progressive elaboration   The process of providing or discovering greater levels of detail as the project moves toward completion.

project   A temporary endeavor undertaken to create a unique product or service.

project acceptance agreement   A document that is typically written very early in the project timeline and in alignment with the defined project deliverables. The document is a clearly written explanation of what qualifies for an acceptance of the deliverables. These are typical of application development projects and often consist of a checklist of the required features of the project.

project calendar   A calendar that defines the working times for the project. For example, a project may require the project team to work nights and weekends so as not to disturb the ongoing operations of the organization during normal working hours. In addition, the project calendar accounts for holidays, work hours, and work shifts the project will cover.

Project Change Request form   This form formalizes requests from anyone to the project manager. It requires the requestor to not only describe the change, but also to supply a reason why this change is appropriate and needed. Once the requestor has completed this form, the project manager can determine if the change is indeed necessary, should be rejected, or should be delayed until the completion of the current project.

project charter   A project charter is similar to the goal, but more official, more detailed, and in line with your company's vision and goals. The project charter authorizes the project.

project closure phase   This phase of project management is the sigh of relief. It requires proof of the project deliverables, approval from management, and satisfaction from the customers or end users.

project control phase   This phase of project management is a continuous cycle to oversee the project. It allows the project manager to manage task reporting, team meetings, reassignment of resources, change, and quality through software, communications, and the project team.

project deliverables   Project deliverables are the end result of the project. They are what the project produces.

project execution phase   Once the project has been approved, the project manager may then create a PND to map out the required tasks, assign resources, and organize the project team.

project genesis   In the origin of the project, there is a reaction to a need or an idea to improve operations within an organization. This realization of an opportunity to fulfill a need is the concept of the project.

project goal   The clearly stated result a project should meet or deliver.

Project Information Center   This centralized room is a collection of all materials related to the project. The size of your project and the available real estate within your office building will determine your ability to create a Project Information Center.

project kickoff   A project kickoff is a meeting or an event to introduce the project, the management backing the project, the project manager, and the team members. It should be casual, organized, and used as a mechanism to assign ownership of the project to the team.

Project Management Information System (PMIS)   PMIS is typically a computer-program that assists with project management activities, recordkeeping, and forecasting.

Project Management Office (PMO)   The role of the PMO is twofold: it offers traditional project management services for an entire organization, and it serves as governing committee for all projects throughout an organization.

project manager   The individual accountable for all aspects of a project.

Project Network Diagram (PND)   A fluid mapping of the work to be completed. PNDs allow the project manager and the project team to tinker with the relationships between tasks and create alternative solutions to increase productivity, profitability, and the diligence of a project.

project planning phase   The cornerstone of a successful project is the planning phase. The project manager and project team must identify the required activities and estimate the time required to complete the activities in order to reach the project goal.

project resources   Project resources can be employees, contractors, or equipment that is used on a project.

project scope   The defined range of deliverables a project will produce. The project scope is concerned with the work and only the required work necessary to complete the project.

project sponsor   Typically the initiator of the project and the project manager's direct link to management.

project vision   In project management terms, the ability to clearly see the project deliverables and recognize the actions required to produce them.

projectized structure   An organizational structure where the project manager has the greatest amount of authority. The project team is assigned to the project on a full-time basis. When the project is complete, the project team members move on to other assignments within the organization.

purpose statement   A statement indicating why the research was initiated and reflecting the proposed project.

qualitative risk analysis   An examination and prioritization of the risks based on their probability of occurring and impact on the project if they do occur. Qualitative risk analysis guides the risk reaction process.

quality assurance (QA)   A process in which the overall performance is evaluated to ensure the project meets the relevant quality standards.

quality audit   A quality audit is a process used to confirm that the quality processes are performing correctly on the current project. The quality audit determines how to make things better for the project and other projects within the organization. Quality audits measure the project's ability to maintain the expected level of quality.

quality control (QC)   A process in which the work results are monitored to see if they meet relevant quality standards.

Quality Management Plan   This document describes how the project manager and the project team will fulfill the quality policy. In an ISO 9000 environment, the Quality Management Plan is referred to as the "project quality system."

quality policy   The formal policy an organization follows to achieve a preset standard of quality. The quality policy of the organization may follow a formal approach, such as ISO 9000, Six Sigma, or Total Quality Management (TQM), or it may have its own direction and approach. The project team should either adapt the quality policy of the organization to guide the project implementation or create its own policy if one does not exist within the performing organization.

quantitative estimating   Estimating based on mathematical formulas to predict how long an activity will take or how much it will cost, using the quantities, units, or other metric of work to be completed.

quantitative risk analysis   A numerical assessment of the probability and impact of the identified risks. Quantitative risk analysis also creates an overall risk score for the project.

quote (or quotation)   A document from the seller to the buyer. Quotes are used when price is the determining factor in the decision-making process.

receiver   The recipient of the message. The receiver is part of the communications model.

referent power   Power that is present when the project team is attracted to, or wants to work on the project with, the project manager. Referent power also exists when the project manager references another, more powerful person, such as the CEO.

Request for Proposal (RFP)   A formal request from your company to a client to create a proposal for the work to be completed and provide you with a cost estimate. An RFP does not guarantee anyone the job; it simply formalizes the proceedings of the selection process.

Request for Quote (RFQ)   A document from the buyer to the seller asking the seller to provide a price for the procured product or service.

residual risks   Risks that are left over after mitigation, transference, and avoidance. These are generally accepted risks. Management may elect to add contingency costs and time to account for the residual risks within the project.

resource calendar   The resource calendar shows when resources, such as project team members, consultants, and Subject Matter Experts, are available to work on the project. It takes into account vacations, other commitments within the organization, restrictions on contracted work, overtime issues, and so on.

resource constraints   A project manager may elect to schedule two tasks as FS rather than SS based on a limitation of a particular resource.

resource histogram   A bar chart reflecting when individual employees, groups, or communities are involved in a project. It is often used by management to see when employees are most or least active in a project.

resource leveling heuristics   A method to flatten the schedule when resources are over-allocated or allocated unevenly. Resource leveling can be applied in different methods to accomplish different goals. One of the most common methods is to ensure that workers are not overextended on activities.

resources   Resources can be both workers and physical objects such as a bandwidth, faster computers, and leased equipment.

return on investment (ROI)   Return on investment is the attitude that IT projects are not an expense but an investment that will allow an organization to become more profitable.

reward power   The project manager's authority to reward the project team.

risk   An unplanned event that can have a positive or negative influence on the project success.

risk database   A database of recognized risks. The planned response and the outcome of the risk should be documented and recorded in an organization-wide risk database. The risk database can serve other project managers as historical information. Over time, the risk database can become a risk Lessons Learned program.

risk management plan   A subsidiary project plan for determining how risks will be identified, how quantitative and qualitative analysis will be completed, how risk response planning will happen, how risks will be monitored, and how ongoing risk management activities will occur throughout the project lifecycle.

risk owners   The individuals or groups responsible for a risk response.

runaway project   A project that starts out well and then gains speed, momentum, and scope, causing runaways with your budget and increased man hours, and possibly hurting your reputation or career. The biggest element of a runaway project is the budget.

scales of probability and impact   Each risk is assessed according to its likelihood and its impact. There are two approaches to ranking risks: Cardinal scales identify the probability and impact by a numerical value, ranging from .01 as very low to 1.0 as certain. Ordinal scales identify and rank the risks from very high to very unlikely.

Schedule Management Plan   A subsidiary plan within the overall project plan. It is used to control changes to the schedule. A formal Schedule Management Plan has procedures that control how changes to the project plan can be proposed, accounted for, and then implemented.

Schedule Performance Index (SPI) This index reveals the efficiency of work. The closer the quotient is to 1, the better: SPI = EV/PV

schedule variance The difference between the planned work and the earned work.

scope creep A process that happens when a project manager allows small changes to enter into the project scope. Eventually, the scope of the project swells to include more deliverables than the project budget or team is able to deal with.

scope statement A document that describes the work, and only the required work, to meet the project objectives. The scope statement establishes a common vision among the project stakeholders to establish the point and purpose of the project work. It is used as a baseline against which all future project decisions are made to determine if proposed changes or work results are aligned with expectations.

scope verification The process of the project customer accepting the project deliverables. Scope verification happens at the end of each project phase and at the end of the project. Scope verification is the process of ensuring the deliverables the project creates are in alignment with the project scope.

secondary risks Risks that stem from risk responses. For example, the response of transference may call for hiring a third party to manage an identified risk. A secondary risk caused by the solution is the failure of the third party to complete its assignment as scheduled. Secondary risks must be identified, analyzed, and planned for just as any identified risk.

semiflexible constraints Semiflexible constraints do have a date value associated with them, but require that the task begin or end by the specified date. Use these constraints sparingly.

sender Part of the communications model. The sender is the person or group sending the message to the receiver.

should cost estimates These estimates are created by the performing organization to predict what the cost of the procured product should be. If there is a significant difference between what the organization has predicted and what the sellers have proposed, either the Statement of Work was inadequate or the sellers have misunderstood the requirements. Should cost estimates are also known as independent estimates.

simulation This exercise allows the project team to play "what-if" games without affecting any areas of production.

single source A specific seller that the performing organization prefers to contract with.

smoothing A conflict resolution method that "smoothes" out the conflict by minimizing the perceived size of the problem. It is a temporary solution, but it can calm team relations and temper boisterous discussions. Smoothing may be acceptable when time is of the essence or any of the proposed solutions would work.

soft logic   The preferred order of activities. Project managers should use these relationships at their "discretion" and document the logic behind making soft logic decisions. Discretionary dependencies allow activities to happen in a preferred order because of best practices, conditions unique to the project work, or external events. Soft logic is also known as discretionary dependency.

stakeholders   The individuals, groups, and communities that have a vested interest in the outcome of a project. Examples include the project manager, the project team, the project sponsor, customers, clients, vendors, and communities.

standard costs   Your budget department may have preassigned standard costs for labor to do certain tasks like programming lines of code, installing hardware, or adding new servers. This preassignment of values helps you estimate labor costs of a project easily and without having to justify each labor expense as a line item.

STAR method   One of the best interview methods, especially when dealing with potential integrators, is the STAR methodology. STAR means Situation, Task, Action, Result.

Start No Earlier Than (SNET) constraints   When you specify a task as having the SNET constraint, you are assigning a task to start on or after a specific date. This constraint is semiflexible.

Start No Later Than (SNLT) constraints   This semiflexible constraint requires that a task begin by a specific date at the latest.

start-to-finish (SF) tasks   These rare tasks require that the predecessor doesn't begin until the successor finishes. This relationship could be used with accounting incidents. For example, the predecessor task is to physically count all of the network jacks that have been installed—once they have been installed.

start-to-start (SS) tasks   These tasks are usually closely related in nature and should be started but not necessarily completed at the same time. An example is planning for the physical implementation of a network and determining each network's IP addressing configurations. Each are closely related and should be done in tandem.

Statement of Work (SOW)   This fully describes the work to be completed, the product to be supplied, or both. The SOW becomes part of the contract between the buyer and the seller. The SOW is typically created as part of the procurement planning process and is used by the seller to determine whether it can meet the project's requirements.

statistical sampling   A process of choosing a percentage of results at random for inspection. Statistical sampling can reduce the costs of quality control.

status reports   These reports provide current information on the project cost, budget, scope, and other relevant information.

status review meetings   Regularly scheduled meetings to record the status of the project work. These commonly employed meetings provide a formal avenue for the project manager to query the team on the status of its work, record delays and slippage, and to forecast what work is about to begin.

subteams   Project teams in a geographically diverse project. Each team on the project in each site is called a subteam.

system or process flowcharts   These show the relation between components and how the overall process works. They are useful for identifying risks between system components.

task list   A list of the major steps required from the project's origin to its conclusion. A task list is created after the technology has been selected and before you create the implementation plan.

team leaders   Each subteam has a team leader that reports directly to the project manager and oversees the activities of the team members on the subteam.

tiered structure   In a tiered structure, the deliverables are released over multiple dates, allowing the IT project manager to agree to meet new requirements for the project scope.

time and material (T&M) billing method   Most technology integrators like to bill time and materials because there may be some additional problem discovered in the midst of the project that can result in the vendor working extra hours to solve it. T&M contracts should have a not-to-exceed clause (NTE) to contain costs.

total budgeted costs   The amount of dollars budgeted for your project prior to the start of the project implementation phase.

Total Quality Management (TQM)   A process that has all employees within an organization working to fulfill their customers' needs while also working to increase productivity. TQM stems from Dr. W. Edward Deming's management principles, which the Japanese adopted after WWII. In the U.S., these principles were readily adopted in the 1980s after proof of their success in Japan.

total slack   The total time an activity can be delayed without delaying project completion.

top-down estimating   A technique that bases the current project's estimate on the total of a similar project. A percentage of the similar project's total cost may be added to or subtracted from the total, depending on the size of the current project.

transference   A response to risks in which the responsibility and ownership of the risk is transferred to another party (for example, through insurance).

trend analysis   Trend analysis is taking past results to predict future performance.

triggers   Warning signs or symptoms that a risk has occurred or is about to occur. An example is a vendor failing to complete its portion of the project as scheduled).

upper management   The chief executive officers of an organization, such as the CEO, CIO, and COO.

usability laboratory   A place where the project team can test the technology prior to implementing it in production.

utility function   A person's willingness to accept risk.

value added change   A change that positively impacts either the scope, schedule, or cost of a project without adversely impacting the other two aspects.

variance   The difference between what was planned and what was experienced; typically used for costs and schedules.

Variance at Completion (VAC)   The difference between the Budget at Completion (BAC) and the Estimate at Completion (EAC); its formula is VAC = BAC – EAC

war room   A centralized office or locale for the project manager and the project team to work on the project. It can house information on the project, including documentation and support materials. It allows the project team to work in close proximity.

withdrawal   A conflict resolution method that is used when the issue is not important or the project manager is out-ranked. The project manager pushes the issue aside for later resolution. It can also be used as a method for cooling down. The conflict is not resolved, and it is considered a yield-lose solution.

Work Authorization System   A tool that can control the organization, sequence, and official authorization to begin a piece of the project work.

Work Breakdown Structure (WBS)   The WBS is a deliverable-orientated collection of project components. Work that isn't in the WBS isn't in the project. The point of the WBS is to organize and define the project scope.

Work Breakdown Structure (WBS) dictionary   A reference tool to explain the WBS components, the nature of the work package, the assigned resources, and the time and billing estimates for each element.

Work Breakdown Structure (WBS) template   A master WBS that is used in organizations as a starting point in defining the work for a particular project. This approach is recommended, as most projects in an organization are similar in the project lifecycles and the approach can be adapted to fit a given project.

workaround   A workaround is an unplanned response to a risk that is not identified or accepted.

work unit   A chunk of work that must be completed to ensure a phase ends on schedule so the next phase can begin.

zero-based budgeting   Zero-based budgeting means that the budget to be created must always start at the number zero rather than factoring new expenses into a budget from a similar project.

INDEX

See "Glossary" for a comprehensive list of terms.

Numbers

8/80 Rule, applying to projects, 160–164

"98 percent done is not complete," significance of, 426

A

AC (actual cost)
 explanation of, 292
 role in EVM, 295
 tracking, 292–293
acceptance agreement, example of, 431–432
accounting skills, importance to IT project managers, 360
achievement orientation skills, importance to IT project managers, 360
Adams, Rob interview, 437–441
aggressive team members, characteristics of, 395
agility skills, importance to IT project managers, 360
ALAP (As Late As Possible) constraints, explanation of, 265
analogous estimating, using in top-down estimating, 121–122
AOA (activity-on-the-arrow) method, development of, 251
AON (activity-on-the-node) method, development of, 251–252
arguments, impact on projects, 205–206
Arndt, Jennifer interview, 95–98
ASAP (As Soon As Possible) constraints, explanation of, 265
assignments, reviewing with project teams, 282–283

audits, conducting after completion of projects, 432–433
Aunt or Uncle personality type, dealing with, 210
authority and responsibility, role in project management, 391

B

BAC (Budget at Completion). *See also* budgets; cost estimates
 explanation of, 292
 overview of, 122–123
backward pass, completing, 258–261
benchmarking, role in planning for quality, 365
benefit-cost analysis, role in planning for quality, 365
Best Enterprises, project charter for, 17–19
bid document, purpose of, 217
bosses. *See* managers
bottom-up cost estimates
 allowing for change in, 114–120
 implementing, 114–120
 including best- and worst-case scenarios in, 119
 tolerance for budget variance in, 120
bottom-up WBS approach, explanation of, 165–166
budget basics, 112–113
budget dollars, obtaining, 48–51
budget estimate, explanation of, 114
budgetary expenses, tracking, 138–144
budgets. *See also* BAC (Budget at Completion); cost estimates
 creating, 116–118, 124–125
 dealing with increases in, 336
 determining most expensive part of, 127
 factoring cost variances into, 127

523

Q

R

S

INTERNATIONAL CONTACT INFORMATION

AUSTRALIA
McGraw-Hill Book Company
Australia Pty. Ltd.
TEL +61-2-9900-1800
FAX +61-2-9878-8881
http://www.mcgraw-hill.com.au
books-it_sydney@mcgraw-hill.com

CANADA
McGraw-Hill Ryerson Ltd.
TEL +905-430-5000
FAX +905-430-5020
http://www.mcgraw-hill.ca

**GREECE, MIDDLE EAST, & AFRICA
(Excluding South Africa)**
McGraw-Hill Hellas
TEL +30-210-6560-990
TEL +30-210-6560-993
TEL +30-210-6560-994
FAX +30-210-6545-525

MEXICO (Also serving Latin America)
McGraw-Hill Interamericana Editores
S.A. de C.V.
TEL +525-1500-5108
FAX +525-117-1589
http://www.mcgraw-hill.com.mx
carlos_ruiz@mcgraw-hill.com

SINGAPORE (Serving Asia)
McGraw-Hill Book Company
TEL +65-6863-1580
FAX +65-6862-3354
http://www.mcgraw-hill.com.sg
mghasia@mcgraw-hill.com

SOUTH AFRICA
McGraw-Hill South Africa
TEL +27-11-622-7512
FAX +27-11-622-9045
robyn_swanepoel@mcgraw-hill.com

SPAIN
McGraw-Hill/
Interamericana de España, S.A.U.
TEL +34-91-180-3000
FAX +34-91-372-8513
http://www.mcgraw-hill.es
professional@mcgraw-hill.es

**UNITED KINGDOM, NORTHERN,
EASTERN, & CENTRAL EUROPE**
McGraw-Hill Education Europe
TEL +44-1-628-502500
FAX +44-1-628-770224
http://www.mcgraw-hill.co.uk
emea_queries@mcgraw-hill.com

ALL OTHER INQUIRIES Contact:
McGraw-Hill/Osborne
TEL +1-510-420-7700
FAX +1-510-420-7703
http://www.osborne.com
omg_international@mcgraw-hill.com

Sound Off!

Visit us at **www.osborne.com/bookregistration** and let us know what you thought of this book. While you're online you'll have the opportunity to register for newsletters and special offers from McGraw-Hill/Osborne.

We want to hear from you!

Sneak Peek

Visit us today at **www.betabooks.com** and see what's coming from McGraw-Hill/Osborne tomorrow!

Based on the successful software paradigm, Bet@Books™ allows computing professionals to view partial and sometimes complete text versions of selected titles online. Bet@Books™ viewing is free, invites comments and feedback, and allows you to "test drive" books in progress on the subjects that interest you the most.

LICENSE AGREEMENT

THIS PRODUCT (THE "PRODUCT") CONTAINS PROPRIETARY SOFTWARE, DATA AND INFORMATION (INCLUDING DOCUMENTATION) OWNED BY THE McGRAW-HILL COMPANIES, INC. ("McGRAW-HILL") AND ITS LICENSORS. YOUR RIGHT TO USE THE PRODUCT IS GOVERNED BY THE TERMS AND CONDITIONS OF THIS AGREEMENT.

LICENSE: Throughout this License Agreement, "you" shall mean either the individual or the entity whose agent opens this package. You are granted a non-exclusive and non-transferable license to use the Product subject to the following terms:

(i) If you have licensed a single user version of the Product, the Product may only be used on a single computer (i.e., a single CPU). If you licensed and paid the fee applicable to a local area network or wide area network version of the Product, you are subject to the terms of the following subparagraph (ii).

(ii) If you have licensed a local area network version, you may use the Product on unlimited workstations located in one single building selected by you that is served by such local area network. If you have licensed a wide area network version, you may use the Product on unlimited workstations located in multiple buildings on the same site selected by you that is served by such wide area network; provided, however, that any building will not be considered located in the same site if it is more than five (5) miles away from any building included in such site. In addition, you may only use a local area or wide area network version of the Product on one single server. If you wish to use the Product on more than one server, you must obtain written authorization from McGraw-Hill and pay additional fees.

(iii) You may make one copy of the Product for back-up purposes only and you must maintain an accurate record as to the location of the back-up at all times.

COPYRIGHT; RESTRICTIONS ON USE AND TRANSFER: All rights (including copyright) in and to the Product are owned by McGraw-Hill and its licensors. You are the owner of the enclosed disc on which the Product is recorded. You may not use, copy, decompile, disassemble, reverse engineer, modify, reproduce, create derivative works, transmit, distribute, sublicense, store in a database or retrieval system of any kind, rent or transfer the Product, or any portion thereof, in any form or by any means (including electronically or otherwise) except as expressly provided for in this License Agreement. You must reproduce the copyright notices, trademark notices, legends and logos of McGraw-Hill and its licensors that appear on the Product on the back-up copy of the Product which you are permitted to make hereunder. All rights in the Product not expressly granted herein are reserved by McGraw-Hill and its licensors.

TERM: This License Agreement is effective until terminated. It will terminate if you fail to comply with any term or condition of this License Agreement. Upon termination, you are obligated to return to McGraw-Hill the Product together with all copies thereof and to purge all copies of the Product included in any and all servers and computer facilities.

DISCLAIMER OF WARRANTY: THE PRODUCT AND THE BACK-UP COPY ARE LICENSED "AS IS." McGRAW-HILL, ITS LICENSORS AND THE AUTHORS MAKE NO WARRANTIES, EXPRESS OR IMPLIED, AS TO THE RESULTS TO BE OBTAINED BY ANY PERSON OR ENTITY FROM USE OF THE PRODUCT, ANY INFORMATION OR DATA INCLUDED THEREIN AND/OR ANY TECHNICAL SUPPORT SERVICES PROVIDED HEREUNDER, IF ANY ("TECHNICAL SUPPORT SERVICES"). McGRAW-HILL, ITS LICENSORS AND THE AUTHORS MAKE NO EXPRESS OR IMPLIED WARRANTIES OF MERCHANTABILITY OR FITNESS FOR A PARTICULAR PURPOSE OR USE WITH RESPECT TO THE PRODUCT. McGRAW-HILL, ITS LICENSORS, AND THE AUTHORS MAKE NO GUARANTEE THAT YOU WILL PASS ANY CERTIFICATION EXAM WHATSOEVER BY USING THIS PRODUCT. NEITHER McGRAW-HILL, ANY OF ITS LICENSORS NOR THE AUTHORS WARRANT THAT THE FUNCTIONS CONTAINED IN THE PRODUCT WILL MEET YOUR REQUIREMENTS OR THAT THE OPERATION OF THE PRODUCT WILL BE UNINTERRUPTED OR ERROR FREE. YOU ASSUME THE ENTIRE RISK WITH RESPECT TO THE QUALITY AND PERFORMANCE OF THE PRODUCT.

LIMITED WARRANTY FOR DISC: To the original licensee only, McGraw-Hill warrants that the enclosed disc on which the Product is recorded is free from defects in materials and workmanship under normal use and service for a period of ninety (90) days from the date of purchase. In the event of a defect in the disc covered by the foregoing warranty, McGraw-Hill will replace the disc.

LIMITATION OF LIABILITY: NEITHER McGRAW-HILL, ITS LICENSORS NOR THE AUTHORS SHALL BE LIABLE FOR ANY INDIRECT, SPECIAL OR CONSEQUENTIAL DAMAGES, SUCH AS BUT NOT LIMITED TO, LOSS OF ANTICIPATED PROFITS OR BENEFITS, RESULTING FROM THE USE OR INABILITY TO USE THE PRODUCT EVEN IF ANY OF THEM HAS BEEN ADVISED OF THE POSSIBILITY OF SUCH DAMAGES. THIS LIMITATION OF LIABILITY SHALL APPLY TO ANY CLAIM OR CAUSE WHATSOEVER WHETHER SUCH CLAIM OR CAUSE ARISES IN CONTRACT, TORT, OR OTHERWISE. Some states do not allow the exclusion or limitation of indirect, special or consequential damages, so the above limitation may not apply to you.

U.S. GOVERNMENT RESTRICTED RIGHTS: Any software included in the Product is provided with restricted rights subject to subparagraphs (c), (1) and (2) of the Commercial Computer Software-Restricted Rights clause at 48 C.F.R. 52.227-19. The terms of this Agreement applicable to the use of the data in the Product are those under which the data are generally made available to the general public by McGraw-Hill. Except as provided herein, no reproduction, use, or disclosure rights are granted with respect to the data included in the Product and no right to modify or create derivative works from any such data is hereby granted.

GENERAL: This License Agreement constitutes the entire agreement between the parties relating to the Product. The terms of any Purchase Order shall have no effect on the terms of this License Agreement. Failure of McGraw-Hill to insist at any time on strict compliance with this License Agreement shall not constitute a waiver of any rights under this License Agreement. This License Agreement shall be construed and governed in accordance with the laws of the State of New York. If any provision of this License Agreement is held to be contrary to law, that provision will be enforced to the maximum extent permissible and the remaining provisions will remain in full force and effect.